FARTHEST FRONTIER
The Pacific Northwest

THE MACMILLAN COMPANY
NEW YORK · BOSTON · CHICAGO
DALLAS · ATLANTA · SAN FRANCISCO

MACMILLAN AND CO., LIMITED
LONDON · BOMBAY · CALCUTTA
MADRAS · MELBOURNE

THE MACMILLAN COMPANY
OF CANADA, LIMITED
TORONTO

FARTHEST FRONTIER

The Pacific Northwest

Sidney Warren

THE MACMILLAN COMPANY · NEW YORK · 1949

For Sylvia

Preface

This book would never have been written had not chance brought me to the Pacific Northwest several years ago. Before that time my knowledge of the region was derived mainly from general historical works or an occasional article, none of which had stirred in me any special concern about either its present or its past. But after I had lived there for a short time, I became as intrigued by the country as the most infatuated of the pioneers who had found it their land of promise. That led me to a closer examination of its history. The aspects in which I was particularly interested had to do with the people—their social attitudes, their amusements, their intellectual pursuits, their cultural development—and this volume is the result.

It was with some trepidation that I considered embarking on this study, for some Northwesterners feel, and with some justification, that only those who have lived in the region for a substantial number of years could truly understand it and its heritage. My reasons for proceeding nevertheless were based on the belief that a relatively short residence and the lack of intimate ties should not be deterrents, if these could be balanced by other factors and qualifications which would help give insight and perspective.

A word is in order as to what is meant by the geographical term, the Pacific Northwest. Opinions on that vary. It has been regarded as all the land which lies between the 42nd and 49th parallels and from the Rocky Mountains to the Pacific Ocean; this would include the states of Oregon, Washington, Idaho, and the western portion of Montana. Setting the exact bounds is perhaps a matter of arbitrary choice. Since Montana lies more precisely within the mountain region, it has been excluded from treatment here. British Columbia is also sometimes included in the general territorial designation, but since this study is concerned with the beginnings of *American* settlement and the development of *American* society in the Northwest, this area, too, has been omitted. For the purposes of this study, the Pacific Northwest will include Oregon, Washington, and Idaho. The first two, as the scenes of the earliest settlements, more numerous and stable populations, and more varied and permanent industries, comprise a more significant part of the region than their sister state, Idaho, and greater attention will therefore be given them.

This is the story of the Pacific Northwest during its pioneer phase of development, its growing-up process. The coming of the transcontinental railroads accelerated the pace of development in the region, but even for a generation after the "iron horse" reached the Northwest, it was still mainly a pioneer area. After 1910, however, the region was well on the way towards maturity and had already acquired many of the features of twentieth-century life found in the older sections of the country. For this reason, that year has been selected as the terminal point.

This is a chronicle of beginnings—the beginning of a society by pioneers who came westward and, in time, created out of a wilderness the towns and cities that comprise the Pacific Northwest. It is a story of how they set about building homes, establishing schools, and launching newspapers; of what they read, how they played, and of the manner in which an indigenous cultural tradition was developed. How the Pacific Northwest came to be discovered, why American men and women came to be there, what they did to establish social institutions and provide for the means of intellectual growth are, then, the main themes.

I wish that it were possible to thank the many people who so generously assisted in the preparation of this work. Many pleasure-filled hours were spent with native Northwesterners, who not only provided the writer with an array of invaluable data, but conveyed to him something of the spirit and flavor of the country. My thanks, also, to the many newspapers for their wholehearted cooperation.

Without the generous award by the Library of Congress Grants-in-Aid for Studies in the History of American Civilization, made in 1945, this work could not have been undertaken. My sincerest gratitude, therefore, to the Library and its head, Dr. Luther Evans. I am especially obligated to Professor Allan Nevins of Columbia University for his constant encouragement and his careful criticism of the completed manuscript; to Professor Dan E. Clark of the University of Oregon for his friendly interest in the project and who, along with Professor Nevins, helped to launch it; to Lancaster Pollard, superintendent of the Oregon Historical Society, who generously made available all the resources of its library, and whose friendship is one of the happy aspects of my research experience. My warm appreciation to Professor Oscar Osborn Winther of Indiana University for his helpful suggestions and comments; and to Richard L. Neuberger of Portland for his keen interest throughout. The academic scholars of the region were most liberal with their aid, and to them, collectively, my thanks. I am indebted, also, to my many good friends—Vera R. Thompson in particular—who assisted with the laborious details in preparing the manuscript for publication.

The officers and staffs of the numerous libraries I visited were exceedingly cooperative. I want to express my gratitude especially to Charles W. Smith and Ronald Todd of the University of Washington Library and to the officers and staffs of the following institutions: The Library of the Oregon Historical Society in Portland, the Oregon State Library at Salem, the Library Association of Portland, the State College of Washington Library at Pullman, the University of Oregon Library at Eugene, the Bancroft Library at Berkeley, the Columbia University Library, and the New York Public Library.

To my wife I owe the greatest debt of all for her unflagging patience and her able assistance in more ways than I could possibly enumerate.

S. W.

GAINESVILLE, FLORIDA
May 10, 1949

Contents

One

For Furs and Fortunes

In the days of the white-sailed vessels, it took many long, dreary months to plow and toss and drift halfway round the world, through treacherous storm-tossed waters and becalmed tropical seas, from the continent of Europe to the mystic Orient. So insatiable was the greed for the exotic spices and priceless jewels of that fabulous land that kings and merchant princes risked fortunes and lives to obtain them. Ships with their crews were frequently lost, the interminably long route made the journey costly in men and matériel, and trade rivalries among the nations added to the hazards of the voyage. It was obviously essential to find a more direct course.

One bedeviled mariner, convinced that the Indies could be reached by sailing due west, set out into unknown seas reputedly inhabited by terrifying monsters. He found no legendary creatures and he stumbled across a new continent, but he failed in the original purpose of his quest. Other audacious navigators followed, ranging the largely uncharted seas. Out of their occasionally fanciful reports developed the conviction that a Northwest Passage, linking the Atlantic to the Pacific, existed around or through the northern part of the American continent. A legend circulated about a Strait of Anian somewhere on the northwest coast of the newly discovered land which was supposed to lead into the Passage.

The story was strengthened by the narrative of a Greek seaman, Juan de Fuca, which appeared in a book published early in the seventeenth century. De Fuca claimed to have sailed for twenty days on a strait which he had discovered that flowed directly into the Passage.

During the years that followed, the search for a Northwest Passage continued. Russia, Spain, and England—offering a reward of £20,000 to the finder—sent out ships, but, though their explorers circum-

navigated the globe and reached the hitherto unknown western coast-
line of the New World, the location of the mysterious Passage remained a mystery. Finally, in the early years of the nineteenth century, a Russian, Baron Wrangell, ended the frantic quest by proving
conclusively that the Strait of Anian and the Passage existed only in
legend.

In the meantime the searchings led to a discovery which resulted
in a struggle for empire among the three old nations and one that
was but newborn: that the pelt of a little mammal which inhabited
the Northwest coast could bring as rich returns as jewels or spices.
And that came about, as such things often do, entirely by accident.

When the survivors of the shipwrecked Russian expedition which
had been led by Vitus Bering reached Kamchatka, they found to
their amazement that the sea-otter pelts which they had contrived
into makeshift clothing were considered almost priceless by the
Chinese merchants. By a strange and remarkable coincidence another
group of sailors, thirty-five years later, also discovered the value of
the sea otter under similar circumstances. These were Captain James
Cook's men who, having survived an Indian massacre, sailed on to
Canton. As had happened before, they received a munificent sum for
the worn and abused remnants of the otter skins.

Reports of the Canton adventure were published widely in English newspapers. The record of the voyages by the official chronicler,
Captain King, achieved tremendous popularity in England and on
the Continent, where it had been translated into several languages.
King had devoted considerable space in his narrative to an enticing
picture of the possibilities for lucrative trade; so had John Ledyard,
an American member of Cook's crew, in his book published the year
before. The result was to be expected—a mad scramble for the pelts
of the unfortunate mammal.

The Russians had gone scurrying back for the golden fleece as
soon as they realized the value of the otter, and had chartered a
fur company to exploit the area. Spain claimed rights to the coast by
virtue of the explorations of her mariners. England entered on the
scene, followed shortly thereafter by the United States. And all because of a mythical passage which was supposed to have joined two
oceans, and a little animal "of the genus *Lutra*, having webbed and
clawed feet and dark brown fur."

The first Americans to venture the journey to the Northwest coast,
an expedition of thousands of miles around South America, were

Captains John Kendrick and Robert Gray. It took them a year to reach it. Gray returned several years later, this time exploring a bit, and succeeded in taking his ship, the *Columbia*, across the treacherous, wave-lashed, and foam-sprayed bar that hid the mouth of the river he named after his vessel. While in the region, he met a British naval officer, Captain Vancouver, and told him about the river which led into the interior. The Englishman sent one of his men to investigate and afterward recorded in his journal that he was the first white man to reach its mouth. Largely on the rival claims of both men rested the rights to all of the vast Oregon country subsequently contested by their governments. At the beginning of the nineteenth century, Spain and Russia withdrew from the area following peaceful negotiations. This left England and America, by agreement, in joint possession for the next twenty-eight years.

Neither nation knew much about the land which they held in common. Interest centered on the temperate coast, which is watered for six months—from October to May—by almost continuous rain. This, together with the mild breezes blowing in from the Pacific, keeps the grass green throughout the year. Some distance inland, on the other side of the soaring Cascade Mountains, the winters are dry and cold, the snowfalls heavy. The entire region is a study in topographical contrasts: rugged, towering mountains and gently rolling hills, jagged chasms and smooth, rich-soiled valleys, turbulent rivers and quietly flowing streams, barren plains and densely wooded forests. Two great rivers flow through the land—the mighty Columbia, rising high in the north and draining a vast area until it empties into the ocean, in one place rushing through a gorge flanked by crags of terrifying majesty; and the picturesque Snake, winding a tortuous course through some sections that men have yet been unable to penetrate.

The magnificence of the Oregon country was revealed to the fur trappers who followed the seamen. Explorations of the westernmost reaches were begun by the Northwest Company, which had been operating in eastern Canada since about the middle of the eighteenth century. Alexander Mackenzie, one of its officials, found the region abounding in fur-bearing animals that, in addition to the otter, would yield lucrative rewards. Mackenzie began to have dreams of empire. He visualized overland trading routes extending from the eastern to the western oceans, with a chain of integrated fur posts along the way and throughout the Northwest. The company expanded, its members spread out, penetrating and investigating the area and establishing posts. Foremost in the roster of these pioneers of the wilds are Duncan McGillivray, David Thompson, Simon Fraser, John Stuart —names which live on in the annals of adventure.

In addition to their explorations, the hardy, lusty Nor'westers have to their credit playing host to the first white woman to set foot in the Northwest. While in England, Donald McTavish, an executive of the company, stopped in at a Portsmouth pub for a glass of ale. He was waited on by a lovely, vivacious young barmaid with inviting blue eyes. McTavish was enchanted. Before he left, he had invited her to accompany him to America and, to his amazement and delight, the wench accepted. The hardheaded Scotsman bought her a complete trousseau, and when they set sail, Jane Barnes had a wardrobe more suitable for cosmopolitan London than for a land inhabited by a handful of white men and hordes of red-skinned aborigines.

Jane remained in the wilds of the Northwest for only a month and a half, but during that time she managed to create quite a bit of excitement at Fort George. Among her conquests was an Indian chief who wanted to make her his chief squaw and pursued her so persistently that she was unable to walk on the beach alone. While McTavish was temporarily absent, Jane—finding life lonely or dull or both—moved into the quarters of the young trader, Alexander Henry. Not long thereafter, both McTavish and Henry were drowned while crossing the Columbia to the *Todd,* a supply ship stationed on the side of the river opposite the fort. It may have been that the longboat leaked, or perhaps that the two men got into a quarrel over the fickle Jane—history, alas, does not say. Though there must have been many other gallants at the fort who would have been delighted to offer Jane their protection, she had apparently had enough of the place where the only women who could envy her clothes were ignorant natives. At any rate, we next hear of her sailing away on the *Todd* with a young lieutenant, bound for China. Not for another thirty years was the Northwest coast to be graced by a white woman.

At the other end of the continent, American interest in an overland expedition to the far reaches of the land was slow to kindle. Nothing was known of the country beyond the Mississippi except that it was vast; and anyone with some imagination could have ventured to say that great deserts, thick forests, impassable mountains, and swift rivers would have to be crossed on the way to the western ocean—not to mention the hazard of treacherous redskins who roamed the land. Thomas Jefferson as early as 1783 recognized the potentialities of the Northwest trade, especially after the publication of John Ledyard's *Journal*. He made a number of attempts to have the area explored, but it was not until after he became President that he was able to launch an expedition by persuading Congress to make an appropriation of $2,500. The declared purpose of the undertaking was to "extend the external commerce of the United States," which meant to develop trade with the Indians as far as the Columbia.

Jefferson selected his private secretary, Meriwether Lewis, and a frontier fighter, William Clark, to act as leaders and maintain military discipline. The expedition of forty-five persons, which included army men, *voyageurs*, and frontiersmen, was well equipped. It was necessary to take along not only certain basic foods and scientific instruments, but also a varied assortment of gifts with which to ensure the friendliness of the Indians encountered along the way. The group acquired one female member, a young Indian woman named Sacajawea. She and her French-Canadian husband, Toussaint Charbonneau, who understood the Hidatsa tongue, had joined the party at what is now Bismarck, North Dakota. When they left, Sacajawea had a newborn son strapped to her back, and she carried him throughout the entire march. This is the fabric out of which legends are cut, and Sacajawea has been immortalized in the Northwest as the guide of the Lewis and Clark expedition, without whom it could not have succeeded. This is, of course, an exaggeration, for, while the young woman was extremely helpful on a number of occasions, she was familiar with only a small section of the country through which the party passed. Once, by her coolness and presence of mind, she saved a boatload of instruments, maps, medicines, and other valuable supplies from being lost while crossing a stream during a squall. She performed various tasks about the camp and taught the men how to supplement their diet with edible roots and berries. Most important, she acted as interpreter to, and ensured the friendliness of, not only the vitally important Shoshone tribe who guided the party and whose chief was her brother, but of other tribes along the way. Her son, Baptiste, was later educated by Clark and taken to Europe by a German prince. He returned to America to become a noted guide, interpreter, and champion of the American West.

The epochal journey to and from the coast took two years and four months. During that time, the Lewis and Clark party experienced almost everything that a wild, unmapped country has to offer those who seek to penetrate its virgin fastness. The physical feat of crossing the vast area in all seasons and in all kinds of weather, over swiftly flowing, treacherous streams, through forest undergrowth so thick the men had to hack their way through foot by foot, with their ears always attuned and their eyes strained for wild beasts or unfriendly Indians, was a truly stupendous accomplishment. Considering the vicissitudes, it is amazing that only one member of the party died—a sergeant Floyd succumbed to "bilious colic" three months after the expedition got under way.

The Lewis and Clark undertaking was not merely a march across a continent. It was a sociological mission in the valuable and interesting data it collected on Indian customs and folklore; it was a biological excursion in the important information gathered on the flora and fauna; it was a geological venture in the great storehouse of knowledge assembled; it was a trade mission in paving the way toward later profitable exchanges with the Indians; and, above all, it was an experience in human relations, for the paths of the white men and the red converged at many points, and friendly intercourse was established not only because the Americans frequently left trinkets for the natives, but because their behavior was courteous, wise, and diplomatic.

Though the accounts of Lewis and Clark should have been enough to discourage another overland crossing, and the way by sea to the coast was a long one, their stirring reports of the rich and lucrative trade possibilities in the far-off land proved an irresistible lure to those interested in amassing wealth. They intrigued the New York fur merchant, John Jacob Astor, who saw a magnificent opportunity to establish a mercantile hegemony over a vast empire and at the same time give the British, from whom he had been purchasing skins at outrageous prices, some keen competition.

Astor formulated a brilliant plan for a triangular trade, with a fur-trading post on the Columbia to be supplied by a boat from the East which would then go on to China, laden with the furs obtained at the post. An overland route from St. Louis would supplement the sea passage. In addition, a coastwise trade would be maintained. He began by sending out two expeditions, one overland and one by the sea route.

The venture seemed doomed from the beginning. The first ship, the ill-fated *Tonquin*, which reached the Columbia in 1811 after an internally stormy passage of ceaseless quarrels among the hot-tempered

Captain Thorn, his crew, and the passengers, was blown to bits after it had been in the area a few months. It was believed to have been destroyed by two members of the crew, survivors of an Indian massacre provoked by Thorn's striking a chief with whom he had been trading.

A year after it had set out, the overland party, composed of Wilson Price Hunt and a group of French-Canadians, finally straggled into the fort built by the *Tonquin* crew. It was a decimated group of exhausted, beaten men who had endured incredible hardships vividly described later in Washington Irving's *Astoria*. They subsisted for five months until the second ship, the *Beaver*, arrived with supplies and reinforcements of men. With renewed hope, they dug in and prepared to compete with Alexander Mackenzie's Nor'westers. Two years later, Fate struck her next blow: war between the United States and Great Britain. The position of the Americans became untenable, particularly when they heard that a British sloop-of-war was on the way toward them to take over. Hoping to salvage something before all should be lost, they sold out completely to the Nor'westers, bringing a grandiose venture to its end.

With the Americans temporarily out of the way, the Northwest Company held sole possession of the field. They also continued their trading operations throughout Canada, but there they came into competition with the old Hudson's Bay Company, which had been dealing in furs for a century and a half. Though it would seem that the area was large enough to permit both to operate without treading on each other's toes, a contest for supremacy had begun almost as soon as the newer organization had been formed. Both companies stopped at nothing, including murder, pillage, kidnapings, duels, and the only beneficiaries were the Indians for whose furs they vied with liquor as their weapon. The violence reached its height when a small English settlement that lay in the path of the Nor'westers' trade was almost destroyed and twenty-one colonists slaughtered in cold blood. The reverberations of the Seven Oaks Massacre, as it was called, reached Britain, and the two companies were ordered to clean house, under threat of an official investigation. The net result was a merger; the name Hudson's Bay was retained, and Mackenzie's dream was at last brought to a successful fruition.

The company began to expand its operations and re-form its organization. John McLoughlin, formerly a doctor and trader for the Nor'westers, was appointed chief factor of the Columbia River district. The "White-Headed Eagle," as the Indians called him because of the thick, prematurely white hair which hung down to his shoulders, was well suited to his job both in personality and appearance. A man of Herculean proportions, six feet, four inches tall, with an erect, dignified carriage and charming, courtly manners, he was, as Hubert Howe Bancroft put it, "fitted to govern men by both awe and love."

McLoughlin was placed at a new post, Fort Vancouver, built at the mouth of the Columbia, which developed into the center of fur-trading activities in the area. The chief factor's control reached to the remotest outpost. He was not only the Law, but Church and State as well.

The fort was actually a small village enclosed by a heavily built timber stockade and containing offices, living quarters, and ware-houses, as well as McLoughlin's two-story house, consisting of his private quarters, a spacious dining room, a smoking room, and several guest rooms. Scattered throughout the rest of the protected area were various workshops, a mill, a dairy, a barn, a granary, and a salmon storehouse. Outside of the stockade was the community proper, which consisted of the houses of company servants, a Catholic church, a schoolhouse, a stable, more workshops, and even a crude hospital.

Like the medieval manor of which it was reminiscent, Fort Vancouver became almost entirely self-sufficient within a short time after its establishment. Food for the table came from the forests and streams, from the vegetable and fruit gardens (later extended into the Willamette Valley), and after some years, from herds of cows, hogs, goats, and sheep that multiplied rapidly under McLoughlin's careful super-vision. The chief factor was skillful at husbandry. He sent to California for seed and cattle, imported a Scotch horticulturist who initiated apple, strawberry and rose culture, added horses to the other livestock, and made his domain comfortable and prosperous.

An occasional supply ship brought clothing and other essentials not available locally and, most welcome of all, an assortment of current periodicals, books, and newspapers. Fort Vancouver was a cultural outpost in the wilderness, with a library containing, among other classics, Shakespeare and Walter Scott, specialized books on medicine, theology, astronomy, and other areas of scientific and philosophical thought. Distinguished visitors to the region—botanists, scientists, artists, explorers—stopped at the fort and enjoyed its excellent table and the urbane conversation around it.

A social hierarchy was rigidly maintained. Only officers were permitted to dine in the big house; their Indian wives and half-breed children ate in their own quarters. Infidelity was emphatically discouraged. McLoughlin himself had married the Indian widow of Alexander MacKay, a victim of the *Tonquin* disaster, and had adopted their four children. She was always treated with the utmost respect and courtesy and remained his life partner to the end.

A number of other Hudson's Bay Company trading posts were strategically placed throughout the area. Some of the furs were obtained from the Indians, who received in return a variety of items such as thread, needles, scissors, mirrors, knives, cloth. The natives, however, could not be depended upon for a steady supply, and so the brigade system was instituted. A group, varying in number from fifty to as many as four hundred, consisted of the chief trader, hunters, trappers, clerks, storekeepers, and a host of Indians, often with their entire families who were taken along to perform the menial tasks of caring for the equipment, the horses, and the provisions. The departure was always festive, with bugles or hornpipes blowing and the company lined up as though on parade. Brigadiers penetrated the mountain fastness and the thick forests and some leaders carved new routes or cut passes through hitherto impenetrable country.

For the decade and a half following Astor's disastrous venture, Americans offered the English little competition in the fur trade of the Northwest. Only an occasional expedition ventured much beyond the Divide until 1828, when Jedediah Smith—sometimes called the "knight in buckskin," because he was reputed to have carried a Bible in one hand and a rifle in the other—opened routes from Salt Lake to the present Los Angeles and from the Sacramento to the Columbia while he and his party trapped the area.

The next to appear was Captain Bonneville, who, for about three years, did some trapping and trading. He met a few men from the Rocky Mountain Fur Company—which operated on the other side of the mountains—who had wandered across the Great Divide during that time. Bonneville was followed by the imaginative Nathaniel J. Wyeth, a New England ice merchant who had been inspired by an Oregon enthusiast.

Wyeth organized a group of some twenty farmers and artisans, put them into woolen jackets, pantaloons, striped woolen shirts, and rawhide boots. Before the group left, it spent ten days on an island in Boston Harbor getting some "wilderness" experience and setting staid

Bostonians by the ears. Equipped with three amphibious monstrosities, part wagon and part canoe, which were supposed to be able to travel on land and on sea, ten bugles which he ordered his company to learn to play, and food, clothing, equipment, and trinkets, the party started merrily off. The "amphibiums," as they were dubbed, were junked at St. Louis when Wyeth, who had obtained his information about the West from the libraries of Cambridge, was told the facts of life about travel across country.

To their great good fortune, the travelers met William L. Sublette of the Rocky Mountain Fur Company, who was on his way to the company's rendezvous, and he took the band of innocents under his protection. The crossing was rough, food and water gave out, some of the men contracted mountain fever, and some deserted. By the time Fort Vancouver was reached, twelve discouraged travelers remained. When it was learned that the supply ship which Wyeth had sent out had been wrecked, the already wavering group disbanded.

Wyeth, however, was persistent. No sooner had he returned to Boston than he began to make plans for another excursion, even contracting to deliver $30,000 worth of supplies to some fur men. The following year he was off again. When he arrived in the Northwest, he built the later famous Fort Hall and trapped and fished for salmon. Like Astor, however, his ventures seemed destined to fail. Goods were stolen, a number of men became ill and died, others deserted, and his small profits went into liquor consumed by the trader at his fort. At last Wyeth himself became ill and, now completely disheartened, he sold Fort Hall to the Hudson's Bay Company and returned home.

With Wyeth's failure ended organized commercial efforts to establish permanent fur-trading posts in the Oregon country. But for some years individual Americans had trapped and traded for furs in the Northwest, using Missouri as their base. They were a peculiar breed all their own, these fur men, but akin to the adventurers of all ages. Living within four walls would have suffocated them, and they were unable to remain long in one spot without getting an incurable itch to wander elsewhere. They were a tough breed, with something of the devil and something of the hero in their makeup. They had the kind of courage which, while holding life cheap, still holds it beautiful, and would fight for it to the last gasp. Their knowledge of the lore of their chosen habitat was combined with such ingenuity as is developed by creatures of the wilds, which, essentially, they were. They were masters at reading signs—how many Indians had passed along a trail, when and of what tribe, or the significance in the unusual chatter of birds, and other such minutiae. They had the skill of the savage, too, in hunting, trapping, fishing, in knowing how to survive off the earth if necessary. Their appetites were gargantuan—six to eight pounds of buffalo at one meal were wolfed easily down and followed by a dessert several hours later of the same. They were a lusty breed who took their pleasures where they found them.

The mountain man lived hard and risked his neck daily to secure the precious pelts. A standard dress and equipment were developed to meet his needs. He wore a flannel, cotton or antelope shirt, leather breeches, and buffalo-skin leggings under which his legs were wrapped with pieces of blanket, moccasins, a coat made of a blanket or buffalo skin, and a woolen or buffalo-skin hat. His horse carried a saddle, a bridle, a sack containing beaver traps, a pouch for pipe, tobacco and flint, beaver bait, a blanket, powder horn and bullet pouch, a hatchet and a butcher knife.

Some Indians were friendly and some were not. Joe Meek, one of the most famous of the Rocky Mountain Fur Company trappers, related an incident of his encounter with a band of redskins. Meek, Kit Carson, a third trapper, and three Delawares were on a hunt about a hundred and fifty miles from camp, trudging along with mules and rifles on the broad plains. Suddenly one of the party spotted a band of about two hundred Comanches riding rapidly toward them in war formation. The plain stretched unbroken and barren between the white men and the hostile Indians, without a single rock or clump of bushes behind which the trapping party could take shelter. After a hasty council of war, Meek and his comrades quickly killed their seven mules and created a fortification out of a ring of carcasses within which they dug a trench. The Indians charged the little group with wild whoops and yells, but, as had been anticipated, the redmen's horses were frightened by the smell of the blood of the slaughtered mules and refused to come within yards of the ring, despite the cruelest urging. The savages kept circling around, hurling spears and shooting arrows. The battle went on all day, three of the defenders firing while the others kept recharging the rifles. They were good marksmen, and toward evening the Indians found their ranks seriously depleted. Finally, the once formidable group of warriors wheeled and rode off.

Tom Fitzpatrick, another trapper, survived an even more hazardous adventure only because he was one of the most expert mountain men in the business. He had delivered a message to the head of a wagon train some distance from the trappers' rendezvous and started out alone to return. This was exceedingly risky, but he had made the trip to the caravan safely and besides, risks were an everyday affair.

Fitzpatrick traveled mostly at night, catching a few hours' sleep in some carefully selected thicket which could hide him and the two horses that he used alternately. He was making his way through a small valley when he ran into a wandering village of Indians. A lone white man was always fair game to the redskins, and these were the bloodthirsty Blackfeet. Fitzpatrick abandoned one horse, turned, and made a hell-for-leather dash in the opposite direction on the other. His mount, which had been pushed hard since the beginning of the journey, soon gave out, and Fitzpatrick clambered up a cliff on foot. He managed to remain hidden in a crevice in the rocks for two days while the Indians searched for him furiously. On the second night he eluded his pursuers and started off into the mountains. He was in the wild Snake River country, and in attempting to cross the river on a small raft he had built, he lost all his tools except a belt knife. For the next five days he walked in the direction of the camp, having found his bearings with the uncanny instinct of a creature to whom the wilds is a native habitat. Without a rifle or tackle, he subsisted on roots and berries. At last, half starved, his clothes in shreds, his bare feet bleeding, he staggered into camp.

It was a dangerous life, but it was a good life too, for those to whom freedom meant more than home and family, who enjoyed the daily tests of skill, and who, though they would have laughed had you said this to them, had a bit of the poet's appreciation of the magnificent country through which they roamed. The trappings of civilization meant nothing to them. They pitched their tipis in a sheltered spot, preferably near a stream, and after the day's toil they returned to eat, to sit around and talk, to tell stories, to sing. One of the songs which the fur men were reputed to have sung is "The Fur Trader's Ballad," though its literacy seems incongruous when the nature of the men is considered:

> Bold and merry Astor men are we,
> We scour the valleys and sail the sea;
> From swift St. Lawrence to Columbia's main,
> From Mohawk's vale to Willamette's plain.
> We traverse the country o'er and o'er,
> From forest to forest and shore to shore—

Yo-ho for that soldier and sailor, ranger and raider,
So dauntless and daring, the fearless fur-trader.

Leaders of civilization are we,
Ranging the land from sea to sea;
We trade with the savage and make love to his maid,
By campfire's glow and in green forest glade;
We trade, fight and frolic, and hunt for gold,
As free as Robin of Hood [*sic*] of old—
Here's to the venturesome, rollicking raider,
The gallant, true-hearted, care-free fur-trader.

And, of course, there was the annual company rendezvous to which the trappers and traders came to turn in their hauls and to make up in wild carousing for the many months of solitude.

It was a carnival with running, jumping, shooting, wrestling contests, fighting, singing, laughing, and the endless drinking. Fur men rarely drank while on the job. It was too risky, for they needed all their wits about them. At the rendezvous, liquor flowed in abundance, raw alcohol generously mixed with water at about $5 a pint, but it slid down thirsty throats like the finest Scotch. Men squatted or sat around trying to outlie or outbrag each other about their adventures. Joe Meek, who was no slouch at telling a tall tale, related that at his first rendezvous he saw four trappers playing cards with the body of a dead man as a table.

Indians were there, also, to buy and sell. Their most important article of trade to the trappers was their women. Indian girls were sometimes radiantly beautiful, and those that were not could make themselves appealing in ways known to women from time immemorial. A few trinkets could buy almost any one for the night, and for a little more a trapper, if he wished, could have a wife. A native girl was more useful as a mate to the fur men than the most accomplished white woman. She could prepare his furs for market, sew his clothes, take care of his horses, mules, and equipment, carry wood and water, make a clean, orderly home of his tent—and be grateful for the privilege of being allowed to work like a slavey. As a companion, she was ideal. He need not curb his tongue, for innocent-looking Indian maidens could sometimes go him one better in jokes and stories. She was always gay and cheerful and she was ingenious in devising ways to amuse and entertain her lord and master. Best of all, should he grow weary of his wife, he could send her home with a little something and start all over again.

Joe Meek related an entertaining tale of his wooing of an Indian maid. "You see," he reminisced, "there was [*sic*] no white women west of the Mississip' in those days, and my forefathers were great on raising families, so naturally I wanted a wife. My first wife, Umentukket, had died, and the second wife, both being Nez Percés, had left me, and after a few months I took quite a shine to Virginia. From the way that girl looked at me I half suspected she liked me, and so, one day, says I, 'Virginia, I want you.' Virginia gave me to understand that I already had one wife and it took me a long time to convince her that I was a widower to all intents and purposes. I finally overcame her scruples and she consented, provided the chief-father was willing—and there's where I had the tussle.

"Do you know, that old chief had been talking to the missionaries, and he wouldn't stand for Virginia marrying a man who already had a wife. For a whole month I argued with him; I wrestled and threw every Indian of the Nez Percé tribe, to show him that I was strong and capable; I outran every Indian in the plateau region, and one day caught the chief's big black stallion in a straight foot-race—and still he said, 'No good; you one wife now; no two squaws.'

"And right here is where I closed in on Virginia's dad, for I pulled the Bible on him one day when the missionary was there, and I read of David and Solomon, and their many wives, and all this time I translated the Bible story I was asking the missionary if I wasn't reading right, and what could he do but say that I was?

"Then the father walked over, took Virginia by the hand and said, 'Go with him, he not so bad as David and Solomon, and he heap stout; he take many skins in his trap.' And that's the way I got Virginia."

When silk and felt replaced beaver for hats, the fur era in the Northwest came to an end. It had existed for about twenty years, and, it is estimated, about two thousand men were in the area during that time. "Judged by the volume of business . . . ," says Chittenden, "the fur trade was of relatively insignificant proportions; but its importance and historic interest depend upon other and quite different considerations." These considerations, according to another historian, were numerous, including "the saving of Oregon to the United States," and when a number of the trappers settled down among the pioneers who came to the region in later years, they were the " 'hearts of oak' on whose firm loyalty the young empire when in peril always depended."

Some of the trappers and traders remained loyal to their squaws, became good family men, and made homes for their wives and children. Joe Meek, for instance, took a donation land claim on Tualatin Prairie and participated in the formation of the provisional government at Champoeg. His friend Robert Newell also retired to the Willamette Valley and actively engaged in the cultural life of the community. He was one of the directors of the Oregon Printing Association, which published the first paper in the region, and the organizer of the first debating society.

A few found themselves unable to leave the wilds which had been home to them for so long and they joined the tribes of their squaws. Others became guides to the emigrant trains which began to roll across the country after 1840, and counselors to military expeditions. "A trapper . . . was able to make a map of the region he roamed over which the reader of explorers' reports would be glad to possess to-day."

And some of the top-notch mountain men became officials of the Bureau of Indian Affairs, working hard and earnestly to protect the bewildered and unhappy aborigines who were steadily being squeezed out, hunted down, and destroyed. The treatment of the Indian by the white man's government is a tragic saga all its own.

Two

Conflict in Cultures

When the early explorers arrived in the Northwest, they found the natives a generally friendly people who stared with childlike wonder at their white skins, their clothing and the other accoutrements of civilization, and their white-winged boats. They were a simple, primitive people not lacking, however, in cunning and with moral standards which kept the white men constantly on their guard to prevent the disappearance of cooking utensils or other shiny objects. Unless the red men were abused or mistreated, they acted cordially toward their visitors and frequently helped them find their way through the wilderness or provided them with food.

The coastal natives had not advanced very far up the ladder of civilization, and those of the inland region were even more backward. They were all, of course, expert hunters and fishermen and knew how to preserve sea food to last until the next season's run. They made clothes out of animal skins or the bark of trees. In their woodwork, however, the tribes of the coast achieved a high degree of skill. They constructed houses, some of them of tremendous size, which endured for generations, using bone or stone wedges together with an ingenious cutting tool to shape the planks. They built canoes sturdy enough to hold sixty men and travel several hundred miles in ocean waters. They fashioned wood into cooking utensils and burial caskets.

In some respects the social structure of the natives was not strange to the white men. The economy of most of the tribes was geared to war, and slavery was a well established institution. Slaves, however, were treated humanely, apparently no worse than were poor relations. The society had rigid group distinctions. Wealth, social position, and membership in religious orders were inherited and, consequently, standing in the community predetermined for the individual before birth. The family structure was patriarchal, with women holding an inferior position but seldom abused or degraded by their husbands, and polygamy was frequently practiced.

The Indian, like his culturally more advanced brother-under-the-skin, had need for ego satisfaction and used time-honored methods to obtain it. The wealthy man flaunted his earthly possessions and when celebrating a marriage or birth or the acquisition of a new wife, lavished a varied assortment of gifts on his guests. According to custom, however, the recipients were expected to reciprocate with interest the following year. At a festival, or "potlatch," tribal chieftains or men of means attempted to surpass one another in orgies of extravagant display, destroying valuable pieces of property, such as canoes which took months to build, or even setting fire to one of their houses.

Sexual mores permitted Indian women to be promiscuous, which, with the coming of the white man, was partly responsible for the later physical deterioration of the race. The early English sea captains, the sailors who frequently lost their way on the Northwest coast, the New England trading captains and their crews, the English and American trappers—none were slow to take advantage of such unaccustomed generosity. Captain Bishop of the ship *Ruby*, which traded with the Chinook Indians on the Columbia River in 1795, remarked that gratitude for little trifles given by the white men was expressed not only in the form of foodstuffs, but in furnishing the men with the daughters of the tribe, some of whom were well featured young women. Possibly Captain Bishop's first officer, Mr. Williams, was one of the first to take advantage of the Indians' courtesy during a trip which he had made on the ship *Jenny* three years before. The captain discerned visible evidence of his mate's earlier call. "Shelathwell, chief next to Taucum, has a child by one of his Woman Slaves, which he ascribes to Mr. Williams, the 1st officer, who was here four years ago."

Lewis and Clark found signs of venereal disease when they traveled through the region, but Clark apparently did not consider it a serious matter, for he comments quite casually:

Several Indians and squars came this evening I beleave for the purpose of gratifying the passions of our men. These people appear to view sensuality as a necessary evill, and do not appear to abhore this as crime in the unmarried females. The young women sport openly with our men and appear to receve the approbation of theer friends and relations for so doing. Maney of the women are handsom.

As the explorers and the trading vessels gave way to the fur men, the problem was aggravated. By the spring of 1814, syphilis had already reached epidemic proportions among the fur traders. The policy of friendly relations with the Indians which the Hudson's Bay Company at Fort George had cemented by means of the union of its men with the squaws of the region produced also the undesirable effect of undermining the trade effectiveness of the company. More and more men were becoming disabled as a result of their escapades, and business was suffering thereby. Alexander Henry, then head of the company's fort, was so disturbed by this trend that he threatened to place every obliging squaw visitor to the company's property in shackles and to withhold pay from the men unable to work because of their disability. His successor to the post, Donald McTavish, was more considerate of human frailties than of company profits, for he relaxed these proscriptions. Physical intimacy with the Indian women by the British and American fur traders and trappers continued long enough for the effects to be felt by many a descendant of the red man.

In addition to the spirochete, the white man brought debilitating illnesses. Contrary to popular belief that the outdoor life of the Indians rendered them immune to ills of the flesh, they suffered from many common ailments. They were, however, able to cope with these more or less successfully with a combination of weird, ritualistic exercises, complicated herbal remedies, and other devices. But such a simple ailment as measles, which incapacitates white men briefly, proved fatal to the natives, often wiping out whole tribes. A measles epidemic in 1847 among the Cayuse Indians of the inland area was one of the contributing factors in a bloody massacre at a mission station.

Tuberculosis and the more dreaded "fever and ague," probably a form of influenza, took a heavy toll. John K. Townsend, an ornithologist who accompanied the Wyeth expedition, described what he saw in 1835:

The depopulation has been truly fearful. A gentleman told me that only four years ago, as he wandered near what had been formerly a thickly populated village, he counted no less than sixteen dead men and women, lying unburied and festering in the sun in front of their habitations. Within the houses, all were sick; not one had escaped the contagion; upwards of a hundred individuals, men, women and children, were writhing in agony on the floors of their houses, with no one to render them any assistance. Some were in the dying struggle, and clenching with the convulsive grasp of death their disease-worn companions, shrieked and howled in their last sharp agony.

Probably there does not now exist one, where five years ago there were a hundred Indians; and in sailing up the river from the cape to the Cascades, the only evidence of the existence of the Indian is an occasional miserable wigwam, with a few wretched half-starved occupants.

The Indian population was estimated at around 100,000 in about 1780; within fifty years, as a result of epidemics, it had shrunk to only about 20,000.

Smallpox was another and deadly contribution of the white man. This dread disease had apparently been brought to the new land by the sailing vessels from New England which plied the waters from Boston to Canton. During their explorations of the Columbia River region, Lewis and Clark had been told by a Clatsop Indian of a malady that had come to his people some time before from the sea; on their journey eastward they encountered, near the Willamette River, Indians with pitted faces who had survived the pox. President Jefferson had apparently been concerned about the disease among the natives, for among his detailed instructions there was a specific order to Lewis to "carry with you some matter of the kine pox, inform them with whome you may be of its efficacy as a preservative from the smallpox; and instruct and encourage them in the use of it." Ross Cox, clerk at Fort Astoria, commented in 1814 that about thirty years before, smallpox had "committed dreadful ravages" and that the vestiges were still visible on the faces of the elderly men and women. It is not surprising that at a council convened in 1855 to sign peace treaties with the various tribes of the inland region, Kamiakin, chief of the Yakimas, explained that his early opposition to white settlement of the country had been due to the smallpox epidemics which had swept his area in former years.

By the time the missionaries and settlers came into the region, the Indians were only a miserable fragment of their former numbers and, consequently, the wars against the white settlers were inconsequential when compared with other frontiers. One Northwestern historian makes the interesting comment that but for the visitation of the various scourges on the tribes, American settlement would very likely have been delayed at least a decade or two, in which case the outcome of the Oregon question between England and the United States would not have resulted so favorably for this country!

It was the white man, also, who introduced liquor to the Indians—

another factor responsible for sapping their vitality. Vitus Bering, the first European to set foot on the West coast north of California, recorded in his *Journal*, under date of September 5, 1741, that, while anchored off the Schumagin Islands, he dispatched one of his aides to interview the natives. Upon his return, the officer reported that he had offered one of them "a glass of liquor, but as he tasted it he spat it out and returned the glass." This was the first recorded case of a Northwest Indian tasting the white man's famous "firewater." From then on, the beverage, which to a certain extent influenced the course of history in the region, became more palatable to the Indian, and within a short space of time he developed a definite craving for it.

Although it was the policy of the Hudson's Bay Company to discourage the use of intoxicants as bait in its trading enterprise, liquor was consumed by the red man wherever and whenever he was able to obtain it. The Nor'westers and the American fur traders constantly employed liquor as a valuable ally in their trade with the natives, who needed no inducement to accept it. A new element had been added to the existing culture pattern, and, if the American settlers in later years complained and protested against the excesses to which drink sometimes led the Indians, they could read Bering's account and conclude that this was one of the by-products of a Caucasian civilization's impingement upon an aboriginal one.

Even after the era of the fur men had ended, some of the settlers found that great profits were to be obtained in the liquor traffic. One hundred and fourteen years after alcohol was first introduced into the region, an Oregon newspaper carried the following account, of which there were many in a similar vein during that entire pioneer period:

The bluffs back of our residence have been made vocal with howls, yells, and a jargon of English and Indian blasphemy, on several nights during the past week. King Alcohol is now in the habit of making frequent nightly visits to the abodes of the poor savages, stirring up brawls, and turning the palaces of the "salmon eaters" into perfect bedlams. In their drunken sprees, the weaker part of them are often compelled to flee in all directions for safety. On last Sunday night, about 9 o'clock, we found an Indian with a double-barreled rifle in hand making his bed under cover of our stable. He told us that the Indians were frantic on "lum" and he had been compelled to flee the roost. On the same night two other Indians stood for nearly an hour within a few rods of our premises, belching forth the most horrid oaths and bestial obscenity, threatening each other with all sorts of tortures, and acting very much as other drunken men do under similar provocations.

Almost as quickly as the natives learned to appreciate liquor, they learned how to ask for it as a form of barter. Language is rarely an obstacle to trade and the fact that the red men's speech was completely incomprehensible to the Yankee and English traders and the white man's to them proved only a slight handicap to a profitable commercial intercourse. Linguistically, the situation was complicated by the various dialects, such as Nootka, Nisqually, Chinook, and Chehalis, each exceedingly complex in sentence structure and spoken within a very limited area.

First, at the port of Nootka, the traders picked up some of the words used by the local tribe, and the Indians, in turn, added some strange words to their vocabulary. Later, when the traders began to frequent the Columbia River, the Chinooks quickly mastered the trading vernacular that was in use, a combination of Nootkan and English. Still later, when permanent fur-trading posts were established and business conducted on a regular basis, the new language, or Chinook Jargon, as it came to be called, was enlarged by borrowing more words from the native tribes and from the French-Canadian voyageurs.

Words were continually added as the necessities of the situation required, and thus an extensive trade language comprising as many as five hundred words developed. About half were Chinook, forty from the dialects of other Salish tribes, about two dozen from Nootkan, some derived from corrupted French and English with possibly some Russian, and about forty formed by onomatopoeia. Among the latter, for instance, a duck was "quack-quack," a crow was "kaw-kaw," a heart, "tum-tum"; a clock, "ding-ding"; a laugh, "tee-hee." In many cases an adjective was prefixed to a noun, thereby forming another word. "Tenas" in Chinook meant small, "moos-moos" was a cow, "waum" was warm, "klootchman" was woman, "cole" was cold, "snass" was rain; therefore, "tenas moos-moos" was a small cow or calf; "tenas waum" meant spring, or the season when warm weather sets in; "tenas klootchman" was a small woman or a girl.

Gabriel Franchère, clerk at the fur-trading post at Astoria, said of it: "The Chinook language is spoken by all the nations from the mouth of the Columbia to the falls. It is difficult for strangers to pronounce, being full of gutterals like the Gaelic. The combination of *thl* or *tl* and *lt*, are as frequent in the Chinook as in the Mexican." Despite this and its limited vocabulary, the Jargon was used extensively and served well the need for which it had come into existence. Its great flexibility made it adaptable to all kinds of situations.

The missionaries who followed the fur traders to bring the word of God to the heathen quickly picked up the Jargon. They used it in daily intercourse and translated parts of the Bible, as well as many songs and hymns, into Chinook. A passage from one of the hymns reads:

> Kwansesum Jesus hias skookum (repeat twice)
> Kahkwa yaka papeh wawa.
>
> (Always Jesus is very strong
> So his paper [the Bible] says.)
>
> Chorus: Delate, nawitka . . . (repeat twice)
> Kahkwa yaka papeh wawa.
>
> (Truly, yes . . .
> So his paper says.)

Chinook Jargon dictionaries were printed for popular use throughout the Northwest, and eastern travel and guidebooks of the period often contained a section devoted to its vocabulary. During the gold rushes into the region, California newspapers published listings of Chinook words. Prefacing an enumeration appearing in one of its issues, the San Francisco *Evening Bulletin* declared that "It [the Jargon] will be found of great use to miners and all parties traversing the Indian country on the Northwest coast, who may have occasion to come in contact with the natives."

During the Civil War, the Chinook Jargon almost created an incident in the nation's capital. One day the Secretary of War summoned Oregon's Senator Nesmith and, fuming with rage, handed him a telegram, demanding an explanation of its contents. It read: "KLAT-A-WA NI-KA SIT-KUM MO-LITSCH WEGHT O-COKE KON-A-MOX LUM." The wire, sent to the senator by General Ingalls from the front, had been intercepted by the authorities. The Secretary shouted vehemently that he was going to do everything possible to stop code messages which made speculation on the stock market possible on the basis of secret information regarding troop movements. Quietly, and hiding a smile, Nesmith explained that the message was in Chinook, and he enlightened the Secretary on the nature of the Jargon, and how General Ingalls and General Grant and other army officers had become familiar with it while stationed at Fort Vancouver. Whereupon he proceeded to translate: "Send me half barrel more that same whiskey." "You see," Nesmith concluded, "Ingalls always trusts my judgment on whiskey. He thinks I can tell the quality of the liquor by feeling of the head of a barrel in the dark."

As late as 1870, more than a hundred thousand people, it was estimated, were conversing daily in the Jargon. Many words were also in common use, evidently having replaced their English equivalents, such as "klootchman," "skookum," "potlatch," "siwash," "cayuse." A decade later, these had been reduced to about a half-dozen and they sometimes were printed in quotation marks until, with the passing of the Indians from the scene, the Jargon died out.

Though the missionaries could successfully overcome the handicap of language, weaning the Indian from his own religion to that of the white man's was a different matter. They had to cope with a collection of myths and legends about the origin of the sun, the stars, the mountains, the role of the various animals which inhabited the land, the meaning of the river and ocean currents. It was a religion of animism coupled with a belief in gods ruling from on high whom the aborigines had constantly to propitiate. Mount Tacoma in Washington had the same significance to them as Mount Olympus had to the early Greeks, in the sense that both peoples regarded with awe and fear the omnipotence of the gods who ruled supreme from atop their sacred province.

The various tribes of the Northwest had their own legends and their own ruling deities, but none of the myths contained any reference to the existence of a benevolent god. Tyhee Sahale of the Columbia River Indians came closest to being an omnipotent spirit ruling from the skies, although there was no sure feeling regarding his friendship. In this respect there was no figure comparable to Manitou, the great kindly spirit found in the mythology of the Eastern tribes.

One of the major Indian gods was Tatoosh, the Thunder Bird, a mighty power who lived in the sky. He was so strong that he shook the mountains when he flapped his wings, and the flash of his eye caused the sky to crackle with lightning. So enormous was he that he caught great whales instead of salmon for food. Only by crushing a huge rock into powder so fine that he could not see it was it possible for Thunder Bird to create spears for the Indians to use for salmon fishing. He had made the mountain peaks which towered to the sky, had carved tremendous canyons out of the mountain barriers, had cut passes out of the obstructions and blocked the passage of stormy rivers by placing great rocks and boulders in their way. Tatoosh was a god of wrath and, to propitiate him, his picture was painted or carved on houses, canoes, canoe paddles, and other objects the Indians used. Often he was represented by a single eye flashing fire.

There were other, lesser gods living beyond the mountaintops whom the Indian sought to placate. In his human helplessness, he was impressed with the cunning and guile which enabled the smaller and weaker of the animals around him to outwit the larger and more powerful. In this frame of reasoning, the small, crafty animals became his earth gods. Coyote, one of the weakest but smartest, became the chief, with the fox ranking second. In some legends Coyote is even credited with the creation of human beings. The story is told that once the universe was inhabited only by animals, but Coyote decreed that there should be people and, lo and behold, they appeared. Then he ordered the sun to shine and so there was light. But his greatest achievement was the theft of fire from Mount Tacoma where it was guarded by the Tomanowas, the angry and vengeful spirits of whom the Indians were in mortal fear. The Tomanowas, they believed, were responsible for avalanches, earthquakes, storms, the eruption of volcanoes, and the Indians, therefore, derived considerable consolation from Coyote's success in outwitting them and kindred evil spirits.

The biblical tale of creation and man's fall from heavenly grace had to be made comprehensible to a people whose own explanation of this theme was the popular myth of the "Bridge of the Gods." This legend also accounts for the origin of the Cascade Mountains. Several different versions were current. In one, the Indians relate that when the Great Spirit created the world he erected a bridge at the Cascade locks which was to be a connecting link between earth and heaven. On it he placed fire, guarded by an old woman as wise as she was ancient, which was to be given to the people when they proved themselves worthy of it.

To help man develop wisdom and merit, the Great Spirit dispatched to earth his three sons, Multnomah the warrior, Klickitat the builder of totems, and Wayeest the sweet singer. An evil spirit, Kakahete, was determined to defeat the plans of the Great Spirit and began to taunt the old female watcher of the fire about her wrinkles and age, contrasting her to the young and beautiful Indian maidens, until she began to regard her withered face and body with loathing. In despair, she pleaded with the Great Spirit to restore youth to her, and, reluctantly, he finally did so. Her radiant beauty attracted the three sons of the Great Spirit, a fierce jealousy developed, and they began to quarrel violently among themselves.

Kakahete, the evil spirit, informed their mighty father of the state of affairs, but, when he came to investigate, he found to his great grief that his sons had slain one another. Infuriated and half mad with despair, he seized the pillars which supported the Bridge and pulled them down. The Bridge crashed into the river and the broken rocks formed the mighty Cascade Mountains. Then he began to pursue Kakahete, and the deep gorge of the river at The Dalles resulted when the evil spirit tripped. He fell with such violent force that the earth trembled to its very bowels from the impact. The Great Spirit then changed Multnomah into a waterfall, Wayeest into Mount Hood, Klickitat into a group of hills, and the female watcher of the fire into Mount St. Helens.

Another version of this story has as its central theme the destruction of the Bridge by the Great Spirit because the various Indian tribes were unable to learn how to live at peace with each other. When they took to fighting among themselves, he tore down the Bridge, which had been a symbol of peace, and transformed his sons into mountains whose tops were always to be covered with ice and snow. The Indians called these peaks Loo-Wit, Klickitat, and Wiyeast; the white men named them Mount St. Helens, Mount Adams, and Mount Hood. The tale of the "Bridge of the Gods" thus became a symbol and a warning to the red men of what happens when discord and strife replace peaceful living.

During the pioneer period of settlement, the Indian legends and folklore formed the romantic background of numerous stories published in the local periodical press, in the newspapers, and in some of the first novels. They were used as a backdrop against which the Indian was frequently idealized and glamorized, a tendency which prevailed in the white man's literary treatment of the native, despite the fact that he was generally regarded with contempt and hostility. The many lines of poetry and the many pages of fiction dealing with the red man offer little evidence of the underlying animosity and antagonism which characterized the relationship of the two peoples.

The settlers clashed frequently with the Indian, defended themselves against his attacks or lived in a state of armed truce, and steadily pushed him off the land which had been his as far back as anthropologists have been able to determine. It was the sad misfortune of the Indians to be the human obstruction on a road over which history was traveling. They were guilty of the cardinal sin for which many before them and many since have been condemned—that of blocking the progress of this mighty force.

The coming of the white man and the introduction of the white man's culture made the native an anachronism, a relic of the past, a representative of an archaic institution. Civilization produced settlements and settlements resulted in agriculture and the domestication of animals and plants, and this, in turn, led to a restriction of the hunting grounds which the Indian had roamed freely. There were, also, great profits in land speculation which made it necessary for the white man to sweep on and acquire additional holdings, extend the frontier of settlement even further, even if it meant the elimination of one property right in order to establish another. Apparently, there was not enough room for two completely diverse civilizations to exist side by side. Chief Seattle once poignantly told some white friends: "The very dust under your feet responds more lovingly to our footsteps than to yours, because it is the ashes of our ancestors." But the white man inherited that dust and, though it was alien, he nevertheless prospered upon it.

The story of the Indian retreat in the face of a superior advance was repeated many times over. The natives were driven farther and farther back, until there was no place left for them to go, and then they were placed on reservations to live in poverty and squalor, a free and nomadic people penned in like a herd of recalcitrant sheep.

In 1897 the once mighty Nez Percé tribe, who had befriended and dealt kindly with the invaders of their land, were a decimated handful of starving men, women, and children, huddled and crowded on a strip of barren soil in Kansas, hundreds of miles from their homeland. Desperate and heartsick as he saw his people dying before his eyes, Chief Joseph pleaded for leave to come to the nation's capital, and, after many weary months of delay, he was allowed to leave the reservation. Accompanied by his friend Yellow Bull and an interpreter, he came to Washington not to demand favors and special privileges, as did most of those who invaded government offices and besieged harassed officials, but to plead for simple justice. In a speech that for dignity and eloquence ranks with the finest in world literature, he addressed the white man's lawmakers:

At last I was granted permission to come to Washington and bring my friend Yellow Bull and our interpreter with me. I am glad we came. I want to shake hands with a great many friends, but there are some things I want to know which no one seems able to explain. I can not understand how the Government sends a man out to fight us, as it did General Miles, and then breaks his word. Such a Government has something wrong about it. I can not understand why so many chiefs are allowed to talk so many different ways, and promise so many different things. I have seen the Great Father Chief [the President], the next Great Chief [Secretary of the Interior], the Commissioner Chief [Hayt], the Law Chief [General Butler], and many other law chiefs [congressmen], and they all say they are my friends, and that I shall have justice, but while their mouths all talk right I do not understand why nothing is done for my people. I have heard talk and talk, but nothing is done. Good words do not last long until they amount to something. Words do not pay for my dead people. They do not pay for my country, now overrun by white men. They do not protect my father's grave. They do not pay for my horses and cattle. Good words will not give me back my children. Good words will not make good the promise of your War Chief, General Miles. Good words will not give my people good health and stop them from dying. Good words will not get my people a home where they can live in peace and take care of themselves. I am tired of talk that comes to nothing. It makes my heart sick when I remember all the good words and all the broken promises. . . .

If the white man wants to live in peace with the Indians he can live in peace. There need be no trouble. Treat all men alike. Give them all the same law. Give them all an even chance to live and grow. All men were made by the same Great Spirit Chief. They are all brothers. The earth is the mother of all people, and all people should have equal rights upon it. You might as well expect the rivers to turn backward as that any man who was born a free man should be contented when penned up and denied liberty to go where he pleases. If you tie a horse to a stake, do you expect he will grow fat? If you pen an Indian up on a small spot of earth, and compel him to stay there, he will not be contented nor will he grow and prosper. I have asked some of the great white chiefs where they get their authority to say to the Indian that he shall stay in one place, while he sees white men going where they please. They can not tell me.

I ask only of the Government to be treated as all other men are treated. . . . I see men of my race treated as outlaws and driven from country to country, or shot down like animals. . . . If I can not go to my own home, let me have a home in some country where my people will not die so fast. . . . We only ask an even chance to live as other men live. We ask to be recognized as men. We ask that the same law shall work alike on all men. If the Indian breaks the law, punish him by the law. If the white man breaks the law, punish him also.

Let me be a free man—free to travel, free to stop, free to work, free to trade where I choose, free to choose my own teachers, free to follow the religion of my fathers, free to think and talk and act for myself—and I will obey every law, or submit to the penalty.

Whenever the white man treats the Indian as they treat each other, then we will have no more wars. We shall all be alike—brothers of one father and one mother, with one sky above us and one country around us, and one government for all. Then the Great Spirit Chief who rules above will smile upon this land, and send rain to wash out the bloody spots made by brothers' hands from the face of the earth. For this time the Indian race are waiting and praying. I hope that no more groans of wounded men and women will ever go to the ear of the Great Spirit Chief above, and that all people may be one people.

In-mut-too-yah-lat-lat   [Thunder-traveling-over-the-mountains]   has spoken for his people.

Thus spoke a tired and defeated man who, twenty years before, had accomplished a military feat which for courage and magnitude can be compared with the greatest in the annals of warfare. It began when, under pressure from Americans who wanted the land of the Nez Percé in the Grande Ronde country of eastern Oregon, Grant ordered the enforcement of the Treaty of 1863, by which large tracts of that land had been given to the settlers. Chief Joseph did not consider his tribe as signatories of the pact, but he entered into negotiations. The white squatters were not content to wait, however, and began committing outrages. The situation became critical, and Chief Joseph decided not to fight but to escape to Canada with two hundred warriors and six hundred women and children.

That retreat is a saga of incredible skill, endurance, and fortitude. Pursued and flanked by two armies and numerous mobile units, the Nez Percé, after two victorious engagements, managed to elude their pursuers for more than a thousand miles, through southwestern Montana, Idaho, Wyoming, and to within thirty miles of their objective, the Canadian border. Though they were a hunted group of people who had suffered a grave injustice at the hands of the white men, they destroyed no property and injured no inhabitants and even paid for their food obtained from farmers along the route.

General Miles finally caught up with them and shortly thereafter

General Howard joined him. It would have been possible to continue the flight only if the women, children, and wounded were left behind, which Chief Joseph was unwilling to do. Too bitter to surrender, he decided to fight. The outcome was inevitable: though the Indians fought bravely and well, they were greatly outnumbered in men and matériel, their provisions were gone, and their clothing inadequate for the cold climate. "My heart sick and sad," Chief Joseph capitulated. The handful of survivors was placed on a reservation in Kansas, and thus another tribe came to the end of the long trail that had begun when missionaries with high hopes came to save their souls.

Three

The Word in the Wilderness

The benighted state of the heathen Indian's soul brought the missionaries to the far Northwest, but they might not have gone when they did were it not for a dramatic and touching story that acted as the fuse to set off their offensive. The largely unknown region held little appeal for church groups who regarded it as wild and inaccessible, and only feeble flickers of interest appeared in their press. Concern for the spiritual welfare of the aborigine in that distant land was, however, expressed in the theological seminaries of the East; and in 1829, after two years of intensive discussion, the Prudential Committee of the American Board of Commissioners for Foreign Missions sent the Reverend Jonathan S. Green on a reconnaissance. Although he brought back a lengthy and detailed report on the moral depravity of the native tribes, it failed to elicit a response from the laity.

Then, about a year later, the religious world was shaken by a letter from a New York merchant which was published in a Methodist paper. The writer quoted a communication he had received from a Christianized half-breed, relating the pathetic story of four Flathead Indians who had made the long, difficult trek from the Pacific Slope to St. Louis for the sole purpose of finding the white man's "Book of Heaven." It seemed that the natives had become deeply distressed when they learned from a religious white man that they were worshiping the Great Spirit incorrectly and would never reach the Happy Hunting Grounds unless they knew the proper method.

The pages of the religious press of the time were filled with story after story of this dramatic hegira, and pictures of the Indians with their artificially malformed skulls—the forehead slanting back from the eyebrows in a straight line so that it came to a point at the crown —were widely circulated. The heart-rending plea of four savages for salvation was in itself tremendously moving to conscientious Christians, but the horrible practice of distorting the heads of babes added the final note of urgency.

It matters little now that the report which was swallowed so avidly was mostly fabrication—that only one of the four aborigines was of the Flathead tribe (three were Nez Percés); that none of them had malformed heads; that the Flatheads did not bind their children's heads; that they had not traveled eighteen hundred miles in a desperate quest but had probably followed, out of curiosity, a fur-trapping party, or had come to learn about the white man's "magic" which produced guns, liquor, tools, beads. Furthermore, all accounts indicate that no one in St. Louis at the time could understand their dialects. What is important is that the myth caught hold and, like a forest fire jumping its traces, leaped from paper to paper of the church press.

When the initial excitement subsided, the legend had become fixed in the minds of sympathetic Christians as gospel and proved to be the strongest incentive yet to an organized missionary movement to the Oregon country. From then on, the American Board pursued the matter energetically and the Methodist Church was no less zealous. Financial obstacles would no longer exist, for the appeal to the heart which the "Flathead" mission to St. Louis so graphically presented transcended mere monetary considerations.

Wilbur Fisk, the influential president of Wesleyan University, gave the impetus to the first organized Oregon mission. In a letter to the editor of the New York *Christian Advocate and Journal*, he wrote: "The Communication of brother G. P. Disoway including one from the Wyandotte agent, on the subject of the deputation of the Flathead Indians to Gen. Clark, has excited in many in this section intense interest. And, to be short about it, we are for having a mission established there at once." His appeal brought an almost immediate response.

First among the missionaries to venture forth was Jason Lee, who, at the warm recommendation of President Fisk, was appointed to his post by the New England Conference of the Methodist Church in June, 1833. Lee was especially suited for missionary work in a lonely, primitive area. He was thirty years old, strong, with a driving energy and a ready adaptability to all kinds of conditions and situations. Though intensely devout, he had none of the austere, hidebound qualities of some of his brethren.

Lee was accompanied by his nephew, a lay missionary, and two young "hired hands" who had joined the party to see the Oregon country. In St. Louis they made contact with two groups of fur traders and trappers, one led by Nathaniel Wyeth and the other by Milton Sublette, and together the strangely assorted company of the pious and the irreverent made the hazardous journey. Five months later the missionaries arrived at Fort Vancouver.

Lee lived for only eleven more years but in that time succeeded in founding a mission colony that developed into permanent settlements in Salem and Oregon City. He organized branch mission stations at Nisqually near the modern city of Tacoma, Clatsop near the mouth of the Columbia, and at The Dalles. He soon became concerned with more than the task of Christianizing the Indian, turning his attention to the desirability and feasibility of American settlement. He urged influential officials to launch a sea trade with the Northwest and even entered into a commercial treaty with King Kamehameha III of Hawaii. He spent considerable time in securing land and was also instrumental in bringing cattle and other livestock into the region to aid in the development of the rich and fertile farming lands of the Willamette Valley.

Jason Lee possessed a keen sense of "manifest destiny." In forceful terms he presented to Congressman Caleb Cushing the case for the extension of American jurisdiction of the Oregon country at a time when joint occupation by this nation and Great Britain made the formulation of a clear national policy on the subject impolitic. During visits to the East, reporting to his church superiors, he lectured repeatedly in an effort to arouse the public to an understanding and an appreciation of the so-called Oregon question.

Not long after Lee had blazed the missionary trail, Samuel Parker was dispatched by the American Board to explore the land beyond the Rocky Mountains. From 1835 to 1837 he toured the Northwest, examining the natural and human resources so as to determine for the board the advisability of sending additional missionaries and establishing stations. Parker was accompanied on this journey by a young physician from New York State, Marcus Whitman, whose religious impulse had excited in him a deep interest in missionary labor among the far-off Indians. Whitman went as far as the Green River region and then returned East to convince the Prudential Committee of the board of the need and practicability of setting up mission stations in the Columbia area, and to offer his services.

With the authorization of the board, Whitman promptly organized an expedition, the first projected under non-Methodist auspices. He was to be accompanied by his bride of a few weeks—the golden-haired and gently reared Narcissa Prentiss, who had also been fired with a desire to serve in the wilderness—the Reverend and Mrs. Henry Harmon Spalding, and the dour, humorless, self-indulgent William H. Gray.

Narcissa's charm and beauty have been commented on by everyone who met her. She was the daughter of a New York judge, well educated, a fine singer, with a lively, vivacious temperament. Several years earlier, Henry Spalding had been captivated by her attractions, but she had refused his offer of marriage. Now, with his wife, Eliza —a contrast in physical appearance and personality (she was plain and dark and inclined to be excessively pious)—Spalding was a fellow traveler on Narcissa's honeymoon. There has never been any question of Spalding's devotion to his Eliza, but he never forgave Narcissa for rejecting him and found it difficult not to show how much he resented her.

Spalding was one of this world's dark, tormented personalities. He could never forget or forgive his illegitimate birth; he could find no rest for his spirit and seemed determined to keep the spirits of those he met as harrowed. A complete contrast was Whitman, whose dedication to his work made personal considerations secondary. He was a man of inflexible will. Across impossible terrain he dragged a lumbering wagon that kept coming apart, when other men would long since have abandoned it. He suffered for years from an undiagnosed ailment that sapped his vitality, but no one would have known it.

This was the group that calmly and optimistically set out on a grueling and hazardous journey into a savage land. It was the first time white women were making the crossing and the first time a wagon was taken over unbroken trails, across streams and through dense, pathless forests. The courage of the two women and their capacity to sustain all kinds of hardships is almost incredible.

Eliza Spalding was an invalid when the party left the East, having but recently recovered from a long illness as the result of a stillbirth. More than once when she felt it was humanly impossible to endure any longer the jolting of the springless wagon or the twisted position of the sidesaddle or the diet of buffalo meat which made her violently ill, she pleaded that the party go on without her. Narcissa, though she became pregnant on the journey, was more fortunate in health and vitality, but little consideration or indulgence could be given to either woman: the group had to push on with the fur-trapping expedition or be left behind to face the perils of possible Indian attack or starvation.

After a stopover at the Hudson's Bay Company's fort at Vancouver, the two couples separated. (Gray returned home shortly thereafter.) The Whitmans settled in an area inhabited by the Cayuse Indians at a locality called Waiilatpu on the Walla Walla River, and the Spaldings among the Nez Percé at Lapwai, about 120 miles away, in present Idaho. Thus the first missionary establishments of the American Board were begun, with others soon to follow under the same sponsorship. Two years later, in 1838, the Reverend and Mrs. Cushing Eells, William Gray with a bride whom he had married in the East, and a bachelor, C. Rogers, founded stations at Tschimakain, some miles north of present Spokane, and at Kamiah in present Idaho.

The Catholic Church was also interested in bringing its message to the red men and in providing spiritual guidance to the French-Canadian fur traders and the employees of the Hudson's Bay Company. In 1838 Father Francis N. Blanchet and Father Modeste Demers arrived in the Oregon country. On a long and difficult journey that took them six months, they had traveled 5,325 miles to reach their destination. Two missions were established: one on the Cowlitz River and the other on the Willamette between present-day Oregon City and Salem. Three years later, Father Pierre-Jean De Smet founded a mission among the Flatheads and, within the next six years, two more at Kalispell and in the Coeur d'Alene region.

Father De Smet was a striking and unusual person, even in a land where physical and mental strength were commonplace. He is said to have traveled 180,000 miles during his lifetime, including several trips abroad, in a day when traveling was an ordeal and a challenge to endurance. He was greatly admired and respected by the Indians and was often called upon to act as mediator when there was trouble between white man and red.

The missionaries whose job it was to save souls found all around them ample cause for discouragement and despair. Only an intense zeal and a deep religious enthusiasm sustained them during the days and months and years of toil in the strange and desolate country. When their spirits sagged temporarily, as was inevitable, for they were but human, they confided their sorrows and their difficulties to diaries or to letters sent home. Reverend Campbell, who came to Lee's station at the Willamette in 1840, reported to a fellow churchman in Illinois on the degraded condition of the heathen's soul, which, he feared, was eternally lost, and on the Indian's laziness, filth, and degeneracy. "All persons who come to this country," he wrote, "subject themselves to numerous ills, and hardships and privations of every character. Many a deep grounded sigh will involuntarily escape from their bosoms, from a fond recollection of what they have left behind them—a civilized country—a beloved family circle—a well organized community—a code of wholesome laws to be governed by and a social and religious community to enjoy." The climate was unhealthy, he said, and there were not enough well persons to take care of the sick and dying at the mission.

The mood of pessimism and despair which colored almost every sentence of the letter reflected the conditions with which the missionaries had to contend at all the stations: isolation, a hostile population, difficult natural conditions, loneliness, and homesickness for loved ones and friends several thousand miles away. They were the only white persons west of the Rocky Mountains, with the exception of the employees of the Hudson's Bay Company and their families who lived at the trading posts, and a small settlement of the company's retired employees and their families in the Willamette Valley. Their only other contact with "civilization" and other white men was provided by the occasional visitors from trading vessels.

The missionary's task was arduous, for, in addition to trying to save the native's soul and teach him the ways of the white man, he had all the duties of farming, fishing, hunting, building, repairing. His wife not only had to run a large household—spinning, weaving, sewing, cleaning, preserving food, often cooking for a houseful of visitors who stopped in at the station—but she also instructed the Indians in domestic affairs and sometimes taught Sunday school for the redskinned youngsters and adults. To make life even more complicated, she was repeatedly distracted by visits of neighboring Indians, who would park themselves on the doorstep of the house and wait to be invited in for meals. If she locked the door, the Indian found the window as convenient a place of entry.

A source of great concern to the missionary was the traditional Indian approach to the treatment of illness. If the sick man recovered, the "doctor" kept the fee which was given in advance, but, if the patient died, the fee would be returned to the family of the deceased and the medicine man was fortunate if he escaped death at the hands of the relatives. One of the primitive methods used in the treatment of a variety of ailments also worried the missionary, because it so often resulted in fatality. This was the sweating oven, which was constructed by digging a hole in the ground at the side of a hill and placing bent poles covered with grass mats and earth over the excavation. Good-sized stones, heated white-hot in a fire, were thrown into the "stove" and water dashed over them, which procedure, of course, resulted in clouds of steam. The patient inside the pit remained until he was almost suffocated. Then he dashed out and immediately plunged into the icy waters of a near-by stream or brook. If he had sufficient stamina or was not seriously ill, he survived this rigorous "treatment"; otherwise it was considered that the evil spirits which had invaded his body were too powerful to be driven out, and he was buried with the customary ceremonies. After the missionaries had won the confidence of the natives, they were called in to treat patients and had varying success in eliminating this and other medical customs.

Many missions were established, but the one whose fame endured longest was the one at Waiilatpu, and its leader, Marcus Whitman, became a legendary figure. The Cayuse Indians, among whom the Whitmans had settled, were more warlike and unfriendly than some of the other Northwestern tribes, but the young couple labored arduously for their conversion. On the surface the red men seemed amicable. They admired and marveled at the lovely Narcissa's red-gold curls, seemed to enjoy learning the hymns she taught them, played with the couple's Alice Clarissa, the first white child born in the Oregon country, and tried to console the grieving parents when the little girl was accidentally drowned.

Whitman taught them the arts of husbandry and put his medical experience to use, although, as a physician, he frequently ran into difficulties because of the primitive methods used by the Indians in their cures and the opposition of the medicine men. The natives were, however, unresponsive to the strenuous attempts to convert them to Christianity. Here and there one would proclaim his spiritual uplift, but it was generally a short-lived, verbal protestation, unaccompanied by any real change in his ways of living. And as they saw their land being alienated to the encroaching settlers, they became steadily more sullen and resentful.

After six years of conscientous effort, the missions at Lapwai, Waiilatpu, and Tschimakain showed little sign of progress. The

American Board in the East began to feel that the money spent on them was being wasted and showed a decided unwillingness to continue financial support. In spite of their own discouragement, the missionaries were loath to give up their work. They all felt, as Elkanah Walker explained in a letter to the board, that the country would be settled in the very near future, and that their services would be required to overcome the influence of the Catholic settlers and priests who were arriving in increasing numbers.

"If this mission should be given up," wrote Walker, "the whole of the upper country would be thrown open to them, and the first influence the settlers . . . would meet would be that of Romanism. If the errors of Romanism are to be met and corrected by the truths of the Bible then it is necessary that there should be the supporters of the truth stationed in this country." And even if settlement did not take place, he said, the missions would still be vital to counteract the influence upon the natives of the Hudson's Bay Company, which had about six hundred men and their families "growing up in all the ignorance of heathen or what is but a little better, a Catholic influence."

At an emergency conference of the missionaries it was decided to send Marcus Whitman back East to plead personally for continued support of the stations. "[With] a feeling that something must be done," Walker wrote the board, "and that with as little delay as possible we came to this conclusion, that if Dr. Whitman could put his station in such situation that it would be safe to leave it, and make proper arrangements, we would consent to his going."

Whitman set out in the dead of winter with only a single companion. It required courage of a unique kind to undertake that journey, over hundreds of miles of forest and wastelands, through Indian territory, seeing no white man except the solitary fur trapper; with the necessity of living off the earth and by the hunt, their echoes the only voices they would hear for months on end. The missionary had that courage. He arrived in the East the following spring, and after brief visits in Washington, D.C., and New York, went to Boston to confer with the American Board. Apparently he presented a forceful case for keeping the missions open, for they were allowed to remain.

On the return trip Whitman joined a wagon train near Independence, bound for the Oregon country. He treated the sick on the way and not the least of his many other services was his guidance of the caravan. He suggested the most desirable routes and, in general, gave the emigrants the benefit of his experience.

Out of this journey to prevent the closing of several solitary mission stations in a wilderness was created one of the most famous myths in the Pacific Northwest. It made a patriotic hero out of a conscientious, ill-starred missionary who lost his life at the hands of a people he had tried with ardor and patience to "civilize."

The spark that ignited into flames the smoldering resentment of the Indians around Whitman's mission was an epidemic of measles in the winter of 1847. It had started at the station and quickly spread to the natives, who naturally found it difficult to understand why the white men recovered and their own people died. They could only conclude that Whitman, who was impartially ministering to the sick of both races, was a sorcerer and using his powers to kill them. Whipped into a frenzy by their medicine men, who hated the white doctor, the Indians swooped down upon the station and in an orgy of violence left a trail of blood and destruction. Those who were fortunate enough to escape being slaughtered were held captive until an enraged populace effected their liberation. Accounts like the following in the *Oregon Spectator* horrified the settlers:

After the supreme solicitude that has filled the public mind since the intelligence of the horrible butchery at Waiilatpu for the survivors . . . it is with feelings of pain and pleasure that we announce their deliverance from captivity and safe arrival in our midst. The pleasure incident to their rescue . . . is marred, however, by the painful intelligence that a portion of them have been subjected to further outrage and insult—the basest—the deepest that can possibly be conceived. . . . We have never shrunk from our duty, in recording events howsoever painful and abhorrent . . . but in this case our pen refuses—we dare not chronicle the terrible story of their wrongs.

The martyrdom of the Whitmans ended the station at Waiilatpu, but Henry Harmon Spalding was not to allow his friend Marcus to be forgotten. Spalding hated "Popery" with all the rancor of which the fanatic is capable. He believed that the Catholics had incited the Indian attack on the mission and that they were supported in their efforts to drive the Protestant denominations out of the region by the Hudson's Bay Company, which considered the Americans an obstacle to British rule.

In an article by Spalding, published in a Western journal in 1865, the "Whitman-saved-Oregon" legend appeared for the first time.

Spalding declared that Whitman had undertaken his ride to the East solely to prevent England from taking over the Oregon country. According to his story, the Hudson's Bay Company and the Catholic missionaries hoped to bring this about by flooding the country with immigrants from Canada. In the autumn of 1842, he stated, Whitman learned that a migration was already on its way, and this information precipitated his departure. He went to try to prevail upon the American statesmen to take immediate action before the land was lost forever to the United States.

So off to Washington dashes Whitman, arriving at the office of Secretary of State Webster just in time to prevent him from concluding negotiations exchanging with Great Britain the whole Oregon country for fishing privileges off the shores of Newfoundland. He dissuades Webster only with the greatest difficulty, for the Secretary considers the Pacific Northwest a "worthless area" and his sentiments are shared by President Tyler. Whitman finally convinces him that thousands of Americans will migrate to the region as soon as they learn more about its great potentialities and pledges himself to spread information about it far and wide.

For the next several weeks he becomes a one-man crusade, speaking wherever and whenever anyone will listen, until it is time for him to go back. After visiting the officers of the American Board, he becomes the principal actor in the famous migration of '43, which laid the basis for permanent American settlement. He inspires it, he leads it, he carries it through successfully beyond Fort Hall, where the Hudson's Bay Company seeks to prevent its passage.

The myth at first was swallowed whole and gained wide currency, even appearing in local histories. Then—some years later—when historians began to investigate the facts, they could find no evidence to corroborate the main strands of the tale in any of their contemporary sources, such as the records of the American Board, the correspondence of President Tyler or Secretary Webster, newspaper accounts, the letters and diaries of the immigrants of 1843, even the letters and other writings of Whitman and his colleagues.

A controversy between the pro and con factions was started when the Oregon historian Frances Fuller Victor challenged Spalding's authenticity. It became more and more acrimonious as time passed, resulting in the publication of hundreds of articles by both factions in Northwest newspapers and magazines. The subject also attracted the attention of some professional historians outside the region who wanted to determine the validity of the account. Finally, in 1900, Professor Edward G. Bourne delivered the *coup de grâce* to the myth in an address before the American Historical Association. His talk was based on data supplied by William I. Marshall, a Chicago high-school principal, who had spent years sifting the evidence and compiling a formidable amount of material.

But myths die hard. Whitman, through the years, had been all but canonized by his admirers. His grandniece wrote to a friend: "To me the supreme moment of all his remarkable life was when he knelt upon the open Bible, raising the American flag as high as he could with the means at hand and tragically said, 'In the name of God, Christian civilization and the American Flag, I take this country.' Mr. Spalding . . . has often told me how he and the two brides stood by the flag and wept. The summit of the divide—the Rocky Mountains—is sacred ground."

The romantic aspects of the tale caused it to linger on. From time to time it was revived in articles in popular magazines. As late as 1943, an American publication which has the largest circulation in the world published a gushy, melodramatic article on Whitman in which the legendary aspects of the story were again revived. "Into the office of the Secretary of War, in Washington, there stalked this man in an old fur hat worn to the skin, his heavy beard now growing gray. What he said there must have opened the eyes of the government to Oregon's danger. What he told Horace Greeley of the New York *Tribune* was sure to be broadcast the breadth of the land. What he urged upon the board of missions in Boston we can guess from their decision that Waiilatpu was to stay open, with funds to run as Whitman saw fit. Then he turned back west for the tide of settlers he had prophesied was already rising, promising to flood the British claims out of Oregon if they could get through to it. They must get through, so Whitman undertook to pilot them in person." That same year, a popular pictorial magazine carried a more restrained account on Whitman, but also repeated a little of the legend.

Whitman's death dramatized not only the missionary cause in the Northwest, but also the rivalry existing among the various denominational groups. Those who came to labor in behalf of God and their respective churches were beset, from the very beginning, with the task of counteracting the influence of their theological competitors. The Methodists believed that the wilderness of Zion ought to be their sacred preserve, while the representatives of the American Board feared the challenge to their efforts; both agreed that "Popery" was a danger next to which all others paled into insignificance, while they, in turn, were held in contempt by the objects of their distrust.

Each of the denominations claimed superior success in converting the Indians. A powerful argument advanced by the American Board's missionaries to secure financial support was that their stations were creating a bulwark against the threatened inundation of Catholic propaganda and influence. Catholics were accused of inciting the Indians to attack the Protestant missionary groups. Henry Harmon Spalding, who became obsessed by the subject, continued to write and talk about the Whitman massacre as though he had been there. In one address he related that a Catholic priest had informed him of having baptized some Indian children near Waiilatpu after the orgy of violence: "Thus the new missionary, this priest of God in the vestments of God, commenced his mission work in his new field, which he had emphatically gained by American blood, by baptising these blood-stained children of these bloody, savage murderers, the dead bodies yet lying unburied about him. For the last eighteen years I have not ceased to ask the unprejudiced what effect this baptisement in those circumstances had upon the minds of the Indians. There can but one answer be given. They understood the priests as approving what they had done and were doing."

The Catholic missionaries were not much kinder in their opinion of the Protestant churchmen. A Canadian priest stationed at the Columbia characterized them as "pretended propagators of the faith" who occupied themselves only with commerce and trade. He contended that they had made no progress in converting the Indian to the Gospel; that their authoritarian approach in compelling the native to yield to their will, and the arbitrary manner with which they imposed their conception of law and justice upon the red man succeeded only in arousing the enmity of all the Indians with whom these Protestants came into contact. And, he stated, they were also antagonizing the settlers who were migrating to the region. The atmosphere became so charged that the Catholic mission retired from the field.

As it began to appear that Indian conversion was a failure, the American Board became increasingly reluctant to support its stations. The situation had deteriorated by the time the Cayuse Indian War broke out. After it was over, the missions found that their positions were untenable and left the field.

Of all the important church groups only the Methodists remained; as settlers, they became farmers and merchants. They, too, had come to realize fairly soon that their goal of Christianizing the native tribes was almost impossible of attainment. The red man, by and large, was not receptive to the teachings of the Gospel. Some attributed this to his inherently savage nature, while others, critical of missionary tactics, contended that the instructional methods were based upon an emotional appeal, without giving the pupil any understanding of the abstract thought which constituted the theology of the Christian religion. As an example of the native's mentality and approach to religion, the tale is related of the Indian who came to a missionary and asked for the best way of praying for a coat which he would like to have. "Praying alone will not get it for you," the servant of God told him, "you must work in addition." The Indian looked at him quizzically and replied, "Of what use, then, are prayers?" But, even more important, the preaching of the missionary was soon accompanied by his policy of land encroachment at the expense of the natives.

Discouraged by the lack of results, the missionaries early abandoned hope for the salvation of the heathen and embarked upon another task: spiritual guidance for the American settlers who had begun to pour into the region. They envisaged a great future for the country and regarded their labors as essential to the preservation of morality and Christianity. At the same time they began to acquire land, each man taking for himself a section amounting to 640 acres and for the church an aggregate of 36 sections. This made imperative for them a government policy designed to pave the way for widespread immigration and settlement. The flag followed the missionary, as it always does, but workers in the vineyard of the Lord had begun to agitate for its protective influence almost immediately after their arrival in the wilderness of the West.

The missionaries became farmers and business proprietors and newspaper publishers, and they launched religious academies. Now they were concerned with protecting their holdings as well as maintaining their spiritual dominance. They regarded the Puget Sound Agricultural Company, a subsidiary of the Hudson's Bay Company, as a threat to their own agricultural trade, and the great commercial domain of the latter as a challenge to American national policy.

The animus against the British company infected the settlers and was carried on in the early pioneer historical writings. To some

Americans John McLoughlin, though he had become a citizen of their country, personified the Hudson's Bay Company, and much of their animosity was directed against him. They ignored or disparaged the invaluable assistance which he had continuously given the immigrants, who, strangers and alone in a strange and lonely land, might not have been able to survive without it.

The last years of McLoughlin's life were embittered by the struggle to vindicate his name and redeem his properties of which he had been deprived by the American settlers. He was never able to collect more than a fraction of the huge sum that he had generously loaned out of his own pocket to destitute immigrants, nor did he ever regain his lost lands. In addition to all this, he was vilified by the British for having renounced his native citizenship.

From time to time the McLoughlin controversy cropped up until —as was inevitable with a maturing society—it was no longer of popular interest. It is significant today only to the historian as an example of how much of the early history of the region was inextricably bound up with the prejudices and special interests of the conflicting groups. The conflicts assumed proportions large enough to affect the writings of a number of pioneer historians, so that their works were characterized by distortions and bias. Without the missionaries, they said, the Oregon country would never have been settled and would have been lost to the United States. Later, the trend was sharply reversed. It was Hubert Howe Bancroft's opinion that the missionary work in the Pacific Northwest "never did any good. What did Lee, or Spalding, or Whitman do that left any mark?" he asked. "They all gave it up, & one of them at least took the sunday [*sic*] school contributions to start a store with and I think it was the most sensible act of his life. That was Lee." John W. Nesmith, ex-senator from Oregon and himself an early settler, told an audience of former pioneers at an annual gathering that the missionaries had been hired by a wealthy organization in the East, sent out in comfortable ships, and provided with food, clothing, and shelter for themselves and their families, so that they suffered none of the hardships of the average immigrant. They not only failed completely, he said, in their avowed purpose in coming—to convert the heathen— but the clothing which had been donated by charitable persons for Indian use was sold or bartered to the natives.

Eventually, the role of the missionary came to be regarded in a more balanced perspective: The zealous disciples of Christ *were* the first Americans to settle in the Pacific Northwest. They *had* ventured forth into a wilderness where no American save the explorer, trapper, and trader had dared to tread. They were among the first to enlighten their countrymen in the East on the nature of the life that awaited the immigrant. The wagon trains would undoubtedly have rolled westward without the presence of Whitman and others, but some impetus was given to the movement by the missionaries, who propagandized in favor of settlement—especially after the futility of their efforts to achieve Indian salvation became clearly evident.

Four

Prairie Schooners Westward

On a lonely hilltop in a small town in Massachusetts, the epitaph on the stone above the solitary grave reads: "He led a colony over the Rocky Mountains to settle Oregon and experienced many perilous scenes. . . ." Ironically, it was the one thing the man whose bones lie moldering there did not do in his efforts to settle Oregon. Even before the missionaries began to wend their way westward, Hall Jackson Kelley, the "prophet of Oregon," became obsessed with the region whose shores are washed by the great Pacific.

Kelley, a New England schoolmaster, was stirred by reading the narratives of the explorers and pathfinders. The exciting tales of adventure, the descriptions of the magnificent land, opened new vistas to the pedagogue whose world was limited to the four walls of his schoolroom. Whether, like many a man, he felt stifled by his narrow existence, or whether there was some latent Messianic impulse in his personality, it is difficult to say. In later years he wrote: "In the year 1817 'the word came expressly to me' to go and labor in the fields of Christianity in the dark and cruel places about the shores of the Pacific," and that seven years after, "I announced to the world my intention to settle Oregon and to propagate in regions beyond the Rocky Mountains, Christianity." And from that time to the end of his long, frustrated life, his entire existence revolved around this objective. He gave up his home, his family, his position, to devote himself exclusively to his mission.

Kelley began his long literary crusade in 1830 with a pamphlet called *A Geographical Sketch of that Part of North America Called Oregon*. He had visions of planting another New England settlement on the shores of the Columbia, and the booklet was written to further the work of the newly organized American Society for Encouraging the Settlement of the Oregon Territory. He was the prime mover in the organization whose membership consisted of a number of important people in the Boston area. Kelley actually began to organize an expedition, inviting women and children to participate, but the grandiose project failed when the man who was to lead it, Nathaniel J. Wyeth, broke with the movement.

An agitator for westward migration was not popular in New England in those years. Any effort to drain the Northeast of capital and labor power was regarded with distinct disfavor, for the area was not yet faced with the problem of surpluses. Moreover, the Oregon country was too remote and unfamiliar, and the voice of a lone crusader of opportunity out yonder was scarcely audible above the hum of the factory machines. Those who paused long enough to listen to Kelley dismissed him as a ranting visionary, an idle and obsessed dreamer.

One severe critic was Solomon Bell, or William Joseph Snelling, as he preferred to call himself in print. In several newspaper articles, pamphlets, and in a full-length book, this member of the Boston literati attacked Kelley and the emigrants' organization he had founded.

That a party of young, brave hardy men may cross the continent to the mouth of the Columbia, [he wrote] we know; but that a large body of the inhabitants of New England, wholly unacquainted with Indian life, and encumbered with baggage and their families, can do so, we hold impossible. We think we have proved that it is so. Our facts cannot be disputed, and the inference is as clear as a geometrical demonstration. We do not know that the prime mover of the folly we have exposed is actuated by an evil motive; we do not believe it. We look upon him as an unfortunate man, who, deluded himself, is deluding others, and conceive it our duty to warn those who are about to follow him on the road to ruin.

Neither opposition nor indifference could turn Kelley from his path. Since he could not go overland to Oregon with an expedition, he went alone by sea and reached it by traveling up from California with a party of traders. When he came to Fort Vancouver, to his bewilderment and dismay he was rebuffed by John McLoughlin, who had been erroneously advised that Kelley and the group were a band of horse thieves. Ill and exhausted, he lingered at the fort until he recovered and then left, again by sea.

When Kelley returned East he began to turn out innumerable leaflets on the Oregon country, deluging Congress and talking to whoever would listen to him. In the meantime, his personal life was beset with difficulties. His wife, tired of being left alone while her husband roamed the land and in financial straits because of his nonsupport, went to live with a relative who refused to let Kelley see his family. His money was gone and the world had repudiated his noble efforts. Time was passing and the westward migrations had already begun, but nowhere could Kelley get any credit for the years of tireless effort he had spent in trying to promote the movement.

Disheartened and disillusioned, Kelley began the long campaign of petitions and memorials to Congress for recognition and financial relief which continued until the end of his life. What he wanted above all else was public acknowledgment of what he regarded as his historic role in the settlement of Oregon. As the years passed, he developed paranoiac delusions that society was conspiring against him and that he was being deliberately ignored out of sheer malice. He died a lonely, unhappy, and forsaken man, his energies spent in a cause that was destined to succeed even without his aid.

Several years before the "word" came to Kelley, Henry Brackenridge, in his *View of Louisiana*, wrote about the possibilities of establishing settlements on the Columbia, probably the first man to do so; and in 1818 Thomas Hart Benton began his championship of westward expansion with a series of articles in the *Missouri Enquirer*. Benton advocated the establishment of a chain of trading posts from St. Louis to the Columbia in order to facilitate migration. "Nothing is wanted," he said, "but a second Daniel Boone to lead the way."

Later, before his own election to Congress, Benton persuaded Congressman John Floyd of Virginia to introduce a measure into the lower house which provided for the occupation of the Columbia River territory. Floyd was chairman of a committee instructed to investigate the question and he submitted a report unequivocally advocating American occupation. Although it was not even discussed by the legislature and the Secretary of State declared it to be "a tissue of errors in fact and abortive reasoning," and that "nothing could purify it but the fire," the President brought the Oregon question before the nation in his annual message to Congress in 1822. Sixteen years later, Senator Linn of Missouri took up where Floyd left off when the latter had become governor of his state, and from then on the Pacific Northwest remained an issue in national politics.

In the early forties, the strange virus which caused the "Oregon fever" attacked the nation. America was in an expansive mood. The boundaries of the continent seemed limitless and men and women everywhere strained to see the farthest shores. Only a little while earlier, pioneers had crossed the mountains from Virginia and Connecticut into the Ohio Valley country and had built homes on cheap and fertile land. In turn, this land of promise had become barren to many, and eyes were once again turned west, stimulated by addresses in Congress and the glowing reports published frequently in the local press.

America was young and wonderfully underdeveloped and men could still dream of a better world a-comin', if not on the shores of the Hudson, the Sangamon, or even the Ohio, then on the shores of the Columbia. The spirit of manifest destiny was in the air:

They go to plant a new people in a new and active country, [wrote one newspaper] to create new states—to open a new field to the growing energies and wants of our expanding Republic—to carry civilization around the world. . . . They go to confront and dislodge British invasion and to stop British conquest, which vanquished in front upon the Atlantic, has gone round our flanks and round the world to crush and destroy from behind. It is a wonderful impulse this, combined of patriotism, curiosity, and a war-like spirit of adventure, which is pressing our people onward to the Western Seas. They depart burning with high hopes of benefits to accrue both to themselves and the general country.

A more impelling motive, perhaps, was the fact that farmers had never quite recovered from the devastating panic of 1837, and the corn which they had sweated to plant and harvest was selling for only ten cents and wheat for fifty cents a bushel. The people of the Old West were also plagued by lung ailments, rheumatism, ague, and malaria. As an Iowa minister wrote: "So much sickness is indeed distressing. There are very few families in which some are not or have not been sick. . . . I saw this afternoon a gentleman from Rock River who says there is much more sickness there than here. . . . The sickness of the country is hindering every kind of labor." The climate was harsh—extremely hot or cold—and Midwesterners listened with longing to descriptions of an area where the weather was moderate.

Streams of oratory gushed forth at mass meetings called to popularize the Oregon country and to recruit personnel for projected migrations. And those who yearned for adventure or responded to the mystic strains of patriotism or were lured by the promise of free land—a whole section to farm and adjacent land for pasturage—responded with alacrity. Talk of free land had been in the air for some time, and, in 1843, Senator Linn's bill providing for 640 acres to settlers in the

Northwest country passed the Senate. Not for seven years was the bill to become a law, but, in the meantime, the mass migration had already begun.

The emigrants were going to an almost unknown country that was not even exclusively American property. The portion that would come under control of the United States was not yet known; it was hoped that the controversy with Great Britain would be decided soon. Between the settled frontier and the Pacific slope lay a vast, un-preempted region of plains and prairies belonging to this nation; but for the time being, the Indians were in possession of it by treaty, and so the pioneers who looked west had to jump this barrier and go on.

"The true western pioneers," wrote an Iowa citizen, "have pushed beyond us or if here and there one still lingers, it is only that he may dispose of his farm 'improvements' to push on for a 'new country.'" Many small towns were almost depopulated by the Oregon fever; in some communities only those too old, too ill, or too poor to go remained behind, and even they hoped to be able to pull up stakes at some time in the future. The impoverished farmer was unable to undertake the journey. Crossing the country involved the loss of a season's sowing and reaping. The purchase of a covered wagon and a sufficient number of oxen and horses, plus all the foodstuffs essential for a six-months' journey, made the venture a costly one and eliminated all but those who were fairly comfortably situated or were able in some way to scrape together the necessary funds, or those who had been promised profitable employment in the new country.

For months the expedition to Oregon was virtually the only topic of conversation in the community, as the emigrants were generally among the "best" citizens, representing a fair cross-section—ministers, a physician or two, the editor of the newspaper, the village blacksmith, the farmers. Meetings were convened in schoolhouses, in churches, in halls to listen to reports gathered by committees who had been instructed to investigate the prospects of settlement.

A typical meeting was the one held in a little Bloomington, Iowa, schoolhouse one spring day in the year 1843. According to information gathered from various sources, reported the chairman of the committee, the Oregon territory was superior to any section of the country in climate, timber, water facilities, and marketing conveniences. It was ideal for agriculture and stock raising, and mechanics would find no lack of inducements. All enterprising citizens were urged to migrate. After some discussion, resolutions were proposed

and adopted unanimously that a company start out on May 10. The
route was carefully mapped out and each individual was advised exactly what to take along to meet all contingencies.

The services of a physician were engaged and a chaplain was also
expected to accompany the group. Officers to command the party en
route were to be elected, one captain, four sergeants, and, at the Continental Divide, a first and a second lieutenant, if there were at least one
hundred men. The funds of the company were to be entrusted to
them and a clerk assigned to keep a complete journal of the march.
"Every man ought to carry with him a Bible and other religious books,
as we hope not to degenerate into a state of barbarism." A corresponding secretary was elected to communicate with individuals and similar
groups throughout the country to obtain additional information about
the journey. This expedition was, perhaps, a little more carefully
planned than most, but in all cases thorough preparations were made.

Weeks were spent in acquiring data about the route, studying books
and pamphlets of instruction written by previous travelers, building
stout wagons and gathering paraphernalia necessary for the journey.
The last alone required considerable time. All the appurtenances of
living had to be taken along, including food, since it was risky to depend entirely on game or fish.

Joel Palmer, who had crossed the trail in 1845, listed in his *Journal*
the items considered essential and recommended that each family
form a self-sufficient household unit. Travelers were advised to take
along two hundred pounds of flour, thirty pounds of pilot bread,
seventy-five pounds of bacon, ten pounds of rice, five pounds of
coffee, two pounds of tea, twenty-five pounds of sugar, a half bushel
of dried beans, one bushel of dried fruit, ten pounds of salt, half a
bushel of corn meal, and a small keg of vinegar.

Though Palmer urged the pioneers to travel light, he considered essential cooking equipment consisting of a sheet-iron stove, a Dutch
oven, a cast-metal skillet, tin plates, cups and saucers, two churns, one
for sweet milk and one for sour, a sizable keg for carrying water; and
an assortment of tools, such as a handsaw, a few plow molds, an ax, a
shovel; also a good supply of rope for various purposes, a rifle and a
shotgun. Durable clothing was strongly stressed, particularly tough,
high boots; and, very important, at least one good feather bed and
other good bedding.

The last Sunday before leave-taking was usually devoted to prayer
in the churches for a safe journey. And then the final farewells were

said to friends and loved ones whom many of the wayfarers into the wilderness never saw again. The women secretly shed their last tears and, with dry eyes and tight lips, herded their children into the wagons and climbed up beside their husbands. They had shut forever the doors of the homes into which they had put so much time and labor. Many disapproved inwardly of this wild venture into the unknown but never gave voice to their feelings.

The men cracked their whips over the lumbering oxen and the caravan moved off. On many a canvas its owner had bravely painted the slogan, "Oregon or Bust," and turned his eyes westward, grimly determined not to look back. He saw before him a dream, a vision of a better life, opportunity for his children which the old home could not afford. There were the young men, some seeking adventure, but the majority, like their elders, looking for a better livelihood in the untried land. And a number of young, newly married couples joyfully considered the trip a honeymoon at whose end they would start a fresh, new life together. From dozens of scattered points the wagons converged on the frontier state of Missouri and rolled west in a mighty, endless caravan of white-topped "prairie schooners" that, within a few years, had worn ruts in the road so deep there could be no mistaking the main sections of the trail.

The Oregon Trail was not actually a single road; in some places parallel routes miles apart were used by different companies, and in later years numerous "cut-offs" were attempted in an effort to save time and perhaps avoid some particularly difficult spots. The general route can, however, be described. The "jumping-off place" was almost always Independence, Missouri, from which point the trail twisted northwestward across the Kansas and Blue rivers to the Platte. It continued for many miles along the south side of the Platte, crossed over to follow the north fork of the river, and from there began the gradual ascent toward South Pass. After the Rockies had been crossed, the trail wound along in the direction of Fort Hall on the upper Snake River. At that point the travelers had to go through sage-covered desert and difficult terrain. From Farewell Bend, aptly named, the trail left the Snake River region, cut across the treacherous Blue Mountains to Grande Ronde, and then on to the Columbia.

The trail had been hacked out and roughly charted by adventurous pathfinders, Lewis and Clark, Wilson Price Hunt, Captain Bonneville, Nathaniel Wyeth, and Robert Stuart, who, with his party, was the first to cross the country from west to east. One of the great obstacles in reaching the Pacific coast was the Rockies. They could be crossed but the way was hazardous. It was Stuart who found the gap in the great mountains which would enable subsequent travelers to go over the natural barrier with ease and safety. He was the discoverer of the famous South Pass in southwestern Wyoming—nearly eight thousand feet up between snow-covered peaks on each side—which seems to sink with the curvature of the earth.

Several names were given to this route across a continent. It was called at various times the Platte Trail, the Emigrants' Trail, or simply, the Road to Oregon. Francis Parkman called it the Oregon and California Trail. The missionary, Father De Smet, heard the Indians speak of it as the "great medicine road of the whites." Another group of Indians referred to it as the "white-topped-wagon road." But, whatever it was called, it was the passageway to the promised land.

The men, women, and children who undertook the hazardous crossing in the forties and fifties were, for the most part, accustomed to a hard, strenuous life. For that reason, perhaps, they were not daunted by some of the reports from previous travelers about the rigors of the journey and the difficulties that awaited them at their destination. Local newspapers carried accounts such as this one: "The poor devils who start for Oregon, generally spend all they have to scrape together a wagon, some cattle, and a small outfit of provisions. They will spend the summer in the severest toil in getting there. . . . In truth, no man of information, in his right mind, would think of leaving such a country as this, to wander over a thousand miles of desert and five hundred of mountain to reach such as that." Or they might have been comforted by another report in the same paper on another day: "Say to those who think of emigrating that the trip to Oregon is not half the bug-a-boo it is represented to be. All that it requires is patience and perseverance."

Such contradictory accounts were characteristic also of the countless diaries and journals kept by the emigrants, but those which recounted the trials and hardships greatly outweighed the others. In later years pioneers wrote books about their experiences, sometimes embellishing and exaggerating them with flights of fancy. Probably no others were quite as fantastic as the one by Emmaline L. Fuller, who related an appalling account of what she and her party had endured in the crossing of 1860:

Will the reader of this narrative please to pause a moment and reflect on my situation. A child of barely thirteen years, and slender in build and constitution, taking a nursing babe of one year, and four other children, all younger than herself, and fleeing for life without provisions and barely enough clothing to cover us, into the pathless wilderness or what is worse yet, across the barren plains of the west. . . . Starvation was making sad inroads on our little band and none but those who endured the awful pangs of starvation can have even a faint idea of such horrible sufferings and death. We became almost frantic. Food we must have, but how should we get it? Then an idea took possession of our minds which we could not even mention to each other, so horrid, so revolting to even think of, but the awful madness of hunger was upon us, and we cooked and ate the bodies of each of the poor children, first sister Libbie, then Mr. Chase's little boys, and next my darling little baby sister, whom I had carried in my arms through all that long, dreary journey and slept with hugged to my heart, as though if possible I would shield her from all danger. She too had to leave me.

While this is undoubtedly a wild tale, there can be little doubt that the journey was, for the most part, an experience that often taxed the travelers almost beyond endurance. One particularly wearing and hazardous aspect was the crossing with wagons and cattle of the numerous streams and rivers on the way. All that could be done with the animals was to make them swim over, which was no easy feat, as they sometimes stubbornly refused to enter the water; or, if the stream was swift-flowing, it took expert guidance and control to keep them and the men from being swept away. Treacherous whirlpools and deadly quicksand, both ready to suck down the unwary, had to be watched for. Whenever possible, rafts were constructed on which the wagons were drawn across. Sometimes the wagon boxes were caulked to keep the water from seeping in and were then floated over. Bridges of willow poles were erected over some rivers.

Occasionally a downpour would swell a small stream into a torrent, and the crossing might be delayed for days unless the captain of the wagon train felt they could not afford to lose time and decided to take the risk. Wagons were sometimes overturned while in midstream and a family bereft of all its worldly possessions. Drownings while crossing streams were not infrequent, as indicated by accounts in numerous diaries. One pioneer relates a typical incident. While the cattle were being watered, some of the beasts swam over the river. One of the men went after them, "and before he got across he sunk to rise no more. He left a wife and three children. . . . The man that owned the cattle took the horse and swam after the cattle, and while coming back by some means got off the horse and sunk and was seen no more. He left a wife and six helpless children. . . . It is supposed that there was a whirlpool in the bottom of the river."

Difficult as the river crossings were, a body of water, any kind of water, seemed almost like a miracle after endless days over barren, arid terrain. The dust on the trail is mentioned so frequently in the pioneer accounts that the reader, after a while, almost begins sympathetically to feel it stinging his eyes, clogging and choking his nose, parching his throat, gritting between his teeth. It was sometimes so thick that it obscured the sun. The hair and clothes of the travelers became heavy with it, the beasts dragged themselves along, their blackened tongues hanging out. Joaquin Miller gives a graphic description of what man and animal endured:

> Then dust arose, a long dim line like smoke
> From out of riven earth. The wheels went groaning by
> The thousand feet in harness and in yoke,
> They tore the ways of ashen alkali,
> And desert winds blew sudden, swift and dry.
> The dust! It sat upon and filled the train;
> It seemed to fret and fill the very sky.
> Lo! dust upon the beasts, the tent, the plain,
> And dust, alas! on breasts that rose not up again.
>
> They rose by night, they struggled on and on
> As thin and still as ghosts; then here and there
> Beside the dusty way before the dawn,
> Men silent laid them down in their despair
> And died.

The wagon trains suffered also from wind, rain, hail, and lightning storms that ripped the canvas covers, soaked the food, the bedding, and the exhausted travelers. Chilled, hungry, and miserable, they found it impossible to light a fire to warm some food or themselves. They would gulp down the soggy bread, a bite of dried meat, and struggle on. To add to the tribulations, the frightened cattle on occasion started a stampede, overturning wagons and creating general havoc until they were brought under control.

Childbirth, a frequent occurrence on the trail, was often a harrowing experience. Fortunate was the mother whose baby arrived while the weather was clear and the caravan near water. Even then the train could sometimes stop for only a few hours, and shortly after her ordeal she was being jolted on in the springless wagon.

When the elements or natural barriers were not being contended with, the sheer monotony of creeping along at about ten miles a day for days without end frayed nerves and tempers. Quarrels flared up at little provocation and sometimes led to serious fights and even murder. Justice was speedy. The nature of the covered-wagon expedition made law enforcement a matter of necessity. Individual acts of anarchy and lawlessness could not be tolerated. A jury of twelve men was chosen, sworn in, a trial held, and the verdict promptly rendered. If found guilty, the criminal was hanged from a gallows which had been fashioned out of the tongues of the wagons. There was no temporizing even when, as happened in one case, the condemned man had a wife and four children. Provision was made to have the family taken care of for the rest of the journey and the crime was forthwith avenged. An apprehended thief was usually punished by a severe whipping with an ox lash.

Though the Indian menace on the overland trail looms large in fiction and screen plays about the "Wild West" and the pioneers were apprehensive, the red men, until about 1854, were more of a nuisance than a danger. They had not yet become aware of the meaning of the covered wagons which plodded endlessly across their horizon, and they came to the trains mostly to pilfer. Anything metal was coveted, but animals were an even greater prize, and the Indians frequently managed to make off with some in the confusion that resulted when they succeeded in frightening the beasts by shooting off guns, yelling, or waving blankets at them. No war parties attacked the caravans during those years.

In 1849 the pioneers encountered the gravest danger to life that had thus far threatened them. That was the year of the stampede to the gold fields of California, and it was also the year when cholera stalked the Oregon Trail. The disease, which is endemic to India, had been brought to America by European and Canadian immigrants. In 1833 it had appeared in the Ohio and Mississippi river valleys but, as an epidemic, had finally burned itself out. From then on it recurred sporadically in various cities until it began to rage with renewed vigor a decade and a half later. By the middle of June, 1848, Dearborn County, Indiana, for instance, with a total population of 2,000, was suffering a daily mortality of 14, and the toll in St. Louis alone for that year was between 4,500 and 6,000. Many attempted in vain to escape the contaminated areas, but they carried the infection with them. Nearly

60,000 persons passed through Independence and neighboring outfit-
ting towns on their way to California or Oregon in 1849, and with
many of them went the dreaded scourge.

The early symptoms of cholera often passed unrecognized, and
some who thought they had escaped it found later, to their horror,
that they were smitten. They polluted the camp grounds, leaving a
trail of infection for those who followed. Without any knowledge
of the cause of the disease, emigrants on the trail pressed handkerchiefs
to their noses and fled from the stricken ones, abandoning them to
their fate. In a day or so they, in turn, fell prey.

The disease struck so swiftly and suddenly that the victim who
woke up feeling perfectly well in the morning would be suffering
agonizing pain by noon and be in a hastily dug and covered grave by
nightfall. It caused excruciating suffering because of the violent diarrhea and vomiting which marked the beginning, the severe loss of
fluid, and sometimes blood, which shrank and wrinkled the skin. The
face hollowed and the patient turned blue. He became completely
prostrate and within a few hours either died or began to recover. "It
is sometimes just a case of Death snapping his fingers at you and you
are gone," wrote one emigrant. Another traveler wrote to his wife:
"We passed six graves in one place there was a Company from North
Carolina with seven in it & six died & but one was spared to tell the
tale of woe."

Major Osborne, who accompanied the expedition of mounted rifle-
men from Fort Leavenworth to Oregon in the summer of 1849, wrote
in his diary:

The cholera continued to prevail among the emigrating parties . . . in
many instances [it] raged with such violence as to carry off nearly whole
parties. . . . It would be useless to attempt to enumerate the deaths that
occurred among the emigrants. The graves along the road too plainly told
us that the cholera was prevailing to an alarming extent. . . . When we
arose in the morning it was a question among us as to who might fall a
victim to it before another sun.

The epidemic finally spread to the natives along the route, who, believing that they were being victimized by the white man's magic,
added to the horror by launching sporadic attacks.

Although the death rate was high along the trail, it did not deter
further migration, for it was probably higher in some of the congested
cities of the East and migrants hoped to escape the plague by running
away. The scourge raged through most of 1850 and then it suddenly

disappeared. But there were other diseases that harassed the travelers. Contemporary accounts mention mountain fever, dysentery, diarrhea, camp fever, bilious fever, flux, typhoid, typhus, gastro-enteritis, scurvy, smallpox, mumps, phthisis. An archaic medical nomenclature and a limited knowledge at that time in diagnosing and identifying ailments make it difficult to appraise properly their types and intensity, but they were numerous. And when the extremely limited medical facilities available on the trail are considered—many wagon trains did not have even a single physician—it can be appreciated how acute was the health problem.

But, whether well or ill, the travelers trudged on. Occasionally a wedding or a betrothal was celebrated on the way with all the ceremony that could be managed. Holidays, such as the Fourth of July, were made festive occasions. On clear, pleasant evenings the wayfarers gathered around the campfire, exchanged stories, told jokes or reminisced about the homes that were now miles behind them. Most trains had a few men who had carried musical instruments along, and there would be some singing and dancing.

> Come along, come along—don't be alarmed;
> Uncle Sam is rich enough to give us all a farm.

was one refrain set to a lively tune that helped to boost flagging spirits.

During rest periods and even on the road many of the pioneers read whatever printed matter they had brought with them. Almost every family had its Bible and some carried copies of the home-town newspaper. Classics such as Shakespeare and Milton were squeezed in with the food and equipment, though living necessaries naturally had to take precedence over literature.

One of the most descriptive and authentic accounts of life on the trail is Jesse Applegate's *A Day with the Cow Column*. He relates, in the following passage, how the covered-wagon travelers began their day:

It is four o'clock A.M.; the sentinels on duty have discharged their rifles —the signal that the hours of sleep are over—and every wagon and tent is pouring forth its night's tenants, and slowly-kindling smokes begin largely to rise and float away in the morning air . . . breakfast is to be eaten, the tents struck, the wagons loaded and the teams yoked and brought up in readiness to be attached to their respective wagons. All know when, at seven o'clock, the signal to march sounds, that those not ready to take their proper places in the line of march must fall into the dusty rear for the day. . . .

It is on the stroke of seven; the rush to and fro, the cracking of whips, the loud command to oxen, and what seemed to be the inextricable confusion of the last ten minutes has ceased. Fortunately every-one has been found and every teamster is at his post. The clear notes of a trumpet sound in the front; the pilot and his guards mount their horses; the leading divisions of the wagons move out of the encampment, and take up the line of march; the rest fall into their places with the precision of clockwork, until the spot so lately full of life sinks back into that solitude that seems to reign over the broad plain and rushing river as the caravan draws its lazy length towards the distant El Dorado.

Five

The Social Fabric

When the battered wagons, with their once white tops gray and dingy from six months of punishment by the elements, limped into Fort Vancouver, their travel-weary occupants knew that the long journey was at last over. There remained only the final lap "up" the Willamette, and for that they knew they could count on the help of Chief Factor John McLoughlin, who generously supplied the immigrants with boats and guides.

In the shelter of the canvas the women tidied themselves and their children as best they could, looking in despair at the frayed and patched garments in which they had lived for half a year. Then, shyly, on the arms of their husbands, the youngsters clinging to their skirts, they set out to examine the famed manor in the wilderness and meet its equally famed lord. McLoughlin was a kindly host and some of the travelers long remembered with gratitude the excellent food he set before them and the restraint they had to exercise to keep from tearing into it after the monotonous diet of the trail. A few days later they were in the promised land.

The early pioneers spread out in the fertile Willamette Valley. The covered wagon, which was still to be their shelter for the next few weeks, was rolled under the shade of a tree, and the job of home building began. Trees were felled, the brush cleared away, and the site for a dwelling prepared. Logs were first cut to the proper length for the walls and floor and then the side which was to go on the interior of the house, hewed smooth with a broadax. A fireplace and chimney were built with sticks and plastered on the inside and outside with a thick coating of clay. Some families had brought along cranes which they installed in the fireplace, and on these were hung iron hooks for the teakettle and pots. Fireplaces were built with great care, for they were to serve for heating, for cooking and baking and, partially, for light. Windows were either just apertures cut out of the logs or, if the man was especially handy, a sort of sliding door.

Log cabins were about twenty by thirty feet, with the fireplace at one end. The settlers who came from Missouri or the region around it built what was called the "dog-trot" house. This was actually two cabins spaced about a cabin apart with a common roof extending all the way across. One cabin was used for sleeping quarters while the other contained the kitchen and dining room. In warm weather the table was placed in the space between the two cabins so that the family could eat outdoors. Later on, the open area was frequently enclosed, making one unit out of the two.

Generally the interior was arranged with a spinning wheel on one side of the fireplace, the bed in a corner, with the trundle bed pushed under it during the day, and the table either in front of the fireplace or in the center of the room. The unadorned furniture, constructed out of cedar trees, consisted of rude bedsteads, a table, and a few chairs. Only the earliest settlers, however, had to resort to log cabins. Sawmills soon came to the region and frame houses were constructed differing little in appearance from those left behind.

A serious problem to the early pioneers was clothing. Most families had started out with as good wardrobes as they could afford, but often baggage had to be left on the road to lighten the wagonloads, and, by the time the Oregon country was reached, clothing was almost beyond repair. Great ingenuity was used in making apparel. Tents and wagon covers, lined with the remnants of some old woolen garments, became sturdy coats, and, for additional warmth, the collars and cuffs were made of beaver or otter skins. Spoons, plates, cups, and other old pieces of tableware that were no longer fit for use were melted down and made into buttons, blocks of soapstone serving as molds.

The symbol of the frontiersman, the buckskin garment, was worn but was never popular and was discarded as soon as fabric became available. While it was strong and served well in a dry climate, it was uncomfortable in the rainy Northwest, because after frequent wetting and drying it assumed a fixed and unalterable shape. "This malformation did not appear when a man was sitting, which was, for this reason, his favorite posture," wrote one pioneer, "but when he arose the appearance to an inexperienced eye was that he was not yet up, for the knees of his trousers did not respond to the straightening of his legs but held the shape of the sitting posture, and the seat of his trousers did likewise."

When heavy unbleached muslin could be obtained, it was dyed and made into dresses and skirts for the girls and trousers for the boys. When wool became available, the housewife carded it herself, washed it with soap she made from wood ashes, wove and tinted it. In dyeing she had the resourcefulness of the primitive. Black was made from the scrapings of burnt logs, brown from the hulls of black walnuts or the bark of an alder tree, bright yellows and reds from the leaves of various trees.

Shoes were made by the menfolk, and almost every family had someone who could construct a last and pegs. Buckskin was used at first, then rawhide, poorly tanned, so that shoes softened and stretched when wet, and the boys would often leave them sticking behind in the mud, which was ubiquitous for a good part of the year.

The pioneers on the whole ate well. The countryside abounded in berries—strawberries, blackberries, huckleberries—trout and salmon could practically be scooped out of the streams and rivers, and the woods were filled with game. The one serious shortage was sugar, and the housewife resorted to all sorts of devices to satisfy the craving for sweets, using to good advantage the garden patch which every household soon acquired. Carrots boiled in a sugar syrup to which ginger had been added formed a base for marmalade. The juice of ripe tomatoes boiled with sugar until very thick and then flavored with honey took on enough of the honey flavor so that it could be used on hot cakes without too much protest. Ripe whole tomatoes, carefully boiled in sugar syrup and carefully removed without breaking, dried and dusted with sugar, were eaten as a confection.

From the same garden patch and from the pantry shelf came a varied assortment of home remedies. Farms were scattered, doctors in effect nonexistent, since there were so few and the area to be covered was so vast, and women, therefore, had to rely on their knowledge and intuition. To cure an earache, a large onion cut up and placed alternately with leaves of strong tobacco was wrapped in a wet cloth and covered by the embers in the fireplace until the onion was cooked. The juice was then squeezed out and, while it was hot, dropped into the ear, three or four drops at a time. Onion syrup, made by mashing diced onions into sugar, was a common cough syrup. A remedy for fever was a poultice of mashed onions applied to the armpits, stomach, palms of the hands, and soles of the feet; and roasted onions were sometimes used to bring boils to a head. And, shades of modern disinfectants and deodorants! onions cut in halves and placed on a plate on the floor were used to absorb the odors of the sickroom.

A spice plaster of powdered cinnamon, cloves, cayenne pepper, flour, and spirits, to which the more imaginative sometimes added for good measure black pepper and powdered ginger, made a poultice for a stomach-ache. It was applied hot, as was the time-honored mustard plaster, made by mixing flour, water, and mustard and used for colds and sore chests. Oil of cloves and oil of peppermint were then the only means of relief for a toothache.

Teas were used for a number of maladies: tansy tea and mullein tea for asthma and bronchial troubles, sage tea for the measles. Vinegar and spices, mixed in various combinations, were considered efficacious for a variety of ailments from coughs, hiccoughs, and sore throats to rheumatism. Next to the cold, the most common complaint was chills and fever, and for that the standard remedy was goose grease and turpentine, also used for innumerable other disorders. "It was all you could smell in a schoolroom," recalled a pioneer. Goose grease or hog's lard formed the base for salves. Mixed with dry sulphur, it was an ointment for boils and sores; with elderberry bark or red clover blossoms, for burns; alone, it was rubbed on the noses and soles of the feet of children who had the sniffles.

Many remedies were based on superstition and folklore, such as a dirty sock tied around the neck to cure a sore throat. Happily lacking any knowledge of germs, cobwebs were used to check bleeding and in most cases apparently left the injured person unharmed. The pungent asafetida, tied on a string and worn about the neck all winter, was considered a preventive of illness. Smoke from burning wool was supposed to relieve inflammations. In the treatment of scarlet fever, the patient's whole body was rubbed with bacon rind and then the rind was tied around the neck.

An important and extensively used item in the medicine cabinet was whisky, taken internally or applied externally. As a treatment for burns, it was combined with essence of peppermint and applied with cloths. It was used as a disinfectant, either straight or diluted with an equal amount of water, for bathing cuts and flesh wounds. And for snake bites, the victim kept himself saturated internally until the danger was considered over. Mixed with salt, it was used as a gargle for a sore throat and mixed in a toddy for the grippe. Sunflower seeds soaked for twelve hours in whisky, strained and drunk a tablespoonful at a time, was supposed to relieve rheumatism. Spirits were often the only relief unfortunate women had for their numerous internal ailments, and they were sipped in secret, the bottle carefully hidden from the menfolk.

Frequently a housewife received an urgent call that a neighbor was ill, and unless she herself was completely incapacitated, she threw a few things together, saddled a horse or set out on foot. She generally remained with the sufferer until her aid was no longer needed.

The pioneer woman's ingenuity extended to the preparation of cosmetics which females the world over—no matter what their age, status or condition of servitude—find necessary for their morale. These were simple and easily compounded. To soften and whiten a weatherbeaten skin, honey soap, made by melting down soap and stirring in a half cup of honey, was used. Sour milk or buttermilk regularly applied at night also served the same purpose. Honey, well rubbed in, smoothed rough, work-worn hands. Another salve was made of white wax, spermaceti, and sweet oil, scented with rose or lavender. No elaborate shampoos were available to clean and brighten woman's crowning glory, but rain water made the hair silky, and a hair wash compounded of alcohol and castor oil scented with lavender left it glossy and fragrant. Sage tea was used surreptitiously by vain ladies to darken tresses which had begun to show telltale signs of gray. These almost pathetically modest attempts to remind the housewife that she was a female took very little time either to make or apply—a few moments snatched from a day filled with countless chores.

In addition to the routine rigors of her daily existence, she had a serious problem with which to contend—the Indian. When they were friendly, these children of nature were too friendly for her comfort. They tracked up her clean kitchen with their muddy feet, stole food and any little household items they could get away with, and embarrassed her by their unself-conscious exposure of their bodies.

Stories are related of women, annoyed beyond endurance by their antics, chasing Indians with anything that came to hand—a poker, a hot ladle, a skillet. One woman is said to have scattered a group of thieving redskins with a tentpole, which so won the admiration of the chief of the tribe that he came back the next day to apologize and to offer $500 in cash for her. When they were hostile, she barricaded herself in the house with a gun if the menfolk were away and waited, her mind distraught by stories of Indian attacks on settlements. Her anxiety was generally groundless, for Northwesterners were rarely victimized by Indian attacks.

Above all, many women were desperately lonely. Weeks sometimes passed before they saw a neighbor, and many years before homes were close enough so that they could indulge in a pleasant exchange of chatter about recipes or child care. Those who lived in clearings in the forest often felt suffocated by the immense trees towering all around them, and the eerie noises of the woodland at night left them trembling with unknown fears.

To some, however, the beauty of the countryside was compensation for all hardships. To be able to stand outside the house and smell the scent of the forest, to reach in spirit to the great, snow-covered mountains instead of seeing the dull, interminable flatlands of the Midwest, was a solace that made the mundane matters of living seem less important. And, added to that, if a couple were in love and enjoyed the blessings of a closely knit and congenial family, even the occasional attacks of loneliness and fear might be discounted. One of these fortunate women was Roselle Applegate Putnam, daughter of an illustrious pioneer of the vanguard of 1843. She died when she was only twenty-seven or eight, and all that remains of what must have been a lovely and shining spirit is the small collection of letters she wrote to her husband's family in the East.

Roselle was a little over sixteen when she married Charles Putnam, a young printer from Lexington, Kentucky, and the following year the first of several children was already on the way. Though she was soon burdened with a growing family, the interminable household chores, and the task of setting type and helping to get out the newspaper her husband was editing, she found time to write long letters to the Putnams. They reveal an exceptionally fine and perceptive mind, a genuinely sensitive personality, and an unusual maturity. The spelling and grammar are frequently poor, for Roselle had little formal schooling and no time to acquire any after her early marriage, but no literary imperfections can detract from their charm.

Though she was separated from her husband's family by thousands of miles, she was intimately concerned with its welfare. In one letter she pleads for her sister-in-law, to whose marriage her mother objected because the suitor was blind: "Like her I chose my companion contrary to the wishes of my parents & had they been as severe with me as you are with her I should have been most wretched indeed, for

I am confident I could not have helped loving my husband had all the world striven to prevent it."

In every letter Roselle urged the family to migrate. Her own life, she said, was a peaceful and contented one, though the nearest family was three miles away and the nearest female companion about six. Her days were full and "we have plenty of reading to pass off the evenings and sundays Charles takes an Oregon paper the New York Tribune & Harper's Monthly magazine." With mature understanding and knowledge she described the advantages of the new country: the wonderful combination of climate, scenery, fertility of soil, the generous land law, the high wages of labor. The family learned from her about the nature of the crops, their output, the prices they brought, the kind of fish found in the streams. Nowhere else, she felt, could one find as rich and satisfying an existence.

Within three years after Roselle came to the Oregon country, there were thriving communities at various points along the Willamette River. Oregon City, which was located on the east bank alongside a waterfall, was the first destination of most of the immigrants. Here they found people who were in a position to guide them, offer them some practical help, and acquaint them with conditions in the new land. It had about a hundred dwellings to house the six hundred inhabitants, two public buildings, a Methodist and a Catholic church, two gristmills, several sawmills, four general stores, two taverns, a hatter, a tannery, three tailor shops, two cabinetmakers, two silversmiths, one cooper, two blacksmiths, a printing office, a lathe machine, and a brickyard. A doctor and three lawyers provided the professional services for the community. Carpenters and masons were employed full time constructing new buildings for residential and business purposes. It even boasted a paper issued twice a month, the *Oregon Spectator*, which was the first in the area west of the Rocky Mountains. Unimproved lots were already as high as $100 to $500 and being snatched up.

Across the Willamette stood Linn City, named in memory of the senator who had contributed so much to the successful outcome of the Oregon question. It was still a hamlet and immigrants were reluctant to settle there, for one man owned a substantial area above and below the falls and he refused to sell the water power which was essential to run mills. Settlers were not, however, restricted to either Oregon or Linn cities.

The claims to the Oregon Territory by the United States and Great Britain had been settled, and immigrants could take any of the land between the 49th parallel to the north and the 42nd parallel to the south, or the Pacific to the west and the Rocky Mountains to the east. The territory had already been divided into eight counties: Lewis County, which comprised the Puget Sound area; Vancouver along the northern side of the Columbia River and which, with Lewis, included all of the land above the river. In addition there were Clatsop, Yamhill, Polk, Quality, Clackamis, and Champoeg. The interior was not opened until the irresistible lure of gold brought men there.

Despite the meager population, some men succeeded in accumulating substantial fortunes from their business enterprises. Not too unusual was the case of Sidney Moss, who, in a few years, became one of the affluent citizens of the community. Moss had come to Oregon City in 1842 and had begun his career in the new land by assisting John McLoughlin, who held a claim of 640 acres on the east side of the Willamette, in surveying the area. He then obtained employment cutting wood at seventy-five cents a cord. With his earnings he purchased a lot on Main Street and the following year erected a "hotel" on the site. It was the first inn west of the Rockies, and when he opened for business there was not a single bed or chair on the premises. Guests slept in blankets on the floor and paid Moss $5 a week for the space and the shelter of a roof. In 1850 he sent his partner east with $63,000 to purchase supplies, having accumulated that great sum from the hotel and a store, also the first in the territory, which he operated in conjunction with it.

Moss's store soon found itself situated in a "city," but Marcel Chappellier located his in a small clearing on the road leading from Cowlitz Landing to Olympia in 1858, and for many years it remained an isolated outpost. Merchandise had to be shipped from Tumwater and Olympia in the north or Monticello and Portland in the south. Produce from the Willamette Valley came by canoe or flatboat along the Columbia to the mouth of Cowlitz Prairie, north through the prairies and dense timberland until its final destination, Puget Sound. The distance between claims was seldom less than half a mile and often through thick woodlands. This made the residents of the entire area dependent on the supplies brought to Chappellier's store, and both the white man and the Indian traded there.

It was a miniature Sears Roebuck in the variety of goods handled. The drug department carried items like camphor, soothing syrup, toothache drops and "pain killer," epsom salts, blister plaster, matches, toothbrushes, and a number of the patent-medicine remedies so popular in those days. In the general department the customer could secure hoops, needles, buttons, gloves, farm tools, butcher knives, candle molds, mirrors, seeds for planting, and so forth. Not to be overlooked was liquor. Magazines and newspapers were also carried.

A good deal of the business was conducted by barter or on credit, as currency was scarce. The Indians were credited for hauling freight, for skins, for fish, and for wages, in return for which they would be given whatever goods they needed. White settlers traded oats, eggs, butter, bacon, hay, and whatever else was of general use. Chappellier's account book listing his bad debts was concise and descriptive:

Henry Miles
1875, Nov. 12, By cash pr Gosnell, $10.00
Bal. gone to Hell

A. J. Simmons
He got mad and quit trading
Profit and Loss Balance $6.81

Capt. Kerns
1869, Jany 13, He is dead and nothing left I believe, $10.55

Doct. D. S. Maynard
July 1, 1868, [sic] My amt. to Bal., $16.00
He is dead and gone.

Chappellier was also an employer of labor, paying about $1 a day to the Indian, $2 to the white man, and about $10 a month to women. He served as a middleman for the farmers of the region in procuring and selling the necessary livestock for them, and acted as banker, lending out money for various purposes. In addition to all this, he rented rooms to travelers, provided meals for them and their horses, and occasionally housed prisoners temporarily for the county.

One important part of the store was the post-office boxes which Chappellier rented, thereby acting as a mail-receiving depot for the settlers in the area. For many years the handling of the mail was a source of continual annoyance to the pioneers. In the earliest days notices would be published in the papers "To Persons Wishing to Send Letters East." Writers were informed that the postmaster general had contracted with a traveler going east who would carry the mail from Oregon City, in one case, to Weston, Missouri, from which point it would be forwarded to any part of the United States. "As the mail sent east, by Mr. Burns, will reach Weston early in the season, it would be advisable for those wishing to correspond with their friends in the east, to avail themselves of this opportunity. Postage only fifty cents on single sheets."

The nearest post office to Centralia in 1846 was Fort Vancouver, about a hundred miles away over winding sheep trails, rivers, and sloughs. The trip there was made only once a year. Not until 1851 did the area have a regular mail carrier who made the journey on horse-back. The following year his route was shortened, for a canoe paddled by Indians carried the mail from Rainier, Oregon, to Cowlitz Landing, and was said to have missed only one trip because of the high water. One carrier was drowned fording the swollen stream near Centralia which, according to some Indians, was named Skookumchuck, Chinook for swift water. It was so much of an event when the mail came through that the newspaper printed a public appreciation to the mailman, who "for sped [*sic*], regularity, and care in carrying the mail is entitled to the gratitude of our whole community." For the next few years, however, deliveries were still uncertain, one pioneer noting in his journal that a letter took eight months to reach him.

Romance was on one occasion a by-product of mail delivery. It seems that one young carrier arrived at the hotel in Monticello on a stormy night to find a dance in progress. Quietly he seated himself in front of the fire to dry his clothes and warm up a bit before retiring to his room. The dancers were having a gay and hilarious time, and while the fiddler was resting, one of the young women jumped up and offered her hand in marriage to anyone in the room, expecting, so the story goes, to add to the festivities by a mock ceremony. With alacrity our youthful mailman stepped to her side and, his clothes still steaming, took the vows. The sequel to this little tale is that he later claimed his "bride" and the couple lived happily ever after.

The nearest post office for the people of Coquille Valley in Oregon was Empire City. Although it was only forty miles away, it took from four to five days to get there by boat if the tide was favorable; if not, as much as a week. There was no regular postman, and so when any-one made the trip to the city, he took along a sack in which to bring back the mail for everyone on the river. Distribution was, of course, haphazard, and the last people on the line were the sufferers. The sack was emptied at the first stop on the way back, the mail assorted, and some effort made to distribute it according to location. The news that the postman had arrived spread quickly through the area, and those closest by congregated at the "receiving depot" to select their own and to take that of the nearest neighbor. The process was repeated at the next point and so on down the line.

Newspapers and magazines were a rarity and those that arrived were so frequently examined that they reached the subscriber well worn, if they reached him at all. "This was done with no intention to be dishonest, but merely a desire to become acquainted with what was happening outside, especially among his neighbors!" recalls one pioneer. Dickens's novels were at that time being run serially in *Harper's Monthly,* and one neighbor told a subscriber to the magazine that he was always very much disappointed when it failed to come through, adding that he hoped she had not minded his "borrowing" them for a while.

This scarcity of reading matter continued all through the early years. Little literature had been brought across the trail, and the cost of ordering books and magazines from the East was prohibitive to most of the settlers. One Washington pioneer read the family Bible over and over again, until the pages wore thin. Humorously, he related that he read every word except the section dealing with the "begats," for there he found the pronunciation of the names too diffi-cult and, besides, he could not see where they figured very largely in the pioneer history of the world anyway. Another settler read Web-ster's dictionary almost from cover to cover, complaining despair-ingly that the subject matter changed too quickly.

Mail, both outgoing and incoming, played a vital part in the lives of the pioneers. It kept them in touch with the outside world, served as a means to urge friends and relatives to migrate, and provided an outlet for those who did not find the Northwest a land of promise and would have returned but for the vivid memory of the long trek. De-spondently, one pioneer wrote home:

When a man gets to raising and selling agricultural products, or becomes established in any other business the profits of which are three or four times the profits of labor, he can prosper—but not till then—That is too true. And you can tell them that if people were not made over, or rather half unmade, by the dehumanising processes through which they go from Kanesville here, they would never submit to living in such houses, with such absence of the conveniences and comforts of eastern life, and such a destitution of intellectual and moral opportunities, if they had not already learned on the plains to submit to anything. You can tell them that too; and tell them they can never, in living here, get paid for coming over the plains. I am not homesick; I am not prejudiced; I only tell you facts . . . much more than half of those, in this country of mild winters, of a fruitful soil and mines of gleaming gold, are dissatisfied and regret having come here.

Although laborers' wages were high, the letter went on, about $2 or $3 a day—a factor to be considered by prospective employers—prices were still higher. Salt cost $0.25 and butter was $1.25 a pound. The city had numerous saloons and gambling dens and "drunkerds" roamed the streets, but there was one encouraging note: schools had already been established, churches were being organized, and five Methodist clergymen were in the field.

The majority, though, were optimistic and regarded their little towns as future Chicagos, St. Louis's, or Milwaukees. The Reverend David Blaine wrote to his brother that Seattle was mushrooming at a fantastic rate and urged him to invest in lots. They were now selling at $15 or $20, but prices were jumping almost daily. He was certain that the city was the future terminus of a railroad, and when that happened the owner of land would make a fortune. Another correspondent in 1858 wrote that he expected Eugene City to be the capital of Oregon. Although only about four years old, it already was the principal trading place in the county. The population was only five or six hundred and it had, among other essential establishments, no less than nine dry-goods stores, two bookstores, a flour mill, and a sawmill, a courthouse "second to none in the territory," a college and a university, a district schoolhouse, one church with others going up, four lawyers, four clergymen, three physicians, and even a jail in the process of construction. The health of his family, he said, was excellent and he had acquired 880 acres of some of the best land in the county, a hundred head of cattle, and a number of fine horses for which there was an especially good market.

The farmer back home, struggling with worn-out soil, must have read with envy that in Oregon, with ordinary cultivation, the land would produce a crop of thirty or forty bushels of wheat and other small grains in like proportion, that one sowing would yield two good crops and sometimes a third, that all the coarser vegetables, with the exception of corn, could be raised easily and fruit grown readily. Everything brought a good price, and as an indication of the growing trade, stated one correspondent, three steamers had been put on the Willamette above the falls that season.

California alone, Northwesterners wrote, could absorb all of Oregon's exports. The "Main Willamette Road," as it was then called, which served as the thoroughfare connecting the populated areas of Oregon with her neighbor to the south, was thronged with freight caravans. Shipments were so numerous that it was impossible to estimate the amount of butter, flour, apples, and sundry other items that were being exported. Travelers reported a constant stream of what looked like steamboats on wheels, with the holds filled with chickens, ducks, and geese and the aft with turkeys.

Towns were springing up so fast that it was difficult to keep up with them. It seemed that where yesterday had been a forest or an empty stretch of prairie was today a full-fledged city, complete with streets, houses, and shops. Cities were becoming too crowded for comfort, wrote one Portlander, "1000 people landed here Saturday, not a house to be hired, taverns all full."

Occasionally, tourists came to see what the new country was like. Theodore Winthrop, a wealthy Boston poet, made a trip through the region in 1853. His impressions were recorded with sensitivity and charm. The forests and the mountains had a majesty and grandeur that California could not approach, he wrote. The scenery of the Columbia "has a breadth and a wild powerful effect every way worthy of it . . . and some thousand years hence, the beauty of its highly finished shores will be exquisite, backed by snow peaks." About the social scene he commented: "There is a heartiness and rough sincerity impressed upon people by the kind of life they lead in new countries. An easy hospitality given and received without much ceremony is a thing of course." In his opinion the new land offered a wonderful opportunity for a man who is "either a world in himself or who can have his own world about him," but those accustomed to sophisticated Boston society would find it difficult to put up with the excessive number of ill bred and ill educated people.

Men of learning and intellect could be found in the new country, though not too many, perhaps, as erudite as Jesse Applegate, who was affectionately and respectfully dubbed "The Sage of Yoncalla." Applegate had left a well established and prosperous farm in Missouri because he loathed the institution of slavery, and it was difficult in that area to manage without it. The West, he hoped, would offer the opportunity for freedom and equality for all men.

On the long journey Jesse Applegate quickly displayed his innate qualities of leadership. The wagon train had left Missouri under the command of Peter Burnett, but after reaching the Kansas River, disagreement arose between those who owned cattle and those who had none. The dispute was understandable, for the men without the encumbrance of livestock saw no reason why they had to perform guard duty over other people's property. The party split and the men with the cattle chose Applegate as their captain.

To have charge of a "cow column" presented the most severe test of leadership. Of Applegate's ability a Northwest historian wrote: "By his accurate knowledge of the difficulties to be encountered, his resourcefulness in overcoming them, his tact and courage, his commanding personality, and withal, the kind, helpful spirit he always manifested, he not only held the uniform respect of all these staunch frontiersmen but won their loyal affection."

After settling in Oregon, Applegate began to survey the country and, among other valuable services he performed, opened the long, southern route. Few other men in the Northwest became as familiar with the wild mountain passes or the dense and lonely forests. Physically, he was well adapted to life on the frontier. Tall—he was well over six feet—strong and powerfully muscled, he could cover forty miles in one day without tiring. Intellectually he had few equals in the new land and quickly took his place as one of the leaders. In 1849, he represented Polk County in the Territorial legislature of the provisional government. Eight years later, he was appointed a member of the convention called to frame a constitution for the proposed state of Oregon. His advice was constantly sought on matters ranging from planting to government, and, until his death, he remained an influential force in Oregon politics.

Like other frontiersmen, Applegate had dug ditches, drained swamps, blazed trails, and fought Indians, but he also managed to find time for literary pursuits. He had a library of several thousand volumes, part of which had been shipped around Cape Horn and the rest acquired through the years. He received newspapers, periodicals, and even the Congressional reports as regularly as the mails allowed. On evenings when he was at home, the family gathered around the fireplace and he read aloud from the literary classics or the latest newspaper or perhaps from some volume of Gibbon or Hildreth or Bancroft.

Applegate's range of knowledge on all subjects—literature, history, science, philosophy—would have done credit to a professional scholar, though his formal education was negligible. In his youth he had studied law while employed as a clerk in the office of Edward Bates, a man of considerable learning and a fine attorney. Years later, when Bates was appointed Attorney-General in Lincoln's cabinet, the two men kept up a steady correspondence, exchanging views on important current matters.

His political sagacity became known to Schuyler Colfax, Speaker of the House of Representatives, who, in the fall of 1865, requested him to submit his opinions on the fundamental political questions of the day. Applegate complied in a series of four letters to the congressman which are a clear and logical exposition of his views. They encompass a spirited and intellectual defense of the Constitution with a keen awareness of its limitations; a faith and belief in the nationalist principle with due regard to the integrity of local and state units of government; a vigorous affirmation of the democratic principle of universal suffrage except for those who would not qualify on moral and intellectual grounds; the suggestion that elections be taken out of the jurisdiction of the states and placed under the Federal government; and support for legislative efforts to accord full civil and political liberties to the emancipated Negro.

A prolific letter writer, his correspondence contained mature and profound opinions, well phrased and cogently expressed, on local and state politics, on slavery, on the Indian problem, on sex and morals, on his fellow pioneers. His views on the marital relationship and on women is surprisingly enlightened and sophisticated for a "backwoodsman." In one letter to a friend he wrote that he had read some books on physiology "and some on secret subjects the public sale of which is forbidden. But thousands of parents live and die as ignorant of these very important subjects as the brutes they imitate, but this is no more a good reason and under pretense of modesty to forbid such knowledge to parents particularly married women than to forbid reading to a slave on the ground that too much knowledge will destroy his happiness." Every husband and every wife should understand these matters, he stated, not only to enable them to secure healthy children, but so that they could "intensify the gratification of . . . 'that supremest pleasure of Sense,' kindly given by the Creator to women as a compensation for the pains of maternity— To men in reward for the love and tenderness he *should bestow* upon both mother and child."

In Applegate's secret life was a correspondence with a young woman whom he greatly admired and respected. To her he poured out his philosophy of living while he attempted to guide and advise her, writing with complete frankness and freedom. One letter is of particular interest in revealing a side of the man which was undoubtedly completely unknown to his contemporaries and even to those closest to him. After an analysis of his emotional nature, he wrote that had circumstances been different, he would have asked her to marry him "and in the regular, orthodox way revelled in the beauties of your person while I aided you in the development of your mind." Or, as his views of marriage were unorthodox, had he been a potentate, "the Pope for instance whose illicit love honors the object," he would have sought her love without the sanction of the Church. Or, had he been extremely wealthy, he would have provided her with enough money to make her independent and above the censure of the world. As he believed that each of them possessed qualities which "might produce an intellect that might walk the untrodden paths of science or sway mankind," he might have asked her "to bear me a son, and take upon yourself as the task of your life his training and education."

With the passing of the years, Jesse Applegate withdrew more and more into himself. It had probably always been necessary for him to make a deliberate effort to meet and deal with people, and his active participation in the life and government of early Oregon was due almost entirely to patriotic motives. He never consciously sought fame or glory and when he felt that there was no longer a need for his services, he retired from the public scene.

Throughout his life he had suffered from, and was handicapped by, a deep-rooted feeling of inferiority because of what he regarded as an unusually homely face. To a friend he once wrote that he had been requested by a historian to supply a biographical sketch together with a photograph for her book. "It was in vain that I urged that I had never been satisfied with my features, never saw them except by accident and was always disgusted when I did." He had never been photographed, he said, and never intended to be. "It was enough to be laughed at for my want of beauty while I lived without being a laughing stock to all eternity." He was also opposed to having his memoirs published because he felt that his life had been commonplace and "barren of thrilling incidents . . . such passages . . . that most nearly approached the romantic were known to few besides myself," and those he would be loath to make public on his own account and that of others.

Applegate kept up his voluminous correspondence and met old friends occasionally, but both his pen and his personality became increasingly irritating to them. His wit had become barbed and caustic and his manners in both letters and person distasteful to many who had once felt very warmly toward him. Mrs. Frances Fuller Victor, Oregon historian, wrote about him to a mutual friend:

Yes, Mr. Applegate is certainly very trying to his friends. I regret his barbarous ways, for I am inclined to like him in spite of them. I should enjoy his friendship if he would give it me—or perhaps I ought to say if he had it to give. . . . He writes charming letters when he's in the humor and insulting ones when he is out, and I've no liking for being petted and abused in turns. . . . But I cannot help feeling sorry for his sad old age, even while I do not acknowledge his right on account of his age to be a discourteous tyrant.

His last years were lonely ones. Occasionally he was invited to address pioneer meetings but, more often than not, he refused to attend. The world which he had helped to create passed him by. It was, in many respects, a far different world from the one in which he had spent most of his years.

For one thing, it was now a stable society and young men no longer had to be concerned about ending their days as bachelors because of the female shortage. Many women, to be sure, had crossed the plains to the Northwest, but they were mostly married women or children. The few young—or old—enough for marriage were quickly snapped up by the numerous bachelors, either while on the trail or shortly after they arrived. The unfortunate men who could not find wives were twice victimized: not only did they have to endure the loneliness of bachelorhood, but they were unable to take advantage of the Federal Donations Land Law of 1850, which provided for a free grant of 320 acres of land to any settler and an equal amount to his wife. What made the situation particularly pressing to the land hungry was the necessity to meet the one-year deadline.

Since few women of the customary marriageable age were available, children of twelve and thirteen were rushed to the altar by avaricious men. Sometimes they were married with their parents' consent and sometimes without. One pioneer recalled a case of a child of four being married to a mature man; another, the wife eleven years old and the husband twenty-eight. When she visited the latter couple on one occasion, the child helped her husband prepare dinner for the guests, but after the meal was over vanished. She was finally discovered in the back yard, playing with a neighbor's little girl, seesawing on a board thrown over a log. The husband returned to the house, cleared the table, and washed the dishes, remarking, "Lizzie's young yet!"

The *Oregonian* lashed out at this widespread practice of "robbing the cradle." It vehemently denounced it as destructive of sound morals, stating that such young girls were not physiologically mature, let alone emotionally or intellectually equipped to assume the responsibilities of marriage and the family. "We design to speak plainly," it wrote, "for we deem it a crime against natural laws, and needing to be discouraged by the indignant voice of public opinion. For God's sake, if any more such sacrifices are in contemplation, let them not be consummated . . . one such example, unrebuked, is worse than a thousand instances of ordinary crime."

With the expiration of the land law, children were no longer in demand as wives, but the dearth of females still remained a problem. Indian women were available, but inter-racial marriages had been frowned on even during the days of the fur trappers, and it was a bold man who could face the community with a redskinned maiden as his bride. Some did, however, and a small trade in squaws went on. Theodore Winthrop made a cynical comparison between the traffic in red women and white:

And now that I am on the tariff for squaws,—dry goods buy them in Siwashdom as sometimes in Christendom. The conventional price is expressed in blankets. Blankets paid to papa, buy: five, a cheap and unclean article, a drudge; ten, a tolerable article, a cook and basket-maker; twenty, a fine article of squaw, learned in kamas-beds . . . fifty, a very superior article, ruddy with vermilion and skilled in embroidering buckskin with porcupine-quills; and one hundred blankets, a princess, with the beauty and accomplishments of her rank. Mothers in civilization will be pleased to compare these with their current rates.

As a blanket cost about $3 at the time, the value in money of these women could be estimated.

Cheaper, even by the standards of the day, was the lovely daughter of an old Indian who was sold in Elk City, Idaho. The Indians came to the city weekly to sell their wares, and one day the young girl was offered as an article of "trade." Three bidders immediately presented themselves. The first offered $0.50 in cash and three deer hides; the second, $3.50 in cash; and the third, two fishhooks. Fishhooks were then an important but scarce item and the Indian tradesman quickly concluded the bargain with their owner. The couple were married and, it is related, lived in connubial bliss all their days.

Whatever the price, native women offered no solution and bachelors congregated to commiserate in their common distress and discuss measures to remedy their plight. Notices such as the following appeared in the local press:

ATTENTION BACHELORS: Believing that our only chance for a realization of the benefits and early attainment of matrimonial alliances depends upon the arrival in our midst of a number of the fair sex from the Atlantic States, and that, to bring about such an arrival a united effort and action are called for on our part, we respectfully request a full attendance of all eligible and sincerely desirous bachelors of this community to assemble on Tuesday evening next, February 28th, in Delin & Shorey's building, to devise ways and means to secure this much-needed and desirable emigration to our shores.

Nine signatures were appended to this notice to which was added, "And eighty-seven others." The paper reported the meeting after it was held and several months later carried an article stating that every city, town, and hamlet in the country must be aware of the female shortage in the Northwest, if one were to judge by the number of papers which reprinted the bachelors' call. Advertisements were also inserted in California and Eastern papers, friends in the more populous sections were appealed to for aid, but in vain. Wrote one forlorn bachelor to his local paper:

Notwithstanding the great inducement held out to single ladies and blooming widows to better their condition here, still they keep away and come not, though every steamer arriving here is looked on to contain the precious and forbidden fruit. The public mind is a little aggravated about the matter, and sundry speculations are on foot to remedy the existing evil, previous to our going down to perpetual celibacy; but the cry is, "they come not." Why should all this be so? is the question naturally asked, answered and discussed, all at the same time.

The following year a group of bachelors leaped to arms when word spread throughout Puget Sound that a shipment of women had been sent from London for the single men of British Columbia. A few desperate souls called a hasty conference and without much further ado made a mad dash into Canada, swept the women off their feet, and returned home with their brides. None were apparently fazed by the fact that the damsels were well past their prime and some old enough to stand more in the relationship of mother than wife!

That, of course, still solved nothing. The pioneers racked their brains. Hardly any obstacles had been too difficult to overcome on the frontier—roads were constructed out of the wilderness with incredible speed, houses shot up overnight, gigantic trees were cut down faster than Skookumchuch could be pronounced, but how to get marriageable females to the Territory seemed beyond anyone's ability. Despair settled on the lonely hearts of the males of Puget Sound until one bright young man, who would have done well today as a public-relations executive, was struck with an idea that was little short of brilliant in its simplicity.

In the West males outnumbered females by nine to one, but in the East women outnumbered men and the situation was aggravated as a result of Civil War casualties. Surely, many of these spinsters and widows would leap at the chance of binding their troth with the fine, stalwart specimens of manhood abounding in the new country who were pining for the chains of matrimony. True, advertisements in the papers had failed, but what gentle, well bred woman would embark on a solitary, perilous adventure even for such a happy fate? It was clearly prohibitive for the average young bachelor just beginning to make his way in the world to go charging east on a quest for a wife as the trip would cost about $1,000 for traveling and other expenses. Ergo! the answer was simple. Why could not one man make the journey, recruit a boatload of women, and bring them back?

So pondered Asa Shinn Mercer, the young, handsome, and affable president (and faculty!) of the new Territorial University. Twenty-two and just out of college, he had come to visit his brother, Judge Thomas Mercer, became enchanted with the vast and beautiful land, and quickly decided to make it his home. Now its problems were his, and no sooner did he evolve his plan, then he presented it to Governor Pickering. It was received enthusiastically and the governor immediately recommended to the legislature that it make an appropriation to finance the project. Unfortunately, there was no money in the treasury, and so Mercer resorted to friends for contributions. He finally collected enough to pay for the trip and set out promptly.

In the East, Mercer centered his activities around the Boston area, delivering talks on the splendid opportunity for jobs, homes, and husbands that awaited women in the land beyond the Rockies. A number responded, but when sailing time came only eleven actually accompanied the matrimonial agent from Seattle. The thought of a seven-thousand-mile journey into the unknown apparently was too much for the others. When the boat docked in Seattle in May, 1864, the "cargo" was warmly welcomed by the community, but there was great disappointment at its small number. The bachelors seemed grateful for Mercer's efforts, for he was unanimously elected to the upper house of the Territorial legislature. Just before the election the *Seattle Gazette* published the following item:

We neglected last week to notice the return home of our highly esteemed fellow citizen, Mr. Asa S. Mercer, from the East, where he has been on a visit for the greater part of the past year. It is to the efforts of Mr. Mercer —joined with the wishes of the darlings themselves—that the eleven accomplished and beautiful young ladies, whose arrival was lately announced, have been added to our population. We understand that the number would have been fifty, as at first reported, but many were not able to prepare for the journey this season. The thanks of the whole community, and of bachelors in particular, are due Mr. Mercer for his efforts in encouraging this much needed kind of immigration. Mr. Mercer is the Union candidate for joint councilman for King and Kitsap Counties, and all bachelors, old and young, may, on election day, have an opportunity of expressing, through the ballot box, their appreciation of his devotedness to the cause of the Union, matrimonial as well as national.

Encouraged by the response to his initial attempt, Mercer, without waiting to finish his term in the legislature, was again on his way east. This time he left with high hopes of securing aid from President Lincoln, whom he had known when he was a child. He would need help from the Chief Executive, for he planned a large enterprise—hundreds instead of a handful of females—and once again he was going with a small purse provided by friends. His plan was to ask Lincoln for a discarded government vessel in which to transport the women. But when he arrived in the capital, he found the city draped in black, mourning the President's assassination.

With his only contact gone, another man might have given up, but not Mercer. For weeks he was almost lost in bureaucratic red tape. At last he obtained an order from General Grant for a ship, *The Continental*, only to meet with disappointment once again when the quartermaster refused to honor it. More detail, more red tape, more pleading until the quartermaster offered to sell the steamer for $80,000. He might have asked a million, as far as Mercer was concerned, and despondently the young man was about ready to give up his project when Ben Holladay, the railroad and ship magnate, came to the rescue. He offered to buy the vessel, which was a bargain at the price, and transport five hundred emigrants for a small sum.

This vital matter settled, or so Asa Mercer believed, he set out on his recruiting expedition. He became a one-man immigration board throughout New England and even found time to write a booster pamphlet entitled *Washington Territory: The Great Northwest, Her Material Resources and Claims to Immigration: A Plain Statement of Things as They Exist.*

Eastern magazines and newspapers gave his venture wide publicity and, according to Mercer, several hundred women signed up for the trip. Then the New York *Herald* published a denunciatory blast that almost wrecked the enterprise. The paper charged that the bachelors of Puget Sound were profligate and immoral, that the maidens would be turned over to houses of ill fame; it slandered Mercer and cast aspersions on his intentions. The story spread and Mercer's heroic efforts to repudiate it made little headway. He claimed that about two-thirds of the women withdrew as a direct result of the newspaper item. And when he finally set sail, after considerable difficulty with Ben Holladay, who demanded full fare for the passengers since Mercer had not provided the number agreed upon, it was with only about a hundred women. In an article taking note of their departure, *Harper's Weekly* began: "No more curious or more suggestive Exodus ever took place than THE EXODUS OF WOMEN TO WASHINGTON TERRITORY under the leadership of MR. ASA S. MERCER. The scheme proposed by Mr. Mercer is in every way original and praiseworthy."

When the *Continental* stopped off in San Francisco harbor on April 24, 1866, before proceeding up the coast, the citizens of the Bear Flag State urged the girls to remain, cautioning them against the uncertainties of life in an unsettled "wilderness." That their motives were not entirely selfless might be gathered from an item which had appeared some months before in the *San Francisco Mercury* congratulating the unmarried men of California upon the prospective arrival of seven hundred women from Massachusetts to cheer the hearts of "our forlorn bachelors." Wishful thinking, perhaps, had given the citizens of that state the idea that the cargo of women was intended for them. The presumptuous *Mercury* even published a "poem" entitled "The Charge of the Bright Brigade."

.   .   .   .

Many leagues, many leagues,
Many leagues onward,
Right for the Golden Gate
Sailed the Seven Hundred

.   .   .   .   .

> Suitors to the right of them,
> > Suitors to the left of them,
> Suitors in front of them
> > Shouted and thudered [*sic*]
>
> •   •   •   •   •   •   •
>
> Flashed all their arms so bare,
> > Brown, black and golden hair,
> Startling the loungers there . . . .
> Right through the line they broke,
> > Broker and merchant
> Reeled from the charge and broke,
> > Every tie sundered.
> Then they rode off, but not
> > Quite Seven Hundred.

The women remained faithful to their agent and continued on to Seattle where they were heartily greeted by the citizens. One or two newspapers grumbled at the whole affair, feeling that such a large contingent of helpless females would prove a liability rather than an asset. Many of the Mercer girls married outstanding men in the community and some became schoolteachers or entered other employment. For many years opinion was divided on the Mercer episode, the "girls" being regarded with favor or suspicion by the inhabitants of the Pacific Northwest. Mercer himself was ensnared by the charms of one of these young women and married her. It was a long time, though, before the female shortage in the area ceased to be a problem, and in the meantime the "belles" had no difficulty in obtaining "dates."

"Oregon, though in its infancy, is not without amusements," wrote the *Spectator* in 1850. "The fun-loving portion of this community had an agreeable entertainment in the shape of a Cotillion Party, at the Oregon House, on Thursday evening last. It was participated in, we are told, by an unusually large number. The turn out of young ladies was far beyond our most extravagant expectations; where they all came from was more than we could conjecture." Young ladies were sometimes booked as much as three months in advance for a dance. Nor was distance an obstacle to the male sex. One young swain who was tending sheep walked eight miles to a ranch to get a horse, rode another eight miles to town for his friend, danced all night, escorted his lady home, returned to the ranch, and then walked the eight miles to where his sheep were grazing.

The pioneers worked hard and played hard. Farmers and their wives took no holidays, but they thought nothing of hitching up the wagon after a back-breaking day in the fields or in the kitchen, driving several miles, sometimes through axle-deep mud, spending the night in dancing and returning the next morning to resume their chores. And dancing in those days required stamina. It was not the modern ballroom kind which seems to consist chiefly of walking around to music, "and if you choose not to walk you may stand virtually in one spot, shifting the body's weight from one foot to the other in time to music," one old-timer commented sarcastically. The old square dances were peasant dances, reflecting all the vitality of people who lived close to the soil, an expression of exuberance and delight in rhythmic movement after a day's toil. Out of simple basic steps whose origins are deep in the past developed numerous variations such as the schottische, Virginia reel, quadrille, and variations of each of these.

Almost any occasion provided an excuse for a dance—a barn raising, a house raising, or just the need for some diversion—and folks would come from miles around, not only the young people, but the whole family. The babies were bedded down in the wagons and the young fry could watch from the benches around the room until they, too, were sent off to sleep. The success of a dance depended on the caller and the fiddler, two of the most colorful individuals in any community and, if good, not without repute and importance. The caller was generally a personable, glib-tongued fellow with strong lungs who was rated according to the new figures or movements he could improvise. In addition to playing, the fiddler livened up the proceedings by a little clowning. Some could toss their fiddles into the air or flip them upside down without losing a beat. Others waved their instruments backward over their heads while they played.

With the exception of certain religious sects, dances were considered entirely proper and respectable. And, indeed, there was no reason why they should not have been. They were always chaperoned and the steps generally required no closer proximity than a momentary touching of hands. In the few movements when the gentleman had to put his arm briefly around the lady's waist, he found her so completely encased in whalebone and steel under layers of clothing that, as one later recalled, "any sensual stimulation resulting from the contact must have been purely psychological." The dances were generally "called" in rhyme and had their own terminology. One old-time quadrille went as follows:

> Balance one—balance all eight
> Swing on the corner like swinging on a gate;
> Now swing your own if not too late,
> Left alamand—right to your partner and hand over hand,
> All the way 'round; promenade eight when you get straight.
> First lady out to right, swing that gent with right hand 'round,
> Partner by left with left hand 'round,
> Lady in the center and seven hands 'round (Circle).
> Bird hop out and crow hop in
> Seven hands up and around agin.

Not until the dancers were exhausted, the fiddler could no longer scrape a tune, and the caller's voice was gone did the affair end. On the way home the young folk still had energy enough to sing the plaintive, often morbid songs popular then. "Do They Miss Me at Home?" was one favorite, and others were "The Dying Nun," "Footsteps That Never Come," "Somebody's Waiting for Me," "Little Nell of Narragansett Bay."

Week-end visiting probably started on the frontiers throughout the world because of the need for social contact and the great distances between dwellings. Saturday-night week ends, as they were called, were almost an institution in some areas of the Northwest. The family started out in a straw-filled wagon on a Saturday eve after the chores were done. When the neighbor's house was reached, it was generally bedtime for the children, who were promptly disposed of, and then the older folks settled down for a gab fest. The favorite theme of conversation for years after settlement was crossing the plains, and, as time passed, the embellishments became so numerous that the teller himself could hardly distinguish fact from fiction. Sunday was devoted to the time-honored custom of amusing the children and to the big dinner.

The outstanding social event in the lives of the pioneers was the Fourth of July celebration which was held in the nearest town. Days were spent by the women in preparation. One pioneer recalls that her mother baked two hundred gooseberry pies, which seems somewhat of an exaggeration, but enough food was brought to feed a regiment. The festivities usually started with a parade featuring a patriotic float with Columbia, Goddess of Liberty, presiding. The prettiest girl in the area was chosen, with preference given to one who had blond hair. She was garbed in a flowing white robe and reigned from a bunting-decorated pedestal on a hayrick. At her feet were little girls, also dressed in white, who represented the states of the Union—the smallest was always Rhode Island. The driver was Uncle Sam dressed in top hat, striped pants, and sporting flowing whiskers.

Dinner was spread on long tables in a near-by grove or vacant lot, and after everyone was stuffed to capacity, the speechmaking began. The main address was generally given by a member of the legislature or a prominent local attorney. Invariably, the speaker "twisted the Lion's tail" and with choice adjectives denounced the British leaders and their government. Then, with even more eloquence, the theme shifted to the oppressed of the earth and the haven of refuge which awaited them on these shores. The big finale was the toasts—"The Day We Celebrate the Birthday of our Freedom"; "Our Country—Dedicated to Freedom by the Blood of Her Fathers. Her Constitution inhibits no liberty consistent with truth and offers to the oppressed of every land a home"; "Woman—Heaven's first best gift to Man"; "Will Amette and Miss Issippi—may they speedily be united by the iron bond of a railroad, and may President Buchanan perform the ceremony." There were other toasts on the Star-Spangled Banner, temperance, education, and so forth. And by then it was dusk and time to go home.

For the faithful, Baptist revival meetings provided both a means of salvation and an opportunity to visit with neighbors. Tent was pitched and for about three weeks the participants reveled in an emotional and spiritual orgy of praying, confessing, and singing. For the young folks it was a courting ground. When a boy reached the age of consent, father would let him use the buggy to go to meetin' and get himself a wife.

In the interim between camp revivals, monthly meetings were held in the schoolhouse. "Sermons lasted for hours and you could smell the hell fire in them," one pioneer related with a shudder, remembering the time spent squirming on a hard bench, the high-pitched, strained voice of the preacher pounding at her ears, and visualizing herself being slowly roasted over an open blaze. Most of the preachers were poorly educated and their English left much to be desired. "Ah, God, Ah, well, Ah, all evildoers, ah," was the vogue. As there were no song-books, the clergyman recited the words of a song two lines at a time, generally some mournful hymn such as "Hark from the Tomb a Doleful Sound." The shrill sopranos of the women and the basso profundos of the brethren mingled in a discordant chorus.

When the singing was over, the praying began. The members of the congregation knelt on the dirty floor and tried to outdo each other in reaching the ear of the Lord. "Glory, Glory Hallelujah," "Praise the Lord," "Amen, Amen," were shouted while the men chewed and spat in the sandbox under the stove and mothers rocked their babies in their arms to keep them quiet. When the meeting was over, the parishioners straightened their disheveled hair and clothing and went outside to chat, shake hands, and invite each other to dinner.

The outstanding revivalist preacher was the famed Joab Powell, "Harp of a Thousand Strings," as he was reverently called by his admirers. Blue-eyed, unruly-haired Joab was five feet ten inches tall, weighed two hundred pounds, and was said to be able to lick his weight in wildcats. On one occasion he challenged a muscular blacksmith of French Prairie, who had warned him to stay away from that vicinity, and beat him hands down, after which, it was said, the two men became fast friends. Another time he bodily tossed out of the meetinghouse the leader of a group of rowdies who had come to disrupt the proceedings. One winter in a backwoods community he dipped four hundred repentant sinners in an icy stream, taking time out only to warm up a bit in between batches.

Powell was as good as any show when he got going, and people of other denominations would often come to hear him preach. He once told a congregation composed principally of young men: "You Salem boys would rather hear Uncle Joab than go to a monkey show. You know it will cost you two bits to go to the monkey show; now fling in." And fling in his parishioners did, once to the tune of several hundred dollars.

Dances, Fourth of July celebrations, and revival meetings were enjoyed by the menfolk, but to many pioneers nothing was more satisfying than to get together with a bunch of cronies and talk politics. And there was a lot to discuss—the latest editorial in the paper on a new road, the shenanigans of some of the legislators, some national event of importance. The Northwest might have been isolated physically, but it was very close to home in its interests.

Six

"To Insure Domestic Tranquility"

Politics, for many of the pioneers, was secondary only to home building and land cultivation. It was natural that this should be so. The people felt a possessiveness toward the new land, which they themselves were helping to tame and fashion, that could not exist in the settled and stabilized communities where the spadework had been done by previous generations. They took a personal pride in every evidence of progress and were eager to assume the responsibilities attendant upon its achievement. Since few recreational facilities existed, more time could be devoted to "politiking."

The first handful of Americans who arrived in the Northwest, while it was still under joint occupation, lost no time in expressing their concern over the jurisdictional question. Eastern journals might consider the fuss about the Oregon country humorous, as did one family almanac:

Reader, you perceive that little spot of earth back of that gallant officer [referring to an illustration above the article] to the right hand that looks like a saddle of swine, or the lower extremities of a man cut in half; well that's the whole of Oregon including hills, hollers, rocks, rivers, vallies, ponds and prairies, wild-woods and wild-cats, wild onions and wild Indians, bears and buffaloes, that's the figure of the leetle spot about which there is so much legislation, negociation, speculation, comboberation, preparation, declaration, disputation, roundaboutation, emigration, fabrication, explanation, little moderation, consternation, humbugation, confederation, including a firm determination of Uncle Sam's nation to defend every station, from all molestation, or innovation, subjugation, or separation up to 54 degrees and 40 minutes, in which the entire twenty-seven states will second him.

But to the settlers, title to the land which was literally being watered by the sweat of their brows was hardly a subject for levity. The powerful Hudson's Bay Company had suzerainty over its employees and former employees, mostly French-Canadians, who had settled in the Willamette Valley and greatly outnumbered the two hundred or so Americans. The latter, however, refused to be subjected to this British authority. They began immediately to agitate for American acquisition of the Territory and for the creation of some form of government.

Nothing happened until one of the settlers, Ewing Young, died, leaving some valuable property which included a herd of fine cattle —and no heirs. Without law there was no means of handling the situation, and so a meeting was called at which an executor of the estate was appointed. At the same time it was felt that this was a good opportunity to do something about establishing a provisional government which would protect those not connected with the Hudson's Bay Company, and before the day was over a number of officers were chosen. The following day the French settlers joined the deliberations, a secretary from each group was selected and a committee appointed to draft a plan for a government and a code of laws.

Although this was an auspicious beginning, no further action resulted until three years later when the French and American settlers were compelled to meet to see what could be done about the wolves which were destroying livestock. At the first of these "wolf meetings," as they were called, attended by both French and Americans, the animals were discussed but politics soon cropped up. According to the minutes, it was decided that "a committee be appointed to take into consideration the propriety of taking measures for civil and military protection of this colony," and a second meeting was scheduled to be held at Champoeg.

Important events, it seems, must have heroes who decisively resolve an issue, and if there are none in fact, one is soon created. So it was with the meeting of May 2, 1843, at Champoeg which, according to legend, was the second time Oregon was saved for the United States. The meeting was held in a warehouse of the Hudson's Bay Company and the rafters rang with excited voices during its progress. Some stories have it that the French-Canadians were unaware of its real purpose, thinking it just another "wolf meeting," and when they realized the implications, indignantly withdrew.

The Americans retired to a near-by grove of trees for further discussion. Many of them were also opposed, believing that such a step would be disloyal to John McLoughlin, who had been generous with loans of money and supplies. An impasse was reached, when suddenly the intrepid Joe Meek, feeling that there had been enough pointless argumentation, stepped aside, drew a line in the dirt with a stick, and shouted: "Who's for a divide? All in favor of the report and an organization follow me!" One hundred and two men were present, and by only two votes, it is related, the government advocates won the day.

Whether or not the Joe Meek story is apocryphal is really irrelevant. What is significant is the early interest in government, though it was largely to protect property rights. Out of the Champoeg meeting came a constitution and a provisional government. This popular participation continued throughout the early years due to the small size of the communities, and the lack of sharply defined social caste lines contributed to greater freedom of expression.

The pioneers were neither taciturn nor inhibited about their manner of speech. Plain speaking and colorful language were not reserved for the intimacy of a family circle or gathering of close friends. They were used all the time—in the press, in the chambers of the legislature, and in the courts. One session of the august Territorial legislature was invoked by a preacher with the prayer, "Lord, forgive them for they know not what they do."

This informality extended to political campaigning. If a man decided to run for office, he merely published an advertisement in the local paper serving notice of his candidacy and he was a candidate. Representatives of the people were truly representatives, without any halo of dignity and awe. Even the chief executive of Oregon was regarded as "just folks." One gentleman addressed a letter to Governor Addison Gibbs which, while perhaps an extreme example of how close the people felt to their government, does give a good indication:

DEAR SIR:
Permit me to trouble you a little in regard to a matter that affects a friend of mine by the loss of a very valuable horse. He has reason to believe that he is in Portland has been kept at Mr. Austin's Stable. I send Enclosed a description of the horse, and also a bill of same to you from my friend, assuring him that you would keep his horse safe if he ever came into your possession. . . . My friend says he would sooner for you to have the horse if he can be found than any one else . . . that he would like to know of the horse being in good hands. He will pay from Fifty to one-Hundred dollars for his recovery. If your Excellency can assist in the recovering of the Horse and get him into your possession, you will not only confer a favor but shall be amply repaid for all trouble.

If a government official had any inclinations toward being overly genteel, he soon lost them in an atmosphere where he might find himself referred to in the press as a "black-legged debauchee," "sneaking hypocrite," or "lying scoundrel," among the milder epithets. He had to be able to give as well as take in verbal and, on some occasions, bodily fisticuffs. On the whole he was cast in the same mold as the average frontiersman, possessing a strong distaste for furbelows or anything that smacked of sham and pretense. One United States senator who attended a ball at the White House given by Mrs. Lincoln in 1862 wrote home to his wife:

I wish that you could have been here, to become totally satisfied with such nonsensical exhibitions. The "East Room," which is about the size of our big red barn was crowded with several hundred of Ladies and Gentlemen. Among the former I did not see one that I thought handsome. They were all distinguished for paint and big Hoops, with dresses a great deal too long at one end, and quite as much *too short at the other*. There were big fat dowagers in *low necked* dresses who would have excited the envy and admiration of a *Dairyman*. Others naked nearly to the waist made a sorry show of skin and bones, with scrawney shoulder blades standing out in the boldest sort of relief. The weak minded Mrs. Lincoln had *her bosom* on exhibition and a flower pot on her head, while there was a train of silk, or satin draging [*sic*] on the floor behind her of several yards in length, as I looked at her I could not help regretting that she had degenerated from the industrious and unpretending woman that she *was* in the days when she used to cook old Abes dinner, and milk the cows with her own hands. Now her only ambition seems to be to exhibit her own milking apparatus to the public gaze.

The bench was equally untrammeled by conventionalities. Courts were held in circuit at different places several times a year. When no appropriate public building existed, a large tree under which a few rude benches and chairs were placed served as a courtroom. A session frequently turned into a public show, with the farmers of the surrounding area turning out as at a county fair. Since cash was scarce, goods of one kind or another were accepted as fines. One prisoner found guilty of contempt was charged a blanket for the judge and a pair of breeches for the United States marshal.

Stories that sound spurious but might well have been authentic are rife about the ways of justice in the early days. There is the one about the Idaho judge who charged the twelve good men and true of the jury to find for the defendant if they believed his counsel, or to find for the plaintiff if his counsel was more convincing, "but if you are like me and don't believe a damned word that either of them says, I don't know what in hell you will do." And with that the jurist gestured to the constable and cavalierly requested him to take the jury. Or the one about the county attorney who was met by a friend and asked why he looked so tired and worn: the advocate replied that he had been trying a case all day but—and his face brightened—he now believed he would win it, for the constable had inveigled the jury into the local blacksmith shop and was arguing his side of the case for him!

As on every frontier, politics was of the cracker-barrel variety, discussion was free and open and every man knew on which side of the fence his neighbor stood. The settlers had come from various sections of the country and naturally brought with them their social, economic, and political predilections. Though they may not have been active in, or vociferous about, politics before, they changed when they reached the Northwest. No local issue was too small to be a matter of intense concern, whether it was a proposal to extend a road another twenty miles, the awarding of a government printing contract, or the location of the capital.

Logrolling was a familiar device. Many a young and inexperienced holder of public office who took his seat in the legislature for the first time was quickly disillusioned as he watched the sorry spectacle of a minority of the legislators intent on promoting their own selfish interests, obstructing the business of the entire assembly until the case was won. Members stood by helplessly while time was consumed with matters of personal favor, such as securing ferry charters for friends, locating county seats, and the like. The man who had the right kind of influence or knew the right men in the legislature need not be concerned about getting special projects approved, even one as difficult as the construction of a wagon road across the Cascade Mountains.

Washington, which became a separate Territory in 1853, experienced the same miniature and constant upheavals, and Idaho, created ten years later, had even more. In 1865 a Washington paper reported: "It appears that the people of Idaho are beginning to be involved in some of the sectional rivalries and difficulties which have so long been a standing curse to our own Territory. An act of their late Legislature removes the Capitol from Lewiston to Boise City. That is, of course, 'gall and wormwood' to the Lewistonians, who can't view the matter in exactly the same light as did the Legislature." The executive office, the article continued, had been moved, but the secretary's, "being a little behind time in taking up its line of march," was placed under an injunction not to proceed until further orders, because the late legislature had not been legally convened. What it did not mention was that the pro-Boise faction had precipitated matters by stealing the seal and legislative records, carrying them off to Boise and designating a rude frame building as the capitol!

Idaho seemed destined from the beginning, and for some time to come, to be almost rent asunder by various conflicts—the war between the cattle and sheep men over the rights to the grazing lands, the disputes with the Mormons, the agitation by the miners of the Panhandle who felt they could be served better by the government of Washington Territory and sought reannexation.

For five decades Idaho's magnificently wild country had known no white men except for the trappers who roamed her forests. It was not until gold, the source of all evil, as some would have it, was discovered in her bowels that the invasion began. For the next three decades the erstwhile peaceful land rang with the sound of pickax and shovel, with lusty cursing and carousing.

The first permanent settlement, named Franklin by a group of thirteen Mormon families who accidentally wandered into Idaho, mistaking it for Utah, was for a while almost unnoticed. But as more Mormons came into the Territory—by 1890 they comprised about 25 per cent of the total population—the violent American prejudice against their practice of polygamy was aroused. In 1884 the legislature passed a law requiring all voters to take an oath pledging opposition to plural marriage. This was construed by the leaders of the Church of the Latter Day Saints as interference with their religious creed and they refused to comply with it. Bitter controversy raged around this question up to the very minute a constitution for the new state, incorporating the antipolygamy law, was adopted. The Supreme Court finally settled the issue against the Mormons.

Not the least of Idaho's difficulties were the executives appointed to rule her. Ill chosen would be a mild understatement. As a matter of fact, for a while it seemed impossible to get appointees not only to stay but even to arrive! Two of them "got lost or stolen on the way out." One who finally did reach the Territory made a quick survey and as quickly took to his heels back to civilization.

Caleb Lyon, appointed by Lincoln simply because he was a good party man, was a fiasco. Lyon was a cultured gentleman, a New York art and literary critic, and somewhat of a dandy. He was not only ridiculous and a complete misfit in an area of mining camps, but apparently figuring that he could spend money for better purposes than for a bunch of crude, illiterate miners, absconded with $50,000 in public funds. The first interim executive soon drank himself to death; the second also died shortly after he took over; the third practiced grand larceny on a slightly smaller scale than Lyon, relieving the treasury of only $30,000 before he precipitately left for China.

To add insult to injury, Lyon was reappointed governor for a second term in 1865. Finding the duties of public office too onerous for his delicate constitution, he is said to have spent most of his time wandering about the country looking for diamonds. The next man, an Oregon physician, was also accused of dipping into the treasury, though it was never proven. The extent of his manipulations, however, may be indicated by the fact that he reported the Federal government's indebtedness on Idaho to be $65,000, whereas records show that only $10,000 had been spent.

And while governors were vanishing or swindling or just enjoying life with their legislative duties incidental, and when the legislators were temporarily not fuming over the Mormon problem, the men of law found other things to worry about. The Chinese who had infiltrated into the area to serve as cooks and laundrymen and as gleaners of what the white miners considered exhausted gold veins were next under attack. Marriage between whites and Orientals was prohibited, and the latter were taxed $4 a month for the privilege of residing in the Territory. The lawmakers as early as 1885 were appropriating money for an insane asylum, an indication, perhaps, of how hectic and wearing life must have been in that frontier society.

National politics influenced local politics in the Northwest almost from the very beginning, despite the barrier of the Rockies and the two-thousand-mile distance from the hub of governmental activity. Party divisions existed in the new land as they did in the old. In the fifties the American party, or "Know-Nothings," succeeded in recruiting enough adherents in the Northwest to emerge as an important factor. It directed its antiforeign prejudice against the remaining influence of the Hudson's Bay Company on American soil as there were too few foreigners among the immigrants to provide the bigots with a target. The Democrats, or "Locofocos," accused the Whigs of being Know-Nothings in disguise, and the war was on.

The bitter and crucial conflict which raged over the issues of slavery and union shook the Northwest as well. While passions could be expected to run high in the East where constitutional interpretation was more than theoretical and impinged on the entire way of life and culture, Oregonians, with no comparable dependence, also found themselves embroiled. The issues penetrated so deeply that they became factors in the advocacy of a separate Pacific Republic. Motives were mixed; they included geographical isolation, economic discrimination by the East, and political sympathies.

The first indication that some Democrats in Oregon were in sympathy with the idea of a Pacific Republic came in 1851. It was promptly denounced by the *Oregonian*. The Democratic victory in the presidential election the following year caused the issue to lie dormant for a while, but three years later it emerged again. Separation on grounds divorced from politics was occasionally advocated in letters to the newspapers. One type of discrimination which some supporters of the region's independence believed would be eliminated, for instance, was the difference in postal rates. East of the Cascades, a letter could be mailed for three cents while the postage on a letter sent from the Far West was ten cents. Usually, however, the views expressed in favor of separation carried political implications—the enhancement of Democratic party interests.

In 1855, when the war clouds were gathering over the country, the *Portland Standard* called for separation principally because it saw no reason why the Territory should enter a Union that was being rent asunder by controversy and bitter sectional rivalry. "If nature ever marked out the division of countries, it has done so in North America," the paper wrote. "The vast chain of the Rocky Mountains presents an unmistakable boundary, and we have reason to believe that these boundaries, laid down by an overruling Providence, ought to be more strictly regarded." Oregon, the paper contended, was too far removed to be expected to participate in that kind of internecine warfare. Her geographical distance had created a natural gulf between her people and the people of the East which could not be bridged by a union with the national government. Distance and isolation had produced different habits and a different social outlook. Oregon should be permitted to live her own way and follow her own destiny without subjugation to a national authority so far removed. There was precedent for bold action. Did not the revolutionary forefathers advocate independence from Great Britain after Lexington and Concord?

Denunciation of these views, which were regarded as treasonable, came swiftly and vehemently, particularly from the Whig press. The *Oregonian*, in an editorial headed "Revolutionary Filibustering in a New Direction," lashed out: "Four years ago we repeatedly told the people of Oregon that the leaders of the self-styled Democratic Party designed at no distant date to throw off their allegiance to the United States government . . . the facts are upon record that these men have been constantly laying their plans for a revolutionary movement. . . . They are endeavoring to create disaffection, anarchy, confusion and discord among the people—urging to rebellion."

The plan provided that the Pacific Republic should embrace the existing states of California, Oregon, Washington, Idaho, possibly New Mexico and Utah and some subdivisions of these territories. California might be split into two or three states, and a similar re-demarcation of lines of Washington and Oregon territories might be effected. No agreement existed on this particular phase, but the con-viction that such a republic ought to be created was shared by most of the Southern Democratic sympathizers in the West.

The influential Senator Joseph Lane of Oregon was charged re-peatedly with favoring separation, probably because his sympathies were openly Southern, but he vigorously denied the allegation. He received the vice-presidential nomination on the Breckinridge South-ern Democratic ticket, which at once caused all the Douglas Demo-crats in Oregon to oppose and denounce him. Lane returned to Ore-gon on the same steamer that brought word of the fall of Fort Sumter and never again entered politics. He had staked his political future on the success of the Southern cause and the outbreak of hostilities spelled defeat for him in the Pacific Northwest. At the mass meetings he addressed on his way home to his farm, many came to express their support, but in a number of cities he was burned in effigy.

With the onset of the Civil War, those who had favored a Pacific Republic became more vociferous, and they were joined by those who hoped that by this means the western states would be spared the obligation of participating in the conflict. Even then they were in a hopeless minority. The legislatures of Washington Territory and of Oregon passed resolutions repudiating all designs for a Pacific Con-federacy. "Let any who propose to speak for this Coast look else-where for sympathy and support in such treasonable plottings, than in the Territory bearing the honored name of the Father of his Country," editorialized the *Washington Standard*. "Such a proposition we regard as sheer madness, the invention of a disordered brain, the conception of a heart lacking fear of God or love to his race."

The movement would probably never have achieved even the small following it commanded were not the West so isolated and remote. Washington, D.C., was a long way off from Washington Territory. It is not surprising, therefore, that some pioneers living in an area that was no closer to the States than the continent of Europe was to the East should have felt little compunction about severing ties with a distant government uncongenial to their views and one that had not yet demonstrated its nationalism.

The agitation over a Pacific Republic provided but a ripple in the political stream compared to other issues such as slavery. During the fifties, the Democrats in Oregon and Washington territories were in control of both the executive and legislative branches of government. Although only a small minority had owned some slaves in their former homes, they were on the whole anti-Douglas Democrats. Their views were shared by Federal Judge Matthew P. Deady, who believed that slavery should be allowed everywhere in the Union and that the principle of squatter sovereignty promulgated by Stephen Douglas should not be permitted to interfere with that right.

Matthew Deady was one of the political and social forces in Oregon. A self-educated and self-made man, he was, like his friend Jesse Applegate, with whom he maintained an extended correspondence for many years, well read in an impressive number of fields. The two men had in common a belief in a mild form of rationalism, but there the similarity ended. Deady labored under no feeling of inferiority, was far more articulate in speech and in writing, and possessed great personal ambition. In later years he acquired a reputation for the amount of attention he devoted to his wardrobe. Deady worked hard to keep up with the Joneses and hide the fact that he had once been a blacksmith. He was also somewhat of a prig, if one is to judge from the views expressed in his public writings. Unlike Applegate, he liked the people but at a distance, though he was active in every cultural and educational movement in Portland. Applegate in one letter chided him for his snobbery: "A Judge of the U.S. Court is or ought to be superior to common people and when he addresses them as 'Chaw bacons' they feel very much inclined to stone him."

Deady was constantly concerned about his possible place in history and meticulously saved not only every scrap of his correspondence, but he even wrote letters with an eye to posterity. Applegate once sarcastically reminded him that

writings designed to be *preserved* does [*sic*] not give an insight into the feelings, impulses and modes of thought, for which the private correspondence of great men are most valued, and sought for. . . . I would advise that so much of your last letter as relates to the preservation of your correspondence be omitted in the preserved copy. For when your admirers are devouring your "remains" and discover that what they had taken as the produce of a hasty moment snatched from official duties, or grave studies . . . received the same careful composition and revision, as your most important decisions, they will turn from them in disappointment, for it is the heart, not the brain that is sought for in such familiar writings.

He was a self-confident individual and often displayed a remarkable lack of sensitivity, so that he could suggest to Applegate, who was a number of years his senior, that when he went East on a lecture and observation tour he should make sure to wear clean linens, see that his boots were kept well polished, and use a toothbrush regularly!

Deady's political opinions and his views on the Negro were typical of the man. Negro slaves, he believed, were property to the same extent as horses or cattle or land. He maintained that view, he said, because he was a man of law, and the law, as he saw it, which created all property made the slave such, too. Governments were instituted for the purpose of protecting the individual in his ownership of any kind of property which it was his good or bad fortune to have, and not, as some felt, to teach or compel citizens to own this or that kind of property. If a citizen of Virginia possessed the right to own slaves, then by what logic could a citizen of Oregon be denied the same right? What right had 26,000 people to say to 25,999 that they could not buy slaves and keep them as property? For Deady there was no middle ground between abolitionism and the proslavery point of view, but when war broke out he became as vigorous a supporter of the Union cause as any Republican.

The slavery and the antislavery forces were constantly jockeying for position in Oregon, and several attempts to establish a state government failed because each side wanted to call a convention when it would be most opportune from its own point of view. When it was finally convened in 1857, the Democrats were not powerful enough to have the constitution permit slavery in the new state, but they did succeed in temporarily barring Negroes. So much significance was attached to the portion of the document dealing with the Negro that instead of submitting the constitution as a whole for ratification, approval was requested on three specific points: Do you vote for this constitution? Do you vote for slavery in Oregon? Do you vote for free Negroes?

When the Republican party was born in the East, the Northwest followed suit and organized one; and when the Dred Scott decision tore the Democratic party asunder in a rift that three years later was to prove fatal, the same dissensions split the Northwest. The region had its share of Copperheads. Hardly had the war begun when the *Oregon Weekly Union* leveled scathing attacks at the Chief Executive which were not surpassed by any of the Southern newspapers. "One would think," it declared, "that Mr. Lincoln and his agents had actually been trained in the school of Machiavelli, and were steeped in the Hell-broth of tyrannical Kingly courts all their lives, rather than in the practise of democratic republicanism. Judging them by their acts, this would be a natural inference." These acts, according to the newspaper, paralleled the worst deeds of the worst tyrants of Europe. Lincoln was compared with the infamous Bomba of Naples, who had destroyed the constitution of his country after he had sworn to support it; who had turned the guns of his forts and ships on Naples, the capital of his own kingdom, bombarded other cities and indiscriminately slaughtered their inhabitants. The entire civilized world had stood aghast at the crimes of this butcher of Naples. But what more had he done, asked the Oregon paper, than Mr. Lincoln intended to do? "How often have we heard that the city of Baltimore was about to be shelled from Fort McHenry? Who believes that the bloody minded crew who rule at Washington would shrink from carrying out that threat, had Baltimore offered any resistance?—Lincoln is another Bomba, at least in intention; and like that infamous tyrant will descend in history

> 'Linked with NO virtue,
> And a thousand crimes.'"

The charges against Lincoln were endless. He had trampled on the Constitution, he had gagged the press, he had caused the sanctity of the home to be violated and made a mockery of private rights; under his despotic rule, quiet, peaceful citizens who did not happen to agree with the views of the abolitionist government in control of affairs were dragged from their homes and imprisoned on slight and flimsy

suspicions; weak and helpless women, hitherto protected by a chival-
rous America, were now made the victims of Mr. Lincoln's persecu-
tion. And, worst of all, an espionage system was being introduced
which threatened to surpass the whole evil structure of spying and
informing for which Europe had become notorious. A few of the
more vicious and scurrilous newspapers were suppressed by the Federal authorities. Papers like the *Washington Standard* or the Portland
Oregonian or the *Salem Statesman,* leading organs of both parties,
reacted vigorously to the Copperhead newspapers and charged them
with being purveyors of treason.

In the Northwest country, too, it was a war of brother against
brother, though the heat that was generated was caused by words and
not by battle. Feelings were naturally intense and bitter in a region
that had been settled by pioneers from both North and South, where
neighbors came from Missouri, Virginia, Texas, and South Carolina,
or Ohio, Massachusetts, and New York. The Free-Soiler vehemently
supported the right of the government to maintain the Union invio-
late against the efforts of slavery expansionists to wreck it. Sometimes
he wished that he could take up arms, feeling that sympathies alone
were an ineffective weapon in the national struggle.

Incidents occurred in the towns and countryside that infuriated
loyal Unionists. Reports were published of Secessionist sympathizers
hauling down a Union flag while the townspeople stood by calmly
and failed to denounce the vandalism and disloyalty. This happened
most frequently in Benton County, in Yamhill County, and in southern Oregon, where a larger percentage of former Southerners lived
than anywhere else in the Northwest. Occasionally a ceremony was
made of raising a new flag, with the local band playing martial
airs and Unionist leaders of the community delivering patriotic addresses.

In the Boise Basin of Idaho the tensions and conflicts were even
more violent, for the miners were generally less restrained and their
conduct less circumscribed by the ordinary dictates of convention.
At first, Union sentiment was in a majority, as most of the new arrivals
were from Oregon and California, with only a sprinkling of Southern
sympathizers who, unwelcome in the Pacific states, had come to the
mining area. The first delegate from Idaho Territory to Congress was
a Republican, but Republican superiority was short-lived, for soon a
stream of Secessionists from Missouri in search of economic opportunity found their way into the basin. Then began a bitter struggle

between the Unionists and the Secessionists. In the saloons congested with miners, most of whom were armed, fierce arguments arose every time news was received of either a Union or a Southern victory. Even in normal times the saloons, which served as the most prominent social centers of the mining communities, were scenes of turbulent outbursts, but when such opposing groups as "Seceshes" and "Black Republicans" were intermingled with booze and guns, the result was violent more often than not. A correspondent of the *Daily Alta Californian* informed his readers that "shooting and cutting affrays are of so frequent occurrence we seldom notice them." Another observer, a man who was later to become a governor and United States senator, stated that the morning menu of a miner usually included "a man for breakfast." On the mining frontier almost every conceivable point of difference served as a pretext for an altercation, and the struggle over secession provided many a pretext.

Traveling through the countryside he loved during that tempestuous period left Jesse Applegate not exhilarated but sick with despair. Everywhere he encountered farmers with seditious and Secessionist views: "This young Oregon which, scarcely out of the shell of Territorial pupilage, stinks with an element foul and corrupt, bordering, I may at least safely say, on actual treason, whose rankness 'smells to heaven.'" It was probably not that bad, but the venomous propaganda spread by papers like the *Corvallis Union*, the *Portland Advertiser*, and the *Albany Democrat* justified his despondent view.

The intensity with which elections were held during the war years indicated that though Oregon was thousands of miles from the capitals of the two belligerent sections, the distance was only in miles. A letter to Governor Gibbs described a scene on election day in Canyon City:

The Copperheads were at the polls early and in force. A perfect understanding seemed to prevail among them, from the most noisy Secession brawler down to the most insignificant saloon bummers. Ike Hare . . . offered to vote. A Union man present challenged him for disloyalty. Hare appealed to the judges of the election but they decided that they had no right to receive his vote unless the challenge should first be withdrawn, or the oath administered. Hare drew his revolver, cocked it and made for the man the [*sic*] gave the challenge. The latter also drew his revolver. Quicker than thought revolvers clicked in every direction. . . . Copperheads great and small flocked around their chief, ready to do his bidding. Union men pressed forward to protect their hero and sustain the laws. . . .

A rush was made toward the man who gave the challenge, when one of the judges requested that the challenge should be withdrawn. It was, reluctantly, and the voting went on.

The election campaign of 1864 was particularly bitter and violent. In Umatilla, Union men were genuinely alarmed. The Copperheads, it was charged, had threatened to make it "warm" for the "Black Abolitionists" should Lincoln be reelected. The "traitors" were arming and increasing their supply of ammunition. It was feared that they might blockade the Cascades and lay waste the region east of the mountains, and in anticipation of an uprising, Union men asked the governor to dispatch troops for their protection.

At last, however, the war ended and passions cooled. Other political issues which disturbed the East were also reflected in the Pacific Northwest. One of these was equal suffrage for women. Its staunchest advocate and most ardent supporter was Abigail Scott Duniway, an intelligent, keen-witted, and courageous woman with the remarkable energy of so many pioneer housewives. She managed to find time to write a novel during the years when, as a farmer's wife in a primitive land, she churned by hand "thousands of pounds of butter every year for market," ran a free restaurant for a neighborhood of bachelors, took care of two youngsters, cooked, washed, and mended for the hired help, in addition to all the other household and farm chores. Her only recreation, she said, was wearing out her wedding clothes or making over her bridal outfit into garments for the children.

Though Abigail had had only a meager formal education, she had been a schoolteacher before her marriage, and whatever intellectual stimulation that supplied, it had made her financially independent. Now her butter-and-egg money went to help support the household, and that factor, plus the drudgery and monotony of the early years, which most women helplessly and hopelessly considered their lot in life, bred in her a spirit of rebellion that found its outlet in the suffrage movement, to which she devoted the major part of her life. In addition she published and edited a family journal which became a leading organ for the cause of female emancipation.

In the Oregon country, as in the rest of the land, a woman had to have courage and stamina to participate in the fight for women's rights. There was considerable support but there was also bitter, vitriolic opposition. When Susan B. Anthony visited the region and went on tour with Mrs. Duniway in 1871, the women had to use a small hall in the back of a saloon to hold their meeting in one town, and in Portland an old theater was the only refuge they could obtain. One man who returned home unexpectedly to find them visiting his wife "treated us as tramps" and ordered them out of the house.

Proselytizing in those years was no mean undertaking from a physical standpoint. "When we returned to Portland," Mrs. Duniway wrote, "the winter rains were deluging the earth. The stage carrying us from Olympia to the Columbia River at Kalama, led us through the blackness of darkness in the night time, giving Miss Anthony a taste of pioneering under difficulties that remained with her as a memory to her dying day." Corrugated roads, dust, heat, wind, rain, jouncing coaches or dirty, crawling trains, nothing fazed the indefatigable Mrs. Duniway, who, like the postman, was not swerved from her course. From 1871 on she traveled throughout all parts of Oregon, Washington, and Idaho. She never neglected the men, who, she was realist enough to know, were basically more important than their wives, because it was only through their votes that equal suffrage could be legislated into existence.

Partial victory was achieved in Washington Territory during a four-year period when an act was passed amending a section of its code by simply omitting the word "male" in the amended section and allowing the construction of the pronoun "his" to mean "her." Conferring absolute equality on women as voters, jurors, and office-holders, it passed the upper branch of the legislature by one vote. Undoubtedly many women felt like Mrs. Phoebe Judson, who recorded in her memoirs: "From 1883 to 1887, the territory [sic] of Washington enjoyed impartial suffrage. I took my turn on petit and grand jury, served on election boards, walked in perfect harmony to the polls by the side of my staunch Democratic husband, and voted the Republican ticket—not feeling any more out of my sphere than when assisting my husband to develop the resources of our country." The beneficial influence of women at the ballot box in that area is claimed by one writer to have sent a delegate to Congress who represented the interests of the people against the predatory demands of the railroads to augment their land grants.

Not only did public opposition or apathy have to be overcome, but the competitive reforming zeal of the prohibition advocates had to be contended with. The two groups were always at daggers' ends. The suffragettes felt that the temperance supporters only served to impede progress with their narrow, bigoted emphasis on what they considered a relatively unimportant question, succeeding only in making women appear ridiculous in the eyes of men. Their opponents, on the other hand, regarded the equal righters as bold and unwomanly and their battle a preposterous one. Clashes between the two groups were frequent, with each jockeying for position at legislative sessions or conventions called to draft constitutions for the new states of Washington and Idaho. When the State Constitutional Convention met at Boise, Mrs. Duniway received an urgent message from suffragettes in that city: "The Woman's Christian Temperance Union is spoiling everything. They have arranged for a hearing before the convention in advance of ours, asking for a clause in the new Constitution to prohibit the liquor traffic. They won't get it, of course, but they will prohibit us from getting a Woman Suffrage plank, if you don't come."

Defeats were many and discouragement great, but eventually the movement for equal rights was won. Idaho adopted woman's suffrage in 1896, Washington in 1910, and Oregon in 1912. It is interesting to note that although the movement had begun long before in the East, where women were participating actively in industry and the professions, the first victories occurred in the West, and even there, in the states last to be settled. All of the Mountain and Pacific-coast states except New Mexico, ten in number, were among the first eleven in the country to provide equal suffrage.

The preoccupation with politics did not, of course, prevent the people of the Northwest from going on with the ordinary business of building a country. The region was rich in natural resources, the exploitation of which was promptly begun. Timber provided a source of wealth. The great forests were rapidly despoiled by men with their little sawmills who came from distant New England. And the towns nearest a logging camp profited from supplying it with hardware, food, and other appurtenances of living. Fishing became a major industry. When the run of Chinook salmon began in the Columbia River, thousands of men, some with their families, came to the valley seeking employment.

Cities like Portland from the very beginning were regarded as the logical centers for building fortunes based on solid mercantile enterprises. Charles Stevens, although yet only a worker for a Portland merchant, wrote to his brother: "I have made a number of enqueries [*sic*] about the kind of business of merchants here, and they all tell the same thing, that is, that a man can loan money on good security, that he can have a good exchange business, and I know that you can do a good business at selling goods. This place is a principal market for

Oregon and a good part of Washington, and if you go into that business, or any of them, I really think that Portland or Oregon Citty [*sic*] is the place for you."

Portland and Oregon City, Seattle and Olympia, indeed all the other cities saw a ceaseless ebb and flow of humanity. Opportunity constantly beckoned, showing her Lorelei face now here, now there. And men were lured on, sometimes to find that the vision was real and good, sometimes to be dashed on the shoals of disappointment.

Seven

Builders and Boosters

No other frontier had so many wanderers, restless and perennially searching for still better opportunities, despite the hazards and difficulties of early traveling conditions. It did not take much capital to hang out a cobbler's shingle or a blacksmith's sign in a new town, and so men wore the trails smooth and paddled or steamboated up and down the waterways, seeking new zones of operations.

When William Wright, a Salem blacksmith, decided to investigate the situation in Olympia, W.T., he realized only after he began the journey what he had undertaken. It started well enough. He took the stage to Champoeg and from there a steamer to Oregon City, where he had to spend the night as the boat to Portland did not leave until the next morning. He waited several days in Portland for the next steamer to Monticello, and at that point he found canoes which conveyed passengers to the upper landing of the Cowlitz River about thirty miles away. Those who were unable to afford the "luxury" of the canoe trip could use a weakly defined trail. Wright chose this alternate route. "After a fatiguing journey, leaping over the trunks of trees, wading through mud and water, &, &, I arrived at the landing only a little worse for wear—cap out of shape, shoes down at the heel, breeches torn and wet up to the middle."

Olympia was still sixty miles away, and although there was a fairly good wagon road between the two points, the only means of getting there was by walking or on horseback, unless he could thumb a ride on a wagon. Wright chose the horse as his method of transportation, and when he arrived in Olympia a few days later, he wrote to a friend: "I have rode but little upon horseback, so that after a day's walk, and one and a half day's ride upon horseback, I felt sore all over and my backside, excuse me if you please, was very much swollen and raw as a piece of meat."

Not only was the journey a test of endurance, but it was expensive. The stage fare was $4.00, the steamers $1.50, $2.50, and $4.00 respectively; the remainder of the trip cost $12.00, and taking board and lodging into account, our traveler's expense totaled $42.00. At that, he had saved $6.00 by walking instead of taking the canoe.

Stagecoaches came to the Oregon country in 1846. Anyone who has ever gone to the movies has at some time or other had to sit through a two-fisted "western" which has the inevitable sequence of stagecoach, generally pursued by masked bandits, lumbering madly and precariously along the edge of a precipice or through a narrow ravine or across a plain, with the lovely, terror-stricken heroine staring wildly out of the window while the invincible hero, still somewhere off in the distance, is galloping lickety-split to the rescue. Stagecoaches were held up, but not nearly as frequently as portrayed on the screen. For the most part they arrived at their destinations when expected—perhaps a few hours late—and with themselves and their passengers as intact as the deep-rutted, corrugated, dusty or muddy roads allowed. The drivers had to be highly skilled to manage the six-horse teams and heavily loaded wagons over those impossible roads—and that they were. It was said of these "knights of the lash" that in their day they were held in higher regard than the merchant prince who rode behind them.

During the winter—the rainy season—the roads in Oregon were almost impassable. The coaches creaked and groaned and crawled at snail's pace through the axle-deep mud, and many a fearful passenger held his breath at some points, fully expecting the conveyance to be swallowed up forever by the black mire. Rumors, no doubt originating from the land of sunshine, frequently spread that passengers on the road from Oregon to Sacramento lived out their lives on the journey and died of old age. In midwinter, even the hardiest driver refused to make the trip, and it was the middle of April before operations were resumed. When there was no mud there was the dust, so familiar to travelers on the Oregon Trail that one remarked that if he shut his eyes he could imagine he was behind his horses in the covered wagon.

Withal, when the day was fine and the road good, it was not an unpleasant journey. The construction of the Concord coach used most frequently was such that passengers rolled rather than bounced, the intimacy of sitting knee to knee was conducive to conversation, and the scenery was good. Stagecoach travel, controlled by Ben Holladay and Wells, Fargo, served to relieve the isolation within the region, but the people of the Northwest were still largely cut off from the rest of the country. And so agitation for a cross-country railroad began early.

It started in the East, a half century before the last spike was driven into the Northern Pacific, with a letter by Samuel K. Barlow of Granville, Massachusetts, to *The Intelligencer* of neighboring Westport. A railroad line was in operation from Boston to Albany; Barlow suggested one between New York and the mouth of the Columbia three thousand miles away. He estimated the cost at $30,000,000 and thirty days for the round-trip journey, allowing for train travel at the rate of ten miles per hour. This completely "mad" idea obviously came from the mind of a visionary, and nothing much was heard further until 1845, when the New York merchant, Asa Whitney, sometimes referred to as the father of the railroad to the Pacific Northwest, tried to stir up interest in Congress in a line connecting Lake Michigan with the mouth of the Columbia. Finally, in 1853, Congress bestirred itself and authorized an appropriation for a survey to be made of four alternate transcontinental routes. Isaac I. Stevens, later to become governor of Washington Territory, headed one group, and when he completed his investigation, in which he was assisted by an army of engineers, officers, surgeons, naturalists, astronomers, draftsmen, and even an artist, he reported that the northern route to Puget Sound was entirely feasible. His report was duly filed and gathered dust for the next ten years.

Northwesterners whose hopes had been raised by the surveys were left with their hopes. To a people accustomed to long, winding trails and crude roads extending into the agricultural and mining frontiers of the fifties and sixties, goods and supplies being carried on pack animals, freight wagons hauling products from depots in Northern California to the mines in British Columbia, from Washington to the Boise Basin in Idaho, from the Willamette Valley to Eastern Montana—to these people the construction of a northern railroad to Puget Sound seemed a much less formidable task. They found it difficult to understand the objections raised against the project: that the heavy snows would prove an impediment or that it would be impossible to blast through the Cascade Range. A wagon road across the mountains had been constructed in 1846 by Samuel K. Barlow, an emigrant from Kentucky. (By a remarkable coincidence he bore the same name as the Massachusetts advocate of a railroad to join the east and west coasts.) The previous year, while en route to the Oregon country, he had demonstrated the possibility of crossing the mountains with wagons. The earlier emigrant companies went to the Willamette Valley from The Dalles by boat down the Columbia, a rough and expensive journey. Barlow had determined to find an overland route. "God never made a mountain that he had not made a place for some man to go over it or under it," he had announced. "I am going to hunt for that place . . ." The "Barlow Road," as it came to be known, was used for many years. What a pioneer could do at that early date with crude materials and little money, reasoned the inhabitants, surely could be done by a government with modern equipment and limitless funds.

A step toward the construction of a railroad line was taken when in 1864 the Northern Pacific Railroad was chartered by Congress. But little was done on the project until the famous Eastern financier, Jay Cooke, became interested in the enterprise and sent an agent out to survey the situation. "What can't be got out of the soil which sustains the growth of sawing firs and cedars 200 feet high?" wrote the agent to his chief. "Salmon are not caught here, they are pitchforked out of the streams. Jay, we have got the biggest thing on earth. Our enterprise is an inexhaustible gold mine." Reflecting upon the tremendous possibilities and the almost limitless extent of land speculation which such an undertaking would make possible, Jay Cooke made his decision and the project was begun.

Cooke invited the "best" people in Washington, New York, Philadelphia, and Boston society to participate in this grand undertaking. The Chief Justice of the United States Supreme Court, Salmon Chase, wrote to Cooke: "I should like to be in the Board of Directors, as to which I suppose there will be no difficulty, and am half tempted to offer myself as a candidate for the Presidency (of the road!). I think I would make a good President and my antecedents and reputation would justify a good salary." Cooke's connections were solid and, like the master strategist he was, he set out to control the state governments of Wisconsin and Minnesota and to dominate the governor of Montana and the delegate of Washington Territory. The inducements for a grasping financier were great, for Congress was even more generous with land grants than it had been to the other transcontinental road project, the Union and Central Pacific. Construction of the line was abruptly halted, however, when in September, 1873, Cooke's banking house failed, causing the worst panic in the history of the nation. The Northern Pacific was deserted at Bismarck, North Dakota, and for a while it seemed that the dream that originated with Barlow of Massachusetts would remain a dream. Laborers on the road were unpaid, the contracts of the rail company defaulted, and the rails were left to rust. Then, as so often happens, another man appeared on the scene, also an Eastern financier, and the future of the Pacific Northwest was changed.

Henry Villard had migrated to the United States in 1853, from his native Bavaria. Within the next twenty-five years he had succeeded in carving a substantial and respectable niche for himself. Five years after his arrival, he was reporting the famous Lincoln-Douglas debates for a New York newspaper. His interest in the slavery question was more than academic, for he had married the daughter of William Lloyd Garrison. Unlike his father-in-law, however, humanitarian causes were not his consuming passion. He was interested in the intricacies of government, corporate finance, and banking operations. His position as president of the American Social Science Association afforded him the opportunity to explore these subjects, so that unlike many of his contemporaries in the world of business and banking, his financial and commercial operations were implemented by a wide, theoretical background.

Villard had been abroad in Germany recovering from a nervous breakdown at the time the Cooke empire collapsed. While there an acquaintance asked him for advice on a bond investment in Ben Holladay's Oregon and California Railroad Company. Villard referred him to a committee which had been organized to protect the interests of German investors in that and two other of Holladay's transportation enterprises. As a result of this incident Villard was sent to the United States some months later as agent of the committee, which had learned that the situation of the companies had been misrepresented. And this, in turn, indirectly resulted in the elevation of a journalist to czar of the railroads of the Pacific Northwest.

For the next few years Villard acted as intermediary in the negotiations between Holladay and the German bondholders. In 1876 he succeeded in obtaining an agreement from Holladay to sell his controlling stock in the Oregon Central Railroad Company, the Oregon and California Railroad Company and the Oregon Steamship Company. Villard was elected president of the latter two organizations and, three years later, when the European investors sold their interests in the steamship company, he became its majority stockholder. The

Easterner now had a personal concern in the railroads of the North-west.

Villard soon began to visualize a vast rail network with Eastern connections. It is not germane to this study to go into all the involved plans and transactions. Suffice it to say that Villard purchased the holdings of the Oregon Steam Navigation Company which monopolized traffic on the Columbia River, and then decided to gain control of the slowly recouperating Northern Pacific Railroad. To accomplish his objective he needed a very substantial sum of money. In a spectacular transaction, which has since become known as the "Blind Pool," he persuaded a group of hard headed Wall Street financiers to subscribe $8,000,000 toward the formation of a new company without giving them a single detail about it.

Villard secured control of the Northern Pacific Railroad and immediately began to push its completion. In 1883 the western line met the eastern at Gold Creek, Montana—the state which only six years before had been a battleground between red men and white. To commemorate the occasion, the staid German and American bankers joined the Indians in an ancient tribal war dance. The latest brigade of empire builders had scored another triumph in the march of civilization. Across the broad expanse of land that had formerly been the exclusive preserve of a primitive people, the Iron Horse would now thunder its way, compressing time and distance.

The greatest transportation mogul in the Northwest before Villard had been Ben Holladay, who owned the California, Oregon and Victoria Steamship Line and a stage line from Atchinson to Placerville, California, before he turned to railroading. For some years Holladay was virtual potentate of the transportation activities of the region. He was a crude, uneducated man, and the difference between him and Villard points up the contrast between the two eras—the one dominated by pioneer enterprise and the other by eastern capitalistic investment. Holladay was described by Villard as "a genuine specimen of the successful Western pioneer of former days, illiterate, coarse, pretentious, boastful, false and cunning."

Henry Villard did a good deal for the state of Oregon. His gift of $50,000 to its university was a tremendous sum in those days and came just in time to save the institution from extinction. But this was the least of his services. The immigration bureau which he organized distributed thousands of circulars in England, Germany, Wales, Scotland, and Scandinavia which contained alluring accounts of Oregon.

His agents met the immigrants as they entered New York Harbor and dazzled them with descriptions of life in the Northwest, inducing great numbers to go to the other end of the continent. They also persuaded owners of run-down farms in New England to abandon them and take up a new life out west. They met travelers in Omaha and Topeka who were heading for the Pacific coast and convinced some that Oregon would be a better destination than California.

The construction of the road had left Villard with more obligations than he was able to meet. Turning over his personal fortune to a receivership, he returned to Europe, leaving Portland, Seattle, and the whole Northwest considerably changed. These cities were now in direct contact with the markets of the Midwest. The resources of eastern Washington and Oregon were made available for exploitation, and migration to the Far West steadily increased.

Traveling was at first uncomfortable and slow. When rail connections between the East and the Northwest were first effected, many families came to the region in what were called tourist coaches. They brought their own bedding and enough food for the duration of the journey. Cooking was done on a stove in a corner of the coach and garbage was continually swept off the train. So slowly did the train meander along that stories were told like the one of the man whose hat had blown out of the window. He got off the train while it was in motion, recovered his hat, and got back on without much loss of wind in the process.

It was also an involved journey. When the representative of Washington Territory addressed the Centennial Exposition in Philadelphia in 1876, he gave the following instructions on the best method of reaching the region:

Parties from the East can leave the Central Pacific Railroad at Kelton, 700 miles east of San Francisco, and by stage reach Walla Walla; from thence they can go to any part of the Territory. Still it is more comfortable, quite as cheap, and about as expeditious, to go through to San Francisco. Arrived there, those bound for Puget Sound will find almost daily opportunity, by sailing vessels and trimonthly steamers of the Pacific Mail Steamship Company, to reach any port on the Sound. Those bound for Eastern Washington (and if expeditious travel be an object, to any part of the Territory) will be best accommodated by the steamers of the Oregon Steamship Company, which make daily trips from San Francisco to Portland. Arrived at Portland, steamers leave daily for the upper

Columbia, by which all parts of Eastern Washington are reached. There is also daily communication, Sunday excepted, by steamers to Kalama, and thence by the Northern Pacific Railroad to Puget Sound.

Nevertheless, the railroads brought immigrants to the tune of about forty thousand a year.

Internecine rivalry among cities over settlers and trade, which had been going on since the earliest days, increased. Even as far back as 1851, when a neighboring village of Oregon and Linn cities planned to put a steamboat on the river and construct a plank road between it and the Tualatin mills, it was accused of trying to divert trade. "Will the people of Oregon and Linn cities remain dormant, while our sister towns are making rapid strides in the way of improvements upon the rivers and roads?" demanded the *Oregon Spectator*. Wake up! it warned the citizens of those cities.

Each town tried to attract immigrants by boasting of its superiority in the purity of its waters, the sweetness of its air, its unequaled business opportunities, the number of its schools, churches, and so forth. Newspapers and individuals acted as their own chambers of commerce before the days when such organizations were established. Later, great sums of money were spent to popularize the region. "A Western town that begrudges an appropriation of a hundred dollars for repairing the pavement of the main street will cheerfully empty its pockets of a thousand dollars for heralding the glories of the place," wrote a visiting journalist.

"Tacoma—The Second Greater New York" was the heading of an item in a local magazine which stated that although it was thus far surpassed by Seattle because it did not have a railroad terminus, it optimistically predicted that Tacoma would nevertheless have a population of at least five million within the next fifty years. A lighter side of the rivalry between Seattle and Tacoma was the controversy over the name of Mount Rainier, which can be seen from both cities. In the latter it was always called "Mount Tacoma," and one traveler was humorously warned that if he called it anything else while he was there, "you can't get anything to eat."

The size of the population was also a source of controversy, with towns boosting their figures and discounting the claims made by neighbors. "The *Oregonian* and the *Statesman* are frothing at the mouth," wrote the *Oregon State Journal*, "because they fear that the census enumerators have overlooked, or perhaps more properly speaking underlooked, a few people who live in the lofts of stables, or the fifth stories of stores or boarding houses." Portland and Salem, it went on, would never be satisfied with the way the census was conducted because they had been systematically lying about their population, making it larger than it actually was. Salem had asked Congress for a post-office building and gave its population as 17,000 when it knew well enough that it did not have half that number. As the census would expose the falsehood, it stated, the city tried to anticipate by complaining about the census takers.

The *Frankfort Chronicle*, in an editorial entitled "Jealous Neighbors," advised Portland and Astoria that if these towns did not want Frankfort's trade, it would get along without it. "We intend building here a city in spite of spiteful and slanderous words from jealous neighbors. . . . We will politely request the *Portland Telegram* and *Astoria Herald* to avoid going out of their way to cast slurs at our young but enterprising city."

Competition was especially keen between Oregon and Washington. Before the areas were separated, the *Columbian* wrote that no one familiar with the subject would deny that *northern* Oregon was the healthiest portion of the territory. That fact, it said, was too well known for even "MISREPRESENTATION" to detract from its reputation; many Willamette Valley residents who had come up to the Sound that past summer, a number almost helpless from disease, were completely cured without any medical assistance. This alone should prove to prospective migrants that not only was the atmosphere free from all kinds of contagious diseases, but that it was "a sort of natural, self-acting, hospital, in which those who may seek a home in it, albeit bringing infection with them from abroad, will be speedily restored to renewed animation, life and vigor."

Self-laudation was indulged in by almost every city and the wildest optimism expressed as to its future growth and development. "Westward the star of empire takes its way and New York will ultimately be superseded by Tacoma," wrote a local magazine. Puget Sound, it stated, was the future center of civilization, destined to be greater not only than the ancient cities but the modern ones, unless the planet collided with a stray comet. "Time was when the future greatness of Tacoma was apparent only to him gifted with prophetic vision," wrote another, "but that time is past. There is no more need of seers and diviners. Tacoma has emerged from the obscurity of prophecy and stands in the broad light of day for all to gaze upon." Her future was assured, the paper felt. It was only the mid-eighties and already the population exceeded seven thousand; the city could be proud of its imposing public and private structures; its grand hotel was the equal of any on the west coast; it had a highly developed system of gas and water works; its terminal facilities were already completed; and, most important of all, the lines of the Northern Pacific were reaching ever closer from across the Cascade Mountains. Tacoma was one of the most prosperous cities, with young, energetic businessmen who pursued opportunity with a progressive vision which left no room for despair or timidity.

Similar virtues were ascribed to other cities in the region with minor variations. The social atmosphere was another factor that was lauded. Portland's education, morality, refinement, and social etiquette equaled that of any Eastern city, according to one journal. The number of people who attended church and could read and write the English language proficiently compared favorably with that of any of the older urban centers east of the Mississippi. Nor did she lack in temperance, stability, and respect for the law.

The climate was always written about as an attraction, though perhaps a little in self-defense. Partisans insisted that the rain which droppeth gently from the heavens from October to May was not rain but "mist." One lady wrote to a friend back home that she was sitting at the window and marveling at the strange phenomenon outside. It was raining, but a most curious "dry" rain—no one was carrying an umbrella and passers-by hardly seemed to get wet! A pioneer author even felt that the moist climate would favorably influence the physical and mental development of the inhabitants:

Think of our humid atmosphere washed and kept pure by the Webfoot rain—did rain, does rain, will rain; gentle rain; rain that comes like a huge joke, ever welcome, ever abundant, and never-failing rain; rain that shortens the days, lengthens the nights, and houses the people, domesticating men who ordinarily grow wild and rough in the free light exhilarating sunshine of the higher altitudes. A heavy, languid, drowsy atmosphere; hence slow thinkers; slower to plan, slow to decide, slow to act,—a people not unlike the Saxons of old, their senses will become blunted, the muscles braced, and the will vigorous. There will be a certain earnestness leading from frivolous sentiments to noble ones—severe manners, grave inclinations and manly dignity.

A Washington magazine noted in October that the long, dry summer was over and Seattleites would actually welcome the rain. If anything, it stated, the rainy season was actually more healthful than the dry. In dry climates disease germs were blown about by the winds, while here residents had the great advantage of a rain-washed atmosphere for six months. "Our winters tend to relieve all nervous disorders, especially insomnia, as nothing can be more somnolent and soothing than the gentle patter of raindrops on the shingles and the window-panes." But lest the reader get an erroneous impression, the article concluded somewhat contradictorily that there was a misapprehension as to the annual rainfall, which was actually less than in New York or Chicago.

Local publications constantly carried items trying to correct the "misapprehension" of outsiders about the coastal rainy season. Even a high-school magazine, in addition to the usual assortment of poetry, short stories, and essays, devoted space to the subject. Easterners, it said, must be disabused of the false notion, circulated perhaps by California propagandists, that all Oregon amounts to is "rain, rain, rain." Many travelers believing this malicious lie returned home by the southern route without having visited the Northwest to see for themselves that it does not rain for 365 days in the year, and that the area east of the Cascades has little or no rainfall.

There were, however, some unpatriotic Northwesterners who felt that the rain was entirely too domesticating and the atmosphere too drowsy for comfort. One of these must have reached the saturation point when he wrote the following ditty which a Portland paper was equally unpatriotic enough to publish:

> Dirty days hath September,
> April, June and November,
> From January up to May
> The rain it raineth every day,
> All the rest have thirty-one
> Without a blessed gleam of sun,
> And if any of them had two and thirty,
> They'd be just as wet and twice as dirty.

It was this type of Oregonian who had the bad taste to indulge in flippancies about so vital a matter, and also those who delighted in characterizing themselves as "ducks" and "webfeet" when visiting California who were responsible for the erroneous impressions about the region, according to one publication.

Booster propaganda poured out in a never-ending stream of books, pamphlets, and articles almost from the beginning of settlement. As early as 1846 the *Spectator* asked some of the "old" Oregon settlers to prepare an article for the paper describing the climate, soil, productions, and anything else that would be of interest to people in other parts of the country. Even children were urged to advertise the region. A Salem magazine noted that each boy and girl in the Baker City schools was writing a letter to a friend or relative in the East, describing the town and country and trying to persuade the recipient to migrate. The names of the addressees would then be turned over to the Development League, which would follow up with literature.

Popular titles of books and pamphlets were *Oregon As It Is*, variously subtitled "By a Resident for Twenty-Five Years," "By an Old Settler . . . A Reliable Guide for All," "Solid Facts and Actual Results, for the Use and Information of Immigrants," "Its Advantages as an Agricultural and Commercial State," and so forth. These, which were the same for Washington, went into great detail, recommending exactly where an immigrant should go, depending on his occupation; how much farm laborers, stonecutters, plasterers, Chinese cooks, mechanics, schoolteachers, domestic help were receiving in wages; the price of livestock, farm and dairy products, the rates of hotels, and the amount of the average rental. Exercising the function of a modern travel bureau, the booster pamphlets described every available route of travel and estimated the cost of transportation to the last penny.

Prospective tourists were not ignored. "Do you wish to hear Nature's Grand Anthem played by the orchestra whose instruments were fashioned by Almighty Powers, whose music has echoed down the ages ever since comets and suns and systems of suns marked the foot prints of God? Then go to . . ." rhapsodized a one-man chamber of commerce in his pamphlet. The attractions of the country were repeatedly emphasized by fillers in newspapers and periodicals, such as the one about the editor who died and, of course, went to heaven. There he saw a man chained to a post and meekly inquired why it was necessary to treat people that way in heaven. "That man," replied St. Peter, "is from Oregon. We always have to keep Oregonians chained up for a while in order to keep them from going back."

The press constantly clamored for an immigration board, and two years before one was finally established in 1874, Oregon sent an "Emigrant Commissioner" to the East to drum up trade. After it had been in existence for a couple of years, the report of the State Commissioners of Immigration noted that the eastern branch had distributed 50,000 pamphlets, 25,000 circulars, had received and answered over

8,000 letters, and advertised the resources of Oregon continuously since its inception in 45 different newspapers throughout the country and in Europe. Its total expenditure for the period was more than $24,000. This, though, was still not quite enough, according to one magazine which suggested that a California practice be emulated. Oregon ought to have an organization similar to the California Excursion Association, which for a number of years had been running monthly excursion trains from Chicago to Los Angeles at special rates for prospective immigrants and by this means had succeeded in attracting thousands each month.

California was a strong competitor of the city on the Willamette. Portland's merchants felt that the neighbor to the south was monopolizing trade and preventing expansion, that San Francisco capitalists had control of the entire coastal trade. Whatever the point of ultimate destination in the West, San Francisco served as the shipping terminus for boatloads of merchandise coming from Hong Kong, Liverpool, Boston, New York, and other points. Oregonians were therefore compelled to pay exorbitant freight charges for imports on ocean vessels from California, as well as the high profits charged by the importer of the city on the bay. Why could not goods be brought directly into the Columbia River? Why not reverse the situation so that Portland merchants acted as the middlemen for the Californians, compelling them to pay the additional charges of wharfage, drayage, warehousing, and reshipping? They realized, of course, that this required a substantial population, but Portland was growing, and a beginning in that direction could be attempted. Trade jealousies, however, were not allayed even after the Columbia began to receive ocean-going vessels which sailed directly to the Northwest. Now cities like Vancouver vied with Portland for commercial supremacy and considered the latter in the same light as San Francisco had earlier been regarded.

With all the internecine bickering, Northwesterners united in their concern for the prosperity of the entire region. Newspapers and magazines continually chastised merchants and native capitalists for their conservatism and backwardness in regard to trade interests. The region, they argued, had sufficient raw materials for finished products so that dependency on the outside world could be reduced. Residents were criticized for failing to patronize home products. Wrote one editor:

The spectacle we daily behold of wealthy men receiving high rents for stores and shops and then sending abroad to purchase the same article manufactured on the very premises that are bringing them this revenue, should cause a blush to gather on the cheek of every man not devoid of the least spark of patriotism. It is not true that such manufactures as we have are not first class. Our wagons and buggies are not inferior to any imported; our machinery is the equal of that produced anywhere; our wooden and willow wares are first class; our furniture is acknowledged to be excellent; our stoves, pottery, canned goods, woolen goods and a score of other things are of standard quality; our shoe makers turn out good boots and shoes; our tailors make fine suits; and mechanics generally in all branches of trade are skillful and competent.

A curious paradox existed in the attitude of the pioneer. He wanted to promote the prosperity of his land and he clamored for measures to bring this about, but a lethargy that he seemed unable to overcome resulted in procrastination and temporizing. Occasionally a thoroughly despondent picture of the future would be drawn by a newspaper in the hope of arousing readers to action. Washington Territory was "plainly on the decline," wrote one paper. Farm, stock, and town property was steadily decreasing in value, with the first mentioned scarcely worth the cost of the improvements made on it. The inhabitants were growing poorer. A thriving metropolitan center would never rise on the Sound, which was really a great shame because it had one of the best harbors in the world, "equal in extent to the Mediterranean, and surpassing it in the safety of its navigation . . . and more accessible in the trade of Asia than any harbor on the Pacific Coast."

This pessimistic view was quite as unjustified as the overly-optimistic predictions; both were aspects of a youthful region eager for growth but, like a colt, not quite sure of its legs. The ambivalence in feeling was natural, but the hopeful always outweighed the other. When gold was discovered in the Inland Empire, Northwesterners looking at California, which had sprung almost full grown from the precious metal within her bowels, confidently expected the same avalanche of people who would remain as permanent residents. They were disappointed. The mining boom did increase the population somewhat, but its greatest contribution was to add additional color to an already colorful history.

Eight

Of Vice and Virtue

The westward-bound pioneers who passed through the Inland Empire on their way to the coastal area of the Oregon country had no indication that within a few years the desolate, forbidding land would be clawed up for miles by hordes of men with pickaxes in a frantic quest for easy wealth. Gold was first discovered in the area between the Spokane and Pend Oreille rivers in 1855, but it required more elaborate equipment to mine than could easily be brought into the somewhat inaccessible region, and the Indians resented the invaders strongly enough to war against them. For the next few years, subduing the unmannerly redskins was a full-time job and discouraged all but the hardiest miners from venturing near the battlegrounds.

In 1860 the Oro Fino Creek in what is now Idaho revealed its riches to a small party of prospectors, and soon the Territory was overrun. By the following year the banks of the Oro Fino groaned beneath the tents and heavy boots of thousands of miners, and at the end of the summer a metropolis existed with flimsily built hotels, stores, saloons, and gambling houses. The streets resounded with the braying of mules, the steady hammering of carpenters and blacksmiths, the shouting of auctioneers, and the dust kicked up by man and beast lay over everything. The usual camp followers appeared so promptly it seemed as though they had been lying in wait in the near-by hills. They paraded the streets in their tawdry finery, managing somehow to look cool and clean, or perhaps it was the contrast with the sweaty, unkempt miners. The dress of the mining population was characteristic and unmistakable. Regardless of how hot it was, the unshaven miner paraded the streets in his heavy flannels and rubber boots, the faithful six-shooter and bowie knife in the belt at his side.

Idaho City in the Boise Basin, a typical mining city, was called

Bannack in the hectic days of 1863, when it was overrun by eager searchers after quick fortunes. The town and surrounding country-side was a mad, frantic area in perpetual motion. Timber was stripped from the hillsides so rapidly that sections which were heavily wooded one day were bare the next. Ditches and sluices ran in every direction, with a forest of hydraulics pumping away over them. From one side heavily laden pack mules from The Dalles jogged on interminably, while from the other rolled a seemingly endless wagon train carrying prospective diggers.

The main street, like all the others in town, was strewn with dis-carded washed gravel and litter. It ran a mile and a quarter in length and consisted of an almost solid line of frame buildings. With utter disregard of personal threats and legal prohibitions, the cross streets were all staked off and blockaded by lines of wagons which made pas-sage in or out impossible. Thirty-three saloons, each jammed to the doors with boisterous, thirsty miners, operated day and night. Imita-tion champagne sold for $8 a bottle and watered-down alcohol mixed with "oil of cognac, ether, or juniper" wholesaled for $8 to $10 a gal-lon, but at the rate they were consumed, it might appear that they were dispensed free. The town's brothels were extremely lucrative, with the average receipts $500 a day.

Lewiston, which became the supply depot for Oro Fino and the other "cities" that sprang up as gold was discovered at various points, experienced a similar wild prosperity. In a few months it had streets that ran a mile in length, with the jerry-built stores and dozens of the inevitable saloons crowding each other. Miners had the same tastes in all sections of the gold fields and they crowded the bars either to cele-brate success at the diggings or drown their disappointment in Tangle-leg, Forty-rod, Lightning or Tarantula juice, as they colorfully named the potent beverage.

Some men made fortunes in the gold fields which many of them gambled or drank away; some accumulated more modest sums; the majority would have done better had they remained at their farms or jobs; and a number wished that the gleaming metal had remained for-ever undiscovered in the earth or the waters beneath which it was buried. One individual with a flair for parody expressed the feel-ings of probably most of the miners:

To dig, or not to dig, that is the question; whether 'tis better to stand in knee-deep water, suffer a boiling sun, and dig, and sweat, and swear, and dig, for a few paltry ounces—or to place one's animated duds upon some neighboring mule and travel homewards. Hold on!—to dig—to find our pile—and by that pile to say we end our poverty . . . 'tis a consummation devoutly to be wished. . . . Who would bear to dig and sweat under a weary life, but that the dread of returning home without the dust—that slippery treasure—puzzles the brain and makes us rather stay and wait our better luck, than "go to hum" poorer than we came.

Mining for gold not only created a blood lust for quick wealth, but was often dehumanizing in its effects. Many of the men who were staid citizens with families in their home towns became as callous and brittle as the atmosphere. "It is astonishing with what facility a man here can not only change his general appearance," wrote the correspondent of a California paper, "but even the language of his country, boyhood and home. Men of talent and education use a jargon of slang phrases, whose only merit is a resemblance to Scotch metaphysics—neither understanding nor understood." And, of course, the mining areas attracted desperadoes, cutthroats, swindlers, gamblers, and any other dregs of humanity which the cities throughout the country spewed up.

Life in a mining town began after dark, when the lights went on in the saloons, gambling houses, and brothels, and the miners, returned from the diggings, made a hasty toilet and went out seeking relaxation. It was apt to be a dangerous life, too, for men had nervous trigger fingers and were quick to take offense at a real or fancied insult. Robbery was the least vicious of the crimes—the victim was glad if he escaped with his life. "Not a day or night passed which did not yield its full fruition of fights, quarrels, wounds or murders. The crack of the revolver was often heard above the merry notes of the violin. Street fights were frequent, and as no one knew when or where they would occur, everyone was on his guard against a random shot."

On Sunday the miners rested from their labors in the diggings, but rested little otherwise. "This is Sunday: the thermometer 92 in the shade—rot gut, twenty-five cents—myriads of mammoth bottle-flies, pregnant with poison, sailing through the air—whisky the beverage, monte the game—angels weep, men curse, dogs fight . . . rapine and murder are in our midst; a breathless corpse lies weltering in his blood, the knife has penetrated him from breast to abdomen, even to the severing of the heart; law is violated and the victim unavenged!" wrote an observer describing a typical Sabbath. Favorite amusements on that day were horse racing and prize fights, but there were no Marquis of Queensberry rules for fisticuffs then. The fight continued until one or both men were blinded by blood pouring into their eyes and their bodies beaten to a jelly.

Organized gangs terrorized many communities. The Updyke and Dixon gangs operated in and around Boise for about three years, until infuriated citizens organized into vigilantes and set out on a manhunt, caught up with the leaders, and strung them up on the nearest tree. Frontiersmen frequently found the orderly processes of law too slow for their purposes and took matters into their own hands. On a number of occasions criminals who were arrested never lived to receive a trial, and the community at large felt that it had saved itself an unnecessary expense.

Leaders of outlaw gangs were sometimes men whose skill in planning and organizing would have brought them profitable returns had they operated in legitimate enterprises. One of the cleverest and most notorious was Henry Plummer, who began his Western operations in Idaho. In 1861 he lived in Lewiston with a "Mrs. Plummer," mingled in respected social circles, and to all outward appearances was an upright citizen.

The code of the West was to ask no questions about the past of a newcomer, to accept a man for what he seemed to be unless it was proven otherwise. Had Lewistonians investigated Plummer's background, they might have discovered that he was wanted for murder in New England, Nevada, and California. While this courteous gentleman walked circumspectly through the town, he was supplying the leadership to a band that pillaged and murdered throughout Idaho. Justice finally caught up with two of its members and they were promptly hanged.

Plummer decided he had better seek less dangerous pastures and soon turned up in wide-open Montana. On the theory that both hands can work more effectively if the right knows what the left is doing, he managed to become sheriff of Bannack and Virginia districts while he was the leader of a meticulously organized band of desperadoes who called themselves "The Innocents." His deputy sheriff was one of its leading members, and it included expert, cold-blooded gunmen, skillful robbers, and others of their ilk.

For some time no shadow of suspicion fell on Sheriff Plummer. His excuse for his frequent absences from town when he went to the meeting place of the outlaws to give them instructions was that he was inspecting his silver deposits. It at last became apparent that Plummer was peculiarly lethargic in investigating crimes, and after one particularly outrageous robbery he became definitely suspect. A vigilante committee was formed which brought about the apprehension and death of a number of Plummer's gang and finally his own.

Gold veins ran throughout the entire Inland Empire and up into British Columbia, and wherever one was opened up, it supplied the nourishment for a town. Settlements appeared full grown, in the middle of nowhere, as though created by the magic of Aladdin's genie. Within ninety days one typical community had a population of ten thousand. Many disappeared almost as quickly; some clung desperately to existence until the deserted shops, the empty saloons, the quiet streets proved that their usefulness had passed and they, too, expired. The West is full of ghost towns, many of which have long since been reclaimed by the wilderness, with perhaps only a few crazy boards still clinging together in the shape of a shack to show where a dwelling had once been.

Leesburg, a few miles west of Salmon City, had first been settled by Southerners who named it in memory of the Confederate general. It once had several thousand inhabitants, a long main street, and even boasted a Chinatown, but by 1910 it was little more than a memory. Pierce City had been a county seat, with a Chinese population of about a thousand and a joss house as imposing as the adjacent courthouse. Mount Idaho, the first town built on Camas Prairie, was a thriving city during the seventies, the county seat of Idaho County, and had been chosen by the Republicans of Idaho Territory as the site for their first party convention. It, too, soon disappeared.

A few towns which resulted from the mining boom remained, but the high hopes for their development never materialized. Their early growth was lush and fabulous, but once the rush to the mines subsided, they withered. Some became centers for a stable population whose citizens discovered that wheat, cattle, potatoes, and other crops could be as profitable as gold mining, even if the returns did come more slowly.

When the gold rush ended, the lawlessness of the mining towns lingered on in the ones that remained. The area around Walla Walla began to be farmed on a small scale about 1864, and two or three flour mills were erected. "It was the winter quarters for the most of the packers and teamsters, and was full of miners, packers, bull-whackers, mule-skinners, stockmen, sporting-men, etc., intermingled with a good sprinkling of roughs and cut-throats who had been driven out of other localities and came there to winter." Life was merry in Walla

Walla with shootings, stabbings, clubbings, robberies, until the "Vigilantes of 1864" took action and cleaned up the town. They made some mistakes, recalls an old-timer, but they were effective.

In a humorous vein, but indicating that life was far from stabilized in the Boise of 1871, the editor of the *Boise News* advised his readers that he was turning over a new social leaf:

All men's wives who have hitherto enjoyed the advantage of our acquaintance are hereby notified that this ceases today, never to be renewed. Men perish ingloriously every day for being on speaking terms with married women, and we're not waiting for our turn. Deeply grateful for the past forbearance of aggrieved husbands, we make our bow and retire. Whoever shall attempt to introduce me to his wife, or to any other man's wife, will be regarded as conspiring against our life and will thus be denounced in the columns of this paper.

Not only in mining areas, but wherever men gathered after a day's or a week's or a month's hard labor for relaxation or dissipation, the same conditions prevailed. The fishing town of Astoria had a "swill" district which was known for miles around as a place where fishermen could deposit the cash earned during several months at sea in return for a little fun. In 1877 it had forty saloons, all doing a lucrative business, and dives and gambling houses flourished. A citizens' committee, aroused by the rioting and disorders in Swilltown and alarmed by the resulting danger to their own business establishments, finally organized into a vigilante force and by threats, intimidation, and physical coercion succeeded in driving out most of the disreputable elements. The reputation for vice and crime which Astoria had acquired, however, clung to it long after its citizens had succeeded in cleaning house.

The open ranges of the Oregon countryside also seemed conducive to terror and lawlessness. The violence appears to have started during the eighties in Wasco County with a quarrel between neighbors over land boundaries. Two men were killed, and the murderer, Lucius Langdon, was shot to death by a masked mob during a stopover at a hotel on his way to jail, while his armed captors stood quietly by. In an adjoining room a man by the name of Harrison, a friend of the criminal, was supposedly overheard to say, when he heard of the slaying of the two men, "Good! There'll be some widows in the country now!" Though he was obviously very drunk, he was seized by the mob, one end of a rope tied around his neck and the other to the end of a saddle-pommel, and dragged to a bridge, where his lifeless body was strung up.

It is believed that there was a method behind the often pointless acts of violence, that it was an effective means by the established and powerful cattlemen to prevent newcomers from invading the ranges. Some said that Langdon, for instance, had shot in self-defense and that Harrison, too, had been a marked man. A whisper, a rumor that so-and-so was a horse thief, a cattle rustler, or just a meddler meant a death sentence. Innumerable other murders were committed: one man was shot in the back through the window of a saloon; two youngsters were lured from their homestead cabin, hung to a near-by tree, and their dangling bodies riddled with bullets; another just disappeared. No one was ever apprehended.

The terror was not confined to this one area. It spread throughout the cattle land and lasted for several years. There were, of course, cases of authentic crimes and just retribution for stealing horses or cattle, though everywhere responsible citizens decried vigilante justice and efforts were made to stamp it out and establish law and order. Peace lasted for a while until, at the turn of the century, the deadly three-cornered war between the cattlemen, sheepmen, and miners began. Death was again in the saddle and masked men were meting out lynch law.

The miners complained that the sheep fouled up their ditches and hydraulic machinery, the cattlemen that the sheep were permanently ruining a fine range country, and together they formed something of an alliance against the sheep owners. Since, they claimed, no law to protect their rights existed, they decided "to shoot down enough sheep to terrorize the sheep owners and cause them to betake themselves and their sheep to other pastures."

And that they did. The slaughter of sheep and sometimes men went on indiscriminately. Lake County was the scene of one particularly wanton and ruthless occurrence. Creed Conn, a merchant and the brother of the district attorney, was supposed to have known too much and talked. After one visit to his brother, his barn burned down and later one of his best horses suddenly died. A few weeks later he started out for a ranch he owned some distance away and vanished. Not until weeks after was his body, with two bullet holes in it, discovered in the snow about a mile from his house. Shortly before his disappearance, several thousand head of sheep were butchered before the eyes of a helpless herder who, tied and gagged, was forced to watch.

The masked sheep slayers were so bold that one gave an interview to a reporter of the *Oregonian* describing a slaughter:

About three o'clock in the afternoon the scouts that had been posted during the entire day had ascertained that the herder was alone and un-armed, and that we ran no chances in getting possession of his band. This was done by our party, numbering some dozen men, after we had indulged in a few preliminaries such as firing off our guns and giving vent to a few oaths, just to make the poor cur stand pat, for if he had attempted to run we would have had to kill him. He was bound and gagged to prevent his getting away and giving the alarm, and was then placed by the side of a tree.

The band of sheep, numbering about 2,000, was then driven to a corral on deeded land, which was done for a double purpose, as we could then shoot without their scattering, and we could also point to the carcasses and say, "Well, they're on deeded land, and whoever killed them did so merely as an act protecting their own property." We then knelt with our knees on the ground, that every shot from our 30-30's might take effect in more than one sheep. . . .

Yes, we had our faces blackened, so that we could not be recognized, and it was a veritable picnic. Had everything our own way from start to finish. You're right, that sheepman will never get within miles of our range again, that's a cinch.

While the mining and fishing towns, the cattle and sheep ranges, were experiencing birth pains in the process of becoming "civilized" communities, the cities had begun to approach that desirable status. They had gone through a hectic period, but the forces of law and order rarely had difficulty in keeping the situation under control. In 1853 the *Oregonian* angrily noted: "Our city has, of late, been the scene of disgraceful midnight rows and bacchanalian revelry, disgusting to every sober mind and disgraceful to those engaged in them." A group of vagabonds, the paper stated, were hanging around the "low groggeries" in the daytime and destroying property at night. If the city police were unable to cope with them and put a stop to such outrages promptly, it hoped that every law-abiding citizen would arm himself and shoot at sight the first drunken brawler who disturbed him. Several people, the paper concluded, had already expressed their determination to do so and that was the only effectual remedy.

In the same issue the paper carried another item about some professional gamblers who had come to the city from the Platte and

Snake River regions. They were the first to appear since card sharks
had been thrown out years before, it stated. Portland had laws to protect its security, and the journal demanded that these men should be
so informed. The owners of any dens of iniquity should be compelled
to leave or follow some lawful occupation—and no doubt they did,
for a time, anyhow.

Cities in the Northwest were striving hard to be counterparts of
those in more settled areas, and their citizens to be as correct in behavior. As early as 1852 the *Oregonian* was concerned with the "very
difficult question" as to whether or not a lady should lift her dress
when crossing a puddle. In the first place, opined the paper, a lady
should never be seen on the streets in muddy or rainy weather. (In
true booster spirit the editor blithely ignored the Oregon rainy season, which would have meant that a "lady" could not set foot outdoors for almost half a year!) That, it stated, would avoid many unnecessary complications; but if she *had* to venture out, it was essential
above all else that she lift her dress very gracefully, for without finesse
she would appear ridiculous. If, when coming to a puddle, the lady
could "just gather the flowing skirts in her hand, revealing nothing
beyond the tip of a well-laced boot, and then spring over," that
"would be more graceful than to dabble with mud both boot and
stocking. Still, to lift a robe in public is a dangerous experiment."
And this in the days when the muddy streets of Portland were either
covered with boards or left exposed to the hoofs of horses and the
heavy boots of the men, when women worked side by side with their
husbands, wielding heavy plows or engaging in other sweaty chores.

Several years later a young woman brazenly rode a horse through
the streets of Olympia *astride*, dressed in what was described by a
horrified newspaper in a scathing editorial as "nearly men's apparel."
Identifying the shameless creature by name, the editor stated: "We
have too good an opinion of the ladies of Olympia to think that such
acts will ever be repeated, and cause the blush of shame to mantle even
the cheek of manhood."

It apparently took little in those days for "the blush of shame" to
mantle the damask cheek of a lady fair or the coarser one of the other
sex. A damsel who signed herself "Betsy Jane" precipitated an extended controversy in the letters-to-the-editor column of the *Washington Standard* by attacking the new form of ballroom dancing
which had been imported from Europe by way of the East. "I maintain," she said, "that an act which would cause the blush of shame to

mantle the face of unsophisticated innocence is most likely to be wrong; and I defy those who may dissent, to select a more fallible test." A correspondent who signed himself "Liberal" retorted sarcastically that the virtuous Betsy pretended to be shocked at the idea of a young man putting his arm around a young lady's waist in the ballroom but wondered "if the fastidious 'Betsy' ever allowed her precious waist to be 'encircled by the arms of a gallant,' either in the ball room or elsewhere. It is to be supposed not, judging from the style of her arguments."

The subject of social dancing was regarded so seriously that three months after Betsy Jane's letter appeared in the *Standard*—which had published dozens pro and con in the interim—the paper prefaced still another with the comment that its correspondence on the subject was becoming as voluminous as the reports of some congressional committees of investigation. The letter published that day was in reply to a previous one suggesting that perhaps the theater might be substituted for ballroom dancing. "Hibernian" took violent exception. "Who are the actors and actresses who perform in this vestibule of hell?" he asked. They were the same type of men and women who performed in the Roman circuses, noted for their impiety and "to whom the epithets virtuous . . . are never applied," he thundered. And the auditors? "Look into the pit and there you will see the quintessence of the scum and dregs of all villanies."

Hibernian undoubtedly would have approved the attitude of the *Weekly Mountaineer* published at The Dalles—which city about twenty years later was to become a notoriously wide-open town—toward the snake in the grass who ran off with his friend's wife. The paper and the town were greatly incensed when it was discovered that a blacksmith and a seamstress, a fine, upstanding couple who had passed themselves off as husband and wife, were living in sin. The real husband discovered their whereabouts and came charging into town one day to unmask them. "Time," declared the paper, "wrights [*sic*] all things, and here at last, like an avenging Deity, has John Harrison been overtaken by the man he had so fouly [*sic*] wronged. . . . In the meantime, to all who may be about to embark on the stormy ocean of Free Love, we commend the couplet:—

> ' 'Tis best to be honest and true,
>   'tis best to be off with the old love before
>   you get on with the new.' "

That Westerners had a saving sense of humor and could indulge in the slightly risqué was apparent from items, like the following, which appeared in the newspapers from time to time:

Hardly any two females kiss alike. There is as much variety in the manner of doing it as in the faces and manners of the sex. Some delicate creatures merely give a brush of the lip. This is a sad aggravation. We seem about to have a good time, but actually get nothing. Others go into it like a hungry man into a beefsteak, and seem to chew up our circumstances. This is disgusting and drives away a delicate lover. Others struggle like hens burying themselves in the dirt. This is won by great exertions, and is not worth the trouble it costs. Now we are in favor of a certain shyness, when a kiss is proposed, but it should not be continued too long; and when the fair one gives it, let her administer it with warmth and energy— let there be soul in it. If she closes her eyes and sighs immediately after it the effect is greater. She should be careful not to "slobber" a kiss, but give it as a humming-bird runs his bill into a honey-suckle, deep, but delicate. There is much virtue in a kiss when well delivered. We have the memory of one we received in our youth which has lasted us twenty-one years; and we believe it will be the last thing we think of when we die.

When, however, they took things seriously, they were very serious. The temperance movement, which was waged from Maine to San Diego, received as fervent support in the Northwest as anywhere else. And since it was a young, impetuous region, the battle was, if anything, fought with more zest and vigor. The crusade against drinking as the root of all evil was launched in the early years of American settlement. In 1846 the first, and as yet only, newspaper in the Oregon country reported on a liquor law which had been passed by the legislature to prevent the introduction, sale, and distillation of liquor. The prohibition of liquor, the *Spectator* commented, would add to peace, happiness, and prosperity. The law was in effect only briefly, but by the eighties almost every community had a local organization of energetic and zealous workers affiliated with the national Woman's Christian Temperance Union.

Testimonials by men who had been "saved" appeared in the papers and public notices of rehabilitation were published. This apparently served a dual purpose: not only to induce others to emulate the ennobling experience of the convert, but also to advise that he was now ready and able to do an honest day's work:

From this date, Harry Conklin wishes to give notice to the public that he has drunken his last drop of liquor in this city. What he now says he means, and what he means he wishes understood by the public generally. For the future he intends to be right side up with care, and no mistake. He makes this solemn declaration to the public as a *fixed fact*. He thinks, yes, he knows it, there is still enough of the man left to make the declaration as firm as the rock of Gibraltar. He now turns a new leaf in life, and henceforth will turn his back upon the *enemy*—ardent spirits. He makes this a matter of record that "he who runs may read." And when there is any Blacksmithing to be done, he is in for a full share, to be done in the best manner, on reasonable terms, and to the minute. Being a stranger in the Territory, and having but a few acquaintances, and fearing that the public may not fully understand his motives and position, he takes this method of informing all who see it that he has spent thousands foolishly, which had been earned by the hardest kind of knocks; and from this out, he intends to be a decent man, and will consider it an insult for any person to give, sell, or even offer him a drink.

I sign myself, in *big letters*,

HARRY CONKLIN

Men were asked to take the pledge in the churches, in the meeting halls, and almost anywhere they assembled, and school children were taught to sing songs like the "The Temperance Call":

> Children all, both great and small
>   Answer to the temp'rance call;
> Mary, Marg'ret, Jane, and Sue,
>   Charlotte, Ann, and Fannie too.

Chorus: Cheerily, heartily, come along,
>   Sign our pledge, and sing our song.

> No strong drink shall pass our lips,
>   He's in danger who but sips.
> Come, then, children, one and all,
>   Answer to the temp'rance call.

> Where's the boy who would not shrink
>   From the bondage of strong drink?
> Come, then, Joseph, Charles, and Tom,
>   Henry, Samuel, James and John.

> Who have misery, want and woe?
>   And who to the bottle go?
> We resolve their road to shun,
>   And in temp'rance path to run.

> Good cold water does for us;
>   Costs no money, makes none worse,

> Gives no bruises; steals no brains;
>   Breeds no quarrels, woes no pains.
>
> Who would life and health prolong?
>   Who'd be happy, wise and strong?
> Let alone the drunkard's bane,
>   Half-way pledges are in vain.

Women periodically made the rounds of the saloons to preach and proselytize. This was not an easy job, for they often encountered vehement opposition and the "territory" to be covered in some cities was great—Portland had forty saloons when its population was only 3,500. One leading citizen who analyzed the situation statistically estimated that there was one saloon for every twenty-four adult males. When it was considered that the city had only twenty-one attorneys, eleven doctors, nineteen hotels, and nine barbers, Portlanders were spending more on liquor than on essential services. Mrs. Frances Fuller Victor, a leading temperance agitator, related one incident which was a sample of what the reformers had to endure. Two women who were on a tour of duty entered a saloon. No sooner had they stepped through the door than the irate proprietor grabbed each one by an arm and, shouting that he did not want any "damned whores" in his establishment, shoved them out. Saloons prominently displayed posters bearing the legend, "All Nations Welcome Except Carrie."

In Washington Territory, a weekly, *The Echo, A Temperance Journal*, "devoted to the cause of temperance, education and moral reform," was issued. Among other things, it published verse on the subject of the demon rum. Shakespeare was popular in the Northwest and poor Hamlet's soliloquy especially so. It was paraphrased for every conceivable purpose, but the bard would probably have turned over in his grave had he read "The Inebriate's Soliloquy" (author unknown):

> To drink, or not to drink, that is the question,
> Whether 'tis nobler in the mind to suffer
> The stings and arrows of outrageous longing,
> Or, to take arms against a sea of trouble
> And by the bottle end them. To drink—and sleep,
> No more? and by this draught to say we end
> The heart aches and the thousand natural shocks
> That flesh is heir to.

.   .   .   .

> Why I tatters wear,
> And drag a useless and shameless life,
> All for this hellish appetite within,
> A flame unquenchable, that burns and seres [*sic*]
> My inmost, pent up soul, puzzles me still!
> And makes me doubt mine own integrity,
> My reason and my soul's supremacy.
> Aye, liquor doth make devils of us all!
> Until the native hue of resolution
> Is sicklied over with the fumes of rum,
> Till enterprises of great pith and name
> Grow dull and die; while we ourselves shrink up
> And lose the name of men!

By the eighties, the frontier cities of the Northwest had so rigid a social caste system that it was difficult to imagine that many had been settled only a generation back. Lavish living, social graces, and Victorian behavior characterized Portland society to an extent where the emulators of Boston almost outdid Boston itself. Great fortunes had been amassed during the early period, and the *nouveau riches* displayed their wealth as ostentatiously as people of their kind anywhere throughout the nation. Since not enough time had elapsed to provide a social aristocracy with a tradition, the aristocracy was based exclusively on wealth. In Boston the Lowells spoke only to the Cabots, but in Portland, it was said, the Ladds spoke only to the Tiltons.

William Sargent Ladd was a typical example of this group and one of its most successful representatives. He had come to Portland in 1851, when it was only a frontier village, engaged almost immediately in merchandising and trading and soon accumulated a sizable fortune. Within ten years he opened a bank in partnership with Tilton, and it soon was a prosperous institution. Ladd's interests became ever more widespread. He acquired three large farms, as well as shares in others, and had extensive holdings in the flour and mill business, the Oregon Iron and Steel Company, the Oregon Railway and Navigation Company, and in Portland real estate. His own dwelling was one of the showplaces of the city, which had a number of beautiful homes, some in the heart of town. Wealthy citizens were not deterred from using an entire block for a residence, despite the fact that the land alone was worth from $30,000 to $100,000.

Though Portland in 1880 was a major city in the region and had advanced considerably from the time, nine years back, when it had a population of eight thousand "nested in primitive homes, among fallen trees and blackened stumps," and one principal street with a hotel or two and several stores, it was still a frontier town in appearance. Horses were tied to hitching posts in the busy shopping streets whose sidewalks were principally made of wood protected by wooden awnings; barbers featured metal bathtubs and provided ornate gilt-edged shaving mugs for regular customers; statues of wooden Indians with feather-decorated heads and holding a bunch of cigars in one hand, a tomahawk in the other, stood in front of cigar stores, and patent-medicine men shouted from street corners, advertising "infallible" cures.

The saloons, with their swinging doors, still outnumbered other business establishments. A horse-drawn trolley clattered through the town. Gaslight had been installed in the business area about 1860, but at night policemen carried dark lanterns as they made their rounds. In the residential areas long-queued Chinese in native dress added an exotic touch as they shuffled along, peddling vegetables in wicker baskets hung at the ends of poles carried over their shoulders. Residents caught their first glimpse of the magical incandescent lights, invented by Edison, on board Henry Villard's ship, the *Columbia*, when it docked in the city that year.

Houses were the last word in elegance, rococo design, and interior decorations. One mansion typical of the extravagant taste had a dignified hall lined in red leather, a drawing room forty feet long with two white mantelpieces and gold-framed mirrors reaching from floor to ceiling at either end. A white-velvet carpet with a pattern of scattered bunches of roses covered the floor, and at the windows hung glass curtains of *point de Venise*, with stiff pink-brocade drapes. Gold love seats and footstools were upholstered in cream-colored satin decorated with painted Cupids. Another house, whose carefully tended gardens stretched for blocks within the city limits, had a top floor equipped not only for ballroom dancing, but for private theatricals, with a stage, dressing rooms, and gas footlights.

Young ladies—and young gentlemen, too—"took the tour" of the Continent and dressed in Paris importations. Balls were affairs gay with the rustle of silks and satins in the latest colors, floating bell skirts, and silver girdles in the most fashionable mode. Gentlemen wore kid gloves of white or palest buff and *boutonnières* in their lapels. One lovely lady stopped traffic, both pedestrian and vehicular, when in her victoria she drove through town behind her uniformed coachman and beautifully groomed horses, bridles jingling, and over her knees a carriage robe of peacock green feathers which set off her fashionable gown.

Women in Oregon had been concerned about their attire when the country was hardly out of its swaddling clothes. In the pioneer days of the sixties, the *Oregon Weekly Union* complained editorially of the general extravagance. Young belles, it said, cannot put up with a bonnet that cost less than $10 or $20, and this had to be replaced every few months. Dresses, naturally, had to be equally costly. In every other new land men and women wore homespun, but not on the Pacific coast. Here it was considered unfashionable to wear anything but imported clothes, and fashion seemed to be more important than the welfare of the region. Money which should have been spent within its borders was constantly being drained out. Even the families of farmers purchased their apparel at the store and manufactured little or nothing at home, concluded the paper. By the eighties, the daughters of the heedless women who had imported their wardrobes from California or the East were even less concerned about their region's well-being and purchased theirs from abroad.

Formal dinners were stiff, correct affairs and impeccably served. No smoking, of course, permitted at the table, and when the gargantuan meal was finished, the ladies modestly retired to the drawing room, leaving the gentlemen to cigars, brandy, and stag conversation. A typical menu included the following: oysters on the half shell, mock turtle soup, fillet of sole, entree of mushrooms and sweetbreads, larded fillet of beef, Roman punch, a lettuce salad with French dressing, ice cream with *marrons glacés*, coffee, nuts, Roquefort cheese, and the finest imported wines and champagnes.

Manners were as formal as the dinners and the chaperoned balls. No lady dared cross her knees; she kept both feet on the ground, one slightly in front of the other. She used no make-up, though buffing the nails with polish was permitted. Excessive drinking, which meant a second glass of punch, was strictly taboo. If (horrible thought!) a risqué joke was by some weird accident told in her presence, the point would quite escape her and she never betrayed herself, even by the flicker of a smile. Under no circumstances would a lady cross the floor of a ballroom alone—apparently she was too delicate to negotiate it without the arm of her escort. She would accept no gift from an admirer other than a box of candy or a book unless he had pledged her his heart and fortune. And to enter the portals of a hotel in the company of a male friend might very well ineradicably blemish her reputation. Using a first name was the rare privilege of long acquaintance —some wives never quite got used to addressing their husbands except as "Mr."

Young men, too, had a set of rules and regulations for proper behavior, though they were given considerably more leeway. A gentleman never called on a young lady until he had received an invitation from either her mama or papa. If he danced more than three times in an evening with the same young woman, that was tantamount to announcing that she was the future mistress of his heart and hearth. Should he be riding through town with a female of not-so-sterling repute, he must never recognize by even a nod or a glance any unblemished lady friend who might be passing.

It was the sentimental age when young ladies wore gold lockets containing a picture and a lock of hair of the beloved, and simpering was in fashion. Autograph albums were inscribed with gems like the following: "There is comfort in the thought, that virtue, modesty, intelligence, industry and heartfelt piety are jewels which adorn woman's soul here, render her life beautiful and valuable and insure a safe passport to immortality. They are gems in the crown of female beauty and loveliness." And hardened men would weep into their beer while a *chanteuse* moaned "The Face on the Barroom Floor," "A Bird in a Gilded Cage," or "The Picture That Was Turned Toward the Wall."

In the rural areas life was still relatively unsophisticated. When going to a dance, young Lotharios called for their girls on horseback, sometimes bringing a horse and a sidesaddle for her. One lady recalling her youth remarked that "A thrill that modern girls miss is sliding off of the horse into the young swain's arms!" Men and boys plastered their hair down with liberal applications of bear's grease mixed with an overpowering perfume. Dances were held in the schoolhouse. The benches and tables were pushed back against the wall, and the orchestra was seated on the slightly raised platform where the teacher's desk ordinarily stood. At the opposite end of the room a table was set with simple but abundant food which was attacked at twelve o'clock. The newer European-styled dances had not yet filtered down to the countryside and square dances were still good enough. Simple games were sometimes played at these affairs. A popular one was played to the tune of "Weevilly Wheat," the words of which went:

> Your weevilly wheat isn't fit to eat
> And neither is your barley;
> We'll have the best of Boston wheat
> To bake a cake for Charley.
>
> Oh, Charley, he's a fine young man
> And Charley, he's a dandy,
> And Charley loves to kiss the girls
> Whenever they come handy.

The "Gay Nineties" were just as gay in the Northwest. This was the era of the Gibson girl and behavior was a little less hidebound. Women played lawn tennis and golf, went cycling in sailor hats, starched shirtwaists, short skirts, and leather boots laced to the knees. Men wore straw hats, striped blazers, and knickerbockers. Spokane society was described by a journalist in *Harper's* as being "leavened by a considerable class of proud and cultivated men and women, who live in charming homes, and maintain a delightful intercourse with one another. They make it a very gay city . . . and are fond of high-bred horses, good dogs, and bright living, with dancing and amateur theatricals, good literature and fun."

Portland had elaborate balls at which expensive favors were distributed, gold hatpins or pencils, gold-topped cut-glass vinaigrettes. Masquerades and fancy-dress balls were popular. "Society" long remembered a Marie Antoinette fete held at the Marquam Grand Theater, when the stately minuet was danced and its participants were in regalia complete with powdered wigs and swords. One young gentleman of fashion gave regular hunting parties, driving friends out into the country in his coach, with the dogs yapping behind.

To the majority of Easterners this aspect of the region was unknown. It was the "Wild West," a land composed solely of sordid mining towns, rough fishing villages, cattle ranges, crude lumberjacks —in short, a section where vice was welcomed and made its home. This prevalent attitude moved an indigenous writer to indignant protest in a local magazine. She was getting tired of all the comment about the unholiness of the West, she said. Vice was vice and it would take a person of godlike brilliance to convince her that Western vice was any worse than the Eastern variety or more in evidence. In the West, "vice goes about openly, unclad, unpolished, open-handed," whereas in the effete East it is "silent, muffled-footed, velvet-gloved, masqued-faced." Let Easterners strip the fine garments from their vice and stand them by the side of ours, she suggested, and they will discover they are twin brothers. For her part, she preferred the obvious to the polished.

The cities of the Northwest were, nevertheless, still frontier cities. As they were in the awkward, coltish stage, the decorum was more decorous than elsewhere and the vice in contrast even a little more pronounced. As was true everywhere else in the country, society existed on two levels. Spokane, with its "cultivated men and women," had one of the best known "box houses" west of the Mississippi, the Coeur d'Alene Theater. It was more than a theater—it was an institution, having under one roof a saloon with three bars, two bowling halls, a restaurant, concert hall, three-story theater, lodginghouse and barbershop and employing a hundred people. The owner and manager was "Dutch Jake," boss of the city's tenderloin and powerful enough to enjoy police protection. A reform wave led by a number of clergymen swept the city in 1904. Mass meetings were held, the papers ran stories and editorials for weeks, and then, as suddenly as it had begun, the agitation subsided. Ladies and gentlemen of the upper strata went on breeding their dogs and horses, and the primrose ladies continued plying their trade.

Portland had its famous or infamous "Skidroad," or North End. Though no respectable citizen was supposed to be aware of its existence, its slime sometimes overflowed. In protest against what it considered the laxity of the law-enforcing authorities, the *West Shore* published a cartoon captioned "Dedicated to the Portland Police Force." This depicted a ten-year-old boy sitting on the curb, drunk, with an empty liquor bottle before him; a prostitute sitting at an open window soliciting a man standing outside; a horse and buggy running over a little girl; a man beating up another man; three Chinese leaning out of windows in a house marked "Chinese Lottery"; a group of men playing cards in a store marked "Faro Bank"; and a policeman walking down the street with a cane and wearing a placard on his chest reading "Please Help the Blind."

The police who patrolled the Skidroad walked in pairs as a precaution against the husky loggers and sailors out to celebrate after months in the wilds or at sea. They closed their eyes to the streetwalkers, the lottery-ticket peddlers, the tinhorns, the barflies, though, contrary to the cartoon, they did their duty when necessary.

The Skidroad had everything on which a man could spend his money—shooting galleries, penny arcades, booths of fortune tellers, phrenologists, astrologists, herb doctors, patent-medicine men, not to mention the saloons, which also had everything. The "House of All Nations" catered to every taste and was one of the more roisterous. Another, Erickson's, occupied half a block, had a bar six hundred feet long, and was equipped to handle a thousand drinking men at one time. An orchestra with female musicians gowned in pink performed on a platform fenced in by a brass rail which was charged with enough electricity to stop short the most venturesome.

Most saloons had an upper story where the daughters of Aphrodite of almost every nationality and color plied their trade. In addition there were the crib houses and the octaroon sporting houses—a social division even in the primrose section. The former were for transient trade, while the latter catered exclusively to white patrons and charged anywhere from $5 to $10, with periodic examinations required by the city health authorities. Streetwalking was relatively rare in Portland until a city ordinance outlawed the cribs.

Periodic reforms were attempted with little result. One had a hilarious outcome. The mayor at the time appointed a vice commission which zealously surveyed the town and published a lengthy report. This included a full-page map of the city, with the streets naturally erased, showing by dots the approximate location of the apartment houses, hotels, rooming houses, and so forth where the crimson damsels lived. Within an hour after the report appeared, draftsmen had filled in the streets, and the places that sold compasses and dividers were suddenly filled with eager men demanding the instruments.

If sedate Portlanders shuddered when the North End was mentioned, they could take comfort in the fact that the city's competitor on Puget Sound was even more damned. Seattle had grown tremendously from what it had been only a generation before, but it was still raw, unfinished, and suffering from growing pains. Where men used to fish for trout in the brooks within the city's limits, now stood magnificent residences and office buildings, though tree stumps were still a common sight. It was the jumping-off place for the gold fields of Alaska after 1896, a week-end resort for loggers, and a port of call for sailors.

Mayor Tom Humes, recognizing the obvious fact that Seattle was the red-light area for almost the entire state, set aside a large restricted district. Through a policy of passive consent, the municipal authorities encouraged the influx of disreputable characters from all over the country to swell the population. To the city's numerous industries were added gamblers, thieves, prostitutes, and "macques," or procurers. A group of tenderloin capitalists arose whose activities were so widespread and profitable that a report of the Federal Immigration Commission designated Seattle as one of the three headquarters in the nation for the white-slave traffic.

A journalist who made a tour of the Northwest and wrote a series of articles on the various cities reported on "slavery among the Japanese" in Seattle. The women, he said, lived in rows of one-story cottages by the waterside in an area locally designated as Whitechapel. The section also contained women from Mexico, China, Japan, and France, as well as American Negro and white women. According to news reports, he related, the Japanese women were probably purchased from their parents in Japan and brought to this country. Seattle, he concluded, is like all the other large Northwestern towns, "but it is livelier than most, in addition to having the most motley population. It is said to be well under police control, and I was told that the gambling there is above-stairs and not too public."

Organized vice was so closely interwoven with politics that a major plank of the platform of "Hy" Gill, who ran for mayor in 1910, was that he would keep Seattle an open town. It was no secret that Gill had been friendly with the gamblers and procurers during the years in which he had been active in city affairs. The underworld turned out to electioneer for him, and he was also supported by the Republican party, of which he was a member in good standing. Hiram Gill was victorious and his election was the signal for a wholesale influx of all kinds of shady characters. It is estimated that about two thousand gamblers, macques, and prostitutes poured into the city within a few weeks.

One of the mayor's first official acts was the appointment of Charles W. Wappenstein, or "Wappy," as the nether world affectionately called him. He had figured in several municipal scandals and, as a former chief of police, had been responsible for the downfall of one municipal administration. With "Wappy" at the helm, the tenderloin operated openly but at a price, a good price. In return for looking the other way, thousands of dollars poured regularly into the pockets of the minions of the law.

The smell became so malodorous that the Seattle City Council secretly hired a former Pinkerton operative, who started his investigation by obtaining a job in a gambling house. When he brought in his report, the conditions he described were made public, and the Seattle *Post-Intelligencer* wrote editorially:

It will be impossible for any fair-minded man to believe that the infamous conditions . . . could have existed without the knowledge and connivance of the police, even if there had been no direct proof. But when policemen are seen going in and out of gambling houses; when gambling house keepers complain that the police are taking too big a share of the profits . . . and when there is a common persistent report that the fat sum of $40,000 has been divided up among officials and others, it is asking too much of the people of the city to ask them to believe that Wappenstein is innocent of culpable connections with these outrageous conditions.

Though the newspaper had supported the election of Mayor Gill on partisan grounds, it now vehemently demanded his recall under the city charter, which provided that any elective officer could be removed by a plurality vote. If 25 per cent of the voters signed the recall petition, a special election would be held, with the name of the man in question on the ballot as well as those of other candidates. The signatures were obtained and the recall campaign was fought with all the passion and ferocity of an aroused people opposed by a group who were determined by every means possible to protect their financial interests. The lives of two clergymen who were active in the campaign were threatened, as was that of the editor of the *Post-Intelligencer*, who was making amends for his earlier support of Gill by publishing vitriolic articles and editorials.

Hiram Gill lost by an overwhelming majority and Wappenstein was dismissed. Then, on evidence gathered by a detective who had been hired by the pastor of one of the churches in the city, criminal proceedings were instituted against the ex-police chief. He was indicted for accepting a $2,500 bribe from some gamblers. During the trial the owners of a house of ill fame testified that they had paid Wappenstein a tribute of $10 a month for every woman in their employ; as they had nearly a hundred, he received a regular monthly intake of almost $1,000. The chief had taken no chances of being cheated. Periodically, his men had visited the restricted district, counted the number of women in each house, and submitted typewritten reports, so that when the owners of the establishments came to pay, he knew exactly what he should receive. Wappenstein was convicted and received a sentence of from three to ten years.

The week following Gill's defeat, Seattle had a mass exodus from its tenderloin. The Union Station was jammed with its erstwhile inhabitants, who realized that for the time being it was no longer the place for them. Seattle had not, of course, solved for all time its vice situation—no more than any other city in the country could—but it had destroyed an unholy alliance.

The two principal cities at the time, and since, were Portland and Seattle. They set the "tone" for their states; all the other cities were pale imitations, their atmospheres and conditions, on the whole, similar but on a smaller scale.

Portland was a New England spinster, cautious, straight-laced, concerned about her virtue and regarding strangers with suspicious eyes. The passions of youth had died down and, though she was still young by any standard, what she wanted most was a placid, orderly existence. She graciously welcomed outsiders into her well kept home, even encouraged them to come, but only if they were mannerly enough not to disturb the routine of her life.

Citizens of Portland took great pride in their conservatism, their stability, and the comparison of the city by visiting Easterners with New England. "A curious social austerity is one of the notable traits of the Oregon character," stated a native writer. Gambling and the lottery ticket had been banned from respectable social circles. Not only was the saloonkeeper ostracized, but also the liquor retailer, he boasted, a very different situation from California, where respectable women did not hesitate to patronize a grocery store that had a bar in the rear. The owner of such a dual establishment could never hope to see "scrupulous Oregonian housewives" step across *his* threshold.

Thus the city on the Willamette, whose strain was predominantly Yankee and, but for the flip of a coin, might have been called Boston, which it strove hard to emulate. Through the years it had received immigrants from many states in the Union—especially after the railroad reached it—but it absorbed them quickly, and soon they neither had nor wanted an identity other than as Oregonians. It was a charming place in which to live, with its neat homes, carefully tended lawns and gardens and well kept streets. The pioneer concern about every minute facet in the local scene still prevailed and was enjoyed by the inhabitants. As an example might be mentioned *l'affaire* Skidmore fountain, which agitated Portlanders for almost half a century.

In 1887 Steve Skidmore, a small businessman, died, leaving a bequest of $5,000 to the city in gratitude for the opportunity Portland had afforded him of living a peaceful and prosperous life. He specified that the money was to be used for a fountain to serve men, horses, and dogs and which was to be placed in the business area. Portland at the time had no public monuments and the city fathers felt it would be a good idea to begin with this. They called in their foremost art expert, Colonel Charles Erskine Scott Wood, and asked him to secure an outstanding sculptor to execute the fountain regardless of cost. He hired the renowned Olin L. Warner, who made the trip from New York just to view the site before he cast the fountain. The price, including transportation and erection, was $18,000, and the amount needed in addition to Skidmore's bequest was privately collected from a number of affluent citizens. With all due ceremonies, the fountain was unveiled the following year and for a time served man and beast.

Neighborhoods change, however, and soon the area around the Skidmore fountain deteriorated as the activity of the city moved uptown. Eight years later the first murmurings began and soon became a roar to move the fountain to a park or a more fashionable section. A story headed "Skidmore Fountain Removal Proposed" could always be relied on to stir up some excitement when the newspaper editor felt that his "Letters" column was becoming a little dull. This *cause célèbre* involved all Portland.

From time to time, C. E. S. Wood had written about the fountain at the urging of interested citizens. In 1933 he was again requested by those who opposed moving it to write a definitive piece which, they hoped, would end the discussion for all time. He complied with a trenchant article that was published in a learned journal of the region. After tracing the history of the fountain, he administered a sound spanking:

I understand that once more the epidemic to move the fountain is agitating certain members of the community. If I may be allowed to say so, this continual recurrence very seriously reflects on the artistic judgment and good taste of these people. At first blush it may seem natural to collect everything that a city has in the way of works of art in its park as a sort of cemetery or museum. . . . If a people's instinct does not teach them to respect a work of art in its original place . . . if they are actually so bourgeois and new-rich that they cannot bear to leave their only work of art where . . . the sculptor placed it . . . that all might be harmonious, then move it. If the city fathers and a controlling element of the city wish to show their ignorance, I suggest that they put the Skidmore fountain on wheels and move it from place to place as the mood changes, with a card "This is our one and only great work of art, the world celebrated Skidmore fountain. Bids will be accepted for its next location."

The Skidmore fountain has remained at the intersections of First, Vine, and Ankeny streets.

Parochial to an extreme, Oregonians compared their society with others in the nation, and always theirs was better. It was impossible, they felt, for an outsider to understand the Oregonian character; only those steeped in the traditions of the pioneer society and an integral part of the milieu from its inception had the requisite insight.

This attitude was frankly expressed by one pioneer leader in offering an explanation as to why the *Oregonian* enjoyed unquestioned primacy in Portland; why, when Portland had a population at the time (1895) of 90,000 and was the metropolis of a state of 350,000, it was the only paper in the city. Outsiders who had studied the situation, he said, simply could not understand how any paper, no matter how good, could consistently crush all competition. The answer was simple: it was impossible for outsiders to comprehend the nature of Oregonians, so that only a native could make a newspaper acceptable to other natives. "A stranger, though combining in himself the highest journalistic talents, and with adequate financial strength, might easily fail in Oregon journalism for want of insight into things peculiarly Oregonian. At every step he would be in danger of giving offense where he meant to please, and of creating antagonism where he sought for favor. He would probably come to grief by the very projects which elsewhere win approval and success."

The peculiar nature of the Oregonian character was a result of a blending of the missionary with the pioneer, according to the same writer. The latter had absorbed the former and remained the dominant element. He made the laws, supplied the political leaders, and was responsible for everything worthwhile in the society.*

The early settlers of Oregon, by and large, were men and women who had come from stable backgrounds and had brought with them a "philosophy of subsistence." Those who came from states like Iowa, Ohio, and Illinois, where they had engaged in large-scale farming, settled in the Willamette Valley and prospered, though they lacked the imagination to undertake the cultivation of crops other than those which they had grown in the past, or to promote the establishment of marketing facilities so that Oregon, like California, might have a world trade. Those who settled in the cities prospered in business. While they wanted their cities to develop and expand, they preferred that

---

* That the first immigrants into Oregon left an unmistakable impress is undoubtedly true, and it can be seen in that significant cultural trait, speech, which is tinted by Southernisms in accent and vocabulary.

the impetus come from within and resented the intrusion of outside capital.

The pride in indigenous products, whether human or material, resulted in the development of the pioneer cult, which had deeper roots and loyalties in Oregon than anywhere else in the Northwest. Adherents of the cult felt that since more Oregonians had migrated in covered wagons than had the settlers who came to other sections, they had endured most and were entitled to greater commendation for building a civilization. It took a special type of person, ran the theory, to make the great trek. One distinguished Oregon scientist, in line with the prevalent mood, stated that the Oregonian was a superior character because he was the product of natural selection. The conditions under which immigration was made, he stated, served to exclude the physically unfit and the indigent, so that Oregon was settled by the element best fitted to lay the foundations of a new country.

Organizations were formed to keep alive the memory of the old days. Annually, the pioneers, like the veterans of the Civil War on Memorial Day, gathered for their meetings. The city which played host to the celebrants had a holiday atmosphere. Banners bedecked the hotels, bands played, parades filled the streets. "Oregon was reconquered yesterday," began a report in the *Oregonian* describing a reunion held in 1897:

All the great struggles were fought over again from the skirmishes and privations of the long trip over the plains across to the establishment of a relatively populous state. The plodding ox teams were guided over waste plains and mountain ranges, by the crack of a bullwhip; the sneaking savages were repulsed in murderous assaults; rescues of beleaguered families were effected; snow and rain, heat and cold were endured with scant clothing and still scarcer food; a provisional government was established, and was followed by a state constitution; the forest was gradually swept back, and with it the den of the wild beast and the damp gloom of the wilderness—all was done again, but not by vigorous, robust and ambitious youth. Tottering frames and white heads did the work and devised the ways, and melancholy reflection over scenes that teemed with friends now gone was the only cloud that marred a day of the brightest and deepest joy.

With the passing of the years, the pioneer spirit became a pioneer cult. In terms of exclusiveness it was as much a distinction to belong to a pioneer association as to be a member of the D.A.R. At one meeting a suggestion was made that the date of migration to the Oregon country which served as a basis for membership eligibility be extended. It was not approved. "I say to you," declared one proud pioneer, "that there was no honor in having come to a country already opened up." After 1855, he said, traveling was comfortable, information about Oregon available in the East, and the journey no longer required heroism and courage.

Historians and newspapers, as well as the pioneer organizations, constantly served to remind Oregonians of the dramatic and heroic role the pioneer had played. Harvey Scott expressed the general feeling of many of his compatriots:

The pioneer spirit makes a slow country in a material sense; but there are other interests in community life far above increase of commodities and multiplication of towns. . . . The social and moral coordination which is so notable of Oregon life—especially notable when Oregon is contrasted with neighboring communities—is a direct achievement of the pioneer spirit. The sympathy which makes of Western Oregon a homogeneous community; the mutual understanding which checks the energies of social disorder before it rises to the degree of social menace; the friendliness of one "old Oregonian" for another; the respect for leadership which has continuously recognized and supported certain men of large talents in quasi-public relationships—these qualities have their foundation in the pioneer spirit.

Under its influence, he boasted, gambling had been banished from all respectable quarters, the trade in liquor discouraged, and all those who handled it ostracized. Outsiders, he said, might criticize this attitude as provincial; perhaps it was, but the Oregon pioneer knew that it resulted in real, positive good—the public credit placed on a sound basis, public extravagance reduced to a minimum, Oregon made safe from the threatened domination of the socialist demagogue, public education and religion secured, and, in general, a higher degree of civilization brought to the Northwest than would otherwise have been the case.

By contrast with Portland, the city on Puget Sound was a vivid, lighthearted, voluptuous maiden in the full bloom of youth. Her home was open to all and the more the merrier. It was not that she was irresponsible or ill bred—she knew and practiced all the social graces. Her upbringing had been as good, but her heritage was different and she took life much less seriously.

Seattle really grew up when she was wedded by the shining bands of the railroad to the rest of the country. Immigrants poured into the Northwest at the rate of forty thousand a year, and most went to Seattle and other parts of Washington, bringing with them capital, initiative, and energy. The city began to expand; and when the Klondike gold rush started, it became a frenzied, seething conglomeration of men passing through who added to its prosperity by purchasing necessary supplies for the gold fields, and others who regarded it as an opportune place for new business establishments. Some of the former returned to stay and many of the latter remained. The pioneers were overwhelmed by sheer numbers and, instead of absorbing, they became absorbed. Something of the pioneer spirit remained, but it never became a "professional" preoccupation nor was it as widespread as in Oregon.

Nine

The Stuff Their Dreams Were Made Of

Not only native white Americans came to pioneer in the Northwest, but native black men, and yellow men who crossed the sunset ocean to the land of gold, and men from the Old World who came to the land of opportunity and, finding competition too great in the older, settled sections of the East, went on to the young, beckoning West.

Some Negroes accompanied their masters to the Oregon country and some came as free men, hoping to escape the curse of their dark skins in the unsettled wilderness and to be allowed to help lay the foundations of a new society. The white men and women who crossed the plains brought with them, however, all their social, economic, and political biases and predilections. Since the majority came from or near slavery areas, the laws they enacted under the provisional and Territorial governments barred additional Negroes from entering the Territory. And when they voted for a constitution for Oregon, they supported by eight to one the following proposition:

"No free negro, mulatto not residing in the state at the adoption of this constitution shall come, reside or be within this state, or hold any real estate or make any contract or maintain any suit therein; and the legislative assembly by penal laws for the removal by public officers of all such negroes and mulattoes, and for their effectual exclusion from the state and for the punishment of persons who shall bring them into the state or employ or harbor them."

By that time some of the Negroes who had settled in the region had become prosperous and worthy citizens. One, William Bush, together with several families, had staked a claim at a time when even a white man in the area was a rarity. He built a home, worked his land, and became a leader in Bush Prairie, as the section was named. When

t was discovered that under the existing Homestead Law he could not
secure title to his land because of his color, prompt action was taken
by numerous citizens. They petitioned Congress for a law which
would give all persons who had settled in the Territory prior to 1850
all the rights and privileges of citizens. A bill incorporating that provision was enacted and Bush was thereby permitted to retain his land.
His son in later years served as a member of the first state legislature.

A Negro, George Washington, was the founder of Centralia,
Washington. He came from Missouri in 1850 with his master, who
later freed him and adopted him as a son. Within two years Washington was able to accumulate $6,000 with which he purchased his
father's claim. He built a home and platted the town, selling lots for
$10 each, offering one lot free to the purchaser who would build a
home on it. According to one story, Washington was a Virginian
who led a group of settlers to the Territory, hoping to find there the
freedom denied him in his native state. Since he had arrived after
1850, the law would not allow him to homestead, and so a white friend
established a claim which Washington later purchased. A number
of years later, when the proposed extension of the Northern Pacific
Railroad passed directly through his farm, the sale of his land and the
acquisition of a town-site from the railroad made him a wealthy man.

A curious and ambivalent feeling existed in the Northwest toward
the Negro. On the one hand, he definitely was not wanted by the
majority of the population, who tried by various means to keep him
out. On the other, many Negro settlers soon earned the respect and
admiration of the community to an extent where they were treated
with greater cordiality than in almost any other section of the country. One of the earliest pioneers of Seattle, for instance, was William
Gross. He had served in the United States Navy in the Orient under
Commodore Perry and had come to the city at the request of Governor Isaac Stevens to operate a hotel. He was so successful with it that
at one time the hotel was Seattle's largest. Gross accumulated a good
deal of property in the city and formed a close association with Seattle's "aristocracy," men like Yessler and Denny. When he died it was
discovered that he had been one of the heaviest taxpayers.

Two newspapers devoted to the interests of the race were published, the *Seattle Standard*, launched in 1892, which seems to have
been short-lived, and *The Republican*, a weekly, founded two years
later, which remained in existence for twenty-one years. Both were
owned and operated by Negroes.

Portland began to have a small concentration of Negroes when it became a railroad and shipping center and when porters, ship attendants, and dining-car waiters took up residence. Others were brought in to serve in the hotels and in the houses of the red-light district. Those who were not property owners or members of the nether world found the going difficult, according to one Negro pioneer who came to the city in 1872. He reported that every Negro had to pay a head tax of $10, that his people had no civil rights, and that it was difficult for them to get any except the most menial jobs. Another stated that on a number of occasions the schools tried to draw the color line, but they never actually succeeded. Churches did not segregate worshipers.

The Negro population remained small. In 1860 there were 128 Negroes in Oregon. A decade later their number had increased to only 1,886. In succeeding years animosity directed against the Oriental and other minority groups drew attention away from them.

The Chinese fared badly at the hands of Northwesterners. They had come to the west coast in profusion during the three decades when the foundations for intensive economic development were being laid. Famine, flood, and other vicissitudes of man and nature drove them from their homeland to a country with an apparently inexhaustible demand for cheap labor. In an atmosphere of friendship between the United States and China secured by a series of trade agreements, the door to the West was thrown wide open. Labor contracts were made directly with American merchants, and thousands of Chinese were imported to work in the canneries, mills, and other industries. The powerful "Six Companies," which represented six provinces in China, were responsible for bringing in about 135,000 of their countrymen. They supplied interpreters for the passengers, met the immigrants when they landed, and saw to it that they were placed in the proper tong.

The discovery of gold in California and later in the Inland Empire held out a glittering lure. During the placer-mining era, the Chinese moved in after the Americans had extracted everything that could be obtained cheaply and profitably, wringing out of the earth the last bit of the precious metal. Their lives were regarded cheaply by the white miners. It was not unusual to find a battered yellow body in or near its owner's shack, and, in general, they were victimized and exploited. Thirty-two Chinese were murdered one day in the Idaho Salmon

River country by a party of cowboys whose only motive was robbery.

When the railroads began to span the continent, thousands of men were needed to perform the menial, backbreaking tasks of cutting through mountain passes and laying the seemingly endless miles of track. The owners of the Union Pacific and Central Pacific imported ten thousand coolies, and the Oregon, Washington, and British Columbia roads were likewise built largely by Oriental labor. The Chinese were excellent workers, tireless, meek, and demanding little. They worked patiently in the scorching heat of the desert and the blinding snows of the northern mountain areas, and when the tracks were down, they turned to clearing the land, gardening, factory work, and domestic service.

By that time the acute labor shortage was over and the Chinese came into competition with white workers. The panic of 1873 intensified the situation and they began to be attacked for characteristics which were either nonexistent or were unimportant ones that had been ignored in the past: they were heathens; they were not citizens; they accumulated great wealth which they sent out of the country; they were opium smokers; they were threatening to overrun the land and to make the west coast a province of China.

Portland's Chinatown in the early eighties contained about twelve thousand Orientals who were employed as seasonal workers in the canneries and mills, on the railroads, as laundrymen, barbers, and domestics. It was crowded with exotic shops and bazaars, laundries, fish markets, and restaurants over which wooden awnings had been built as protection from the rain. The streets were constantly filled with loitering Chinese males, gossiping or shopping while the smoke from their tiny-bowled, enormously long-stemmed pipes hung overhead. The quarter had always been regarded as "colorful" by the white citizens, who frequently visited it to gape or shop. Suddenly it became a den of iniquity.

In Tacoma a mob surrounded the Chinese quarter, forcibly ejected the residents from their homes during a driving rainstorm, herded them down to the railroad and shipped them off to Portland. The next day the quarter was razed. In Idaho the same year, the murder of a white man resulted in the arrest and subsequent lynching of five Chinese who had been accused of the crime. Riots occurred in Seattle and other cities of the Northwest, and when no physical action was taken, the cry "The Chinese must go" was constantly heard, until the animosity finally burned itself out.

Little anti-Japanese feeling existed in the early days. The Nipponese mingled freely with the population; many purchased farms and owned business establishments. When in 1907 the editor of the *Pacific Christian Advocate*, a Methodist Episcopal clergyman, delivered a sermon in which he stated that he would not allow his children to go to school with those of Japanese descent, protest was prompt and vehement. The superintendent of schools and several ministers declared that his statement was ridiculous and unfair, that Japanese pupils were quiet and orderly, that they were bright and learned rapidly.

Another group that was lured from various parts of the country by the promise of the Northwest were the Jews, who began to arrive in the early years. Many of them became farmers, but most settled in the cities and engaged in merchandising. They entered the social and political life of the community and contributed leadership that was often illustrious. One of the outstanding members of the intellectual life of Portland at the turn of the century was Rabbi Stephen S. Wise, who held a pulpit in the city. An energetic social reformer, he helped draft Oregon's first child labor law.

In the fifties the bigoted T. J. Dryer launched a vicious attack against the Jews, with particular emphasis on the merchants. In one article he made base remarks about Jewish business practices, and in another in the same issue he accused Jewish merchants of stealing the *Oregonian* from gentile subscribers. And when the Jews retaliated by canceling their subscriptions to the paper that was maligning them, Dryer became apoplectic at their temerity. For about a month he fumed and raged, dragging out all the old libels and inventing some new ones.

Revolted by this type of editorializing, the *Statesman* and the *Weekly Times* raked Dryer over the coals. The reason for his invective, they charged, was his defeat as the Republican candidate for the legislature in Multnomah County, which was partially due to Jewish opposition at the polls because of his Know-Nothing views. "It is not strange," the *Statesman* wrote, "that the professed organ of a notoriously intolerant and proscriptive party should attack the religion of those who refuse to obey the dictates of that party; nor that one who has long since laid aside even the outward semblance of morality should mock at the religious ceremonials and forms of worship adhered to by others."

About a half century later, when the *Oregonian* was edited by Harvey Scott, a news story reported a gathering to discuss pioneer life among the Jews. Four generations of one family were present, the paper stated, as were three brothers who had come to Portland when it was little more than a group of log cabins. Mrs. Abigail Scott Duniway delivered one of the addresses and another speaker named "the first settlers . . . and many honorary offices held by them at various periods, including those of Mayor, Councilman, State and City Treasurers, United States Senator and Minister to a foreign country."

With the completion of the railroads to Portland and Puget Sound, the new Northwest was completely accessible, and those who no longer found the land of the Great Plains or the old Northwest satisfactory, again pulled up stakes and traveled out to the farthermost reach. During the nineties, Scandinavians began to come to the region, and occasionally small groups decided to migrate and establish colonies, impressed by eyewitness accounts of the region by countrymen in their own language papers. Numerous articles were published like the one in the Madison (Wisconsin) *Vikingen*, which stated that "no section of the country today is attracting so much attention as Montana, Oregon and Washington," or the one in *Nordvesten* describing Seattle's "fortunate situation" and its "magnificent future."

Scandinavians worked in sawmills, logging camps, and fisheries in the earlier days. Later, with the development of the horticultural and agricultural resources of the Puget Sound region and the growing importance of the urban markets of Seattle, Tacoma, Everett, and Bellingham, farming became a major occupation. Many moved into the port cities and manned the crews of vessels which plied the coastal waters or engaged in the Alaskan or transpacific trade. They also migrated to Oregon, moving up the Willamette Valley and settling on the wheat lands below the Columbia River. In time the population was large enough to sustain many language newspapers and a few institutions of higher learning.

By 1910 nationalities from every part of the world were represented in the Northwest. An admixture of peoples was assimilated into the general whole. A few scattered settlements throughout the region contained concentrations of national groups, so that towns like Odessa in Washington came to be known for its German-Russian population, Astoria for the Finns, and southeastern Oregon for the colorful Basques.

The newness of the land had also attracted people who believed that there they could create a society free of the fetters imposed by the older and more traditionally-minded areas of the country. Factors conducive to charting a new social pattern were there—cheap land, a desirable climate, scenic grandeur. They came, hoping to be able to build a utopian order, an Erewhon perhaps, where human nature would be given an opportunity to justify and redeem itself.

America has been the home of many such settlements inspired by aspirations and dreams of a better life. Brook Farm in Massachusetts and New Harmony in Indiana were such experiments, and there were many lesser ones throughout the land, each with its own blueprint for the achievement of the millennium. Patiently, indefatigably, hopefully, and with an imperishable faith in man's better nature, they created their little isles of cooperation in a sea of confusion and competition, small oases in experimental living.

Of the numerous communistic societies in the Pacific Northwest, the one which had the fanciful name of Aurora achieved the greatest degree of success and respectability. Its members were German immigrants who had established a successful and prosperous cooperative society in Bethel, Missouri. Although they owned about 23,000 acres, the Midwest had its drawbacks, and when the leader of the colony heard that good cheap land was available in the beautiful Oregon country, he dispatched a group to investigate. The party spent several months searching for a suitable location and finally purchased two quarter-sections of land, on one of which stood a sawmill and a gristmill. When the surveyors returned, the Bethel community sold its holdings and shortly thereafter set out for Oregon. It was the strangest caravan that had ever crossed the plains. For the entire two-thousand-mile journey the wagon train was led by a hearse containing the body of the leader's child in a lead casket filled with alcohol. The boy had died just before the group left, and his father fulfilled his promise to take him to the new land in the first wagon.

The head of the colony was Dr. William Kiel, a dynamic, forceful, and authoritarian personality. He inspired his followers with a supreme devotion to the principles which he had formulated for the colony: "No man owns anything individually but every man owns everything as a full partner and with equal voice in its use and its increase and the profits accruing from it. But in no other way do we differ from our neighbors. As a community we are one family. 'From every man according to his capacity, to every man according to his needs' is the rule that runs through our law of love." Though power was vested in a democratically elected council, in practice Kiel exercised complete control.

Aurora prospered from the very beginning, due largely to the rigorous, disciplined life led by its members. Both men and women cultivated the thousands of acres the colony acquired, setting out orchards and vineyards until the area looked like a German province. During the winter, the mills and shops were kept busy making clothes and furniture, baskets and implements, all of which were of the finest craftsmanship and artistry.

The most famous building at Aurora was its hotel, where meals were served first to the stagecoach and later to the train passengers. One epicure reminisced: "Why did trains stop for meals at Aurora when the Portland terminal was only twenty-nine miles away? Because the trainmen wanted the better meals they could get at Aurora —better meats, better vegetables, better pies and puddings."

William Kiel had definite ideas on how the colony should be conducted, and he was forceful enough to have them carried out in the face of any opposition. All activities were regulated and behavior was required to conform to the personal tastes and standards of the leader. The doctor disapproved of marriage and so children of the colonists were dissuaded from wedlock—all except his own. Celibacy was encouraged, principally for economic reasons. Single men and women could be boarded and lodged at much lower cost, and with no children as legatees, inheritances would on death revert to the colony, which in large measure was William Kiel.

Education was provided by several tutors who, in the German tradition of thoroughness, taught elementary and advanced subjects and foreign languages to a select number of children. The others received only a simple schooling in reading, writing, and arithmetic. A product of Aurora, Henry Finck, son of one of the hierarchy, confounded his examiners when he applied to enter Harvard with his ability to translate on sight some of the most difficult passages from Roman and Greek classics. Later the institution awarded him a music scholarship to study abroad, and when he returned he was employed by the New York *Evening Post* as its music critic, a position he held for more than forty years.

Musical education was encouraged and Aurora became the musical center of the state. Two brass bands provided entertainment for the colony and were in great demand to play in neighboring communities on festive occasions, such as Fourth of July celebrations. They also played for the country dances frequently held at Aurora, which were attended by neighbors from miles around.

For about twenty-five years the spiritual force of William Kiel, which had generated the movement, was powerful enough to hold the colony together. Then Kiel began to lose his influence. His autocratic, authoritarian leadership was increasingly resented, particularly by the younger generation, and his drinking, which had become excessive, was demoralizing. His death in 1877 completed the deterioration of an enterprise that had been based upon "equal service, equal obligations and equal reward." The property of the colony was apportioned among the members according to their original contributions and period of service. Aurora still stands, but it is merely another of the small towns in the Northwest.

A less successful communal enterprise was the Puget Sound Co-operative Colony, organized in Port Angeles, Washington, in 1877. It had been conceived by a New York lawyer who died before the experiment could be undertaken, and it was launched by George Venable Smith and a number of others. As projected, it was a grandiose and ideal plan offering "permanent employment in all branches of trade and industry at good wages, guaranteed, free lands, free water, free lights, free libraries, exemption from taxes and rents. All profits paid to colonists." Land was to be held in common and "all money relations between individuals shall be abrogated." A cardinal feature was to be the "associated homes." Under this plan, domestic help would be provided and paid for by the community so that no stigma would be attached to those whose special talents lay in homemaking, and women whose interests lay elsewhere would not be bound to the kitchen and the dust mop.

Mills, docks, stores, a hotel, offices, machine shops, homes, and even a newspaper, *The Commonwealth,* were established. For two years the colony actually functioned, and then rival factions began to fight for control. Recriminations, charges, and countercharges of fraud and mismanagement flew back and forth. The beginning of the end, however, seems to have been caused by the notoriety resulting when *The Commonwealth* put its column rules in mourning for the men who were executed on the charge of throwing the bomb in Chicago's Haymarket Square. During its existence, the usual gossip and rumors were circulated regarding the immorality of some of its members. The colony quietly slipped out of existence, and thus ended another noble experiment.

At the turn of the century, a colony was founded at Edison, Washington, which was sponsored by outstanding reformers of the nation. It had the backing of a national organization, the Brotherhood of the Cooperative Commonwealth, which included such persons as Henry Demarest Lloyd and Eugene Victor Debs. Colony leaders were careful to point out that there was no association between the Brotherhood and the Social Democracy of which Debs was a leader. It was named Equality, after the utopian municipality in Bellamy's *Looking Backward*, and sought to practice what it considered the true precepts of Christ.

Within the first year of its existence, the Brotherhood had enrolled three thousand members dedicated to the task of establishing cooperative commonwealths in as many places in the land as their resources would permit. Equality was intended as the first of a series in Washington. The plan envisaged settlements devoted to agriculture as well as manufacturing and services, which it was hoped would lead ultimately to the transformation of the state of Washington into a cooperative commonwealth predicated upon the principles of socialism.

The object of Equality was to "own, cultivate and improve land, to establish factories and industries, to insure the members against want or the fear of want, to build homes for its members; to provide educational and recreative facilities of the highest order, and to maintain harmonious relations of freedom, equality and unity on the basis of social and industrial cooperation." Most of the officers of the national movement resided at Edison, where the organ of the society, *Industrial Freedom*, was issued. The nucleus of the settlement was a group of one hundred who had left their homes in Maine to participate in this new adventure in the far Northwest. Soon others from various parts of the country were added to the ranks. There were no bars to membership; all that was required was an entrance fee of $160 and a willingness to practice the principles of Equality.

A considerable amount of land was purchased upon which were erected homes and numerous workshops such as a sawmill, a shoe shop, a tailor shop, a shingle mill, a laundry, and a fruit evaporator. The colony also owned a sloop that was used for salmon fishing. Ten departments of labor were established, and each member was permitted to select the one in which he wished to work.

Equality was regarded favorably by Washingtonians, and one magazine published an article on it headed "A Western Utopia." In 1898 the Seattle *Post-Intelligencer* carried a lengthy piece dealing with its aims, purposes, and achievements. Among other things, it mentioned that the "intelligence of the members taken as a whole, is above the average," that many were experts in the mechanical trades, agriculture, and horticulture, and that a number of artists, scientists, writers, and musicians were in the group.

Complete individualism in thought and behavior was the rule, subject only to such restrictions as members imposed upon themselves for the general welfare. In the end, the individualistic views of the participants, each with his own peculiar formula for achieving a socialist utopia here on earth, were responsible for the disintegration of the experiment. When the colony was little more than a year old, an article was published in *Industrial Freedom* which indicated that it was already beginning to be torn asunder. "Right here," it stated, "we will take occasion to remark that we Equalityites do not seek to hide the disagreeable fact that we have had a fair share of the trials and tribulations that almost invariably befall those who have the temerity to quit the beaten path trodden by the multitude and strike out boldly for themselves on a short cut across lots towards a higher civilization." The root of the trouble, the writer went on, was the "childish weakness of human nature," and the indisputable fact that as socialists most of them had been "pulled before we were ripe. We thought we had reduced socialism to a science before we had mastered the alphabet thereof." Furthermore, none had seemed to realize how much of the "old, competitive, murderous, individualistic spite still lingered" in their natures. The time, apparently, was not yet ripe for a successful attempt at socialistic living.

A belief in iconoclastic ideas rather than in a communal enterprise drew a small band of intellectual rebels to the little town of Silverton, Oregon, now better known as the birthplace of the famed cartoonist, Homer Davenport. They were disciples of Thomas Paine, Robert Ingersoll, and other philosophers of rationalism, atheism, or agnosticism. A weekly newspaper, *The Torch of Reason*, was published regularly to disseminate news and articles of interest to its antireligious subscribers throughout the country.

In an attempt to provide a new approach to education, the Liberal University was established, the only institution of its kind in the nation. It offered instruction on all levels, including the doctrinal teachings of rationalism. Freethinkers from every part of the United States gave it their financial support, hoping it would be the first of many similar undertakings. The school remained in existence for several years, until it became apparent that little support from residents of the Northwest was forthcoming. Only about $2,500 of the $35,000 that had been contributed came from the region, nor could enough students from the area be recruited. With considerable regret the sponsors decided to change the locale to Kansas City, where it was felt there would be wider opportunity for its development.

A pleasant relationship existed between the Freethinkers and the other inhabitants of Silverton. The former challenged conventional thought in only one sphere—organized religion. In all other respects they were as men everywhere, running the political gamut from anarchism to stalwart Republicanism, and were progressive, reactionary, or middle-of-the-roaders in their social views. When the town paper, the *Silverton Appeal,* learned that the Liberal University was to close its doors, it expressed its regret that the community was to lose the institution, stating that all had hoped to see it on a sound financial basis. "The good people of the University will be greatly missed in this city where they have made many friends during their stay in our midst. We can heartily recommend them to the people of Kansas City as honorable, courteous and progressive people who attend strictly to their own business. They will make friends in any community." And on occasions such as a Thomas Paine anniversary or a homecoming celebration for Homer Davenport, everyone would turn out to join in the festivities in the hall of the University. With the passing first of the school and later of *The Torch of Reason,* the Freethinkers as a group disintegrated and Silverton lost a distinguishing characteristic.

A completely nonconformist colony was Home, in Washington, once the only anarchist settlement in the country and at its height one of the most talked-about spots in the nation. It was started by three pilgrim fathers who, in 1895, left the small socialist community of Glennis, in Tacoma, which was being torn asunder by internal dissensions, and set out to found another Eden. They located a beautiful, isolated spot on Puget Sound where there were no roads, no human habitations for miles, and, most important, where land was cheap. In 1897 the three men and their families began to make a dent in the forest primeval by hewing down trees from which they built shelters, and the Mutual Home Colony Association was officially established.

The purpose of the colony, as announced by its founders, was simply to obtain land and to achieve "better social and moral conditions." Land was to be owned in common but could be occupied by the individual for life simply by paying the necessary taxes to the state. There was to be no interference in the private affairs of the members. "The love principle of our being is a natural one, and to deny it expression is to deny nature," was a basic plank.

Within a few months six more families joined the group and additional ones continued to come in until the community had over two hundred people. Most were sincere believers in the anarchist philosophy, but the inevitable cranks, malcontents, and Casanovas who hoped to find a congenial atmosphere in a settlement based on the love principle drifted in. The colony had three cooperative stores, a hall, a school, a printshop, and a newspaper which at various times was called *New Era, Discontent: Mother of Progress, The Demonstrator*, and *The Agitator*. An active social life included dances, masquerades, and picnics and, for intellectual stimulation, lectures given at Liberty Hall. Anyone could get up to address a group on any subject he pleased and, on occasion, outside speakers visited the colony. Emma Goldman was warmly welcomed in 1899.

Life at Home was peaceful, quiet, and industrious until the murder of President McKinley by a self-confessed anarchist. The hysteria which swept the nation finally reached far-off Washington when some people in Tacoma remembered the settlement of outlanders only about twenty miles away. An antianarchist meeting was held and a heavily armed mob of three hundred chartered a steamboat and set out to raze Home. Only the intervention of a clergyman and the owner of a steamboat, both of whom had visited the colony and knew that the people there did not carry bombs in their back pockets, prevented what might have been a disaster.

The next thing to disturb the tranquillity was an invasion by a United States marshal sent by an outraged post-office department which had discovered that *Discontent* was preaching "free love." The good people of Home, who were forewarned of his coming, sent a delegation to meet him at the pier. He was wined and dined and a dance was held in his honor. The next day the overwhelmed minion of the law returned to Tacoma with the editor and one or two others in custody to report that it had all been a mistake. A friendly judge acquitted the staff of *Discontent*, but the following year the Federal authorities barred the paper from the mails.

All this put Home into the headlines of the nation, and it rapidly became the mecca for all kinds of weird cultists and an object of sociological study for college professors and students, newspaper and magazine reporters. Everyone enjoyed living or visiting at Home. By 1910, as it seems to happen to all experimental ventures in social living, the association had been dissolved, although the cooperative store and Liberty Hall were still maintained. That year a complaint was entered against the practice of nude bathing, which had quietly been going on for years, and again the law entered. Four men and one woman were arrested for indecent exposure and hauled off to jail. In vehement protest, the editor of the paper, then called *The Agitator,* wrote:

Home is a community of free spirits, who came out into the woods to escape the polluted atmosphere of priest-ridden conventional society. One of the liberties enjoyed by Homeites was the privilege to bathe in evening dress, or with merely the clothes nature gave them, just as they chose.

No one went rubbernecking to see which suit a person wore, who sought the purifying waters of the bay. Surely it was nobody's business. All were sufficiently pure minded to see no vulgarity, no suggestion of anything vile or indecent in the thought or the sight of nature's masterpiece uncovered.

But eventually a few prudes got into the community and proceeded in the brutal, unneighborly way of the outside world to suppress the people's freedom.

Editor Fox followed his neighbors to jail on the charge of aiding and abetting disrespect of the law, having been sentenced to a two-month term. Liberal and radical groups throughout the country immediately jumped to his defense. Dances and rallies were held to raise money for an appeal to the Supreme Court. When the case was reviewed, the stuffy tribunal, alas, upheld the verdict. Fox spent six weeks in jail, was pardoned by the governor, and returned to continue editing the paper.

As the years passed, the fires of anarchy burned low at Home. The colony remained, though most of the young people left, and, while today the inhabitants still discuss Marx and Emerson and Thoreau, they are mostly occupied with farming and livestock, with bee culture and weaving. They are not much concerned with the outside world, and the world outside takes little notice of this once picturesque community on Puget Sound.

The people who came to the Northwest found a land of enormous reaches, of towering, craglike mountains and gigantic trees. Everything was on a vast scale. And the fanciful stories, the folklore, the

legends, and the tall tales that they brought with them were made
even taller, as though in keeping with their new surroundings. As
early as the fifties, newspapers entertained their readers with amazing
stories—not the pseudoscientific kind popular in the later, more sophisticated societies—but tales fabricated out of whole cloth and the
more incredible the better. There was the story, for instance, published on the front page of the *Statesman* in 1857, which began: "A
most wonderful and thrilling adventure has recently occurred in the
southern part of this county. . . ." It seems that a few weeks "since,"
a man and a boy started out in quest of some lost cattle and, being
overtaken by night, lay down to sleep. Toward midnight—the witch-
ing hour—the boy was awakened by "a loud plaintive" cry. He
jumped to his feet, without disturbing his companion, and ran but a
few yards when he saw before him—but let the narrator continue in
his own inimitable words and style:

He observed an object approaching him that appeared like a man about
twelve or fifteen feet high . . . with glaring eyes which had the appearance of liquid balls of fire. The monster drew near to the boy who was
unable from fright, to move a single step, and seizing him by the arm,
dragged him forcibly away towards the mountains, over logs, underbrush,
swamps, rivers and land with a velocity that seemed to our hero like
flying. They had traveled in this manner perhaps an hour, when the
monster sunk upon the earth apparently exhausted. Our hero then became aware that this creature was indeed a *wild man*, whose body was
completely covered with shaggy brown hair, about four inches in length;
some of his teeth protruded from his mouth like tushes, his hands were
armed with formidable claws instead of fingers, but his feet, singular to
relate, appeared natural, being clothed with moccasins similar to those
worn by Indians.

Our hero had scarcely made these observations when the "wild man"
suddenly started onward as before, never for a moment relaxing his grip
on the boy's arm. . . . They had not proceeded far before they entered
an almost impenetrable thicket of logs and undergrowth, when the "wild
man" stopped, reclined upon a log, and gave one shriek, terrific and pro-
longed, the reverberations of which seemed to continue for the space of
five minutes; immediately after which the earth opened at their feet, as if
a trap door, ingeniously contrived, had just been raised. Entering at once
this subterranean abode by a ladder rudely constructed of hazel brush,
they proceeded downward, perhaps 150 or 200 feet, when they reached
the bottom of a vast cave, which was brilliantly illumined with a peculiar
phosphorescent light, and water trickled from the sides of the cave in

minute jets. . . . Above, the cave seemed slightly arched, the ceiling apparently composed of sea shells . . . the bottom was . . . thickly strown . . . with the bones of many kinds of animals. . . .

As our hero thus closely observed the interior of this awful cave, the "wild man" left him. . . . Presently the huge monster returned by a side door, leading gently by the hand a young and delicate female of almost miraculous grace and beauty, who had doubtless been immured in this dreadful dungeon for years. . . . The young lady fell upon her knees, and in some unknown language . . . seemed to plead for the privilege of re-maining forever in the cave. . . . This singular conduct caused our hero to imagine that the "wild man" conscience stricken, had resolved to set at liberty his lovely victim, by placing her in charge of our hero, whom he had evidently captured for that purpose. As this thought passed through [his] mind his ears were greeted with the strains of the most unearthly music. . . . The "wild man" wept piteously . . . and sobbing like a child, his handkerchief moist with grief, he raised her very carefully from her recumbent posture, and led her gently away as they had come.

A moment afterwards, the damsel returned alone, and advanced toward our hero with lady-like modesty and grace, placed in his hands a beauti-fully embossed card, upon which appeared the following words, traced in the most exquisite hand evidently the lady's own, "Boy, depart hence, forthwith, or remain and be devoured." Our hero looked up, but the lady had vanished. . . . He acted at once upon the hint . . . and commenced retracing his steps towards the "ladder of hazel brush" which he shortly reached and commenced the ascent. Upon arriving at the top, his horror may be imagained when he found the aperture closed! The cold sweat stood on his brow, his frame quivered with mental agony, when . . . he bethought himself of a small barlow knife . . . with which he instantly commenced picking the earth. . . . After laboring in this manner . . . he was rejoiced to see daylight through the earth, and he was not much longer in working a hole large enough through which he was enabled to crawl.

The adventure ends with our hero wandering around for a day and a night until he met a small party of miners, prospecting on the head-waters of South Umpqua River, to whom he told his story. They lis-tened in silence, apparently not believing a word, but they were un-able to account for his presence in that desolate region and, after feed-ing him, directed him home. He related his tale to his father, who called in the neighbors and the circuit preacher. "At first they smiled, then doubted, then believed; and the whole neighborhood are now prepared to make affidavit to the principal facts. The boy is a mild, modest, moral boy . . . his parents are moral and religious people,

and it is hoped that out of respect to their feelings, the story will not
be disbelieved as a general thing, although many parts are truly wonderful."

And there were the stories dealing with the cunning of insects or
animals which went the rounds and frequently turned up in the local
press. An entertaining little tale on this order is the one about the
pioneer who crawled into bed after a hard day's work and had just
gotten comfortably settled when "I kinder felt sumthin' tryin' to pull
off my shirt and diggin' their feet into the small of my back to get a
holt. Wiggled and twisted and doubled and puckered—all no use;
kept agoin' it like all sin." Certain that sleep under those conditions
was hopeless, the weary man got up and struck a light. To his intense
disgust he found himself covered with bedbugs which, having stormed
the fortress of his nightshirt, now besieged his body. Whereupon the
dismayed bedroom captive shook them off, cleared a place on the
floor, wrapped himself up in his blanket and prepared to go to sleep.
"No use; mounted right on me like a passel of rats on a mealtub, dug a
hole through the kiverlid and crawled through and give me fits for
tryin' to hide." Determined to see this thing through, the victim got
up again, obtained the slush bucket from his wagon, made a circle of
tar on the floor, and lay down inside. He left the light on and watched.
"See 'em get together and have a camp-meetin' 'bout it, and then they
went off in a squad, with an old gray headed he one at the top, right
up the wall out on the ceiling till they got to the right spot, then
dropped right plum into my face; fact, by thunder!" Still undaunted,
our hero swept them up again and made a circle of tar on the ceiling. That, he thought, surely would get them. But, lo and behold, if
those infernally ingenious bedbugs didn't pull straw out of the bed
and build a regular bridge over the tar! Noting that the listener by
that time was looking more and more incredulous, he ended: "It's so
whether you believe it or not, and some of 'em walked across on stilts.
Bedbugs are curus critters and no mistake, 'specially the Oregon
kind."

Told to this day by men who ride the Union Pacific across the
Idaho country is the story about Old Man Hubbard, an Idaho sheepman, and his dog. A short time after the Oregon Short Line Railway
was completed, Hubbard went to Omaha to sell some sheep, and after
he had spent all his money but $5, he decided to buy a dog and ride
the blinds back home. By mistake he landed on the observation section
of the train, where he was soon accosted by the conductor, who sput-

tered angrily that he hated dogs and to get that damned pooch off the train pronto. Reluctantly, the master complied. He tied one end of a long rope around the animal's neck and the other to the back of the train. The dog seemed not the least bit disconcerted and loped merrily and effortlessly alongside the car. Annoyed at the ease with which he kept up with the train, the conductor had it speeded up. At eighty miles an hour, the dog trotted gaily along, hardly panting, sometimes on three legs, sometimes on two.

Almost apoplectic with rage and frustration, the conductor yelled for more steam. At a hundred miles an hour, the dog still trotted along serenely. Determined to get the dog or bust, the conductor had the train speeded up another fifty miles. Though the telegraph poles looked like teeth in a fine comb as the train flew by and the dog had to use four legs, he still followed unperturbed, with the rope sagging loosely between him and the car. And then, suddenly, the dog vanished. Triumphantly, the conductor turned to Hubbard, but before he could say anything, the train ground to a sudden stop, the box cars piling atop each other. Dashing ahead, the two men saw the dog standing in front of the engine with a red flag between his teeth. He had broken the rope, seized the flag from the cowcatcher, and run ahead to warn the engineer of a washout!

Simple stories of this nature were popular on the Northwestern frontier, as they had been on preceding ones. The tall tale, the impossible or romantic adventure were only one small part of the rich storehouse of American folklore. A particular brand was developed on the frontier, originated by the fur trappers, influenced by the Indian legends, brought by the various national groups. American folklore, in contrast with the folklore of other countries, has few outstanding picaresque heroes, though many tales about the picaresque. On the whole, the people of this country preferred to endow their heroes with noble virtues. The rogue as he appears in European literature was generally too subtle and unpalatable a characterization for unsophisticated and moralistic Americans, who may have been influenced by the Calvinism of the Puritan tradition. Folk heroes were almost always kindly supermen who could perform incredible feats.

One of the most popular and colorful products of vivid imaginations was the mighty Paul Bunyan, the Master Lumberjack. His original habitat was the Maine woods, where stories about him were spun in bunkhouses steaming with mackinaws drying about the red-hot stove. Then he was passed along to the gangs moving west across the country who were laying the foundations of a civilization by blasting mines open, cutting through the mountains with the endless track which was to bind a continent, riding herd on the ranges, or tying the land together with bridges. Inevitably he reached the great woods of the Northwest.

Paul was a giant in stature, a logger extraordinary, and a leader of the woodsmen. His lifelong companion, the Big Blue Ox Babe, was equally gargantuan, "a 'normous critter—forty ax-handles and a plug o' Star terbacker between the eyes. Paul, he allus toted 'long a field glass with him so's he could see what Babe wuz a'doin' with his hind feet."

An oft-recounted story is about the time Paul was unable to supply Babe with his favorite food, hot cakes. Paul tried to deceive him with shredded wheat biscuit, but the ox was not to be fooled and so his master let him out to graze. Babe had eaten about forty or fifty acres of Douglas fir when along came a forest ranger and ordered Paul to tie him up before he ruined the lumber business.

"Paul, he sez, 'I don' aim to make no onnecessary trouble, but I ain't got nothin' to tie him with.'

" 'Thar's a big ship anchor chain,' sez the Ranger. 'That'd orter do.'

" 'Guess sh'll do,' sez Paul. 'But what'll I tie him to?'

"An' the Ranger, he sez, 'Y' kin try tyin' him to that thar rock; guess that'll ballast him.' "

Well, Paul was doubtful, but he was willing to try, so he tied Babe to the rock and went to bed. Toward morning he heard a terrible rumpus and he got up and found Babe pawing the ground and snorting fiercely. Paul tried to quiet him, but it was no good. Babe had gotten a whiff of hot cakes being cooked over in Vancouver and there was just no holding him. "He give one beller an' out come the rock. An' the hole it left filled up with water and made Lake Washington."

The next day, when Paul started to track down Babe, he found a big waterfall in the Skomackaway River where Babe had pawed up a bed when he crossed it. Paul named it Snoqualmie Falls. A little further on, Babe had dropped some of the dirt he dragged along—"an' that's Mount Li. An' the rock he was hitched to—wal, when that thar anchor chain busted, it flew off an' kept goin' a spell 'fore it settled, an' afterwards a feller named it Mount Rainier. Yeh, Paul wuz purty well satisfied with what Babe'd turned off in a day; but when he heard that that thar beller capsized six steamers offn the coast an' all hands drowned, he wuz some distressed."

One day a gang of workers going to a job found they couldn't cross Rock Creek because it was swollen with melted snow. So they sent down to Skomackaway for help to build a bridge. "Paul, he come up an' looked her over. 'Give me a day and a half,' he sez, 'an' I'll have a bridge fer you.' " The company pitched tents and prepared to spend a month. "Next day Paul, he went on up the crick a ways to whar thar wuz a nice straight red cedar seven foot thru for seventy foot 'bove ground, an' right crost the stream was a sharp-pointed rock. Wal, Paul, he just felled that thar tree onto the rock, an' she split open clean's cheese an' made a bridge fourteen foot wide; an' the hull gang got crost 'thout losin' a day."

Paul needed plenty of food to stoke his massive body. When he and his company logged on the Little Gimlet in Oregon one winter, the cookstove covered an acre of ground. Four men fastened the side of a hog on each snowshoe and skated on the griddle while the cook flipped the pancakes. The mess table was three miles long and elevators carried the cakes to the end where boys on bicycles rode back and forth on a path down the center, dropping the cakes where demanded.

So the tales went, and it is impossible in the telling to transpose their full flavor into print. With the sophistication of our civilization, they were lost for a while, and how they came to be revived is a story in itself. During the twenties, Jim Stevens of the West Coast Lumbermen's Association heard about Paul Bunyan from a lumberyard superintendent in Washington who had heard the tales from a Minnesota lumberman who had come across them in Canada in the 1840's. At about the same time a roving reporter of the *Detroit Times* was visiting Seattle and wrote a front-page feature story, "Paul Bunyan, the Epic Lumberjack," for the *Seattle Star*. He asked for contributions from readers of any stories they had heard. A year later the *Oregonian* ran a series on Bunyan for almost two months.

Paul Bunyan had become literature, but as a subject of spontaneous talk he no longer exists. Stevens commented that "In the woods Paul Bunyan is dead. . . . The old tales mean nothing to the loggers of today. Some of them appreciate the books and pictures . . . But all would gag at any suggestion that my stories are ever told in camp by actual loggers."

That folklore has been placed between the covers of books, that folk tales have become collectors' items instead of the spontaneous expression of those with perhaps uncultivated minds but rich imagina-

tions is an indication that our society has aged. On the path to sophistication has been lost a certain wholesome naïveté, a trusting youth-
fulness that would permit the un-selfconscious enjoyment of Paul
Bunyan and his kind should they be met outside of print. And those
who are unworldly hide the fact with care, lest they be thought simple
or credulous.

The pioneers had none of these inhibitions because the need for
them did not exist in their unsophisticated society. They were the
youth of the nation—exuberant, eager, trustful—for whom there were
no obstacles that could not be overcome. They set out to turn into
reality the stuff their dreams were made of—some, a new type of
society that existed thus far only in imagination's blueprints; or a
better home and a richer life in a new land. These dreams, these aspirations brought them to America's farthest reaches.

Ten

Medicine Men and Men of Medicine

Many of the settlers had migrated to escape the ailments that were endemic to their areas. But illness occurs everywhere, and in their new home they were faced with a special problem—the unprincipled, illegitimate doctors. An Eastern medical journal in the sixties commented on the state of medical progress in Oregon by quoting a letter it had received from a subscriber who lived there: "In some respects this is a good country to practise medicine in. The prices are almost double those charged East, payable in coin, but no attention is paid to medical ethics; each does what he considers right in his own eyes." The writer greatly understated the case.

The lame, the blind, the sick of the Northwest were besieged by a plague of locusts in the shape of men who promised them miraculous cures. With each wagon train from the East or stagecoach from the South, these purveyors of worthless nostrums poured in. The urban East had many such charlatans, but they were beginning to feel the pinch in some areas where attempts were being made to set up standards and in general regulate the practice of medicine. The West was wide-open territory, with no examinations to pass, no state licenses to obtain, and therefore it was virtually impossible to distinguish the quack from the bona fide doctor. Many a shrewd town cobbler or village peddler suddenly blossomed forth as a "physician" when he arrived in the Oregon country.

Reputable medical practitioners believed that part of the reason why Oregon and Washington suffered from a deluge of quacks was that a California law required a state examination for physicians, which drove many of them north. They constantly agitated for a similar law, believing that was the only effective method of keeping out "druggists, clerks, quacks and pretenders who set themselves up as physicians." It was many years, though, before such a law was enacted, and, in the meantime, not only did the public waste money on useless remedies, but frequently the result was permanent injury and even death because serious ailments were not properly treated.

The quacks wandered from town to town, staying just long enough to accumulate profits and leaving when personal safety or dwindling returns made that advisable. Or they would operate from a distant base, concentrating exclusively on advertising in the newspapers—a rewarding medium, for the papers circulated widely, reaching the remotest hamlet and farm. The reader of the *Lewiston Tribune*, the *Pioneer and Democrat*, the *Washington Standard*, the *Morning Oregonian*, the *Astoria Gazette*, or any other local paper would find a prominent advertisement, profusely worded in small type, offering a "certain" cure for cancer, diphtheria, gonorrhea, syphilis, and dozens of other ailments to which the flesh is heir.

The advertisements were frequently written in flowery language; one "doctor" even prefaced his with a quotation from "Shaks.," adding a few pertinent words of his own:

> I can administer to a mind (and body) diseased
> And with a sweet oblivious antidote
> Cleanse the foul system of its perilous stuff.

He urged his readers to "Read my THEORY of LIFE AND DEATH," which, in essence, was that people suffer not from the disease itself but from an "inability in nature . . . to maintain life through the ravages of disease." His Sanguiferous Nervine Tonic was guaranteed to act on the "blood, heart, brain, intestines, sinews, nerves, the fluids and semi-fluids and the whole physique and BENEFITS ALIKE the gloomy hypochondriac, the dyspeptic, the nervous, debilitated and feeble, the over-doctored invalid, the bilious and liver-diseased sufferer, the gourmand, the debauchee, the intemperate, and all who suffer ill health!" And if the reader had not yet been convinced, he issued a dire warning: "OH HORRIBLE! OH HORRIBLE! MOST HORRIBLE!!! When worn-out nature succumbs to DEATH, because she has not strength to resist. Now, Dr. Jacob Webber's Invigorating Cordial causes strength—that is its main quality. . . ." Lest the reader who suffered from any of the numerous ailments listed should want to consult a physician, Dr. Webber stated: "Doctors may tell you that you have such and such a disease, but until medical practice becomes a science (and it is not yet), disease cannot be described to a certainty. This singular medicine gradually strengthens the system, enters the blood, which from sluggishness is rapid, courses through the veins and heart." In addition to all these things, "one of the beautiful properties possessed by DR. WEBBER'S INVIGORATING CORDIAL is that it removes all longing or taste for liquor." Truly, it was all things to all men. The advertisement ended, as almost all of them did, with a testimonial.

If the sufferer exhibited none of the symptoms described by Dr. Webber, perhaps he had some other ailment, and he did not even have to turn the page to find a description of a preparation to help *him*. Dr. William Hall's Balsam was advertised to cure "all diseases of the lungs and throat. For the cure of consumption, decline, asthma, bronchitis, wasting of flesh, night sweats, spitting of blood, whooping cough, difficulty of breathing, colds, coughs, influenza, phthisic pain in the side . . . is safe for use among children, yet pewerful [*sic*] in cases of chronic pulmonary disease."

And if he felt that neither of these remedies was inclusive enough, he might try "THE PEOPLE'S FRIEND—PERRY DAVIS' VEGETABLE PAIN KILLER—*The Greatest Family Medicine of the Age!*" This was a double-barreled product:

Taken internally, it cures sudden colds, coughs, etc., weak stomach, general debility, nursery sore mouth, canker, liver complaint, dyspepsia, or indigestion, cramp and pain in the stomach, bowel complaint, painters' colic, Asiatic cholera, diarrhoea and dysentery. Applied externally, Cures felons, boils and old sores, severe burns and scalds, cuts, bruises, and sprains, swelled joints, ringworm and tetter, broken breasts, frosted feet and chilblains, toothache, pain in the face, neuralgia and rheumatism.

It was also "a sure remedy for Agur [*sic*] and Chills and Fever." Could one ask for more in a medicine?

Some of the advertisements sound so ludicrous today that we wonder how they could have been taken seriously. There was, for instance, the one which began: "Have you a hurt child or a lame horse? Use the Mexican Mustang Liniment." It was good for "cuts, sprains, burns, swellings and caked breasts . . . rheumatism, neuralgia, stiff joints, stings and bites . . . for spavined horses, the poll evil, ringbone and sweeney . . . for wind galls, scratches, big-head and splint." Mr. S. Litch, of Hyde Park, Vermont, according to the advertisement, wrote the following testimonial: "My horse was considered worthless, (spavin,) but since the use of the Mustang Liniment I have sold him for $150. Your Liniment is doing wonders up here."

Though the papers printed these advertisements, they would sometimes poke fun at the "cure-all" properties, as in the item which bore the caption "A Rich Puff":

A manufacturer and vendor of quack medicines, recently wrote to a friend living out west for "a good strong recommendation" of his, the manufacturer's, "Balsam." In a few days he received the following, which we call pretty "strong":

"Dear Sir:—The land composing my farm has hitherto been so poor that a Scotchman could not get his living off it; and so stoney that we had to slice our potatoes and plant them edgeways, but hearing of your balsam, I put some on the corner of a ten acres lot surrounded by a rail fence, and in the morning I found the rock had entirely disappeared, a neat stone wall encircled the field, and the rails were split into oven wood and piled up symmetrically in my back yard.

"I put half an ounce into the middle of a buckle bury swamp—in two days it was cleaned off, planted with corn and pumpkins and a row of peach trees in full blossom through the middle.

"As an evidence of its tremendous strength I would say that it drew a striking likeness of my eldest daughter, drew my eldest son out of a mill-pond, drew a blister all over his stomach; drew a load of potatoes 4 miles to market, and eventually drew a prize of ninety-seven dollars in the lottery."

It is not surprising, though, that the public was gullible enough to swallow the claims of the charlatans, considering the state of medical knowledge at the time, and when articles such as the following were published in the papers:

remedy for cancer.—Col. Ussery of the parish of De Soto, informs the editor of the Caddo Gazette that he fully tested a remedy for this troublesome disease, recommended to him by a Spanish woman, a native of the country. Take an egg and break it, pour out the white, retain the yoke in the shell, put in salt and mix with the yolk as long as it will receive it, stir them together until the salve is formed; put a portion of this on a piece of sticking plaster, and apply it to the cancer about twice a day. He has tried the remedy twice in his own family with complete success.

The same paper also published another remedy:

A man named Edgar Fluker has a new recipe for the cure of those painful excrescences, cancers. The remedy is cheap, and easy of obtaining and applying and cannot possibly do any harm. It is simply to hold a toad or frog, either dead or alive to the afflicted part for the space of one hour, repeating the application as occasion requires. With six frogs Mr. Fluker says he cured a very painful cancer upon his nose, of six years standing, and now considers himself well and sound.

One of the most prominent and consistent advertisers was a "Dr." L. C. Czapkay of San Francisco, whose copy frequently occupied a third of a page. His specialty, as that of a good many others of his ilk, was venereal disease. The doctor was modest. He could not promise a permanent cure in the secondary stages; he would guarantee success only if the disease were in the primary phase. His method, he said, "combines all the latest improvements by the Medical Faculty, with discoveries made by himself, more effective than anything yet known, which secures the patient from the possibility of secondary symptoms, and removes the disease in the shortest possible time." He was so confident that "for a cure of all these forms of disease the Doctor guarantees a cure or asks no compensation."

Another San Francisco "specialist" warned: "Beware of the San Francisco quacks and pretendrus [*sic*] who, with bogus sworn-to certificates, dupe the unwary. Some of the self-styled doctors whose pames [*sic*] are to be found in the daily and weekly newspapers of San Francisco are tradesmen, and besame [*sic*] too lazy to work at their trades." According to Dr. Gibbon, he had just returned after a year's stay abroad spent in visiting all the principal hospitals of Europe, and he had spared neither time nor money in seeking out new remedies for the alleviation of human suffering. He claimed to have made a special study of social diseases and promised a cure for any case, no matter how far gone, without using mercury or any injurious drugs. He also cured "seminal emissions, the consequence of self-abuse," which, he warned, "is practiced by the youth of both sexes . . . producing, with unering [*sic*] certainty, the following train of morbid symtoms [*sic*], unless combatted by scientific medical measures, viz: Sallow countenance, dark spots under the eyes, pain in the head, ringing in the ears, noise like the rustling of leaves and rattling of chariots, uneasiness about the loins, weakness of the limbs, confused vision, blunted intellect, loss of confidence . . . a disposition to shun society, loss of memory, hectic flushes, pimples . . . furred tongue, fetid breath, coughs, consumption, night sweats, monomania and frequent insanity." He offered a written guarantee that there would be no charge if he did not effect a cure. It was not even necessary to see the doctor. Medication would be sent promptly on request to any part of the country, and assurance was given that it would arrive "free from damage and curiosity." In addition to all this, the reader was offered "The newly invented Patent French Safe, a sure Preventative against Diseases and Pregnancy, sent by mail. Price $2.00."

On the lighter side, and characteristic of modern advertising, were such products as hair restorers. One company anticipated, by about eighty years, our radio commercials in an advertisement written in verse to urge the purchase of its product:

> Tell me not in mournful numbers
>   Life is sinking to decay,
> Should there come in frightful numbers
>   O'er your heads the silver gray.
>
> Life is real, life is earnest,
>   Why should any one despair,
> "Dust thou art, to dust returnest,"
>   Was not spoken of the hair.
>
> .   .   .   .
>
> In the world's sublimer calling,
>   Where we each our race must run,
> If your hair be falling, falling,
>   Use the "Martha Washington."
>
> Trust no other, howe'er pleasant,—
>   None can do what this has done;
> Try it—always keep it present,—
>   Use the "Martha Washington."

Occasionally a local newspaper or magazine urged its readers not to be duped by the misleading copy to which they were constantly being subjected. One publication warned repeatedly that the Pacific Northwest was flooded with fake doctors to an even greater extent than other regions, that an ethical doctor did not have to roam from town to town, and that those who did lacked professional ability. It cautioned readers not to be deceived "when some fellow takes up a large amount of newspaper space in telling you what a skillful doctor he is, that he can tell all about the patient's disease by simply looking at him and that he is just from Berlin, Paris, or Dublin, and comes here to Oregon or Washington out of pure love for mankind and to alleviate human suffering." But a later issue of this same publication carried an ad by a Dr. T. A. Slocum of New York, who offered "a positive remedy for consumption" which had cured thousands of cases in advanced stages of the disease. He was so confident of the efficacy of his product that he was willing to send two bottles free, together with a booklet dealing with the malady.

Although some newspapers and periodicals objected to the nature of the quack advertisements, they were too lucrative a source of revenue for ethical scruples to stand in the way. Even in the twentieth century, advertisements in virtually the same vein filled their pages. Many columns of the *Oregonian,* most dignified of all Northwest papers, were taken up with copy promising fantastic cures. In one issue a Dr. Kessler used a half-page for his advertisement, which was headed, in 24-point, bold type, "HOPE FOR THE AFFLICTED." The copy contained an illustration of a building which bore the legend "St. Louis Medical Dispensary." One side of the page was addressed to MEN and the other to WOMEN, and Dr. Kessler informed both sexes that "Every trouble that is curable I will cure." In one corner was a newspaper extract, purportedly an account of an interview with the doctor:

The following clipping is published for the purpose of showing the public the esteem with which Dr. Kessler is held by the press and the public throughout the entire Northwest: "Dr. Kessler has just returned from an extended tour throughout the United States, and during his absence the Doctor has visited most of the large hospitals and world-renowned specialists in search of any information that might be of value in the practise of his profession. Dr. Kessler is a physician from choice, nature having intended him for no other calling. . . . Dr. Kessler has made a number of original discoveries that stamp him as one of the foremost medical men of the present century. He possesses the faculty of almost reading a patient's feelings, and is invariably correct in his diagnosis of the most complicated cases. It is remarkable the number of seemingly hopeless invalids that are treated and cured by this scientific physician. . . . The Doctor . . . talked entertainingly and modestly of his many discoveries."

The modest doctor urged the reader not to become discouraged "when other doctors fail. Your physician may be a well-meaning man, who did all that he could to help you, but he probably lacks the thorough knowledge of your case that constant practice and constant research imparts." He also claimed to be "full of the milk of human kindness, and is never so happy as when he is doing good to his fellow man." To "weak men" he promised, "I will restore you to your full vigor or forfeit $1000. . . . I have seen middle-aged and elderly men cry with delight when they felt assured that my treatment was restoring them once more to a vigorous manhood." To women he offered a cure for any internal disorders "without the use of the knife."

There were also the quacks who toured the region lecturing on medical subjects. A Dr. N. Hudson, "A.M.," who stated that he was formerly of New York City and lately of San Francisco, advertised in a Washington newspaper that he was going to deliver a series of lectures every night for an entire week on "Anatomy, Physiology, and Pathology as the Foundation of the True Principles of Hygiene and Diet for the Sick and Well!! Embracing an Analysis of the Temperaments, as Founded on the Natural Constitution of Man." Each lecture "will be followed by an examination of certain persons selected by the audience, in illustration and proof of the Physiological, Pathological, Hygienic, Dietetic and Temperamental doctrines advanced in the Lectures." Single admission was fifty cents, $2 dollars for the course, and tickets could be obtained at the post office or the local drugstore.

Unfortunately for the genuine medical practitioners, nothing could be done about these charlatans in their midst as long as professional standards were not enforced by statute. Organizations like the Medical Society of the State of Oregon deplored the situation, but their pleas for effective controls went unheeded, for the locusts were too numerous and the feeding grounds too rich for them to be dislodged without a struggle. At a meeting of the organization, the president bewailed in verse the plight of bona fide practitioners:

> But quacks there are of many sorts and kinds,
> As dupes we see of many grades and minds.
> One class ignore the rostrum, but presume
> To claim all honors. Titles they assume
> More noble than those conferred by prince,
> Or king, in palmy days of yore, or since.
> They fill with false certificates of cure
> The press; and oft from men of sense secure
> Endorsement. How and why, I must confess
> Are problems solved by nothing I can guess.
>
> Thus fortified, from place to place they rush,
> False hopes inspire, which time, alas! must crush;
> Then, like the "Kansas hoppers," disappear,
> When all things *green* are nipp'd, both far and near.

If laws protective shall not e'er be found,
To cunning wiles and tricks of quack confound;
Then plain our duty. Shall we hesitate,
The public mind at large to educate
Upon deceptions, which concern us all,
When sick; the young and old, both great and small?
If such a course alone to us remains,
Humanity at stake! Let's spare no pains.

Medical societies in the state and its sister Territories actively pursued their programs for the improvement of health and medical standards through committees dealing with the practice of medicine, surgery, obstetrics, the treatment of endemic and epidemic diseases, public hygiene and state medicine, and the treatment of mental diseases; but not until the state directed its legal artillery against the quacks were they driven from the scene. That came about when the medical profession became strong enough to compel the adoption of measures which it deemed vital to its own welfare. Meanwhile, the pioneer physician did as well as he could in competition with the quacks.

Legitimate doctors were to be found in the Pacific Northwest even before any American settlers had come to the country. Discounting the brief stay of Dr. Swan at Fort George and the transient ship surgeons and other medicos who visited the fort, the regular practice of medicine dates back to 1833. In that year, Drs. Tolmie and Gairdner came to Fort Vancouver, at the request of John McLoughlin, to take up posts as resident practitioners. There they found a number of Indians and fur trappers in dire need of their attention. They got to work as soon as they unpacked their medical bags, though they themselves were at the point of exhaustion after their protracted eight-months' journey, the last stage of which had been made by canoe. The medical headquarters consisted of one room, the same one in which they lived. At the first opportunity Dr. Tolmie took inventory of the laboratory equipment placed at his disposal. "There is," he remarked, "an excellent supply of surgical instruments for amputation, 2 trephining, 2 eye instruments, a lithotomy, a capping case, besides two midwifery forceps and a multitude of catheters, sounds, bandages, probings, 2 forceps, etc. not put in order."

Dr. Tolmie played an important part in the development of the Northwest, where he remained until his death in 1886. He taught Christianity to the Indians, went on expeditions to establish trading posts, discovered coal on Vancouver Island, took a prominent part in the Indian War in the Puget Sound region, and continued his medical practice even after being appointed chief factor of the Hudson's Bay Fort at Nisqually. When he moved to Victoria, he gave up the practice of medicine, but many of his former patients from Washington Territory came to visit him whenever they required treatment. A man of considerable culture, he established a circulating library in one of the company's posts which was continued for about a decade. After he retired from the service of the company in 1870, Dr. Tolmie made a trip to Oregon and brought back shorthorn cattle which laid the foundation for the livestock industry of British Columbia.

Dr. Forbes Barclay was appointed surgeon to the Hudson's Bay Company and was sent to the Columbia in 1840 to relieve Tolmie. He remained in charge of medical activities at Vancouver for ten years, then left for Oregon City, and, shortly after, became an American citizen. For the next twenty-three years, until his death, Dr. Barclay engaged in active medical practice. He received calls from patients which took him miles away from his home, over almost impassable roads and to places which could be reached only by canoe. On many occasions he had to use Indian guides to lead him through the wilderness of heavy brush and wooded forests. Dr. Barclay was one of the few well educated physicians in early Oregon and, in addition to his medical practice, he took an active part in the community life. He was the city superintendent of schools for a number of years and also the mayor of Oregon City. When he died, the community mourned the loss of one of its outstanding citizens as well as the "kind, skillful and devoted physician in our midst."

The first nonmissionary doctor who came directly to the American settlement was Ralph Wilcox, a practicing physician from Missouri. He arrived in the region in 1845 and, two years later, settled in Portland, which at the time had only seven houses in the entire town. The population was too small to sustain a medical practice and so, after a very brief and unprofitable interlude, he opened a school and became the city's first teacher. Within the next few years he was a farmer, a judge in Tualatin County, in charge of the government's land office at Oregon City, and an official in the United States customs office at Portland.

Wilcox served as a doctor for only a short period, and his chief claim to distinction as a member of the medical profession in the Northwest is that he was its first American member. A number of pioneer physicians who arrived during the first years of settlement continued in practice. Among these, the following were outstanding: R. B. Wilson, Rodney Glisan, J. H. Wythe, Horace Carpenter, and Henry A. Smith. They were the practitioners who laid the foundation for a sound medical practice.

All the legitimate doctors hoped to devote full time to their professional work, but there were simply not enough people in the early period to require their services, and many turned to other fields of endeavor to supplement their incomes. In those days a doctor could perform any type of labor and still command the respect of his patients and the community. Whether or not Dr. W. F. Allen, who came to Oregon City in 1850, was a regular physician, he was certainly enterprising and ambitious. When he found that the cost of living was too high for his means—rent for a single room from $25 to $75 a month, flour $15 a barrel, sugar $0.25 to $0.30 a pound—he quickly decided to do something about it:

> The 150 [dollars] was nearly out. . . . In a week or two I got a call to see a sick woman went to see her twice about 100 yards charged them twenty five dollars it was several days before she was able to work I Hired my Black Girl to them for several days at $3 pr day making at the end of the week 46 dollars all paid over with a very cheap bill Dr you must charge more than that or you cant live in this country in a week or ten days after I was called to see a young man who was deranged mentally about thirty miles I took him home and soon cured him for which I charged $100 this Helped considerably in the mean time Rose was washing for persons at $3 pr day and some days she washed at home by the doz pieces at $3 pr doz making from 6 to 12 dollars pr day My wife got some sewing at which she made from $1.50 to 2.50 pr day.

When the Christmas holidays arrived, a ball was planned in town, but no musicians were available. Dr. Allen, who could play the violin, offered his services and was promptly hired for the occasion. He received a fee of $50. "Towards the close of the ball," he wrote, "I concluded I would shake my leg once after which the young ones insisted that I would give them a few lessons in dancing so in a few nights I commenced a course of lessons, thirteen lessons in six weeks for which I charged Two Hundred dollars."

The doctor quickly became a very popular man whose services were continually sought for dances and parties, and in between there were the usual number of patients to attend: "Two small parties at which I charged $25 each cured one man and his wife of gonorrhea or clap for which I charged $5." As though all that were not enough, he was lending money at interest, speculating in cattle, considering the purchase of an interest in a steamboat business on condition that he be given the position of clerk, and he was also preparing to go to the mines.

Dr. Allen was doubtless a unique personality and given to exaggeration, but the frontier doctor was often a man of diversified talents. He had no conventional pattern to follow and had to improvise as he went along. Thrown completely upon his own resources, it was left to him to blaze a medical trail.

David Swinson Maynard, the first medical practitioner in the Puget Sound area, was such a trail blazer. The story goes that he was responsible for naming the city of Seattle after the Indian chief with whom he had a warm friendship. He was the first in more fields of endeavor than any of his contemporaries in the region. In addition to being Seattle's first physician, he was its first merchant, first fisherman, first blacksmith, first real-estate dealer, first justice of the peace, first notary public, first port commissioner, first Indian agent, first man to be admitted to the practice of law, and the first to open a hospital.

The doctor was an individual who would have made his mark in any society and, as a matter of fact, had achieved a measure of success before coming to the Oregon country. Maynard was a native of Vermont and he began his medical practice after he received a diploma from the Academy of Medicine of that state, granted for serving an apprenticeship in the office of the town's leading physician. Temperamentally restless, he moved with his bride to Ohio, where, in a short time, he founded a medical college and became involved in several business deals. The enterprise was profitable until he became liable for a friend to the extent of about $30,000. Maynard was now almost penniless, but what made him even more unhappy was the constant nagging of a disgruntled wife. At the age of forty-two, he decided to try his fortune in the gold fields of California.

Leaving his family behind after making whatever provision he could for them, he joined a wagon train. On the way he became enamored of a widow whose destination was Olympia. Love proved more powerful than the lure of gold and he decided to follow her. When he arrived in the Northwest, Maynard felt that the newly organized city, later to be called Seattle, possessed great possibilities and decided to make his home there. His close friendship with Chief

Seattle was largely responsible for saving the city during the great Indian attacks in the winter of 1855–1856.

Maynard ministered to the whites and Indians alike, and frequently his calls took him away for days to far-off places accessible only by canoe. During the years when the city on Puget Sound was a frontier outpost, his name was a household word. He was a little too fond of the bottle, but so kindly, helpful, and generous that even the advocates of temperance ignored his failing. On one occasion he set the city by the ears when his first wife, whom he had divorced, came to Seattle at his persuasion to help him settle a land claim, and he walked down the street "with a wife on each arm." As a token of his services to the community, a street in Seattle today bears his name.

The Northwest had pioneer physicians of all kinds, but Mrs. Bethenia Owens-Adair was unique even among them—she was the first woman in the Pacific Northwest to have graduated from a medical school. This was no mean achievement in those years, for whether in the urban East or the pioneer West, a woman physician was a rare phenomenon and one to which the community did not take too kindly.

Bethenia Owens began her career of rebellion against the mores of society by divorcing her husband after four years of marriage. Like many girls at the time, she had been a bride at fourteen, but unlike most she did not hesitate to sever the relationship when she found it intolerable, despite the fact that she was left completely on her own with a two-year-old son. More than anything else, the young woman wanted an education and, as she was too proud to accept financial help, she resorted to the only means she had of earning a living—washing other people's laundry. As she put it, "the only occupations open to a respectable woman were sewing, nursing, teaching or taking in washing. I had no education and most of the women were too poor to have their sewing done so I took in washing." She spent every moment away from the tubs at her studies, and after a year's hard work she got a position as a schoolteacher. Her salary was $11 a month. That year she worked even harder. "I got up at four each morning and milked the cows where I was staying and after school I did washing. Next year I went to Astoria to school. I took care of my boy, took in washing and by working till midnight I was able to keep up with my classes."

Her next venture was to open a millinery store, but, feeling that she lacked sufficient skill in the craft, she saved some money, went to San

Francisco, and apprenticed herself to one of the leading milliners there. After her return to the Northwest she was soon earning $1,500 a year, a substantial sum in those days, but she was still dissatisfied with her life. When her son was of age, she sent him to college and decided to go back to school herself to study medicine. "When I announced I was going to become a doctor it broke the heart of all my friends. They felt I had disgraced myself so they refused to recognize me when we met. I was a pariah and an outcast. Men pointed me out, jeered at me and made insulting remarks." The young woman went to medical school nevertheless. She studied at the Philadelphia Medical College, the University of Michigan Medical School, did hospital and clinical work at Chicago, returned to Ann Arbor as a resident physician and took post-graduate work, went abroad and studied in the hospitals of Berlin, Munich, Paris, London, and Edinburgh.

When Bethenia first returned to Oregon after her stay in Philadelphia, she found living very difficult. It was only because she had several sturdy brothers in town that she was spared even more overt expressions of disapproval than were flung at her. On one occasion an autopsy was to be performed on the body of a man, and, as a "lark," one of the doctors invited the young woman to do the work, never expecting, of course, that she would come. When she did appear at the shed where several physicians were gathered to witness the operation, they were aghast at her brazenness and embarrassed for themselves, because, as it happened, it was to be a dissection of the genital organs. Several objected to her staying even if she did not perform the autopsy, but she insisted and executed the job very creditably. Word of this unprecedented behavior quickly spread, and once again her brothers had to protect her from the opprobrium of the community.

Bethenia Owens-Adair must have been an unusual woman in many respects. For a number of years she kept up a correspondence with the venerable pioneer Jesse Applegate. She had known him from childhood and, though he was about twenty years her senior, there was a great mutual admiration and on his part an even deeper feeling. His encouragement was probably partially responsible for her determination to pursue a medical career. She had written for his advice and Applegate replied:

It seems to me the oracle you consult is a frail one indeed. But as I do love you dear as the "bone of my bone and flesh of my flesh" my great partiality for you may lead me to hope more from your remarkable intellect than you will realize. . . . You are right in deciding that your mind was not given to be frittered away in frivolity—I was right in deciding that marriage and motherhood was not intended for you by the Creator, he designed you for a higher destiny,—and you *will* attain it. Let your motto be "Excelcior" [*sic*] avoid love, marriage and all other entanglements, and relaxations until you have attained the high distinction you aspire to. Fame and fortune will then await you, and there will still be time to indulge in the tenderness of your heart and the warmth of your affections.

She also apparently took his advice to avoid marriage and other entanglements, for it was not until she was well into her middle years and an established physician that she married again. While an unattached young woman, her occasional meetings with Applegate apparently were responsible for some gossip in the community and also insinuations by a rejected suitor, for Applegate wrote her: "It seems I cannot even visit you without subjecting you to foul ditraction [*sic*] and suspicion! Under these circumstances my duty is plain. . . . If I visit you no more, do not think I love you less. Or if I cease to correspond with you do not suppose my interest in your prosperity and happiness has abated."

Bethenia Owens-Adair fulfilled Jesse Applegate's high hopes for her. She succeeded in winning over the community and built up an excellent practice. She became one of the outstanding women in the Northwest and her services were so much in demand that she found it difficult to keep up with all her calls. Many who had originally sneered at her later tried to obtain her professional help. Even after her second marriage, to a wealthy man, she continued her practice. She also participated actively in the suffrage and prohibition movements in the Northwest and claimed to have spent $5,000 of her own money on the latter. Despite an extremely rigorous life, she lived until well past eighty, keeping up with many of her activities until the very end.

To be a doctor on the frontier meant hard work; it meant not only the sleepless nights which are the lot of most physicians, but riding a horse at top speed in all kinds of weather over crude trails and swollen streams, through thicket, briar, and bush. Even after the railroad lines joined some of the cities together, many doctors in the Northwest still had to contend with frontier conditions. Dwellings were scattered, and many of the doctors had to serve the inhabitants within a radius of a hundred miles of their homes.

Often a trip into the "country" necessitated an extended stay until the patient began to recover, as the distance from the doctor's residence was too great and the roads too poor to make return visits feasible. The physician, therefore, prepared for all eventualities and carried his hospital with him. One reported that when he made distant calls he took along a medicine case "which contained fifty-four different drugs of an assortment sufficient for any case of sickness. An obstetrical bag was stocked with everything required in a confinement case. A large canvas . . . was filled with plaster bandages, splints, gauze bandages, and everything needed in a fracture case. Another bag held an amputating outfit and all instruments needed for an operation of any kind. In addition to these I equipped an emergency bag with anaesthetics, antiseptics, soap, sterile towels and dressing; a series of enameled basins of graduated sizes that fitted one into the other; and everything needed in an emergency not provided for in the other bags."

Races with the stork occurred frequently. One pioneer mother recalling those days relates: "It was midwinter. . . . We were living on a ranch six miles from Lakeview and were expecting our second child. We kept the horses harnessed so that my husband could go for the doctor at need. There were no telephones in the county as yet. At midnight that January I woke my husband and sent him for Dr. Daly. He drove away in frantic haste while I waited alone in pain and anxiety in that remote ranch house." Fortunately, the doctor was at home. He heard the pounding of the horses' hoofs and the clatter of the buggy, and before the husband began to bang on the door he was already out of bed and dressed in some makeshift garments, ready to start.

Professional training of medical doctors during the pioneer period ranged from reading a few medical books and a brief apprenticeship to graduation from an Eastern school; and the school often required only serving an apprenticeship with a physician for a few years, several courses of lectures combined with the ability to dissect a body, and demonstrations in physiology, chemistry, and other related medical subjects.

This situation was prevalent throughout the country. The standards at Harvard's Medical School were representative of most medical colleges. In 1869, when Charles William Eliot assumed the presidency of the university, he found the medical students undisciplined and illiterate—many had not had even a good high-school education

Medical training was such in name only. Candidates for the doctor's degree bought tickets to the lecture courses as they might to a concert series and attended or not as they pleased though, theoretically, they were supposed to sit in on five or six a day. The so-called examination at the end of a three-year period consisted of oral quizzes given by nine professors, each of whom was allotted ten minutes. If the student passed five of these, and presented a certificate from any regular practitioner stating that he had studied with him for three years, he was awarded his diploma and could begin practicing medicine the following day. Appalled by this state of affairs, Dr. Eliot promptly proposed a number of drastic reforms, one of which was that students must pass written examinations at the end of each year. His whole program was bitterly opposed by the older members of the faculty, and on this particular feature the objection was raised that "students should not be expected to pass written examinations, since half of them could hardly write." Eliot finally won out and his system was adopted in 1871, but not for another six years were entrance examinations required.

The Johns Hopkins Medical School, which was established in 1893, pioneered in requiring a bachelor's degree for admission at a time when the overwhelming majority of recognized medical schools required only a high-school diploma or at best one year of college work. The Council on Medical Education of the American Medical Association reported that as late as 1906 many so-called "medical colleges" had as their only material equipment "a blackboard and some chairs"; others "were quiz classes, where students were given just enough textbook knowledge to attend state board examinations, and where the teacher looked for his compensation in consultations sent him by his ill qualified pupils."

Placed against this national setting, it is little wonder that when the medical department of Willamette University was established in 1867, its facilities were so modest that all the institution could boast of in the way of equipment were a few cadavers, a dissecting room, several chairs, and a blackboard for the lecture room. This was the first effort to offer medical instruction in the Pacific Northwest, and, naturally, it was extremely difficult to find competent instructors. After scouring the city, two members of the faculty who were assigned the task of assembling a staff reported:

In pursuance of our trust we found the chief difficulty to arise from the circumstance that a sufficient number of physicians resident in Salem could not be found to fill the professorships, without appointing some whose educational qualifications were evidently defective. For the sake of founding the department, however, we consented to waive the objection and every regular physician in the town who had a diploma or who declared that he was a graduate of some Medical College, was appointed to a professorship.

Most of the members of the faculty were poorly equipped for their work, and only one had ever taught at a medical school before— Dr. J. H. Wythe, who had been a professor of physiology, pathology, and microscopy at the Philadelphia Medical College. Courses were short, only twenty weeks, and the requirement for graduation was simply proof of having attended two courses of lectures.

Two years after its founding, a class of ten was graduated, and six years later, the great sum of $200 was allotted by the board of trustees for the purpose of renting suitable quarters in town. As Portland had a considerably larger population than Salem, more practicing physicians, two general hospitals, and one for the insane, all of which would afford the students more opportunity for practice, the school was moved there. It was established in rooms above a livery stable, but nine years later it was moved again to a building especially constructed and equipped for an institution of that nature.

Some years after, difficulties and misunderstandings arose among the faculty of the Willamette Medical School which were serious enough to cause a number of its members to resign. These men, together with several Portland physicians, decided to organize a medical department at the University of Oregon and obtained a charter in 1887. They borrowed $1,000 from a Portland bank for a building which, when constructed, had two stories, each consisting of one room. Lectures were given on the first floor and dissections performed on the second. The Northwest could now boast of two medical schools, both of them in Portland.

In line with the rest of the country, the terms of admission at both institutions were extremely modest. To enter the Willamette school, the aspiring medical student merely had to present a diploma from a good "literary and scientific college or high school," or a first-grade teacher's certificate, and have good moral character. Or, in lieu of these, he was required to pass an examination in mathematics, English composition, elementary physics or natural philosophy. The medical department of Oregon University listed its qualifications for admission in the first announcement as "satisfactory evidence of knowledge of the common English branches, including reading, writing, spelling, grammar, geography, arithmetic, etc." As a condition for graduation, its students were required to attend two full courses of lectures, at least one course in practical anatomy and clinical instruction, study medicine for three years, and pass examinations in the various branches of the medical curriculum.

Efforts were constantly made to improve standards, and, in 1880, the Willamette Medical School, adopting the requisites of the Association of American Medical Colleges, was admitted to membership in the organization. Requirements for admission as announced in 1902 were still vague, except for the specific prohibition of students who were less than twenty-one years of age; six years later a high school education was definitely stipulated. Enrollment increased slowly but steadily, and when in 1913 it merged with the University of Oregon Medical School, 213 students had been graduated since its founding.

The medical department at the University of Oregon enjoyed the advantage of being connected with the two leading hospitals of Portland. By 1895 it showed marked progress in its standards when the school was placed on a graded basis, the term of instruction extended from three to four years, and a knowledge of physics and elementary Latin was added to the qualifications for admission. With pardonable pride but some exaggeration, the *Oregonian* wrote on the school's tenth anniversary that it "has advanced steadily in the estimation of the medical profession, as well as the general public . . . until now it stands abreast of the best schools in the United States. . . . The corps of lecturers numbers the very best material as medical educators and successful practitioners in the Northwest." The article listed a faculty of fifteen who taught the various branches of medicine and surgery, and, in addition, seven special lecturers. Three years later the institution became a member of the American Association of Medical Colleges and adopted its standards for admitting students.

New techniques in medical study were introduced through the years, but in some instances instructors were hampered by lack of equipment. As late as 1903, many departments in the medical school offered instruction in a slipshod manner, with classes irregular and students passing the time in card games while waiting for the instructor, taking the precaution of posting a sentry to warn of his approach. In 1913 the modern phase of its development began when the medical department of the University of Oregon was transformed into a full-scale medical school.

The Territorial University of Washington was supposed to include a medical department in 1855, but no instruction was given until 1914, when courses in anatomy and related subjects were introduced in connection with a premedical course that had been offered for some years. Washington had no medical schools until then.

Sporadic efforts were made throughout the region to establish medical schools, most of which were unsuccessful. At La Grande, Oregon, in 1874, the cornerstone of Blue Mountain University was laid. The school operated for a while, but the colleges of medicine, law, and theology which had been envisaged in the plans never materialized and it soon closed its doors. In 1889 a Washington Biochemic Medical College was organized in North Yakima. Three years later it moved to Spokane, assuming the name Northwestern College of Biochemistry. It proved to be a fraudulent institution, for almost immediately after the charter was obtained, the "students" were issuing diplomas to themselves, and it was soon compelled to go out of business. An attempt to get a legitimate medical school established in the city was made in 1890 when the University of Spokane Falls announced a College of Medicine. No sessions were ever held, however, and the university itself soon went out of existence.

State medical associations were established, beginning with the Oregon Medical Society in 1872. At its second meeting a committee on medical education was appointed and instructed to "prepare an annual report on the general condition of medical education in the state of Oregon as compared with the advancement of medical science in other states of the union." Its members were assigned the task of surveying the existing medical institutions of the state, inquiring into such factors as curriculum, requirements for graduation, examination procedure for the conferring of degrees, the number of students and graduates, and other pertinent matters. The organizations were, of course, concerned not only with medical education, but medical standards in general.

There is, perhaps, no better guide to the advances made by the medical profession than its publications, which serve as a medium for the dissemination and exchange of information on the latest findings by practitioners and researchers. It was symptomatic of the times that the first medical journal issued in the Northwest should have been one devoted to exposing "fallacies and impositions practiced by the 'regular profession.'" This organ, the *Oregon Physio-Medical Journal*, began publication in Salem in 1866 under the editorship of J. C. Shelton, M.D., who was a follower of so-called "botanic" medicine.

In announcing his purpose to prospective subscribers, Dr. Shelton declared: "We shall labor assiduously through its pages to lead the people away from so constant a dependence on poisonous drugs and patent medicines, to a greater reliance upon natural remedies . . . pure air, sunshine, bathing, sleep, exercise, rest and all the hygienic agencies and innocent vegetable medicines . . . for their recovery from disease when sick." This was fine as far as it went, for undoubtedly too much reliance was being placed on injurious drugs and patent medicines; but it took no account of diseases which could be treated only with drugs, and in that sense Dr. Shelton's practices could be as injurious as the others.

Although the *Physio-Medical Journal* was published in the same city in which the Willamette Medical Department was located, Dr. Shelton did not serve on its faculty at a time when every available doctor in the community had been appointed to the staff. All the articles were written by the editor, who managed to keep the magazine going for two years, after which it expired.

Shortly thereafter the medical faculty of Willamette University began publication of the *Oregon Medical and Surgical Reporter*. The journal would conform to the customary arrangements of medical publications, the editor announced, but in addition to publishing original pieces, it would also carry descriptive accounts of diseases and the most suitable treatment. Each issue contained analytical articles on some serious maladies, reports on surgical cases, reprints of articles from the better-known medical journals of the East and Europe, and editorials on a variety of professional themes.

Some of the articles indicate that isolated as the Northwest was during the pioneer period, conscientious physicians tried to, and to a great extent did, keep up with developments in medicine throughout the world. One physician wrote of his experiments with carbolic acid in cases of diphtheria and syphilis, though "the mode of action is yet a mooted point" as the acid was used mainly for external application. He also used it, he wrote, with complete success in treating a severe case of inflammation of a synovial membrane, saving the patient's arm without leaving the joint stiff. Several years earlier, Lister had first used carbolic acid and published his results in the London *Lancet* of 1867, which the Oregon physician had doubtless read.

Despite the enthusiasm of its publishers, the *Reporter* seemed unable to muster enough support from subscribers. It could not even obtain enough original articles to fill its pages. Exasperated, the editor wrote in the last number of Volume I: "The gentlemen who were selected to assist us in the writing for the *Journal* will please return their thanks for having their names published to the world, none contributed a single article, hence the above request." The publication went out of existence in 1871.

Five years later the *Oregon Medical Journal* was launched with the backing of the Marion County Medical Society. This quarterly featured excerpts of articles from other journals, as well as original contributions by local physicians, and reviews of the latest literature in the field. Apparently, however, the time was still not ripe for a medical publication as there were not enough physicians to support an indigenous one and this, too, went the way of its predecessor after the end of Volume I.

For the next seventeen years the field was vacant, until the *Medical Sentinel* (called the *Pacific Medical Record* during its first issues) appeared. Its declared purpose was "to supply a well organized and pressing requirement of this vast North Pacific region [and] to gather and publish a monthly review of current medical events . . . and general medical intelligence . . . from the writings of other regions." It listed seventeen of the leading physicians of Portland as collaborators and was officially endorsed by four state medical societies.

Although the *Sentinel* experienced the usual financial difficulties at the beginning, it gradually began to make its way, probably aided by the large amount of advertising it carried. In an early sworn statement the average monthly circulation figure was given as 1,791. It reached nearly every active practitioner in the entire Northwest and through its personal columns many physicians in Washington were brought into contact with their colleagues in Oregon for the first time. It reported the proceedings of local medical societies throughout the region, and the articles supplied information on medical progress everywhere. As an illustration of its contribution to medical progress in the area might be cited the first printed account of Rocky Mountain spotted fever, which appeared in an article entitled "Some Observations on the So-Called Spotted Fever of Idaho" by Dr. E. E. Maxey of Caldwell, in the October, 1899, number.

Not until 1903 did the journal have any competition. In that year *Northwest Medicine* began publication in Seattle and became the official organ of a number of medical societies. With the increasing trend toward medical specialization in later years, the name of the *Medical Sentinel* was changed in 1930 to the *Western Journal of Surgery, Obstetrics and Gynecology. Northwest Medicine* was adopted as the organ of nearly all the medical societies of the region.

The pioneer period in the development of medicine in the Pacific Northwest was relatively brief; and by 1910, there was little to distinguish medical practice in this farthermost reach from that of any other rural and urban areas of the nation. The horse-and-buggy doctor, the real old-fashioned country physician, the medical practitioner who was a family friend and often remained in the patient's home for days until recovery was assured were still in evidence in the more rural localities. But the telephone and the automobile and, above all, modern therapeutic methods caused the members of the medical profession in the Northwest to become as "streamlined" as they were in the more populous and older established sections of the East.

Eleven

Pioneer Papers and Periodicals

The frontier produced many innovations, but perhaps few as unique as the procedure of using shingles, hung on trees and posts, to disseminate news and opinions. That novel idea required a rich imagination—a quality that Charles E. Pickett, who later started the first "newspaper" on the Pacific coast, possessed in full measure. A cultivated and educated Virginian, he came to the Oregon country with the immigration of 1843 and almost immediately became involved in the intellectual and political entanglements of a pioneer community. At first Pickett would neither toil nor spin in a land where every able-bodied man had to work for himself and the community so that both might survive. He was an intellectual and he felt that he could contribute most by using his mind instead of his muscles.

Discords and difficulties of one kind and another soon arose, even in the land which was so new that the bark still clung to the logs out of which the cabins had been built. Pickett became the self-appointed conscience of the community. Lacking paper, he prepared shingles on which he worked laboriously—his only form of labor thus far—to make them smooth so that they would take ink. On them he wrote his "pronunciamentos," which he posted about the town.

One of the iniquities against which Pickett battled, and in which he was supported by many of the newer settlers, was the excessive land claims of the missionaries who had appropriated the most desirable sections of the Willamette Valley as church property. The only way he felt he could break the monopoly was by staking a claim on their land and thereby issuing a direct challenge. He was so keenly concerned with the injustice that he was even willing to work, and on his 640 acres he built a cabin and planted a vegetable garden. He lived there alone until he won out, though the missionaries brought suit against him and, it is said, even tried to incite the Indians to kill him.

That over, Pickett gave up his claim and returned to matters of the mind. In 1845 he began a biweekly manuscript "newspaper" which he called the *Flumgudgeon Gazette and Bumble Bee Budget*, subtitled "A Newspaper of the Salmagundi Order, Devoted to Scratching and Stinging the Follies of the Times," edited by "The Curtail Coon." The only extant copy of the twelve issues which he carefully wrote by hand contains, for the most part, satirical barbs directed at the legislators. The other numbers undoubtedly continued in this vein, gibing and thrusting at any evils in the society.

Pickett did not remain long in Oregon. California beckoned and he moved on to the land of gold, where he edited a regular newspaper in San Francisco. A man with a sharp, incisive mind and a rebellious spirit, he acted as a leaven in early Oregon society.

For six months after the *Flumgudgeon Gazette* ceased publication, Oregon was without any means of learning what was going on in its own back yard. The year before, a group of settlers had formed an organization in Oregon City called the Oregon Lyceum, which issued a document: "Whereas there is at present no press or public paper in this territory, therefore we the undersigned in order to promote science, temperance, morality and general intelligence, to secure a press and to establish a monthly, semi-monthly or weekly paper, do hereby severally promise and bind ourselves to pay the sum set to our respectives names." Stock shares valued at $10 each were sold and the first group of subscribers contributed $645. When about $1,000 had been raised, the press, type, and paper were sent for. At a meeting of the stockholders the name selected for the newspaper, which was to be a biweekly, was the *Oregon Spectator*, and a Southern Democrat, W. G. T'Vault, was chosen editor at $300 a year.

The first copies to roll off the press that had been imported from New York were snatched up eagerly, although the type was almost microscopic and the content dull. Almost three columns of the front page were taken up with the Organic Laws of the Territory and more than three-quarters of a column with the new liquor law. The rest of the page contained miscellaneous items such as "An Infallible Remedy for Lowness of Spirits" (composed of a mixture of "oil of good conscience, a tablespoonful of salt of patience," and similar ingredients), and some "Good Advice"—"If you have no wife, get one; if you have, God bless her, stay at home with her, instead of spending your evenings with expensive fooleries. Be honest, frugal, plain—seek content and happiness at home—be industrious and persevering; and our word for it, . . . if your circumstances are now embarrassed, they will soon become easy, no matter who may be editor, or what may be the price of flour." Page two contained more laws, an item on "The Fall of Empires," and "Morse's Electro Magnetic Telegraph." The third page had an editorial, an item on city government, a few assorted brief items and letters to the editor; the final page, another miscellany and advertisements.

As immigration increased and communities sprang up, newspapers were launched one after another. In a new land the opportunity for publishing was virtually unlimited. The field was virgin and unpreempted for many years, and since at the beginning the cost was not too great, any man who had some extra cash and an urge to express himself could obtain a press and start a paper. Many journals professed to be nonpartisan; others were avowedly supporters of a political party or the organ of a religious group; some championed labor, the farmer, temperance, and, in later years, the railroad monopolies.

Politics was the major issue of great personal concern in the fifties and sixties, and with passions at a fever pitch, the appearance of a self-styled Democratic organ inevitably resulted in the launching of a Whig paper. Or a newspaper championing the Union cause during the Civil War made necessary the creation of a Copperhead journal. The *Oregon Spectator* began as a nonpartisan sheet, though it leaned toward the Whigs, but it became definitely political in 1852. The *Western Star*, founded at Milwaukee in 1850, was strongly pro-Democrat, and the *Oregonian*, established in Portland that same year, soon became the chief organ of the Whig party. In its "prospectus" of a weekly newspaper which was to be published in Oregon City and called the *Oregon Statesman*, the group of New Englanders who launched that paper in 1851 announced: "*In Politics*, we are democratic— Democrats we ever have been, and Democrats we ever shall be; but still, we shall not seek to excite party organizations. So long as the citizens of Oregon are disposed to let partizan fires lie dormant, we shall not attempt to kindle them into flame; but should others rake open the coals and attack Democratic Principles, Measures, or Men, *we shall defend them.* . . . And whenever the people themselves, shall deem it proper to organize Parties and draw party lines, we shall array ourselves on the Democratic side, and, with our colors nailed to the masthead of Democracy, sink or swim with the party."

Newspapers played a vital role in the politics of the new country.

The *Statesman* moved to Salem, when that city became the capital, so that it could be closer to the scene of action. Its editor, Asahel Bush, a cold, calculating, and ruthless power-behind-the-throne, dominated Oregon politics for the next decade, making and breaking politicians at will. He waged a bitter and relentless fight, in the pages of his paper, against the Know-Nothing group which had infiltrated the Territory. He published the party's secrets and lists of its members, and with his associates forced through the Legislative Assembly the viva-voce ballot law, the purpose of which was to destroy the movement. This also resulted in strengthening the power of the Democratic leaders, and, under Bush's guidance, an inner circle, known as the "Salem Clique," was created which dominated the party in the years preceding the Civil War. Despite threats and attempted intimidation, the American party nominated a candidate who received the fervent support of W. L. Adams, a preacher turned newspaper editor. Adams began publication of the *Oregon Argus* shortly after the *Spectator* breathed its last. The campaign in the press was "personal and virulent beyond description."

During its brief life of thirty-seven numbers, the *Oregon Free Press* agitated against the practices of the provisional government. It was published by George Law Curry, who had edited the *Spectator* until 1847, when he was fired. His little four-page sheet was frequently concerned with the adjudication of land claims by the settlers. He urged that the financial affairs of the provisional government be made public and that government documents be carefully preserved.

The Columbian, the first newspaper in the region north of the Columbia River, which was launched in 1852, also started as a "neutral in politics," according to its owners. A year later it was sold, and the new editor changed its name to *Pioneer and Democrat*. For the two years following, it was the only paper in the Territory, and then the *Puget Sound Courier* was issued at Steilacoom, struggling along for about twelve months before it expired. Printing plants were too rare to remain idle for long, and political issues required championing; so, in 1857, the plant of the defunct *Courier* was utilized to turn out a campaign sheet called the *Washington Republican*. It was founded solely to promote the election of a party candidate to Congress and endured only as long as the campaign issue.

A year after the Civil War began, the *Pioneer and Democrat* changed hands and was called the *Overland Press*. It devoted considerable space to war news, using the fastest pony express to obtain it, and became one of the most popular journals in the entire region. The Inland Empire's first paper was the *Washington Statesman*, published in Walla Walla, of whose editor a contemporary historian wrote: "Mr. Newell made the *Statesman* a vehicle for very bitter and insane abuse of the Republican Party and of every Union man of note who took part in the Rebellion; in other words, he published a copperhead journal of the most virulent stamp, and one which would not have been tolerated in California or New York."

When the Boise Basin was settled as a result of the rush to the Idaho mines, two enterprising gentlemen who had been in the packing business launched the *Boise News* in 1863. This was the only paper in the entire area and sometimes sold for as much as $2.50 a copy. As it was independent in politics, two other sheets were issued from the same office, one a Republican and the other a Democratic organ! The editor of the *Golden Age*, published at Lewiston at about the same time, was a Republican, and so violently was exception taken to his views by Secessionists in the section that on one occasion the Union flag flying above his office was riddled with bullets.

If a paper did not intend to be political, it made its position very clear at the beginning. In its "salutatory" in 1853, the *Journal of Commerce* announced that it "follows in the wake of no party or individual . . . [but] soars above party or faction. It has no affinity with the dirty ropes by which political machinery is served." The paper intended to publish nothing but original matter and to be a correct and thorough commercial paper. That same year, the Portland *Commercial* began publication and also proclaimed its independence of party politics, requesting the support of those who believed in a paper which represented *all* the people. The paper was founded, its editorial stated, because it was felt there was a need for an organ devoted solely to the interests of merchants, mechanics, and traders.

The first issue of the *Labor Gazette* (1878) contained the customary salutatory which declared that it disapproved of strikes and believed the only remedy for the evils of which the workingman complained was the ballot box. Elsewhere, under the caption "Laws of Life," the editor outlined his personal objectives: "Having devoted many years to the study and observation of the laws under which we live, suffer and enjoy, are idle or industrious, we shall endeavor, as opportunity offers, to impart the information to our readers. We have been a 'moderate drinker' for more than twenty years, but are now a Good Templar. We used tobacco most excessively for forty years, but gave it up more than four years ago. So the reader can judge whether or not we are competent to counsel the young." At all times, the editor continued, readers could be sure that the paper would contain nothing to distress families of "moral and intelligent people."

The Portland *Daily Standard* was sharply attacked by another paper for being subservient to, or in the employ of, the Villard railroad interests. Though its bias was no secret, "It was not supposed that it would ever expose the cloven foot to the public so as to damage its property." But now it had thrown off all disguise and came out squarely as an advocate of special favors to this "overwhelming monopoly."

The weakest aspect of the pioneer press was the reporting of local news. Papers depended on the townspeople to supply it, and the stories were written in a formless, uninteresting fashion, generously interspersed with editorializing. Little color or detail was given to events which today would rate, if not a headline on the front page, then generous treatment. A murder which had shocked the community and the apprehension of the alleged criminal might be reported in one terse sentence: "Duncan McLean was committed to jail on Friday last (17th inst.) on suspicion of having murdered a Mr. Owens." Newspapers in those days apparently regarded the education of the public as their most important reason for existence, for in the same issue in which the murder was treated with such English understatement, the first page carried a three-column article justifying the annexation of Mexican territory.

Significant events which affected the lives of every member of the community were frequently reported in a casual, nonchalant manner. The first issue of the *Oregon Spectator* acknowledged the existence of the local government with a brief, offhand comment and then ignored its activities for weeks. Wrote the newspaper: "The time has come for a thorough and complete reorganization of our city corporation. Our mayor and trustees are doing business in the right way. Our advice to them is, first: Be sure you are right, then go ahead. Gentlemen, dig up the stumps, grade the streets, tax dogs, prohibit hogs—and advertise in the Spectator." Readers bought their local papers for the political editorials, for the news from the East, for the hints to the housewife, for the humorous bits, in short, for everything but what was going on in their own town.

Advertisements, which were generally carried on the last two pages, were prosaic and stereotyped; they were a mere listing of commodities received by the various business establishments and the "cards" of professional people. The quack advertisements, which were especially prominent in the later years of the pioneer era, discussed the most intimate matters with a frankness astonishing even to modern, sophisticated readers. They were so common and so lucrative a source of revenue that they were accepted even by the denominational press. The governor of Washington Territory in 1878 was impelled to send a letter of protest to a religious periodical about its inconsistency in advocating brotherly love and carrying advertisements of products the use of which might result in permanent injury or death.

Advertising standards on the Northwestern frontier were not unique. The low level was fairly characteristic of newspaper advertising throughout the country. The New York *Herald*, during the middle of the nineteenth century, frequently contained pages devoted entirely to "medicine ads." One issue, for instance, featured no less than nineteen such advertisements, all but one designed to attract the attention of those afflicted with so-called "private diseases"; the exception was an advertisement offering a cure for worms. Newspapers generally accepted copy for anything that was at all mailable and were inclined to use *caveat emptor* as their motto.

Almost all the papers published some "poetry," which was usually of a highly sentimental and saccharine nature. "The Graves of a Household" is a typical example:

> They grew in beauty side by side
>   They filled one house with glee,
> Their graves are severed far and wide,
>   O'er stream and mount, and sea.
>
> The same fond mother bent at night
>   O'er each fair sleeping brow;
> She had each folded flower in sight,
>   Where are those dreamers now?
>
> The sea, the lone blue sea hath one,
>   He lies where pearls lie deep;
> He was the most loved of all, yet none
>   O'er his lone grave may weep.
>
> .   .   .   .
>
> One 'midst the forest of the West,
>   By a dark stream is laid;
> The Indian knows his place of rest
>   Far in the forest shade.

The writings of poetasters poured into the newspapers in such volume that the *Oregon Argus* protested in self-defense: "Our hills and dales, murmuring brooks, cascades, and roaring cataracts, are inspiring everything with song." The paper lacked space, it continued, to publish all the contributions, though, no doubt, their authors felt that the editor displayed bad taste in his selections when theirs were not included.

Occasionally a humorous and clever piece of verse appeared, such as the one written by Elizabeth Markham, mother of the famous Edwin:

A Contrast on Matrimony

1 The man must lead a happy life
2   Free from matrimonial chains
3 Who is directed by a wife
4   Is sure to suffer for his pains.

1 Adam could find no solid peace,
2   When Eve was given for a mate,
3 Until he saw a woman's face
4   Adam was in a happy state.

1 In all the female face, appear
2   Hypocrisy, deceit and pride;
3 Truth, darling of a heart sincere,
4   Ne'er known in woman to reside.

1 What tongue is able to unfold
2   The falsehoods that in woman dwell;
3 The worth in woman we behold,
4   Is almost imperceptible.

1 Cursed be the foolish man, I say,
2   Who changes from his singleness;
3 Who will not yield to woman's sway
4   Is sure of perfect blessedness.

To advocate the ladies' cause, you will read the first and third, and second and fourth lines together.

In lieu of a fashion expert, the editor was frequently his own. "We have described a fashionable female costume," wrote the editor of one paper in 1851. "Some do not wear stays, but they wear what is just as bad—tight dresses stiff with whale bone. Now if there be a man in Christendom who can look upon this prison house instrument of torture and slow murder—this leg-tangling, back-heating, hip-depressing, chest-compressing, arm-imprisoning, breath-stopping, disease-inducing apparatus known by the name of 'woman's dress'—and not exclaim 'away with the miserable humbug' he is a very small pattern of a man."

When "bloomers" were in vogue, a lively controversy ensued in the Northwest press. One editor went into detail about the many advantages and comforts of the new fashion. Women, he said, would now be able to perch their feet on high-back chairs, mantelpieces and window sills without difficulty; they would be able to "sprawl about promiscuously, miscellaneously, masculinely and generally."

Social news—marriages, births, deaths—were faithfully reported, but in a way which left no doubt as to the intimate relationship of the editor with the community. "Miss Susan is a blooming Oregonian, having as many friends as acquaintances," began one description of a marriage ceremony, "and Mr. Gist . . . has shown himself of the right material to carve out success in affairs of love. . . . May they live a thousand years, and their shadow never grow less—and if any more of our friends . . . conclude to obey Scripture by going and doing likewise, may they as courteously invite the printer to rejoice with them."

Early newspapers contained more words per printed page than could be found in the modern press, for comic strips, illustrations or cartoons did not exist to provide any break. Nor had the Sunday edition, with its rotogravure section, feature supplements, and pages of colored comics, yet appeared. Churchgoing sentiment was opposed to the publication of a paper on Sunday, and it was not until 1881 that the *Oregonian* dared defy it. The Sunday edition, however, was little different from the one issued the rest of the week.

Since he was unable to provide any embellishment, the editor tried hard to insert some sort of light touch to amuse his readers. The "humor" was frequently stale, pointless, and not very funny, but it did provide a relief from the solid columns of heavy matter. Occasionally, it was entertaining:

"If a young lady wishes a young gentleman to kiss her, what paper would she mention? No *Spectator*, no *Observer*, but as many *Times* as you like. We wish to add that she would like it done with *Dispatch*, no *Register* or *Journal* kept of it, and for him not to *Herald* it, or mention it to a *Recorder*, nor *Chronicle* it abroad. Her lips shoud [*sic*] be the only *Repository*, and the *Sun* should be excluded as much as possible. Should a *Messenger* get it, the *World* would soon know it, for *News* is now carried by *Telegraph* where it was formerly done by the *Courier*, who was always ready to *Gazette* it. In the act, the *Press* upon her lips should be light and the *Union* perfect—that is our *Standard* of kissing—first assuring ourselves that no *Argus* eye was upon us, and the only *Reflector* present the *Mirror*." One "agony column" contained the following choice items: "Lady with good character would like to meet a gentleman who could loan her $50 for one year, and be a friend." And, "Refined young gentleman wishes lady friend, about 18, for winter amusements; must be good looking."

The editor who had to think up such quips and fancies to keep his readers amused needed to be more than ordinarily resourceful and versatile. He had no staff to assist him, no body of trained reporters to bring in the news. The editor wrote copy, set the type, saw that the papers were delivered, worried about delinquent subscription bills, obtained advertising, and maintained cordial relations with the townspeople. Sometimes readers found a brief notice, in lieu of an editorial, that because of the editor's absence editorial comment would be omitted from that day's paper.

At a time when towns were springing from the earth full-grown almost overnight, when talk of settling in this community or that was constantly in the air, intensive journalistic activity was a phenomenon in keeping with the spirit of the day. Newspapers mushroomed everywhere, but only a few were successful in surviving the hardships attendant upon infancy. With little regard for sound finance, enterprising editors went into communities that had hardly been in existence the day before and set up shop.

In Olympia, one of the most thriving cities of the early period, six papers and one magazine were launched during the years between 1863 and 1870. The high mortality rate for pioneer papers is reflected in the statistics for the period from 1852 to 1859: less than one paper in twenty lasted more than fifteen years.

Some papers were published only because the editor had a great deal of imagination, ingenuity, and sheer determination. When George Law Curry decided to go into the newspaper business, he found that it would be too expensive to obtain a printing press from the East. He went ahead and had one constructed from wood and obtained a meager supply of type from Catholic missionaries in the neighbor-

hood. As they did their printing in French, there were no *w*'s in the
type. Curry whittled some out of hardwood, and when those proved
inadequate, combined two *v*'s to make a *w*. Another editor used a
pine log covered with zinc as an imposing stone. One particularly enterprising chap set up his "office" on the ground floor of a solitary
house in a tiny clearing in the forest, which he could reach from his
own place, about a mile away, only over a narrow and winding trail.
The *Curry County Recorder* was published on a primitive press which
editor Upton had constructed himself, and the imposing stone was a
slab borrowed from a distant sawmill. To some editors the newspaper
field was a completely new one and difficult not only for them, but for
the reader who had to plough through columns unbroken by punctua-
tion or paragraphs and marked by a notable lack of proper sentence
structure.

Finances were a constant source of concern. Many papers were published virtually on a shoe string, and if accounts were not paid, the
hapless editor began to worry about his next meal. Appeals such as
the following were common in the early papers:

TO OUR PATRONS. Unpleasant as is the task to us, we are at length compelled, from the force of circumstances (hard times) to address ourselves
plainly to our numerous patrons, and request of them forthwith to trans-
mit to us the amounts of their respective indebtedness. . . . We have
been lenient and forbearing with our patrons, and we now hope they will
be equally just with ourselves.

The readers of the *Pioneer* can bear us testimony, that a direct "dun"
has not appeared within its columns. We abhor and detest to appeal to
honest men for sums which are honestly our due, believing that "if honest,"
an appeal to their "better feelings" would be unnecessary. A three and a
half years' experience in the publication of this paper has, however, fully
satisfied us that *all* our patrons are not of this class. Taken all in all, they
are sadly and heavily in our debt, and therefore are we constrained to demand our our [*sic*] dues, which we hope will no longer be withheld.

One editor reprimanded his readers for buying more newspapers than
they were willing or able to pay for. The wages of a journeyman
printer in the far Northwest were considerably higher than in the
East, he explained, and if the editor was to meet his costs, the public
should buy only one paper and make certain that they pay for that
one.

Newspapers were compelled to quit because of lack of financial support. The Astoria *Marine Gazette* in 1866 wrote its obituary, stating

that the paper was almost self-sustaining and paid all expenses except the editor's own salary. And under the heading "Dead," the *Statesman* noted the demise of another journal, the *Religious Expositor*. There was not another man in Oregon, it said, who would have made the sacrifices that the editor of the *Expositor* had, traveling on foot, resorting to all kinds of economies, living cheaply, incurring deprivations, and still losing about $3,000 in six months. The cost of printing was just too high. "The Expositor, in its death," the *Statesman* went on, "has but a short time preceded three other Oregon papers . . . which have only lived, one by a system of non-payment of jours [sic], another by ratting for labor and running its publisher in debt and a third by paying nothing for its labor, living from hand-to-mouth and resorting to the most humiliating system of begging and dunning."

The editors who survived both welcomed a new paper and hung out the crepe when it passed away, generally devoting more space to the finish than the beginning. When the Jacksonville *Herald* began publication, Asahel Bush, after a few words announcing it, wrote: "We know the junior partner of the enterprise, and we know a first rate fellow. The senior we are not acquainted with, but presume he is ditto." Three months later he devoted another paragraph, "regretting its loss" because of lack of patronage.

A few of the papers which endured became outstanding journals in the region, as, for instance, the *Spokesman-Review*. It began publication as a weekly in 1883, when Spokane was a tiny hamlet, another of the many frontier towns lacking the bare facilities for newspaper operation. Its editor carted the forms each week to Cheney, where the paper was printed on the old *Sentinel* press. That winter the famous stampede to the Coeur d'Alene mining districts of Idaho took place, and Spokane was in the news of the nation. The publisher began to issue a small daily edition which came out first in the evening and then in the morning, printing them on a small, primitive hand press. From that modest beginning the paper grew until, by the turn of the century, it had a circulation of more than 40,000 in eastern Oregon, Idaho, western Montana, Washington, and southern British Columbia. It therefore had the responsibility of printing the news and discussing the issues of four states and one foreign country, including reports on the legislature, agriculture, mining, fruit growing, lumbering, stock raising, fishing, and irrigation. The paper was delivered to distant communities by stagecoach, pack train, canoe, steamboat, railroad, and even by mountain carriers on snowshoes.

Editors accepted merchandise of various sorts instead of cash for subscriptions. The editor of the little *Silverton Appeal* took cordwood and after a number of years was able to open a wood yard which he ran jointly with the newspaper. This dual enterprise caused readers to remark humorously that Editor Guild was a better judge of cordwood than of news. Guild had one competitor with which no other newspaper had to be concerned—the old covered bridge which crossed a creek in the town. Someone had started the custom of posting town scandals on it, and at times it had more news than the paper. Guild fought this by sneaking out on Saturday nights, before the *Appeal* appeared on the streets, and stealthily tearing down as many of the items as he could!

If the editor was not also the owner, he was relieved of financial worries, but he did have to be concerned about satisfying those who held the purse strings. Many an editor felt the ax because he disagreed with the views of his employers. T'Vault of the *Oregon Spectator* was dismissed for refusing to keep his politics, which were opposed to those of the owners', out of the paper. Bitterly, he wrote his farewell editorial: "The great diversity of opinion in Oregon, renders it impossible for one man to please many. The *junto of aristocracy*, in and about Oregon City, think they have the right to manage matters as best suit their views, and the citizens in the country will tamely submit to whatever mandate the favored few may think proper to issue. My *lords* and *masters*, you may be mistaken; Oregon territory is settling with the hardy freemen—as independent as the air they breathe."

When the next editor, H. A. G. Lee, left four months later, he made his adieu more restrained, sarcastically thanking the board of directors for the privilege of ending his services and stating that he was happy to be able to return "to the more humble and far more pleasant duties of a laboring mechanic." His successor lasted a year and four months before he was summarily discharged, though his contract required thirty days' notice, because, as he wrote, the owners knew that the next edition "would contain some truths very unpleasant to themselves, which is their only apology for thus endeavoring to muzzle the press."

With all his manifold duties and headaches, the pioneer editor had to have a tough constitution, no sensitivity, and, in western parlance, be "quick on the trigger." Some of the "cowboy" movies popular today, depicting the precarious existence of the lone frontier editor, are not too much exaggerated. Bodily attacks were frequent, and as late as 1878 a chance meeting of two editors in front of a cigar store in Portland led to a fracas which resulted in the shooting and killing of one. However, not only did editors have reason to fear attacks from their fellow journalists, but from some citizens whom they might have offended in print. In 1852 Asahel Bush of the *Statesman* wrote a lengthy article describing what transpired one day when he met Governor Gaines on the street:

Upon encountering each other, he instantly said (we use his *precise language*) "You God damn son of a bitch, did you intend to run against me . . ." Some other words of a like character passed, and he commenced flourishing his cane, when we prepared to defend ourself against any violence he might offer, and remained in our place upon the walk while he passed on railing and cursing. . . . If such foul profanity and low-lived scurrility suits his tastes, his years, his station or his excessive dignity, he can . . . indulge in it at all times . . . to his heart's content, so long as he harms not our person. . . . He plays the part of a markethouse bully, and stalks about our streets like a mad imbecile. . . . The man . . . is a sad object of pity, and we refer to his disgraceful conduct . . . more in sorrow than anger.

The editor of the *Newberg Graphic* informed his readers that he had just traded his old shotgun for a new rifle which was considerably less noisy than the other weapon, so that "the man who wants to whip the editor now can be disposed of without people thinking an earthquake has struck town. With a stock of undertaking goods in the back room and this new rifle we feel that the Graphic has the best equipped office in the country." Editor Pengra of the *People's Press* probably regretted that he was not similarly equipped when the principal of Columbia College at Eugene began to blast at him with a Colt. He was able to duck in time, though, and "pitched into the Professor, knocked him down, and was proceeding to give him a severe trouncing, when the bystanders interfered," reported one newspaper. It seemed that Mr. Ryan took umbrage at something written about him in the *Press* regarding his activity in the election campaign held a short while before, and, instead of politely writing a letter to the editor, he took direct frontier action.

The *Democratic Era* in 1871 published an article headed "Shooting Affrays," which began: "This has been an eventful week among newspaper editors in Oregon, and somewhat alarming to the profession in general. On Sunday morning last the editors and publishers of the Roseburg *Plaindealer* and *Ensign* met in front of the Postoffice in that

place and proceeded to bang away at each other in downright murderous style." The quarrel, it seemed, was provoked by a newspaper
article and resulted in one man being shot through the face, neck, and
shoulder, and his side grazed by a bullet, another being shot through
the breast, and the third, badly beaten over the head with a revolver.
Two were in critical condition. That same week, the paper reported,
the superintendent of the penitentiary at Salem tried to cowhide the
editor of the *Statesman*. The latter, who apparently had absent-
mindedly left his trusty pistol at home, drew a knife. Whereupon the
superintendent pulled out his gun and began to fire. He was a bad
shot, and the editor escaped with only a bruise.

When editors were not taking pot shots at each other or being shot
at by readers, they attacked with the pen. There were no libel laws
and no holds were barred. The language of the "Oregon style," as it
came to be called, was frequently so graphic and torrid that it blistered
the paper. Many of the "little" exchanges in which editors indulged
would probably be libelous today. The English language was culled
for the most descriptive epithets, and when the Oregon editors ran out
of words that might be found in a dictionary, they used their vivid
imaginations to make up their own. They became especially picturesque when dealing with political opponents. Some of the milder terms
used were Benedict Arnold, Judas Iscariot, cutthroat Tory, blackleg
debauchee, lying scoundrel, sneaking hypocrite, Ass of Hell, Sewer
man, pensioned hireling.

Most vitriolic were Asahel Bush of the *Statesman*, T. J. Dryer of the
Oregonian, and W. L. Adams of the *Oregon Argus*. If words could
destroy, none of them would have survived. In an editorial reply to
Dryer, who made a "whining complaint" that he had been attacked
by the *Statesman*, Bush wrote:

Complaints of this kind come with a special grace from a paper devoted
from its first to its last number, almost exclusively, to the grossest personal abuse, the most foul mouthed slander, grovelling scurrility, falsehood and ribald blackguardism; insomuch that it has long since ceased to
sustain any but a pot-house reputation, or to receive the countenance and
respect of any party or community. . . . Business concerns, personal difficulties, public and private matters, have all alike been drawn through
the slime and slander of his columns. . . . After showering his personal
abuse and fishmarket slang about him without stint . . . he flies into a
passion about a little newspaper squib.

Dryer himself was not backward in wielding the pen. In one of his editorials he characterized a fellow editor as "a thick-skulled bog-trotter or an addle-brained fool" who was unable to understand the English language. Of the *Statesman*, the *Spectator* said that the public had so little confidence in the paper that it refused to advertise in it, and that the only material the editor had to fill up space was the list of laws, the paper's prospectus, and advertisements of patent medicines which, together with "falsifying" editorials, made up the sheet. Papers accused each other of stealing stories or using them without acknowledging their source. One editor stated that being on unfriendly terms was not a sufficient excuse for such theft. Disgusted by one especially scorching battle of words, the *Washington Standard* commented: "The Statesman and Argus are waging a desperate war of words, in which all the vulgar, not to say obscene epithets, peculiar to Oregon journalism, are freely bandied. What depraved morals the patrons of such papers must possess!"

By the end of the century, the large city newspapers had abandoned this type of journalism, but it could still be found in the small country papers. The rural editors continued squabbling among themselves either because they found it the easiest way to write or because they believed it entertained their readers. In 1907 the *Oregonian*, in dignified language, commented about some of the tiffs of its country cousins in a big-brotherly editorial. Country editors, it wrote, sometimes have quarrels and call their rivals "harsh names." That this was a mild understatement is indicated from the example which followed, reporting one editor's opinion of his rival as the "scum writer who evidently knows from experience what it means to be boiled in the pot, raked off with the scum and dumped into the refuse pile;" another compared a recent electric storm to the "brain storm that sometimes occurs in the Athena Press sanctum when Editor Boyd's gigantic intellect is set to accomplish an impossible task. We then have a sample of an irresistible force in contact with an immovable obstacle, and the office cat, bristling with electric disturbance, proceeds to throw a fit and clear the atmosphere."

The era of personal journalism in its more dignified phase is perhaps best symbolized by the noted editor of the *Oregonian*, Harvey W. Scott. When he came to the paper in 1865, it was a struggling little sheet which had been given to its owner, H. L. Pittock, by the previous proprietor in lieu of $500 in back wages. Scott at the time was librarian of the newly formed Portland Library Association and had been recommended as an editorial writer. Pittock was impressed with his ability and hired him on a permanent basis. Scott eventually became editor and acquired a part interest in the paper. During the years when he was at its helm, the *Oregonian* and Scott were synonymous, and when he died in 1910, it was the leading journal of the Northwest.

It is, perhaps, a commentary on the nature of Oregonians and Oregon society that Harvey Scott should have been regarded with the admiration and esteem he commanded. A conservative, he preached the doctrine of nineteenth century individualism during the high tide of national prosperity and the low ebb of depression. He saw the frontier as the true expression of personal initiative and limitless opportunity. He worshiped at the shrine of *laissez faire* and made of it a doctrinaire philosophy, a fixed star in his ideological constellation.

Scott was a product of the old frontier of Kentucky and Illinois and of the new frontier of the Northwest, to which he came as a boy of fourteen. The family was poor and he suffered the usual hardships of pioneer existence, managing to get as good an education as was possible in those days by "working his way through school." He taught for a while, studied law, and acted as librarian. From the time he was a boy, he was not only self-supporting but helped the family, and his life is a success story in the best tradition of Horatio Alger. He never forgot his early struggles, and though times had changed, the only advice he could give the unhappy victims of unemployment on the breadlines of 1894 was to go thou and do likewise, rebuking and criticizing them for lacking initiative. So vehemently did the *Oregonian* attack Coxey's Army, that in the spring of 1893 the paper was threatened with attack by a mob of bitter, desperate men.

The *Oregonian* "is hated and embraced by everyone," wrote a local magazine. "It is influential. The people have never had any other. . . . The paper is Scott. It is brutal and dictatorial, and the people, dog-like, love the arm that flails them. A strong editorial page is its mainstay. . . . Portland will stick to the Oregonian as a browbeaten wife sticks to a recreant husband, but in the end the city will thank and reward a new paper for bringing about her emancipation." The publication reported a rumor that Hearst intended to establish a morning paper in Portland and, though it was not particularly fond of his type of journalism, it would welcome his newspaper as a competitor to the Scott "institution."

Scott's *Oregonian* participated actively in all important local and national campaigns, but the one which brought the editor into the public eye more than any other was on what he called "sound money." From the very beginning of the controversy over the money issue after the Civil War, Scott flayed the Greenback or cheap-money advocates as undermining the foundations of society, and went on to fight the advocates of free coinage of silver. Bryan and the Populist movement were vehemently attacked. When he was charged with intolerance during the free-silver campaign, he replied: "Somebody asks if there can't be 'an honest difference of opinion about the gold standard.' There can be no honest difference of opinion where one of the parties knows nothing of what he is talking about. There may be honest ignorance. But it is entitled to no opinion." He reserved his special scorn for the philosophy and movement of socialism, which he regarded as a threat to the American way of life. In his own state he led the crusade against the passage of the direct primary law, which he felt would result in the loss to the public service of many of the best men. And he opposed the initiative and referendum as destructive of the established system of representative government. Scott's philosophy and pattern of thinking can, perhaps, best be described to present-day readers by the comment made in a biographical sketch: "It is interesting to note that Herbert Hoover as a boy in Salem read *The Oregonian* and no doubt absorbed some of the individualistic ideas of Mr. Scott as the basis of his present philosophy of American individualism."

Though Scott's formal education by modern standards was meager, he was a voracious reader. His favorite books were the Bible, and works of Shakespeare, Milton, and Burke, and he was well versed in such widely divergent fields as literature, theology, science, economics, and politics. His editorials were liberally sprinkled with quotations, literary allusions, and historical references. His son, Leslie, devoted twelve years to the job of compiling, editing, and annotating his writings and finally issued a six-volume set which he entitled the *History of the Oregon Country*.

During the years he edited the *Oregonian*, Scott was a power in Oregon. "He thundered through the columns of the *Oregonian* and the reverberations sounded from the Siskiyous to Puget Sound, from Astoria to Boise. He held in his strong grasp for 45 years the most powerful thing in Oregon—the public opinion of that broad commonwealth and of a wide fringe around it." As an individual, however, while he undoubtedly had the affection of his intimates, he was too cold a personality to appeal to the broad mass of people. When he ran for United States senator in 1903, he was defeated in the Oregon legislature. One present-day Oregon writer comments that "as a man he was lacking in sympathy and humanity and as a leader he held to outworn social theories. In some ways he was overestimated, his scholarship, for instance, being credited with too great a breadth and profundity." Portland, which Scott served to the best of his ability, erected a huge statue of him which stands in Mount Tabor Park. With his passing in 1910, the era of personal journalism in the Northwest approached its end.

By the beginning of the twentieth century, the pioneer phase of newspaper publishing, with the exception of some small country journals, was already history. Papers now contained illustrations, book reviews, sport news, syndicated news stories and features, and a financial section. News stories no longer began, "John Smith met Paul Jones in front of the barber shop where the former was going to get a haircut," continuing in chronological order and coming to the murder of one man by the other about five paragraphs down. Some of the features, though, were still handled in a countryfied manner. The sport page of the *Oregonian* in 1901, for instance, was headed "In the Sporting World." Under the headline were two single-column illustrations, one depicting a lovely lass, in what was known as gym bloomers, ready to throw a basketball into the hoop; the other, a typical male athlete swinging from a trapeze. The page contained stories about track, handball, bowling, fishing, baseball.

Papers reflected the interests of the community rather than the public ambitions of an editor and, with the rise of big business which supported the press with its advertising, became more cautious and restrained. They were now large financial enterprises, and this is best indicated by the fact that after the turn of the century, fewer and fewer papers were established in proportion to the total population.

The greatest number of newspapers had been launched in Oregon during the decade of the eighties, the period of active immigration, when the land was still being opened by thousands of settlers. As the state emerged from pioneer days and the people became increasingly interested in matters outside their immediate environment, larger papers, with enough financial backing to make comprehensive news coverage possible, began to supersede the smaller ones in influence. The number steadily declined and the circulation of the remaining ones increased, on the whole, as they came to serve wider areas within the region. In 1880, for example, when the population was 174,000, there were 74 papers. Ten years later there were 142 for a population of 317,000, and in the next decade, 218 for 413,000 people. By 1910 the ratio of papers to population continued to decline so that the number now was 248 for a population of 672,000. And the trend continued.

The rapid development of journalism in Washington, too, was a consequence of the influx of settlers after the isolation of the state had been ended by the transcontinental railroad lines. After 1880, in addition to the regular papers, a specialized press began to appear, with foreign-language papers in the Scandinavian communities on Puget Sound, mining, lumbering, professional, and business publications. Washington matured later than Oregon, so that in 1890 the number of weeklies and semiweeklies published in the former were less than one-tenth the number issued in the latter. But within the next ten years, the state to the south was surpassed. Compared to 19 dailies, Oregon had 17, and 162 weeklies to 176. With the growth and stabilization of the state, the inevitable decline occurred in the number of papers proportionate to population.

Idaho's journalism naturally developed more slowly than that of the other two states, for population growth lagged far behind. Only a scattering of weeklies, semiweeklies, and triweeklies were published in 1870, and ten years later the number remained substantially the same. A noticeable increase occurred during the next decade. At the time the Territory was given statehood, more than thirty weeklies and several dailies were issued. There was no marked change in the number of papers for the next ten years, but by 1910 about fifty weeklies and eleven dailies were printed. In terms of the number of papers, Idaho was about thirty years behind Oregon.

In all the states, while the large metropolitan dailies received wide support, the more local weekly, biweekly, or triweekly papers greatly outnumbered them.

If the regularity with which advertisements of Eastern and European periodicals appeared in the newspapers was any gauge, then Northwestern subscribers to those journals were not lacking. A variety of publications solicited readers: *Gleason's Pictorial Drawing Room Companion*, which described itself as "a record of the beautiful and useful in art" and contained sketches, poems, stories, and a digest of events of the day; *America's Own*, a literary magazine; *Harper's Monthly*, *Putnam's Monthly Magazine*, the *London Quarterly Review*, *Westminster Review*.

Although readers had a wide selection of "foreign" periodicals from which to choose, an enterprising bookstore owner and printer apparently felt that a field existed in the Northwest for an indigenous publication. In December, 1851, S. J. McCormick announced in the *Spectator* that on the following month he would distribute the first issue of a monthly journal to be called the *Oregon Monthly Magazine*, which would be devoted to literature, science, art, poetry, moral tales, national biography, sketches, anecdotes, essays, and "useful knowledge." He promised his readers that it would be neutral in religion and politics, "bound to no class, creed, or party,—but its pages shall ever be devoted to the instruction and amusement of the people," and he would do everything within his power to carry out his motto "A FRIEND TO ALL,—NONE A FOE." Literary selections would be reprinted from the outstanding European and American publications, and for poetry the pages of the magazine "will be graced with Original Pieces, together with culled flowers from the bouquets of the sweetest and most popular bards." Terms were $5 a year or $3 for six months. The main object of the *Monthly*, McCormick said in his "introductory," would be to make men wiser and happier, since ignorance bred crime and misery. He hoped it would "instill into the minds of the rising generation the wholesome maxims of morality and virtue, and hold up to their astonishment and horror the misery attendant upon those who follow the practices of evil."

McCormick was not only a printer, editor, and bookstore owner, he was also a poet and short-story writer, as appeared from the first issue of the *Oregon Monthly*. It contained three of his "poems" entitled "An Advice to the Boys," "The Drunkard's Wife," "Hail to Columbia," and a story, "Paddy Phelan and his 'Wonderful Advinthurs.'" Even his address to his patrons, friends, and readers was in verse. There was also a short story by F. Soulie, translated from French, and a few other miscellaneous items, such as an article on the life of Columbus and one on Rebecca Motte, "an heroic woman of the American Revolution." Subsequent issues were on a similar order, though McCormick devoted more time to "culling" and editing than writing. The circulation was fair, considering the small population and the difficult, circuitous routes necessary to reach the widely scattered subscribers.

Two years later the ambitious McCormick began to issue the *Oregon Almanac*, which appeared regularly for more than ten years. It cost 12½¢ in 1864 when Matthew P. Deady commented on it in his column. The *Almanac* could now be regarded as a prominent institution of the country, he stated, and in it the reader could find any information he wanted about Oregon, Washington, and Idaho more correctly and carefully compiled than in any similar publication issued elsewhere. Nor did McCormick stop there. He published the second periodical in the region, a semiweekly, *The Commercial*, devoted mainly to business interests, which appeared in Portland in 1853. The name was changed six months later to the *Commercial and General Advertiser*.

There was a lull for about the next two decades, and then dozens of publications were started. The emphasis was on agriculture, mining, animal husbandry, commerce, education, and a sprinkling of religious, professional, literary, and musical journals. Most of them flickered briefly and died out. One of the most long-lived was the *West Shore*, first issued in August, 1875. It began as a literary and booster magazine whose aim was to make it "*the* literary paper of the Pacific Northwest —to this end, we have secured contributors from the brightest intellects and ablest writers in this State." It originally had eight pages but within a few years increased to thirty-two. By 1877 it claimed a circulation of 7,200 and distribution in over thirty-two states and territories as well as England and Scotland. The contents included short stories, verse, miscellaneous items such as "Woman's Influence in Society," Northwest history and articles on current activities throughout the region and the inevitable "jokes," of which this is typical: "Mother—'Now, Gerty, be a good girl and give Aunt Julie a kiss and say good-night.' Gerty—'No, no! If I kiss her she'll box my ears like she did papa's last night.'" Or, "A young man in Jersey City was urged to marry, but he replied: 'I don't see it; my father was a single man, and he got along well enough.'"

"The Faithless Wife" was representative of the fiction published by the *West Shore*. It was calculated to wring the hearts of its female readers and point up a moral. The entire story was written in the vein of the following excerpt:

Ten years nearly have passed over the sad catastrophe, and, now, alas! poor Andy, too has bowed to his Master's call. He returned from the Casiar mines, and on the fatal trip of the steamer Pacific met his fate, and sleeps beneath the silent waves till Jesus calls.

"What became of the erring woman?" did you say? Ask me not. But the cold and watery grave of the noble-hearted husband is a pillow of golden down compared to the living tomb of "THE FAITHLESS WIFE!"

In 1882 the *West Shore* became concerned almost exclusively with extolling the virtues of the region, its natural resources, climate, and other aspects designed to attract immigrants from all parts of the country. It returned temporarily to its original family and literary content, then resumed its booster characteristics, and so remained. The magazine requested contributions from readers on any subject except religion and politics, offering to pay liberally for any pieces used if the writers desired remuneration, and leaving it up to them whether the article was a free or paid contribution!

Announced as the first purely literary journal ever issued in Oregon was the *Oregon Literary Vidette*, a monthly priced at fifty cents a year. It featured tales, essays, romances, sketches, adventures, satire, anecdotes, poetry, and literature generally. In the hopes of boosting its circulation, the second issue, dated March, 1879, announced that in the next one sketches of living pioneers of Oregon would be published, edited by the secretary of the pioneer association of the state.

Competition was becoming keen and magazines vied with each other to attract readers. The March 4, 1882, issue of the *Polaris*, a home-type weekly, listed eight reasons why it should be purchased: It was the handsomest journal on the coast, printed on better paper and superior typographically; it was the most convenient as it was published in book form; it was the most interesting, covering all fields, including church, temperance, and scientific notes; it was the cheapest, considering its size (sixteen pages); most important, it was the "purest"—"no questionable matter was admitted into its columns. Objectionable details of social immoralities and criminal proceedings, such as parents desire to keep from their sons and daughters, would never be allowed." Advertising was also carefully selected. It prided itself on being the most independent, published in the interest of no church, political party, clique or faction and treating all subjects with a high moral conscience, being loyal to no authorities but God and the laws of the land. And, finally, it had a corps of writers selected from the finest literary talent of the nation.

Women were also in the ranks of editors. For about sixteen years Abigail Scott Duniway, whose family seemed either to have printers' ink in its blood or an overwhelming urge to mold public opinion, regularly issued the *New Northwest*. Of its beginning she wrote: "I was wholly ignorant of the publishing business, into which I was stumbling blindly, but I hired a foreman at twenty-five dollars per week, who placed my type and galleys in shape, using two upper bedrooms of a two-story frame house." The journal began publication in 1871 and appeared regularly, except for a temporary interruption, when the whole typographical force was prostrated by the measles and the editor was badly in need of a rest, as she reported. This eight-page journal militantly supported the suffragette movement and contained articles, short stories, and poems written by Mrs. Duniway and local contributors. According to its editor, it "soon became a household visitor throughout my chosen bailiwick of Oregon, Washington and Idaho."

At the end of the century Abigail Scott Duniway assumed the editorship of *The Pacific Empire*, "A Journal of Freedom," which was a spiritual successor to the *New Northwest*. It was founded in 1893 by Lischen Miller, a poetess, who was said to be "noted for her devotion to the arts, chief of all, fine writing." After a few years it was merged with the literary magazine *Drift*, whose independent existence had lasted for only three months. That, in turn, was combined in 1898 with *The Pacific Monthly*, whose prospectus announced that it would be a monthly literary magazine of the highest order, dealing with the history, romance, and poetry of Oregon and the Pacific Northwest. In 1901 it absorbed another short-lived periodical, *The Oregon Native Son*, which had been "Devoted to the History, Industries and Development of the Original Oregon Comprising the States of Oregon, Washington, Idaho and Part of Montana." The latter had been published for almost two years, and a typical issue contained a few poems, one of which was by Valentine Brown and another by Abigail Scott Duniway, a few short stories, and several articles, including one on the Oregon Historical Society by its then assistant secretary, George Himes, one on Edwin Markham by John B. Horner, A.M., and several biographical sketches of pioneers.

The Pacific Monthly was the leading literary magazine of the region for several decades. It received financial support from a number of prominent people, among whom was Colonel Charles Erskine Scott Wood. He conducted a regular column called "Impressions," and Ella Higginson contributed comments on literature from time to time. One issue contained a short story, "Typee," by Jack London, the reminiscences of Mrs. Lafcadio Hearn, translated from the Japanese, and an article on civic religion by Rabbi Stephen S. Wise. In July, 1906, the magazine claimed to have received orders for 85,000 copies.

The booster magazines flourished briefly and soon died. One of this

large crop, *Resources of Oregon and Washington,* an eight-page journal started in 1878, urged its readers to subscribe, read it, and then
send it to the East or Europe so that it might be "the means of bringing some good, intelligent settler into this far-off, favored and promising Land." Mrs. Frances Fuller Victor, the "Associate-Corresponding
Editor," had been assigned to visit every section of Oregon and Washington to gather material for articles and at the same time solicit subscriptions. The publication contained articles on the various industries,
the schools, Indian agencies, market and meteorological reports, and
descriptions of some of the towns.

The "boon companion" of every home, as it hoped to become, was
the *Northwest Herald.* Its first issue, which appeared in 1899, announced that every number would be a "souvenir" and completely
cover the field of progressive thought. Contributions would be secured from famous authors who would present a digest of the trend
of current events. It advertised itself as "A twentieth century paper
for any century readers. A world of wit and wisdom," published to
entertain the family.

The New West announced its appearance in 1910 with a verbal fan-
fare and promised its readers the best in literary criticism, economic
and sociological discussions, stories and poetry. It also pledged itself
to deal with all aspects of reform throughout the land. A staff of eminent writers and contributors had been assembled, it stated, among
whom was Olga Nethersole, "the most famous emotional actress on
the boards today." She was to write the first piece she had ever attempted, giving her impressions of the Pacific coast. An arrangement
had been made with Miss Adelaide Stedman, "the foremost dramatic
critic of New York City," to supply an article each month on the
New York stage. The first issue contained some sound, critical essays
on Zola and Gorki by a professor at the University of Oregon, and
more in a similar vein were promised.

In outlining its aims, the editors of *The New West* stated confidently, optimistically, and, in part, prophetically:

The Pacific is by far the most important waterway in the world, for
its waters join the shores of ancient and modern romance. *Its islands are
the strategic positions upon which are now turned the eyes of the old and
the new world and about which will be waged the great naval battles of
the future* [Italics mine]. A great industrial war is now on between the
New West and the Far East. It is to the lands of the Pacific that the industrial captain, the warrior, the student of political and economic condi-

tions, the novelist, and the poet must turn for inspiration and it is with these and their doings that our magazine, THE NEW WEST, intends to deal. We intend to chronicle the story of the building of the new Western Empire in comparison with which the splendor and romance of Ninevah and Tyre will seem as simple fairy tales fit for children.

With the development of cultural activities, sanguine devotees of the arts who had editorial ambitions believed the time was ripe for publications on music and the drama. A theatrical daily called *Figaro* appeared in 1887 and survived for three years; the *Northwest Dramatic News*, issued a decade later, lasted only a year, and several other journals on music came and went during the same period. One, the *Northwestern Musical Journal*, attempted criticism of outstanding musicians of the day and featured some sheet music.

And, from time to time, Northwesterners were offered varied periodicals such as the *Chemawa American*, which dealt with Indian education; a magazine published in Boise to advance the cause of farmers' cooperatives; the *Mountaineer*, to record the explorations of mountain-climbing enthusiasts; and a bizarre publication, *The World's Advance-Thought and the Universal Republic*, which ran for a number of years after the end of the century. Each issue contained a "Soul-Communion Time-Table" which fixed a specific day and a time for the leading cities of the world to hold soul-communion "of all who love their fellow-man, REGARDLESS OF RACE AND CREED—the object being to invoke, through co-operation of thought and unity in spiritual aspiration, the blessings of universal peace and higher spiritual light." It published poetry and articles, such as "Bring in the Light," "Mediumship for All," "Dream Life," some of which the editor, Lucy A. Mallory, wrote herself.

Periodicals appeared later in Washington than in Oregon, but there, too, the market was rapidly flooded; many entered the field hopefully but soon departed. *The Dilettante*, which was launched in 1898, aspired to become *the* literary journal of the Northwest. It was compelled to suspend publication for a while because of lack of support and then, having gathered some strength, feebly but stoutheartedly reentered the ranks. It styled itself an esoteric publication to appeal to the "Illuminati," that small but sterling minority which, it declared, Matthew Arnold said is the saving element in human affairs. But perhaps realizing that there were not enough esoterics to keep the magazine going, it hastened to add that it would contain features to appeal to the average man and woman. All "clever" contributions would be gratefully received, the magazine stated. And though it could not afford to pay for them at the present time, a special effort would be made to give writers adequate presentation "before that august court —that choice coterie—our readers," and it would take extra pains to spell the authors' names correctly. In 1900 the editor reported a circulation of approximately five hundred copies.

The February, 1901, issue of *The Dilettante* carried an item on the first number of *The Coast*, which had come out the month before. The cover cut, it wrote, was depressing, but perhaps that was a fault which would be corrected in later issues; it seemed to be prosperous, judging by the amount of advertising it contained, and the editorials were written by two outstanding men in the region; on the whole it seemed calculated to appeal to discriminating readers. *The Coast* was a combination booster and literary periodical. Almost every issue treated a city in detail, giving its history, financial, agricultural, and trade resources, schools, and physical description. It ran to about eighty pages and was profusely illustrated.

An "arty" magazine with a prosaic title, the *Seattle News-Letter*, appeared in 1900. This was directed at middle-class Seattleites and contained a social calendar, woman's club calendar, stories of the street and the town, and reports on musical activities. To carry through a sophisticated effect, the editorials were captioned "*Entre Nous.*" On the same general order was *The Week-End*, which began publication a few years later and branched out to include "society" in other Washington towns. One issue reported the Vancouver horse show, a reception by the Seattle Federation of Women's Clubs, a symphony concert, and a new art society, among other such items.

The State, which was launched in 1898, was a literary magazine with some booster qualities and an editorial policy of commenting on current events. Toward the end of its first year, it announced that it was a success beyond the most sanguine hopes of its most ardent well-wishers, so much so, that attempts were being made from time to time by others to share some of its prosperity. The magazine wished all newcomers well:

The literary fields of the Northwest—inexhaustible in their fertility— are rich enough, wide enough, and fallow enough to yield abundant returns to those who work with a purpose. . . . A brighter day has come and is coming yet to the imperial domain of the Northwest . . . the superior intelligence of men who have hesitated not when there was a wilderness to conquer, hostile tribes to overcome and a civilization to found when once separated from the Diana of gold, will rise superbly to the necessities of the case and support by word of mouth and by material aid anything that has for its honest purpose the building of a yet greater, of a nobler civilization in the three States we call our own.

By 1910, of the dozens of magazines that had been published, only a very few remained. With the end of the isolation of the Northwest and the cheaper postage rates, local periodicals were unable to compete with the established and superior Eastern publications. Nevertheless, during the time they existed, they filled a need in two ways— they provided some outlet for aspiring native writers and a source of entertainment to readers.

Twelve

The Lamp of Learning

Probably no stronger force existed than the pioneer newspapers and magazines to stimulate interest in a sound educational system. Hardly had towns been platted than papers expressed concern about the educational future of the children. One Oregon newspaper in the early years of settlement editorially chastised the citizens of the region for being so absorbed in "such worldly matters as . . . opening farms, building houses and barns, gathering large herds of cattle . . . that some of them we fear have sadly overlooked the great necessity of giving their offspring such an education as will prepare them honorably to bear the burthens of government, [and] exercise a wholesome influence upon their kind." This strong rebuke was less a reflection of the apparent neglect of education than of the high regard in which it was held, so that any seeming lethargy was sharply criticized.

As a matter of fact, a school of some sort was established almost as soon as white men came to live in the Oregon country. The first was at the Hudson's Bay Company at Fort Vancouver and the students were the half-breed children of its fur men. School was taught for a while by a New Englander, John Ball, who had come overland with Nathaniel Wyeth's party and been persuaded by John McLoughlin to remain as a tutor. Instructing those youngsters required infinite patience and more than ordinary skill, for only one child understood the language of the teacher and he was more hindrance than help, constantly interrupting with suggestions as to how the school ought to be run.

After about three months, John Ball decided that he had had enough of this kind of work, and in any case he had not come to the far Northwest to teach the three R's. McLoughlin next induced Solomon Smith, also a member of the Wyeth expedition, to take charge. He struggled along until love came to his rescue in the shape of the alluring Indian wife of one of the Fort's more prosaic employees, the baker. History does not record just how the situation was untangled, but Smith ended by marrying his inamorata and moving with her to French Prairie. There he established a little subscription schoolhouse at the home of a settler for children of the retired Hudson's Bay men. Undaunted, the chief factor then obtained the services of the Methodist missionary, Cyrus Shepard, who carried on for a while.

The missionaries of the various denominations considered education an essential part of their religious program and promptly set up schools at their stations for the Indians and their children. Only an insignificant number, however, responded to their efforts. Jason Lee's school, for instance, opened with three Indians, and after a year of patient striving, only about twenty had been induced to attend.

After the first American settlers arrived in the region, the missionaries began to concentrate on offering their children instruction in reading, writing, arithmetic, geography, and theology. The latter were the first to set up schools, which accounted for the denominational influence that persisted in the educational system long after the area had lost its frontier characteristics. By 1878, Oregon had about twenty-eight parochial academies and Washington had at least one in every important town.

In addition to the denominational institutions, the subscription, or term, schools were rapidly established. Each term was usually of three months' duration and the fee approximately $6 to $8. One after another opened, each using the local press to bring its special qualities to the attention of parents. Advertisements generally followed this pattern:

THE EIGHTH SESSION of Mrs. N. M. THORNTON'S SCHOOL, in this city, will commence on Monday, 25th September, and will continue eleven weeks. All the branches usually comprised in a thorough English education, and taught in this School, together with Plain and Ornamental Needle Work, Drawing, and Painting in Mezzotinte and in Water Colors.

Strict attention will be given, not only to the intellectual improvement of the pupils, but also to their morals and manners. It is Mrs. Thornton's design to make this a permanent School; and her past success and long experience as a teacher, induce her to hope that she will give general satisfaction.

The charge for tuition in this School has been six dollars per session; but with a view to meeting more fully, the convenience of the community, the price, from the commencement of the seventh session, will be regulated as follows:

Orthography, and Reading, and Plain Sewing, if desired $3.50
Writing, Arithmetic, and Geography   4.00
Any additional Solid Studies, and Fancy Needle Work   5.00
Drawing and Painting, an extra charge

Pupils from the country can be accommodated with boarding and washing in the family of the teacher, at one dollar and fifty cents per week.

The above are strictly Mrs. T's cash prices— Persons who make an arrangement to pay in other funds, will be charged in proportion, as such funds may be below par.

For testimonials of Mrs. Thornton's qualifications, as a teacher, and the character of her school, she is happy in being permitted to refer to the gentlemen, among others, whose names will be found below. These gentlemen are respectfully solicited to act in the capacity of a committee to visit the school.

His Excellency, Geo. Abernethy,   Archibald McKinlay, Esq.
Hon. Columbia Lancaster,   Capt. W. K. Kiborn,
Hon. A. A. Skinner,   Joel Palmer, Esq.
Rev. William Roberts,   M. Crawford, Esq.
Rev. Lewis Thompson,   M. S. White, Esq.
Dr. McLoughlin,

Itinerant schoolmasters and 'marms who became pedagogues until they could find more lucrative employment soon presented the problem of separating the wheat from the chaff. The dearth of teachers was acute and many an instructor knew only a little more than the children he taught. He coped as best he could with a class which often consisted of as many as thirty students at different levels of progress, involving references to about eighty or ninety books in the course of a day. A few teachers had surprisingly fine backgrounds, though perhaps not quite as good as that of Bernard Cornelius, who taught at one time at Olympia. He was a graduate of Dublin's Trinity College, a member of the College of Preceptors in London, and had been employed in schools in California and British Columbia.

School activities played a prominent part in the life of the community and were faithfully reported in the local press. When quarterly examinations were held, they were made the occasion for public receptions. Exercises usually consisted of the reading of compositions, orations, declamations, and dialogues, with a band to enliven the pro-

ceedings. The excited student, twisting a handkerchief or the corner
of her dress or of his coat, nervously declaimed from the platform on
such subjects as "Our Present Conditions and Future Prospects," "Our
Territory," or the universal ones of "Time" or "Slander." "The composition of Miss Thompson was beautiful—it could not have been
otherwise—the subject being '*Flowers*'—clothed in chaste and expres-
sive language," reported the town's paper, carefully noting the proceedings and even devoting space to critical evaluation.

Most of the settlers were not satisfied with the parochial and term
schools. They had come from areas which had public-school systems
and demands were soon made for the establishment of tax-supported
schools. Both Oregon and Washington developed a type of educational system patterned after that of New England. It reached the
Northwest by a two-way process: indirectly, through the Iowa law
(influenced by the New England system) brought by the settlers, and
directly, through Massachusetts-born Reverend George H. Atkinson,
the father of education in Oregon.

Atkinson, a Darthmouth College graduate who had received his
religious training at Andover Theological Seminary, had come to the
Northwest as a missionary and remained to engage actively in church
work. Education was his primary interest, and he took a leading part
in the formulation and passage of the important Oregon School Law
of 1849. All the significant characteristics of the New England system
were embodied in this first and basic law: the emphasis upon free education, the reluctance to provide for centralization of control, and the
preference for extreme localization as manifested in the district-school
system, the permanent and irreducible school fund, the certification
of teachers and the efforts to impose professional standards, the state
tax-supported schools and, finally, the religious freedom of teacher
and pupil.

Not for another eight years, however, was actual provision made
for a free public-school system, and that was when the Oregon State
Constitution was adopted. Opposition was prompt and emphatic.
Asahel Bush, editor of the *Oregon Statesman* and an influential politician, denounced the common-school feature as unwarranted and
unnecessary. "We regret the introduction of that provision into the
instrument," he wrote. "Not that we are opposed to common schools
in the abstract, for we are not. But Oregon is a very different country.
Oregon is too sparsely populated. In our opinion we now have and
under the present system for years to come will have schools inferior

to those which would spring up under the voluntary system." Bush and those who shared his views were outvoted.

Despite the apparent eagerness of the majority of the settlers for a public-school program, it was not until 1872 that an effective one was instituted. The office of superintendent of public instruction was divorced from that of the governor, a state board of education was established, provision was made for county-school superintendents, school districts were organized, the duties of teachers were defined, and even the establishment of a full-fledged state university was contemplated. So complete was this legislation that since then there has been no fundamental revision except that which made education compulsory.

In Washington Territory, so-called "public" schools were soon provided for, although none were actually free, a tuition fee of about $5 to $10 being charged for each school session. Common-school legislation was made a condition of Territorial status by the Federal government, and the first session of the legislature enacted laws making this stipulation effective. The Organic Act of 1853 provided that two sections in each township be reserved for school purposes.

The growth of schools was relatively slow for the first twenty years, as the population was sparse and scattered, and in many instances travel over long and tortuous roads was necessary in order to reach the schoolhouse. In 1869 there were twenty-two schools in eight counties, and less than half the children of school age were attending. The average length of the annual school session was approximately four months. From then on, development was considerably accelerated, and only three years later, the Territory had more than 140 schools. The duration of the school year was continually extended; children in some counties were attending class for as long as nine months during the year, though the average was still about five.

In those communities where the term was very short, constant pressure was exerted for the adoption of a longer session. When Walla Walla was little more than a supply base for the mining region of Idaho, demands were raised for a permanent school to replace the temporary ones that had been operating on a three-months-per-year basis. "It seems to us," wrote the town's paper, "that it is time that such schools were dispensed with in this city, and an advanced step taken. There are children enough in this city to justify the inauguration of a permanent school system and the erection of a suitable building, wherein they may be educated, instead of being allowed to grow up on the streets, receiving every-day lessons in idleness and mischief."

Educational development in the neighboring Territory of Idaho was different from that of either Washington Territory or Oregon in one significant respect: there, with the exception of a small school at Franklin established in 1860 by the Latter Day Saints, public schools antedated church schools. No other parochial schools were founded until 1867, when the Episcopal Church established one at Boise, followed the next year by a Catholic school at Idaho City. The tax-supported common school was not opposed by vested church interests, as was the case in Oregon, where clerical hostility did not disappear until almost the close of the century.

Two clearly defined stages marked the development of education in Idaho: the distinguishing feature of the first period, from 1863 to 1880, was the creation and extension of the one-room school, located for the most part in the mining camps; the second saw the emergence of the graded school in the mining, agricultural, and railroad sections and of the one-room schoolhouse in the newly settled rural areas.

The progress of the public-school program in Boise illustrates the nature of the development throughout the Territory. On July 4, 1863, the American flag was raised over the spot which soon became the site of the Boise Barracks. Three days later, seventeen men gathered in a small log cabin, organized a townsite company, and proceeded to lay out a town on the land situated between the barracks and the ranch locations of two of the members. They named it Boise City. No sooner was the main street cleared of a heavy growth of sagebrush than a private school was established. At least three such simple log schoolhouses opened their doors during the first year of the town's existence, at a time when the streets were either almost obscured by clouds of dust or made impassable by streams of mud.

Although the first session of the Territorial legislature failed to enact a public-school law, it did provide for the election of a school superintendent in each of the counties. At the next session, the following year, it made up for this deficiency and also created Ada County, with Boise City as the county seat. The following spring, elections were held for county officials and School District No. 1 was organized. Only a brief statement in the *Idaho Statesman* of June 13, 1865— "A public school will open this morning at the corner of Capitol Square"—noted the opening of the first public school, but the news must have been greeted with enthusiasm by many a parent.

School structures during the first fifteen years were poor and totally inadequate. As late as 1800, the public schools of Boise were housed in one old brick building which was so crowded that pupils could attend only half-day sessions. The following year the legislature passed a law establishing an "Independent School District of Boise City," appointed trustees in charge of the district, and gave them authority to sell bonds for expansion and improvement of the schools. Two years later, a modern structure was opened, containing sixteen classrooms. Classes were conducted on a graded basis and a secondary-school curriculum was offered as well.

Parents who sent their children to the tax-supported schools were able to keep a close check on the progress of their offspring. Not only did they receive regular reports from the teachers, but they could follow the activities of the class by means of notices sent to the newspaper. Under the heading "Oregon City Public Schools," one paper carried the following item:

REPORT *for the Term ending Friday, June 29*, A.D., *1855*

No. of pupils enrolled	78
Average daily attendance	43
No. of pupils *punctual*	35
No. of pupils present *every* day	5
No. of days of *absence* from sickness	46
No. of *communications* noticed	32
No. of pupils engaged in *quarrel*	2
No. of pupils using *profane* language	00
No. of cases of *truancy* detected	5
No. whose general deportment is *very good*	43
No. of lessons recited	650
No. of exercises	812

Names of those in attendance every day: Masters S. Richardson, John Moss, Henry Neitchin.—Misses M. Straight, J. Straight.

R. T. LOCKWOOD, *Teacher*

Common-school education which was tax supported had come to stay and was no longer challenged by any responsible person. Public high schools, however, were still in the nature of an innovation, and considerable opposition to their establishment was expressed. The reasons for the hostility were the same as those prevalent throughout the entire country when the high-school program was being launched. Men like Harvey Scott, famous editor of the Portland *Oregonian*, editorialized repeatedly on the evils of tax-supported high schools, their undermining effects on self-reliance and individualism, and on the fact that they were a luxury which ought not to be paid for by the community:

The belief is expressed that the machinery of the schools has grown to a too cumbrous and expensive system; that there are too many studies; that the high school is not a proper part of the system of public education; that foreign languages, higher mathematics and the several branches of natural sciences, so-called, should not be taught in the public schools, and that those who desire for their children an education beyond the common branches of the old fashioned common school should pay for it . . . effort should be concentrated on the few fundamental branches of common school education.

The struggle over "higher education" was a bitter one and the forces arrayed against it powerful and articulate. Governor Thayer of Oregon believed that if schooling beyond the elementary level were to be provided at the taxpayers' expense, it should consist of teaching the trades. W. S. Ladd, a prominent businessman, believed that all that was necessary was to give a child a good elementary start and, if he developed into a scholar, he would somehow find the means to obtain additional education. Academic subjects had no place, he felt, in a curriculum financed by public moneys; studies should be limited to reading, writing, spelling, arithmetic, history, and geography. Another well known public figure, Sylvester Pennoyer, believed that taxes should be levied only for the purpose of enabling children to master the three R's, and anything beyond that should be at private expense. Simeon Reed, whose later philanthropy made possible the establishment of Reed College in Portland, declared: "It would certainly be better if children were kept in school less and taught useful industry more, as they used to be. It seems to me that our old school system was nearer right than our present one."

Parents countered by turning out en masse at school elections where tax funds were to be voted upon. Notices appeared in the press urging citizens to attend the annual meeting and cast their ballots "in favor of free education for the masses" by voting sufficient appropriations to maintain the schools for the coming year: "The issue to be decided . . . at the election was avowedly High School or no High School; but really it was a fight for the existence of our entire common school system. The people triumphed, and the attack on public education is quelled, for a time, at least. The enemy who anticipated an easy capture of the High School, and who hoped to overthrow the entire system if they could win the first battle, are discomfited and baffled." The high school waged its struggle for existence during the eighties. It was fought out district by district until, in 1901, a general, state-wide system of high-school education was enacted into law in Oregon.

The distances on the frontier created a special obstacle to the efficient operation of the school system. County superintendents reported that because the population was so scattered, many children could not be taken care of; that in some sections the only mode of travel was by water and youngsters were unable to manage boats for a distance of two or three miles. Another handicap was the lack of sufficient community funds. The officials complained about the dilapidated condition of school buildings, some of which, they said, compared unfavorably with many barns; or that the school term was too short to provide an adequate education; or that more equipment was needed, citing as an example a county that possessed only a single geographic globe.

Other problems were essentially the same as those which confronted the rest of the country: lack of uniformity in instruction, textbooks, and teachers' certifications, low salaries, difficulty in securing competent county and state superintendents of schools, ways of allocating school funds so that the poorest counties should benefit equally with the more prosperous ones, means of separating politics from the school system.

Of great concern, especially in the earlier period of the Northwest, was the absence of consistent standards for the employment of teachers. Few restrictions were placed on the county superintendent in the matter of teacher certifications, and no uniform system existed. Occasionally boards of examiners assisted him, but, on the whole, he had virtually complete discretion. With a policy under which he could give either oral or written examinations in public or in private which he made up and graded himself, there was great temptation to be less than objective and impersonal. In addition the examination fee might have influenced his judgment because of the meagerness of his salary. One superintendent stated that he had to supplement his income of $100 a year by farming or clerking.

Candidates were generally expected to be jacks-of-all-subjects, to teach Latin, Greek, and French, as well as all the higher branches of the English studies, which sometimes included philosophy, botany, chemistry, geometry, geology, and so forth. They were tested particularly in the fields of grammar, geography, modern history, orthography, writing, reading, mental and written arithmetic.

As was characteristic of education generally during that period, no premium was placed on the ability to interpret, to analyze, to judge. Almost complete emphasis was given to the accumulation of factual data for its own sake, and all that was needed for scholastic success was a retentive memory. For instance, examination questions in history ran like this: Into how many departments is the government of the United States divided—name them; mention the names of five authors, five inventors, five noted statesmen and five noted events in American history; mention the place and date of the second colony planted in what is now the United States; list the causes and date of the French revolution which occurred during the life of Napoleon Bonaparte.

Impetus to elevate professional standards came in large measure from teachers' organizations and institutes. They were interested, in successive stages, in securing suitable textbooks and establishing uniformity, in achieving better school laws and better pedagogic techniques. When there were no immediate issues necessitating legislative action, the institutes were concerned with instructional problems, such as teaching arithmetic to primary and intermediate classes, object teaching, methods of teaching American history, discipline, and the extent to which oral instruction should be used. The following was a typical program as described in the local paper:

EUGENE, ORE. April 11.—The District and county institute, which promises to be a very interesting one, convened here yesterday afternoon. State Superintendent McElroy, various county school superintendents, and quite a large number of teachers were present. . . .

Primary reading and spelling was [*sic*] presented by Mr. Williams, Principal of the Eugene Public School. He reviewed the several methods, citing the merits of each, and concluded by saying that the word method is the one which should be used in all beginners' work.

Physiology and hygiene was [*sic*] discussed by J. L. Taite, who presented the subject practically and at the same time held the undivided attention of his audience. . . .

EVENING SESSION

After music by the orchestra Hon. S. W. Condon delivered the address of welcome. He spoke at length of the necessity of education for the poor and rich, and of the equal privileges which our schools give to each. He eloquently referred to those great minds whose cradles were rocked beneath the humble roof of the log cabin, and whose early lessons were received in the old-fashioned log school house. . . .

After music by the orchestra, and a recitation by Miss Straight, Prof. Bailey delivered a lecture on the "Solar System," speaking of the number of stars and their distance from the earth, and of the force of gravitation, and closed by referring to the great Power which had so wisely arranged such a system.

An excellent programme has been arranged, and the institute will undoubtedly be very beneficial to the teachers of this state.

In Washington the King County Teachers' Institute presented a more elaborate program, at which the president of the state university spoke on "General and Local Storms," the president of the state agricultural college at Pullman gave an address on "The Relation of Higher Education to the Community," and the president of the state normal school at Terre Haute, Indiana, delivered a talk on "The Ethics of Shakespeare." During the four-day program, papers were presented on "Practical Psychology," "The Child and Nature," "The Elements of Mental Science," "The Bad Boy in School"; discussions were held on whether the vertical system of writing should be adopted and on the advisability for teachers of organizing to protect themselves against reductions in salaries.

The question of salaries became a vital issue at the beginning of the century. Faced with the constantly increasing cost of living, teachers found that the average salary of $50 a month was but a pittance, and they grew impatient with the temporizing tactics of school boards. Professional journals which appeared in the eighties in the Northwest soon began to devote considerable space to agitating for higher wages, though at first they were concerned exclusively with the improvement of professional standards.

Many of them were militant and, for the period, even radical in their views, as, for example, the *Oregon Teachers' Monthly*, which urged members of the teaching profession to organize. It declared that teachers should align themselves with the broad stratum of wage earners and through union muster the necessary strength to prevent underbidding and enforce their demands for higher salaries. Although there were many professional organizations in the field, they evinced little interest in financial conditions, the publication pointed out. A foolish notion was current, it stated, to the effect that teachers found compensation in the glory inherent in their work. When that idea was discarded, it was hoped that salaries would rise at least to the level of those commanded by manual laborers!

A Washington journal wrote: "All over the United States the question of better wages for teachers is being discussed. The people are coming to realize that the only way to get and keep good teachers is to pay them wages commensurate with their services. By and by the teachers will organize, raise the standard of the profession, and ask for and receive living wages." Teachers' salaries may have been inadequate, but it could not be doubted that the people of the Northwest were education-conscious. Nearly every town and hamlet had a "college" or academy, although most of them were only preparatory schools whose instruction did not advance beyond the secondary-school level.

The University of Washington Territory, which opened at Seattle in 1861, was made possible by the Donations Act passed by Congress seven years earlier. According to the law, two townships of thirty-six sections each were to be set aside for university purposes and administered under the direction of the Territorial legislature. During its early history, the university was more of a primary and secondary school than a college. The regents' report for the first year listed thirty pupils in the primary department, thirteen in the grammar school, seven in the preparatory department, and one in the college freshman class. All "departments" were taught by a faculty of one who was also the president.

The newspaper announcement of the opening of the university stated that the girls would be supervised by a teacher and would be offered lessons in piano and voice. "Pupils of both sexes will be under proper restrictions and care . . . and their education in the several branches above named industriously and carefully attended to, *without any sectional bias* or influence whatever."

In Oregon considerable opposition existed to a tax-supported institution of higher learning, as many felt that the denominational academies and colleges were serving the purpose adequately. The influential Judge Matthew P. Deady believed that colleges under governmental supervision always languish and are never as popular as those under the auspices of religious groups or supported by private philanthropy. For a while he actively opposed the idea of a state university but then had a change of heart and, after the University of Oregon was established, he became chairman of its board of regents.

For a number of years after the university opened, Deady's misgivings were confirmed—the student body was so small that those concerned with its welfare were apprehensive as to whether it would be able to continue in existence. In 1881, five years after the establishment of the institution, it could claim a total enrollment of only 186, and four years later the number had increased by only two. Seven students were graduated in 1881 and only four in 1885.

In neighboring Idaho the university, which began to function in 1892, opened in the "unfinished and unfurnished wing of the main building, which stood in the midst of a plowed field." It had a president to supervise a faculty of one, no books or apparatus of any kind, and not a single student on the college level. Some thirty students, who, according to President Gault, could barely write their names, had come from great distances by saddle horse and wagon to enroll, the journey requiring weeks in some cases.

For some time the university provided instruction on elementary, secondary, and college levels. Of the 133 students enrolled during the first year, only six were of college caliber. This was not too strange as at the time there were only three accredited high schools in Idaho. When the newly admitted scholars were being classified, they were asked where they had received their previous training. A number replied nonchalantly, "Oh, something out of a little red book."

The morals and deportment of students and faculty were as much the concern of those in control of educational institutions as were learning and teaching. In an advertisement of the University of Washington in 1863, the section under "Discipline" stated:

No student will be allowed to retain a connection with the school whose habits are such as to render him an unfit companion, or who will not render a ready compliance with the regulations of the School. Frequenting of saloons, and attendance upon theatres and balls, are not allowed, but students are required to be at their respective places of abode at stated hours. A respectful observance of the Sabbath is required, and at 3 o'clock P.M. each Sabbath, the Students will assemble at the University Chapel, to study the Scriptures as a Bible Class. The reading of the Scriptures, regarded as the only safe text [*sic*] book of morals, will be a daily exercise of the school.

One president of Willamette University, although a man of distinguished professional attainment, was not reappointed after two years of service because he smoked a pipe. He had earned an international reputation in the scientific world with the publication of an invaluable treatise on the use of the microscope, the first book of its kind in America and in the English language.

The curricula of the Western universities were patterned on those of the Eastern institutions whose emphasis was on the classics and the natural sciences. The objective was to foster "the dogma of formal discipline." One of the catalogues expressed it thus: "The aim of the college is to cultivate the mind in a general way by disciplining the faculties, to make the young strong in intellect. . . . If this disciplinary work is well-accomplished, the mind may afterwards be applied to any subject, to the study of any profession, art, or business, and it will be able to work with precision, ease, and power."

At Willamette University, which was typical, students in their first year were required to study algebra, Latin and Greek prose composition, ancient history, geometry, Xenephon's *Memorabilia*, Ovid, Virgil, Homer's *Iliad*, anatomy and physiology. During the sophomore year, the course of study included trigonometry, mensuration, Horace's *Odes and Epodes*, classical literature, Herodotus, Greek Testament, chemistry, analytical geometry, Livy, Aeschylus' *Prometheus*, botany, and zoology. If the student survived this plethora of intellectual fare, he was snowed under during his junior year with calculus, *Germania* and *Agricola*, more classical literature, Euripides' *Alcestis*, Greek Testament, mental philosophy, mechanics, logic, geology, *De Natura Deorum*, *Oedipus Tyrannus*. And during the senior year the courses dealt with rhetoric, political economy, Juvenal, Horace's *Satires* and *Epistles*, Plato's *Gorgias*, natural philosophy, natural theology, astronomy, moral science, "evidences of Christianity," Butler's *Analogy*, and physical geography. Interspersed with all these were courses in mental arithmetic, declamation, composition, and orthography.

Changes were made at this particular college during the academic year 1865–1866, and courses in modern history, surveying and spherical trigonometry, physics, philosophy of history, mineralogy, and constitutional history of the United States were added to the curriculum. Elective studies during the senior year now included biblical science and literature, logic, Hebrew, analytical chemistry, mining and metallurgy, higher astronomy and civil engineering. "Co-eds" were not spared. The three-year program they took was essentially the same, except that they could substitute French and English for the classical languages. This generous concession was made, no doubt, in deference to their status as the weaker sex.

In later years the curricula of the various institutions were liberal-ized and courses in music, art, history, and other branches in the hu-manities were introduced, with a corresponding decline in the clas-sical studies. The liberal-arts program was becoming the mainstay of higher education. Extension courses were given and, toward the end of the century, a few schools began to offer graduate work.

It was some time, though, before universities advanced to the point where subjects were taught by specialists in the field. As a rule, when a faculty member was appointed to teach the natural sciences or clas-sical languages, he was expected to offer all the courses within that wide range. For example, at the University of Washington, Professor C. B. Johnson was the head of both the Department of Physical Sci-ence, which included physics and chemistry, and of the Department of Natural History, which included physiology, botany, zoology, biology, mineralogy, and geology, and he alone taught all these sub-jects! When he was asked the nature of the chair he filled, he could hardly be blamed for answering that he occupied a lounge.

The settlers were concerned about the establishment of educational facilities for their children, but they were no less worried about Satan finding mischief for the idle hands of adults as soon as the backbreak-ing labor of removing the tree stumps from their front yards was over. The long, rainy winter evenings were the Tempter's own, they felt, and the *Oregon Spectator* was moved to write that if some means were not devised, "we may surely calculate that very many of these excellent young men will be lured into resorts of vice and gambling, and ere the vernal suns of another spring shall clothe the earth with bloom, they will have fallen into destructive habits, and their inno-cence, that gem above all price, will be lost forever."

The more serious-minded in the community promptly set about protecting the innocence of the younger generation and providing for themselves a source of mental stimulation to balance their days of purely physical labor. Adult education on the Northwestern frontier began with lyceums, debating societies, literary clubs, and general discussion groups. There were hundreds under a variety of names: The Young Men's Debating Club of Portland, the Young Men's As-sociation, the Alphean Society of Olympia, the Franklin Club of Astoria, the Academy of Science, the History Club, Current Litera-ture Club, German Club, Thursday Afternoon Club, the Belles-Lettres Club.

The stated *raison d'être* of these organizations was invariably, as the

Oregon Weekly Union wrote of one called the Calliopean Society, "for the benefit of the young men of our town." (Occasionally special programs were planned for the ladies.) The paper urged all young gentlemen to join and participate in the instructive activities. The group was affiliated with a library from which its members could borrow books without charge.

Announcements frequently appeared in the press about new groups which had just been organized, listing their objectives and soliciting new memberships. The most popular type had as its objective "extemporaneous discussion," recitations from various authors, and essay reading. Cultivating the art of public speaking was fashionable, and rhetoric was studied diligently both inside and outside the schools. All kinds of subjects were debated—that the Sunday Laws ought to be repealed, that intemperance was a greater evil than war, that the Monroe Doctrine was a good American policy, that the suffrage should be made universal, that the "Specific Contract Law is a humbug and ought to be repealed by the next legislature," and so forth. The debates were all faithfully reported in the local paper, with some critical comment such as, "One of the lady members read a short argument . . . which, in our opinion, contained more sense applicable to the question, than all else said upon the question, pro or con."

In later years women took over "culture," and their various organizations, characteristic of most small towns today, began to flourish. In Pendleton, Oregon, the members of the History Club during its first year studied "French history, from the time of the earliest Franks to the downfall of the great Corsican"; the next year, German; and then for three years, the history, literature, and politics of Great Britain. Pendleton also had a Current Literature Club, a Thursday Afternoon Club which studied Shakespeare, music, and early Colonial history among other subjects; a Belles-Lettres Club whose first project was a study of the literature, mythology, art, philosophy, and architecture of the ancient Greeks; a German Club which read and discussed German literature in the original tongue, with Goethe and Schiller among the authors studied. This was during the time when the city's population was about three thousand and when it had almost thirty saloons and wide-open gambling.

Churches were frequently used as meeting places for the groups, and as many of the clergymen were also scholars, they were often invited to address the members. The selection of topics ranged from politics to world history to literature, with Shakespeare a favorite subject. Lecture series extending over a period of months were occasionally organized in the earliest years. The *Oregonian* announced one under the headline "Lectures—Winter Course, 1860–61," and stated that it was to be held in the Methodist Episcopal Church. A $3 subscription fee entitled the purchaser to attend all the talks, which were to be given bimonthly throughout the winter season. The paper urged editorially that the lectures be heard by everyone, as they "blend instruction with delight. . . . We shall regard it as a high evidence of the good taste and intelligence of our citizens to know that they are well attended. How much better for the young men of our city to attend these instructive lectures (the young ladies would be glad to go with them), than to waste their evenings in frivolous amusements."

A number of years later, the Oregon Academy of Sciences, supported by many of Portland's leading citizens, was organized as a center for the study and discussion of the sciences. A museum and library were included in the plans. For its opening program an ambitious series of lectures free to the public was announced: "The Nebular Hypothesis," "The Formation of the Earth's Crust," "The Succession of Plants," "The Origin and Distribution of Animal Life," "The Development of Mind," and "The Advent of Man." Arrangements were made with Willamette University to use the museum attached to its medical school, but the organization hoped eventually to have permanent quarters of its own.

Visiting lecturers of all persuasions soon began to tour the region, giving addresses on diverse subjects. When B. F. Underwood, a prominent freethinker and leader of a national antireligious organization, delivered several talks in 1873, the *New Northwest* commented: "As a 'freethinker' he is a decided success, and there is much in his lectures that is profitable to an analytic mind, yet some of his therories [*sic*] are not only far fetched, but are so strongly put that they weaken his argument. But we are no theologian, and if the Portland ministers will not meet this anti-Christian philosopher's logic, we don't know that we are called upon to attempt it." Eleven years later, Robert G. Ingersoll, America's outstanding agnostic, was warmly received by large audiences.

Local scholars also traveled around on lecture tours. President Chapman of Oregon State College gave a series of talks on Shakespeare in Portland. Popular interest in the bard is indicated by the critical analysis in the press:

One of President Chapman's most interesting lectures is on "Hamlet." His view of the prince's insanity is of interest in connection with the recent utterances of Beerbohm Tree, who maintains that Hamlet's madness was wholly feigned. President Chapman holds to the original view that Hamlet's eccentricities, when not due to his dissembling, are to be accounted for on the ground of the melancholy Dane's extreme youth . . . and that his actions are not to be judged, therefore, as those of a mature person.

The Chautauqua was undoubtedly the greatest effort in organized adult education in the Pacific Northwest. In its early days it provided cultural advantages that were seldom enjoyed except in large cities. Each season, for a week or two, it offered programs that ran the gamut of formal instruction, lectures, music, and athletics. Families frequently planned their vacations to coincide with the dates of the nearest Chautauqua.

In Washington one large Chautauqua was held regularly, beginning with 1889, at Vashon Island on Puget Sound. In Oregon the one held at Gladstone Park, which was organized in 1895, was the third largest unit in the country. Others were later founded at La Grande, Albany, and The Dalles. Thousands of persons traveled many miles and paid admission fees to hear William Jennings Bryan, Sam Jones of Georgia, Henry Watterson of Kentucky, Senator Dolliver, Champ Clark, Bob Burdette, and many others.

Following the turn of the century, Northwesterners became increasingly concerned with large and vital issues, such as imperialism or economic crises or immigration, and groups were organized to deal exclusively with these controversial questions. One of these was the Sunday Forum of Portland founded by Rabbi Stephen Wise, who held a pulpit in that city, and Colonel Charles Erskine Scott Wood. Single taxers, socialists, anarchists, nationalists, and champions of almost every orthodox and unorthodox social viewpoint participated in the lively and frequently stormy sessions held every week, at which the problems of the world were considered and analyzed.

Apart from intellectual group activity, many pioneers considered books an essential part of living and reading one of the most enjoyable ways of spending their rare evenings of leisure in the solitude of the frontier farm. Reading matter had been hauled across the plains, squeezed into every available bit of space between articles of food, household equipment, and bedding. Though it often arrived battered, wet, stained or torn, it was treasured in the new home as a mute link with the civilization and world of knowledge left behind.

The wilderness to which the settler had come was not completely barren of literary collections. In the spring of 1839, the missionaries at Spalding's Lapwai mission established a library consisting of about five hundred volumes. Most of the books were, naturally, religious in nature, but there were titles like *Alice and Her Mother*, *A Child's Story*, and *Burns's Principles of Midwifery* by W. W. Luchanan.

Bookstores appeared during the first years of settlement and the wide variety of titles which they advertised and sold reflected the constant demand for knowledge. Emphasis was on the classics, among which the favorites seemed to be Shakespeare, Coleridge, Shelley, Wordsworth; biographies of Washington, Jackson, Bonaparte, Mozart; ancient and modern history, such as Gibbon's *Decline and Fall of the Roman Empire*, Macaulay's *History of England*. They also sold volumes on geography, physiology, chemistry, philosophy, government, anatomy, mineralogy, mathematics, debating, oratory, medicine, theology, temperance, rhetoric, grammar, arithmetic, astronomy, travel, and books of humor. S. J. McCormick of Portland advertised that his stock "comprises EVERY USEFUL BOOK! From that of a Child's Primer to a Family Bible! Not forgetting a few thousand novels!" This book-seller also took subscriptions for magazines such as *Harper's Monthly*, *Graham's Magazine*, *Godey's Lady's Book*, *Leslie's Weekly*, and *Putnam's Monthly Magazine* and for newspapers published in any part of the country.

Under the act creating the Oregon Territory, Congress made provision for a Territorial library with an appropriation of $5,000. The first shipment of books and legislative documents arrived shortly thereafter from the East, consisting mainly of legal works and about two hundred volumes on historical and scientific subjects. The Territory's newspaper expressed pleasure at the selection of titles, which, it said, "are of the most approved character for correct and standard literature." Included in the miscellaneous assortment were classics such as Goethe's *Faust*, Locke's *Essays*, and Gibbon's *Decline and Fall of the Roman Empire*. A number of volumes, the paper stated, were injured by dampness during the long journey, but fortunately not enough to impair the collection, which would constitute an "excellent foundation for a noble library." The following year, when a batch of congressional documents and a copy of the narrative of the exploring expedition under Captain Wilkes was sent to the library, it devoted an item to this news, ending with the comment that the donation would make a valuable addition to the collection.

A similar appropriation was made for Washington Territory, and the newly appointed governor, Isaac Stevens, spent considerable time purchasing books before he left the East to take up his assignment. In his first message to the legislature, he proudly reported that 1,850 volumes had already arrived and that the balance, which was on the way, would bring the total to about 2,000. Despite this auspicious beginning, the library made little advance in the years preceding statehood.

No provision was made for a Territorial library in Idaho, and though some local historians portray the miners as a literate, educated group of men who held learned discussions around the campfire, the first public library was not established until 1901. With permanent settlement, however, the interest in education became as keen as in other parts of the Northwest.

Small private or semipublic libraries opened in the towns and cities throughout the region. Oregon had three in 1850. A decade later there were ten, including a college library, most of them under the control of religious denominations. One private library had a thousand volumes. Dues in the private libraries were nominal and the membership fee entitled unlimited borrowing.

Libraries served not only to diffuse "useful knowledge and sound morality," but provided a meeting place for public lectures and debates. Typical was the Steilacoom Library Association, which was organized in 1858 in what was then one of the leading communities of Washington Territory. For an admission fee of $5 and monthly dues of twenty-five cents, members were given the privilege of the reading room and library and were afforded the opportunity of attending lectures, debates, and other such public functions. This was by no means an impersonal civic organization, but in a real sense a community enterprise. If funds were lacking—and that was the case more often than not—balls and various other entertainments were held to raise money. For about fifty years the library served not only as a repository for books, but as the headquarters for regularly conducted study circles at which anyone interested in edifying his townspeople was given a platform. The decline in importance of the city resulted in the disappearance of this pioneering library institution.

As the population of the region increased, demands were made that libraries be supported by tax funds, but achievement was a slow process. Washington passed a law in 1890 providing for a tax levy for the maintenance of public libraries. Many established after that year were nevertheless supported partially by subscription fees, though these were considerably reduced when aid was given by the city treasuries.

Local library commissions did attempt from time to time to offer free service to borrowers, but sometimes the funds available for such purposes were so meager that recourse to subscription levies had to be taken again. The Library Commission of Seattle reported unhappily in 1895 that on the first of the year the treasurer's office had had the sum of $15.85 for library purposes. Even a general appropriation of $250 by the City Council had not been sufficient to defray expenses, and with great reluctance it had been necessary to resort to the undesirable expedient of imposing subscription fees as an alternative to shutting down the library and reading rooms. Having had a taste of free service, the library patrons in Seattle were no longer content to pay for their books, and the number of borrowers declined drastically.

A number of private libraries became public institutions. The Library Association of Portland, for example, which had been organized in 1863 under the sponsorship of several wealthy men in the community, became a free institution in 1901. Its first benefactor had been W. S. Ladd, who had donated funds and turned the second floor of his banking house into a library. In 1868 it owned 3,000 volumes; by the end of the century the number had increased to 35,000. Its first librarian was Harvey Scott, who held the position until he joined the *Oregonian.*

The scattered nature of the population impeded library development throughout the Northwest. As late as 1905, eastern Oregon, which comprises two-thirds of the physical area of the entire state, had an average of only one and one-half persons per square mile. The same general situation was true for Washington, and Idaho was even more sparsely settled. Under those circumstances the cost of furnishing adequate free library facilities to the inhabitants was prohibitive, even if the obstacles of transportation could have been overcome. Nevertheless, the development of the region as a whole made it imperative to invoke the aid of the state legislatures to improve the existing situation.

The Oregon legislature in 1901 enacted a number of laws designed to regulate and coordinate the loosely connected system. These provided for the establishment of school and district libraries and for the supervision of county units. Four years later, the State Library Commission was established and assigned the task of expediting the creation of local libraries, traveling libraries, and, in general, "to do all things necessary to help the people of Oregon obtain good books and libraries." Thus Oregon became the twenty-first state to encourage and stimulate a library movement.

Progress was also made in the mechanics of library procedure. When the secretary of the Oregon Library Commission arrived to assume her duties in 1905, she found it necessary to make frequent trips to teachers' institutes, many of which were held in places accessible only by stage, in order to explain basic techniques. No catalog system existed in the entire state outside of Portland, and none even in the universities and normal schools. A program for professional training of librarians had to be instituted, and this was shortly undertaken. The first mail-order system in the nation was started in Oregon, and books were sent to distant parts of the state by express before parcel-post service was available. Encyclopedias and reference books were cut up into sections so that the material in them could be made available to the largest number of readers.

Libraries began to assume a greater responsibility toward the public and coordinated their work with that of the school systems. The Debate Library, a collection which was set up in 1905 by the Oregon Library Commission, furnished the various high schools, colleges, academies, and granges with material necessary to enable them to conduct well informed debates. During the early years, schools and colleges borrowed more than 250 such debating libraries on a variety of topics, including city government by commission, municipal ownership of railroads, ship subsidies, tariffs, trusts, Asiatic immigration, strikes, trade-unions, industrial arbitration, injunctions, woman suffrage, proportional representation, direct legislation, and direct primaries.

The introduction of traveling libraries was another of the commission's extension activities, bringing books to the isolated, rural sections. Titles were selected with a view toward stimulating popular interest in literature. About one-half were fiction, but every traveling unit had a substantial number of classics which usually circulated well.

In one of its reports, the Oregon Library Commission outlined the progress that had been made during the two years following its organization. There were, it stated, fourteen free public libraries in the state which received some of their funds from taxation, and four had their own buildings. There were four free libraries not tax supported, nine subscription libraries, and three city reading rooms. Within those two years, free libraries had been opened in such widely scattered communities as Albany, Bend, Jacksonville, Medford, Newberg, Springfield, Sumter, and Tillamook. Subscription libraries had been established in several cities and a number already in existence had been transformed into free libraries. One city was allocating $10 a month for the local school library. In two cities Carnegie library buildings were under construction.

The growth of a free-library movement in Washington was also a natural concomitant of population development. Throughout the entire Territorial period, that is, up to 1889, only two libraries, the Territorial library and the university library, received any financial support from the government. But after statehood had been achieved, the situation changed, due in large measure to the continuous pressure brought to bear by public-spirited citizens. The state librarian, in his report of 1900, urged the adoption of a traveling-library system, and a bill providing for this was passed the following year. A free traveling library with ten stations, which had been in existence under the sponsorship of the State Federation of Women's Clubs, donated its cases and books to the state. Six years later, the traveling library was made independent of the state library and acquired its own superintendent. Its appropriation and the number of its books continued to increase steadily.

Literary taste in the Northwest was essentially the same as that in the rest of the country. Of the books loaned by the Portland library in 1868, 73 per cent were romances. This was explained in part by the fact that many people in the city had private collections for more serious reading. When they purchased books, which were expensive, they wanted those that they felt would stand the test of time, and they relied on the library for lighter reading. Mrs. Emma Southworth was a favorite author in the latter category. She was described in later years as "a joy, a very well in the desert to that type of romantic, poorly educated woman who at that time filled the position now held by the average female frequenter of the movies." The comparison is not entirely valid, but the point is clear. Penny novels were in great demand, as well as those dealing with temperance and religion.

Popular books in the eighties were the romances of H. Rider Haggard, the melodramas of Mrs. Humphry Ward, William Clark Russell's sea stories, *David Copperfield, Ivanhoe, The Scarlet Letter, Ben Hur*. At the turn of the century, semihistorical fiction of the heavily romantic kind ranked first, followed by adventure stories and such character studies as *David Harum* and *Ben Holden*. Reading tastes were still simple and superficial. Women enjoyed weeping over the trials and tribulations of the gentle heroine, and men enjoyed identifying themselves with the stern, noble hero. Only a small percentage of the population had discovered Ibsen, Bellamy, or Upton Sinclair.

By 1910 the people of the Northwest were as well read as any in the land. Of the ten cities whose population numbered between 200,000 and 300,000, Seattle, with the third largest population of the group, was second in the number of books circulated, and Portland, with the smallest population, was fourth in book circulation. This was the region where only a generation before the sound of the ax had broken the stillness of the great forests and where there were men who remembered the long crossing in a covered wagon.

Thirteen

The Literary Frontier

In a pioneer land the ax is unquestionably weightier than the pen and more essential in the process of establishing a new community. "The era of intellectual productions comes only in the full and ripe age of a people, who have accumulated sufficient intellectual capital to engage in the production of such exquisite luxuries and stimulants," wrote one of the leading pioneers of the Northwest. Oregon was still in the state of a half-grown boy, "busy with building, begetting, delving, and . . . physical labor," which was entirely natural for a people who still had to improve and adorn a land. Book publishing, therefore, had not gone beyond a few ephemeral pamphlets, and the newspaper literature, "like Caliban, smelling strongly of the virgin soil— full of uncultivated natural vigor and truculent politics," could not be considered more than "a branch of physical labor, where so much blank paper is wrought into printed sheets, full of advertisements, dispatches and miscellaneous clippings."

It did not take too long, however, for intellectual productions to appear. From the beginning the pioneers were prolific writers. They poured out a torrent of letters to the folks back home, reminiscent accounts about the experiences in crossing the plains or rounding the Cape, and about life in the new country. Innumerable letters and diaries were carefully preserved by families and historical societies and in later years published in newspapers, quarterlies, and as pamphlets and books. They are warm and human documents, many vividly descriptive, poignant accounts of hopes and fears, of frustrations and achievements, of desperate loneliness in the solitudes of the great Oregon forests, and of neighbors' generous hospitality. Some display a natural gift for words, as, for example, the letter of Mrs.

Amelia Stewart Knight, who somehow managed to steal time to write on the journey across, despite the care of a brood of seven children:

> Traveled 14 miles over the worst road that was ever made, up and down, very steep, rough and rocky hills, through mud holes, twisting and winding around stumps, logs and fallen trees . . . these mountains are a dense forest of pines, fir, white cedar or redwood. . . . Many of the trees are 300 feet high and so dense to almost exclude the light of heaven, and for my own part I dare not look to the top of them for fear of breaking my neck. . . . It would be useless for me with my pencil to describe the awful road . . . (let fancy picture a train of wagons and cattle passing through a crooked chimney . . .) steep, winding, sideling, deep down, slippery and muddy, made so by a spring running the entire length . . . and this road is cut down so deep that at times the cattle and wagons are almost out of sight, with no room for the drivers except on the bank.

Written because of an impelling need for self-expression, or as a record for coming generations, un-selfconscious and unsophisticated, these early writings can more properly be classified as journalism than literature. Much on the same order were the tracts and books written by the explorers and missionaries.

Literature began with a novel, *The Prairie Flower; or, Adventures in the Far West*, whose authorship is in dispute among Oregonians to this day. It was published in Cincinnati in 1849, and the author on the title page is given as Emerson Bennett, who was an Eastern writer of popular fiction. A prominent businessman of Oregon City, Sidney Moss, claimed, however, that he had written the book. He said he had entrusted the manuscript to a friend bound for the East to turn it over to a publisher, that the friend had given it to Bennett, who unscrupulously appropriated it after he had changed the names of the characters and made some other slight alterations.

The controversy over the question of authorship became extremely involved. Frances Fuller Victor in her *History of Oregon* gives Moss credit for the book and states that the characters were modeled after well known pioneer figures. One present-day writer says that there is historical evidence that parts of the manuscript were read by Moss at meetings of a literary society in Oregon City in 1843. Moss's daughter, in an interview given in 1901, made the same statement. Moss himself told Hubert Howe Bancroft in 1878 that "J. Emerson Bennett claimed it [the book] for a while but withdrew his claim finally." Some weight has been attached by supporters of Moss to the fact that in his introduction Bennett has an imaginary dialogue between the author and one of his characters, the "Wanderer," who left the manuscript with him. To add to the confusion, one Oregon historian alleged that the book was written by still another Oregonian, a Samuel Allen!

In and of itself, *The Prairie Flower* has only antiquarian interest, though over the years it sold more than a hundred thousand copies. Too saccharine for the tastes of modern readers, who prefer more sophistication in their "westerns," its great popularity at the time is not surprising. As one contemporary reviewer wrote, "It is brim-full of life, love, passion, sentiment, humor, pathos; and its glowing descriptions, romantic incidents, daring adventures, fearful perils, thrilling exploits, dreadful accidents, and hair-breadth escapes—all run through and interweave with a deep, ingenious and intricate plot." The scene was laid on the trail to Oregon and in the Oregon country, and it is claimed that the book stimulated interest in migration to the region during the fifties. The style is sentimental and slushy in the tradition of the romantic novels of the period. The following, which is a typical example, would probably bring a snort even from the present-day reader of dime novels:

It was a lovely day in the spring of 1843. On the banks of the romantic Willamette, under the shade of a large tree, I was seated. By my side— with her sweet fact averted and crimson with blushes, her right hand clasped in mine, her left unconsciously toying with a beautiful flower, which failed to rival her own fair self—sat Lilian Huntley. . . . It was one of those peculiar moments which are distinctly remembered through life. I had just offered her my hand and fortune, and was waiting, with all the trembling impatience of a lover, to hear the result.

"Say, Lilian, sweet Lilian, will you be mine?"

Her lily hand trembled, I felt its velvet-like pressure, but her own had lost the power of utterance. It was enough; and the next moment she was strained to my heart, with a joy too deep for words.

"And when shall it be? when shall my happiness be consummated, dear Lilian?" I at length ventured to ask.

For a time she did not reply; and then raising her angelic face and fastening her soft, beaming eyes, moist with tears of joy, upon mine, she said in a low, sweet, tremulous tone:

"On the day when we are all made glad by the presence of my brother."

"Alas!" groaned I mentally; "that day may never come!"

The first literary work undisputably by an Oregonian was a play called, *A Melodrame Entitled "Treason, Stratagems and Spoils" in Five Acts, by Breakspear*, originally published in several installments in the *Oregonian* in 1852. It was written by a Whig farmer and school-teacher, William L. Adams, who possessed a barbed wit and a facile pen. He cleverly patterned his style on that of the great English play-wright whose name inspired his own *nom de plume*. What made the work especially appealing to Oregonians was the fact that it was a trenchant satire on the politics of the day, making the Democratic clique of politicians in the Territory the target. Each character represented an actual person powerful in the ruling political group at Salem, thinly disguised under another name. The play become so popular that Adams issued it in pamphlet form, and he became so well known as a result that three years later he launched a Whig newspaper in Oregon City to compete with the Democratic organ in Salem. Adams published another work, a *History of Medicine and Surgery from the Earliest Times* (1888), which exposed "All frauds, medical, theological and political, by which kingcraft and priestcraft have fattened on ignorance in the world's history." This was probably a result of his medical studies—he became an M.D. at the age of fifty-two—but it sank into oblivion and, as one literary historian says wrathfully, is not even listed in a compilation of Pacific Northwest Americana.

For two years after *Breakspear*, there was a lull on the literary front, and then the women entered the field with a novel by Mrs. Margaret Jewett Bailey. Most of the early novelists and poets were women, some of whom undoubtedly found in writing—especially poetry—an escape from the tedium, the drudgery, and the stultifying loneliness of their daily lives. They were not too graciously welcomed into the literary fraternity or even by the reading public, and most of their books have self-conscious introductions humbly apologizing for any deficiencies in style.

Mrs. Bailey had come to the Northwest as a teacher with the early missionaries of 1837. Nothing is known about her before she arrived in the region or the inner reason for her having left civilization, but she was undoubtedly a sensitive, intelligent woman. She married Dr. William J. Bailey and the couple settled in French Prairie at a time when most of her neighbors were fur traders and their squaw wives. Even after Americans came to the region in great numbers, her life did not change appreciably, for her home was located in an isolated area. To add to her desperate loneliness, she soon found that she was married to a sot who tried to strangle her while in an intoxicated fit three weeks after their marriage, and she experienced the bitter humiliation of knowing that she shared her husband with any and every Indian squaw who came his way.

The couple quarreled constantly, separated and reunited about a dozen times. Bailey always promised to reform, but when he returned home one day, shortly after a reunion, with evidence of having been with an Indian woman, Margaret decided that she had had enough and obtained a divorce. To her bewilderment and despair, she, and not her husband, whose character and activities were well known, became the pariah in the community. She found herself completely ostracized by society to the point where she could find no employment. "I am avoided and shunned and slighted and regarded with suspicions in every place," she wrote in the introduction to her book, "till my life is more burdensome than death would be."

After years of having suffered in silence, this was indeed draining the cup to the bitter dregs. In an attempt to mitigate her loneliness, Margaret Bailey had previously written bits of verse which were published in the *Spectator*. Now she decided to write a novel based on her life and perhaps thereby drain the gall of being rejected out of her system and at the same time try to right the score. *Grains, or Passages in the Life of Ruth Rover* (1854) was the result. It was issued in two volumes, the first containing thirteen chapters and the second, fourteen. The latter, dealing with her life before she came to the Northwest, has completely vanished.

If Mrs. Bailey hoped to obtain sympathy as a result of her book, she failed to reckon with Oregon. As with one voice, the press ripped it to shreds. The review in the *Oregonian* by "Squills" was especially vitriolic. He began by congratulating the printer on his typography and the neatness of the cover. Then he tore in, commenting first that he seldom read books written by women because he believed their province was in the kitchen. It was bad enough, he fumed, to be plagued with unjust laws, bad lawyers, incompetent judges, and taxes with no money to pay them, without having to contend with an authoress. He devoutly hoped that this unnecessary visitation would be the last. It would be impolite to call the book trash, he said, because it was written by a woman. He objected to the plot; he objected to the style; he further objected to quotations from the heroine's diary. Private biographies in general were intolerable, he continued. They might be justified for a prominent character, "but who the dickens cares, about the existence of a fly, or in whose pan of molasses the insect disappeared." And on that note the review ended.

Mrs. Bailey had been bruised too badly to allow herself to be crushed by this type of comment. She issued the second volume a short time later, taking the opportunity to retaliate against Squills in a biting preface headed "The Monster." Enraged, Squills launched a vicious attack. "The immorality, not to say the indecency of the work, is far too much in advance even for the fast ideas and morals of young Oregon," he wrote. "We have a law in Oregon regulating the morals of publications to be uttered in the territory and at the end of this article we shall quote it, leaving it to common judgment whether the 'Grains' comes under the statute or not." He compared the book with a pornographic supplement to a literary work published in New York which had been suppressed, stating that Mrs. Bailey's volume "only lacks the illustrations to be twin to it," and ended with a citation of the law against "any book . . . containing obscene language or other things tending to the corruption of youth . . . [the author] shall on conviction be punised [*sic*] by imprisonment . . ."

The reviewer of the *Oregon Weekly Times* dismissed the work with the statement that from a half-hour's hasty glance he concluded that it did not warrant a review; that the only worthwhile part of the book was the section dealing with the missionary movement and early settlement of Oregon. He ended with the promise "more anon," but that was his last word.

Margaret Bailey was by no means a literary genius nor is the book a work of art. It did, however, deserve a fairer reception than it received. *Grains* made entertaining reading and was on a par with popular works of a similar kind published in the East at that time. There is no doubt that the reviewers were prejudiced by the fact that the author was a woman, and worse still, a divorcée; and accustomed to the romantic pap of the novels of that era, they objected to the book's realism. The reading public seems not to have shared their prejudice, if any significance can be attached to the fact that each volume, containing about a hundred pages and selling for $1.50, quickly disappeared from the bookstores. Only one copy of one of the volumes is known to be in existence today. Perhaps that is the final commentary of how *Grains* was regarded in the last analysis by Oregonians.

The next woman to dare the criticism of a male-dominated world was Mrs. Abigail Scott Duniway, sister of the man who was later to become the famous editor of the *Oregonian*. She published her *Captain Gray's Company: Or, Crossing the Plains and Living in Oregon* when she was twenty-five and already the mother of several children. In her introduction she begs the reader for his indulgence: "When a frontier farmer's wife undertakes to write a book, who has to be lady, nurse, laundress, seamstress, cook, and dairy-woman by turns . . . 'want of time'—is a necessary, unavoidable excuse for fault of style or discrepancy in composition." Mrs. Duniway was more successful than her predecessor. Her book contained nothing to offend the sensibilities of her contemporaries and, as it dealt in a sympathetic manner with familiar scenes, its appeal was understandable. Newspaper notices, if brief, were favorable.

Captain Gray's Company is, of course, hardly a great novel. The characters are wooden, it lacks suspense and most of the other ingredients that make for good writing. The plot is a simple one: a mother and two children leave their home to make the grand trek to the Oregon country and there experience the vicissitudes of pioneer life. With all that, it is a faithful, if too literal delineation of the period, and the pioneer could relive his own experiences on almost every page. When Mrs. Duniway wrote of the efforts of Gustavus Willard to obtain additional land by marriage to a thirteen-year-old girl, she was describing a practice with which her readers were familiar either through personal experience or observation:

Gustavus Willard soon found himself immensely rich. But as the rapid accumulation of property too often increases a desire for more, he became eager to hold more of the valley prairie than as a bachelor, he was entitled to claim.

Gustavus Willard must have a wife. That was settled. If he couldn't get *somebody*, he must take nobody, or her sister. A squatter lived about three miles from our bachelor's *ranche*. He had a daughter thirteen years of age, "verdant" as the grass she trod; more thoughtless than the cows she milked. Our bachelor called at the residence of the mountain lassie. He thought she wasn't much like the dark-eyed niece who kept house for him at his *ranche*, neither did she suit his fancy like Fanny Waters, who wouldn't have him.

"But then," he mused, "she'll hold that splendid half section of land in the bottom, if I'll marry her, and I can't think of giving it up. I'll be compelled to, though, by next December, if I don't marry somebody."

Although Mrs. Duniway's life was more than usually hard as the result of a permanent injury her husband had sustained and which made it necessary for her to support the family, she had the vigor and spirit which was to make her an outstanding personality in the region.

She wrote several volumes of prose and poetry after *Captain Gray's Company*, among which are *My Musings* (1875), *David and Anna Matson* (1876), and an autobiographical account of her part in the women's suffrage movement. For many years she also edited a literary journal, *New Northwest*. Not as a novelist was she best known, however, but as a leader in the fight for women's rights and as editor, and so is she remembered today by Oregonians.

By 1871, when Belle W. Cooke's 250-page volume of collected poems, *Tears and Victory*, was published, Mrs. Abigail Scott Duniway no longer had to be concerned about the reception of her books. She was then editing her magazine and, remembering the days when she was a novice in the writing game, she hastened to review the book, though, as she said, "We have not as yet had opportunity to give it that thorough perusal which we are satisfied that its ability . . . will amply repay." However, "the few shorter poems that we have read sparkle all through with originality, good taste, cultivation, and that noblest quality in woman, common sense." She went on to describe the edition, for which Mrs. Cooke, incidentally, had herself paid, and ended by urging readers to encourage the poetess by buying the book "and you will not regret having made the investment."

Mrs. Cooke was another of the pioneer housewives who wrote with one hand while she rocked a cradle with the other. She also managed to teach music on the small folding melodeon she had brought across the plains, teach school, give art lessons, act as clerk in the Oregon legislature, and as a correspondent for the *Oregonian*. A woman of deep sensitivity, as her verse reveals, she apparently found the greatest measure of release and satisfaction in her writing, which shows some degree of talent. Bret Harte reviewed *Tears and Victory* harshly in the *Overland Monthly*. Her poetry, he said, "is merely a simulation, a counterfeit. . . . Occasionally there flits a pleasing fancy, a felicitous expression . . . but it proves a . . . meteoric flash; yet who knows but these hints of genius may prove buds of promise?" The buds never blossomed, for though Belle Cooke continued to send an occasional bit of verse to the magazines of the region, she never published again.

In Washington Territory nothing appeared in print until 1853, when R. H. Hewitt's autobiographical *Notes by the Way—Memoranda of a Journey Across the Plains, from Dundee, Ill. to Olympia, W. T.* appeared. It was distributed locally and for private circulation, as the editor of the *Washington Standard* regretfully announced. He felt that a wider circulation would have been profitable both to the author and to "those who have seen what he so glowingly depicts." The newspaper apparently took its cue in style from the author in its review: "It is a volume of 58 royal octavo pages and is written in the obscure yet captivating strain peculiar to many works of the present age. The change from the gay and sprightly tones of 'The murmuring streamlet of the sylvan grove,' to the low notes of melancholy and despair, is happily blended by the author; and anon, catching inspiration from the mighty emblems of Omnipotence strewn with a lavish hand in his pathway, the narrator soars aloft in majesty and grandeur. The hardships and hair-breadth escapes incident to the trip, are depicted in a manner which few may equal, none excel. It is the warp of truth entwined in the woof of romance."

Until the appearance of Joaquin Miller in the literary firmament, the constellations moved in their orderly courses. No one in the Northwest before him had created even a ripple in the national stream of belles-lettres. Joaquin was as picturesque a literary frontiersman as ever emerged from the border regions, and the splash which his presence caused in an otherwise quiet brook was paralleled by no other writer in the region for many years. He was also one of the most colorful characters this country has ever produced, and though largely forgotten today—he never achieved his dream of being a Western Whitman—in his own time he was a figure of note.

In a technical sense Miller cannot be considered a Northwestern poet, for, with the exception of several minor works, his major contributions in his long, vivid career were outside the region, in California, Europe, and the East. Oregon, where his first book of poetry was published in 1868—five hundred copies of a slender volume entitled *Specimens* that attracted little attention and was soon consigned to the oblivion of the back shelves in bookshops—regarded him with mixed feelings. Even after he had achieved national and international recognition, certain elements in the community could not forgive him for the heinous sin committed in his youth—deserting his wife. There were others, however, who welcomed him eagerly and resented attempts to identify him with any other locality but Oregon. One paper, under the heading "Another Oregon Poet," wrote: "The San Francisco *Bulletin,* with characteristic fairness gives 'honor to whom honor is due' in the following: 'California has not the honor to claim Mr. Miller as a citizen. His residence when at home is Oregon.' " And the author of a history of Oregon literature published in 1899 wrote: "He may have written in the Sierras and sung of their grandeur; he may have bowed to the muses in the East; his soul may have been mellowed with the sentiments of the vineclad Italy, yet he is an Oregon poet,—simply a child away from home."

During his lifetime, an incurable wanderlust took Joaquin Miller to Oregon, Washington, Idaho, Montana, the East, Europe, Hawaii. His first journey was from his birthplace, Indiana, to the Oregon country. Because of his penchant for romanticizing himself and distorting facts, the exact date of his birth is not known; but it is believed to be 1841. He was christened Cincinnatus Hiner Miller, but he early changed his given name for the more euphonious "Joaquin." He spent his early youth in the Northwest participating in gold stampedes, Indian wars, altercations with stagecoach bandits, and earning his living as a teacher, editor of a newspaper (suppressed during the Civil War for Secessionist sentiments), lawyer, judge, and pony-express rider. But the craving for self-expression would not be stilled, and he was undeterred by the fact that his first brain child, *Specimens*, was stillborn. The following year he published, again at his own expense, another volume, *Joaquin et al*.

Apparently his verse was too heady a mixture for some parts of the Northwest press to swallow, for the papers which printed the trivial, sentimental "poetry" of hopeful would-be writers criticized it severely. One newspaper devoted its entire "review" to finding fault with his grammar: "We find beautiful thoughts and splendid imagery mingled with vulgar idioms and a total disregard of the properties of English grammar . . . the harmonies of poetry illy accord with improprieties in language, and a poet of aesthetical taste, as all poets should be, would not array heroic verse in vulgar verbiage or illiterate idiom." Other papers in the region either ignored Miller or treated his volume with equal disfavor. The *Eugene City Guard* was one of the few which displayed enthusiasm: "A careful perusal of the contents proves that the poet possesses true genius and real poetical fire. He is among the poets that are born, not made, and with experience and study, Judge Miller will rank among the first poets of the age."

Without honor, thus far, in his own country, Joaquin Miller left for Europe in quest of literary fame and fortune. In London, between pilgrimages to literary shrines, he compiled a manuscript of his previously published poems. He made the rounds of the publishers, tried to persuade the venerable house of Murray to issue it, and finally, when it became plain that no one would handle the work, printed one hundred copies of the book which he called *Pacific Poems* at his own expense. Its success was phenomenal. One poem was even compared by a reviewer to some written by Browning. The publication by Longman's shortly afterward of his *Songs of the Sierras* (1871) made his triumph complete. Although critics called attention to the faults in his rhyme, meter, and diction, that did not detract from the overwhelming response the volume received. In *The Academy*, W. M. Rossetti, brother of Dante Gabriel, asserted that the book was truly remarkable and called Miller an excellent and fascinating poet. *The Westminster Review* referred to Miller as "a Whitman without the coarseness. . . . America may well be proud of having discovered a new poet in Mr. Miller." Copies of the book were snapped up, and almost overnight Joaquin Miller was the rage of literary London.

Never modest, he was his own best publicity agent in interpreting and singing the praises of his poetry. And with the skill of a modern practitioner of ballyhoo, he always went attired in the colorful frontiersman's dress—"sombrero, red shirt open at the neck, flaming scarf and sash, trousers tucked into spurred boots, long hair down over his shoulders, and a great blond beard." With disarming candor, Miller explained to members of a literary group that his costume "helps sell the poems, boys! And it tickles the duchesses." He was invited everywhere and the climax of his year in England was a dinner given in his honor by Dante Gabriel Rossetti on the eve of his departure for America.

Back in his native land, Miller found that his private affairs had received a thorough going-over in the press. His ex-wife, Minnie Myrtle, a poetess in her own right, had written a sarcastic "defense" of Joaquin that was published in the *Oregonian* and reprinted in the *New Northwest:*

It had been his sole ambition for years, to go to Europe and acquire a literary fame; he felt, and justly that he was gifted, and his mind being of fine, poetic structure, and his brain very delicately organized, the coarse and practical duties of providing for a family, and the annoyance of children, conflicted with his dreams and literary whims. So, when he wrote to me that he would be absent in Europe five or six years, and in the meantime, I need not expect to hear from him often, as he should be very busy, I asked for and obtained a divorce . . . and your singer was loosed and free, and no longer chained to the annoying cares of a family; he could give his whole attention to his poems. I, myself, sympathize with him in his desire to "tamper with the Muses," and cultivate his taste and talent for literature, and I feel that all poets and authors will also sympathize with him.

Minnie Myrtle had cause for bitterness. An exuberant woman with a zest for living and experience, and burning with the poet's fire, she found herself deserted, penniless, and saddled with two children, while the man whom she had inspired was "loosed and free" to wander the earth and gather its laurels. Her poetry has never been collected and most of it was lost. All that remains is the verse published in the *New Northwest*. Joaquin said at one time that much of what she wrote was superior to his, but that she "lacked care and toil and sustained thought."

The same issue of the *New Northwest* that published Mrs. Miller's letter also contained a vitriolic attack on not only the bard but his poetry. While conceding that his poetry had merit, the article stated that "its construction and sentiment are alike often deserving of severe criticism." His success, greater in the Old World and in the Eastern states than in his old home of Oregon, the magazine went on, was due to the novelty of the scenes he dealt with, the

wild and wierd [*sic*] and rugged in nature, so general on the Pacific slope . . . rather than to greatness of thought or depth of sentiment. . . . We who live here need no poet to sing to us of glorious old Mt. Hood and stately Jefferson, for those mountain giants as we gaze at them are grander poems than were ever penned, and baffle all description. Neither do we care to have sung the rippling flow of the beautiful Willamette . . . these subjects are in themselves so surpassingly grand that it need not be wondered at if he fail to do them complete justice. It would take a Homer or a Milton indeed to do that. In the Old World and the Eastern States, where sketches of this far Western country read like romance, "Joaquin" Miller's poems have elicited very commendatory criticisms, while in the West they are not so favorably regarded. Hence we infer that much of the laudation bestowed upon our poet by the press of England and the Eastern States is made in the enthusiasm of the moment, and cannot be considered the deliberate judgment of the critics.

Although the severe criticism of the frontier poet by the *New Northwest* was probably colored by the fact that it was a feminist magazine, edited by one of the foremost suffragettes of the region and one whose sympathies were undoubtedly with his hapless wife, it was not entirely erroneous, as the test of time was to prove. Miller was not a great or profound poet, but there was a passion, a fire, a wealth of imagery in his poetry that appealed to the senses. There was apparently enough in it—or perhaps it was its frenzied, barbaric, wild quality—to make him a success in the England of the great Victorian poets.

When he arrived on the Continent, he was almost penniless; he left a comparatively wealthy man. It was, perhaps, his hedonism which militated against him among his own countrymen, who, where literature was concerned in those years, were more chaste in their tastes than the great English queen. They threw up their hands in horror at Walt Whitman, an incomparably greater poet, and this wild westerner appealed equally little to them. Miller, none the less, continued to write and to hope that he would gain the recognition in his native land that he had received in Europe.

His next work, *Life Amongst the Modocs: Unwritten History* (1873), subtitled "Joaquin Miller's Romantic Adventures Amongst the Red Indians," was published in London. (The title was later changed to *Paquita*). In this pseudo-autobiographical prose work, Miller allowed his ever fertile imagination to run riot. It is filled with incredible, heroic adventure, but, as one biographer of the poet wrote, "one feels in reading the book that Miller poured the whole of his love for the West into that volume, that the emotion of the book is honest, that it presents, accurately, an attitude of his youth." In later years the truth caught up with Miller and he revised the work, which was then published in Chicago under the title *My Own Story* (1890). In the preface the author confesses that there was a good deal of fiction in the original work and states that he is now presenting the naked truth. The story, with some minor exceptions, though, remained the same; the fiction still peeps out behind the façade of fact.

Joaquin kept shuttling back and forth from America to Europe in the years between 1871 and 1878. In Rome he was asked by the king to address the Italian Parliament on the subject of draining the swamps of the Campagna. He moved in the best social circles there and was a constant companion of Mrs. Leslie, whose husband was the founder of *Leslie's Weekly*. She is the heroine of his second novel, *The One Fair Woman* (1876), supposed to contain some autobiographical material. It was received no more warmly than his previous fictional work, *First Fam'lies of the Sierras* (1875), published in London and of which one critic observed that it would not increase Miller's fame in England, and another, that it had no plot, no action, and no characters—was, in short, no novel.

Songs of Italy (1878), a volume of poetry composed in that country, was his next publication, and then Joaquin Miller came home. He returned to England for one last visit, in 1880, when his play *The Danites in the Sierras* was produced at Sadler's Wells. It was also apparently staged in California, for a leading Northwestern magazine wrote that as a dramatist Joaquin Miller was a failure, that the entire California press had snubbed his *Danites*, and that his latest production, *Vigilantes*, was rejected by the producers.

Whether it was because of his flamboyant personality, his marital difficulties, or the lushness of his poetry, Joaquin Miller seemed unable to break through the barrier that had been erected against him in the Northwest. *Shadows of Shasta* (1881), his next work, was dismissed summarily by the *Oregonian* with the comment that it was "Balderdash very characteristic of 'Wakeen'!" The book, which dealt with the unfair treatment the Indian had received at the hands of the white man, was a trivial piece of work and pointed up glaringly Miller's inability to handle prose. It did not merit much more than the few lines given it by the *Oregonian*, but the tone in which the item was written reveals the paper's attitude toward the poet.

To his colorful career of poet, novelist, biographer, short-story writer, journalist, columnist, and editor, Miller in 1894 added historian. He was commissioned to write the textual narrative for *An Illustrated History of the State of Montana*, which was subsequently published in Chicago. Although modern research methods were not used and facts were not always carefully checked, the result is an interesting account containing many vivid word pictures in Miller's best pictorial style.

The last of his poetic works were *In Classic Shades* (1890), *The Building of the City Beautiful* (1893)—both eloquent pleas for peace, tolerance, equality, and the brotherhood of man—*Songs of the Soul* (1896), and his final, *A Song of Creation*.

Although Miller conquered Europe, he wanted more than anything else to conquer America, but it was not until almost the end of his life that he partially achieved the latter. The complete edition of his works was brought out in 1909 and it received almost unstinted praise from the press. He had with great care gone over his poetry, cut, elaborated, changed, eliminated, and the final product could be considered a fair representation of the quality of Joaquin Miller. Characteristic of Miller, the work contains an autobiographical section in which he indulged in his usual romantic self-glorification. Miller believed in himself as a poet and though he never realized his ambition to be the great American poet, he did make a contribution to American letters. His is the voice of the frontier, of the West, of America. His glowing descriptions of the region he loved inspired a number of writers to visit it, among whom were Hamlin Garland and George Sterling. His work can be summed up in the words of one of his biographers: "Too suggestive of a defunct Byronism, too indulgent of the melo-dramatic, too luxuriant in its descriptive passages, the poetry of Joaquin Miller, despite its limitations, is amazingly alive at times and occasionally beautiful. A few of Miller's poems, no doubt, are permanent additions to American literature."

After a lingering illness, Joaquin Miller died in 1913 and in death achieved some of the measure of greatness he had so deeply desired and labored for while alive. Newspapers in America and Europe wrote lengthy eulogies which contained an evaluation of his work by eminent critics. A number of these felt that a true poet had passed, and all of them that a picturesque one was gone. His burial was as dramatic as his life had been. Although the authorities of Oakland forbade his cremation on the stone pyre which he had built on the Heights overlooking the sea and the city, the final services were held there. A large group of friends and strangers had come to bid him farewell. The funeral pyre was lighted, the ashes, brought in an urn from the crematorium at Oakland, were scattered over the flames, and "Good-bye, Joaquin, Good-night" was read. Thus passed a unique personality, a singer of songs who, despite his inadequacies, managed to convey in his verse the freedom and spirit of the West.

One Oregon poet of the pioneer period is remembered today in the Northwest principally because of his poem "Beautiful Willamette," which he wrote when he was twenty-two. During Samuel L. Simpson's lifetime his verse was printed in the region's magazines, but it was not until ten years after his death that J. B. Lippincott published a collection of his poetry in a volume called *The Gold-Gated West*. Simpson had always refused to collect his writings. "I have not even a copy of my poems," he once told a friend. "I have never written anything that satisfies me. There are so many half-way poets deluging the world with so-called poetry that I am disgusted, and do not wish to add to the burdens of the long-suffering public."

Simpson was one of those unhappy souls who consistently failed at everything he attempted. His streak of talent was wide enough to impel him to write, but not wide enough to raise him above the level of the "half-way poets" he scorned. He began to compose poetry while attending Willamette University, but somehow he was diverted to studying law. He passed the bar before he was twenty-one, practiced for only a brief time, and returned to writing. He had married in the meantime and soon there were two sons, an almost overwhelming responsibility for a man of his temperament. Unable to support his family by free-lancing, he went into newspaper work and even owned a paper for a brief while. For years he wandered from one sheet to another, frequently being fired because of chronic drunkenness and scribbling his poetry on scraps of paper whenever the inspiration moved him. Even his marriage was ill starred, for he became estranged from his wife.

Simpson deeply loved the West, where he spent all but the first six months of his life, and he was affected by the pioneer tradition, the mountains and roaring glacier streams which he depicted in so many of his poems. His "Beautiful Willamette" has become almost the theme song of Oregon:

. . . . .

From the Cascades' frozen gorges
　Leaping like a child at play,
Winding, widening through the valley,
　Bright Willamette glides away;
　　　Onward ever,
　　　Lovely River,
Softly calling to the sea,
　　Time that scars us,
　　Maims and mars us,
Leaves no track or trench on thee."

. . . . .

One critic summed up the feeling of many pioneers about the poem: "The Willamette is henceforth more than a river; for us it is the mountain's child wreathed in 'spring's green witchery—softly calling to the sea.' For us it's now a parable, 'Life's old questions, and suggestions, whence and whither? Throng thy stream.' There is a cadence and melody in 'Beautiful Willamette' which certainly equals the sweetness and beauty of Lord Byron. And the poem will live as long as the River flows." It is a testimony to the regard in which Simpson was held that on his death the *Oregonian* editorialized that "The death of Sam. L. Simpson leaves Oregon no poet of merit or reputation," but it is also a rather sad commentary on the state of letters in the year 1904.

A little more than a decade before, Oregon lost a writer of considerably greater talent who is also remembered for one work, a novel, that remains a classic of the region. Frederic Homer Balch began *The*

Bridge of the Gods when he was twenty-six. It was published in 1890 and the following year he was dead of tuberculosis. Between the time the book was issued and 1935, it went through twenty-nine editions.

At the time Balch was writing, the country was still young and the deeply rooted Indian culture, tradition, and folklore had not yet been eclipsed by the white man's traditions. Balch fell under the spell of this ancient culture. It was also his admitted ambition to make Oregon as famous as Scott had made Scotland, to make the Cascades as widely known to the world as the Highlands were, and to make the scenic Willamette the background for romance. *The Bridge of the Gods* was the fruition of that aspiration, for the grandeur of the country which he described and the passion with which he wrote made of him, if not a Walter Scott, then at least an interpreter without equal of the native heritage of his own Oregon.

In *The Bridge of the Gods*, Balch took the old and popular Indian legend of the creation of the mighty Cascades and used that as a backdrop for a vivid portrayal of Indian communal life, habits, traditions, religious beliefs, ceremonials, and clashing concepts in the conflicting cultures of the white man and the aborigines. A minor theme of the novel is the moving romance of the half-breed daughter of the great war chief Multnomah and a young Puritan missionary. Balch's research was exhaustive, including visits to the lodges of old Indians, and he took meticulous care to check on the facts. He gave his novel perspective by projecting himself into the Indian's cultural life and reflecting thoughts, hopes, and aspirations from his vantage point. He treated his subject without glamor or idealization, portraying him as proud, but also cruel and savage:

The air was putrid with decaying fish; the very skins and mats that covered the lodge-poles were black with rancid salmon and filth. Many of the men were nude; most of the women wore only a short garment of skin or woven cedar bark about the waist, falling scarcely to the knees. The heads of many had been artificially flattened; their faces were brutal; their teeth worn to the gums with eating sanded salmon; and here and there bleared and unsightly eyes showed the terrible prevalence of ophthalmia. . . . Half starved horses whose raw and bleeding mouths showed the effect of the hair-rope bridles, and whose projecting ribs showed their principle nutriment to be sagebrush and whiplash, were picketed among the lodges. . . . Prevailing over everything was the stench which is unique and unparalleled among the stenches of the earth,—the stench of an Indian camp at a Columbia fishery.

Frederic Balch's first book was a historical romance which he wrote when he was eighteen, but he subsequently burned it because, as his sister related, it was "interwoven with skeptical beliefs and theories that had no place in the life he had now chosen." He had undergone an intense inner emotional conflict and resolved it finally by discarding his antireligious proclivities and joining the ministry to do home missionary work. In the course of his labors he traveled throughout the countryside and gathered a good deal of the material for his books, especially from the Indians. His religious convictions, though, did not prevent him from handling certain themes realistically. The missionary in *The Bridge of the Gods*, for instance, does not make a single convert to Christianity.

A few years after his death, the *Oregonian* carried an article about Balch in which it stated that the young man had left a large collection of notes on several works that he had planned to write, and mourned his early demise as an irreparable loss to Oregon. The opening chapters for a novel entitled *Kenasket* were completed and there were outlines for six historical novels relating to Indian Oregon. In addition he had left a complete manuscript of a novel called *Genevieve*, whose locale was near Washougal, Washington.

Genevieve: A Tale of Oregon, which Balch was revising when he died, was published more than forty years later. It was probably resurrected only because of the success of *The Bridge of the Gods*, for it did nothing to increase his stature as a writer. The book, written in memory of his sweetheart, who had died during their courtship, is a highly melodramatic work in the tradition of the dime novel, filled with fantastic adventures, with a typically beautiful and unsullied heroine and a gallant hero, and has the stereotyped happy ending after all the difficulties have been resolved. In this work Balch also displays his enthusiasm for his native land. He takes his hero, who is apparently autobiographical, on a tour of the Northwest, describing in detail the country through which he passes.

The only other published work of Balch's, except some poems which appeared in contemporary periodicals, is a small volume entitled *Memaloose*, printed by a friend in 1934. It contains three poems and two short prose sketches, the latter published for the first time. Issuing the book was a labor of love, for the contents are mediocre, though they show more than ordinary skill. The leading poem, "What the Zither Said," is addressed to his dead sweetheart, Genevra Whitcomb, "Genevieve" in the poem as in the book, whom he must have loved deeply. Whether or not Balch would have developed the talent displayed in his major work, despite the failure of *Genevieve*, is, of course, problematical. But if he had, he would have been an outstanding regional writer.

The first Washington author of any prominence was the poet Herbert Bashford, who earned his living as state librarian. His initial work, *Songs from Puget Sea* (1898), is his best known. It was followed in the same year by *Nature's Stories of the Northwest*, and three years later by *Beyond the Gates of Care* and *Wolves of the Sea*. Though some of his verse still remains interesting, it is on the whole undistinguished. Washington, however, pressed him to her bosom. Only one other poet —Joaquin Miller—wrote a critic, had captured the inspiration of Western life as he did. And another: "The most noteworthy Pacific Coast nature poet . . . While uniform excellence may be said to be characteristic of Mr. Bashford's poems, . . . he often takes one by surprise with a line or phrase of transcendent brilliance and power. A few of these magic lines will serve to illustrate: 'An frightened echo flees from hill to hill . . . ;' 'The storm swept ocean: that jars the world with its white cavalry;' 'Big drops of rain that fall in slanting lines— Long glances gleaming from a wall of night.' "

Bashford also wrote short stories that appeared in various minor periodicals throughout the country and, of course, in the newspapers and journals of the region. The *West Shore* in 1890 published another of his poems every other week. Most of his verse dealt with the beauties of his homeland, but he was not entirely an ivory-tower writer. He was profoundly concerned by America's imperialist policy at the end of the century, and since a pen is a poet's voice, he expressed his feelings in a poem that was published in the *San Francisco Examiner* and entitled "The Voice of Conquest":

> I hew my pathway with the sword
>   Slay peace and say I throttled crime,
> Ring round with flame the Savage Horde,
>   Weave crimson in the robe of Time.
>
> I search for gold and gleaming gem,
>   Seize fairest islands of the sea,
> Find simple folk and fling to them
>   From cannon mouth—Humanity.
>
> I seek the realm where dullards dwell,
>   I make each brutish weakling feel

The good there is in shriek and shell
The blessings wrought by fire and steel.

With saber stroke and thrust of lance
I shake the regions of Content,
And teach the hosts of Ignorance
The sweetness of Enlightenment.

What matter if Death's pride be War
Or weakness be the slave of Might?
Is Progress not a conqueror,
And Power another name for Right?

What matter if I crush the free
Or if ten million men be slain?
Am I not lord of Destiny—
The Anglo-Saxon god of Gain?

Female writers, on the whole, seem to have been more successful, financially and otherwise, than the men. A contemporary of Bashford's was Mrs. Ella R. Higginson, poetess, short-story writer, novelist, editor, travel and song writer. She was claimed by both Oregon, where she had spent her childhood, and Washington, where she subsequently lived. (The region had so few outstanding literary artists that there was a tendency to claim as its own those who were successful, even though they had spent only a short time there. For many years Edwin Markham was regarded as Oregon's poet laureate, though he had lived there only until he was five years old.)

With the exception of a few minor works, Macmillan of New York published most of Mrs. Higginson's writings. In 1897 they issued *From the Land of the Snow Pearls*, a collection of short stories about farm and village pioneers, *A Forest Orchid*, also short stories, and a volume of poetry entitled *The Snow Pearls;* and in 1898, another book of poems, *When the Birds Go North Again*. Her only novel, *Mariella of Out-West*, was published in 1902; *The Voice of April-Land*, a volume of poetry, in 1903, and in 1908, *Alaska, the Great Country*. Her fiction appeared in the leading national periodicals such as *Lippincott's Magazine, Harper's Weekly*, and *Cosmopolitan*, and she won $500 prizes in short-story contests sponsored by *McClure's* and *Collier's*. She also wrote extensively for periodicals in the region and almost every literary organ there published her poems.

Mrs. Higginson's prose, for the most part, was in the local color tradition, displaying deep consciousness of her own community environment, but maintaining, however, a sense of artistic objectivity. Her subjects possess a richness of detail and realistic protraiture with very little sentimentality. In a comment on her short stories, the *Chicago Tribune* wrote: "She has shown a breadth of treatment and knowledge of human verities that equals much of the best work of France." And the *Overland Monthly* stated: "Her style is strong, powerful and realistic. . . . She writes from the heart of the plain, everyday folk she meets and consequently touches the heart. Her stories are unpretentious tales of common people, told simply and naturally, yet so vivid and graphic that they charm the reader from the first to the last."

Because of their lyrical quality, a number of Mrs. Higginson's poems were set to music and sung by artists of national reputation. They were the kind popular in the women's magazines then—and today, for that matter. Many are of an inspirational nature with deep religious overtones. Her "Four-Leaf Clover" is a good example:

> I know a place where the sun is like gold
>   And the cherry blooms burst with snow,
> And down underneath is the loveliest nook
>   Where the four-leaf clovers grow.
>
> One leaf is for hope, and one is for faith,
>   And one is for love, you know,
> And God put another one in for luck—
>   If you search, you will find where they grow.
>
> But you must have hope, and you must have faith,
>   You must love and be strong—and so—
> If you work, if you wait, you will find the place
>   Where the four-leaf clovers grow.

A contemporary critic said that her poems "breathe a spirit of piety which commend them to the most refined; and her great spirituality will always win her an increasing patronage among the ever-growing circle of readers who learn to regard her as their friend and adviser."

Historical writing, whether academic or in fiction form, is a field in which men are generally preeminent, but not in the matriarchal-literary Northwest. There the first historical novelist was Mrs. Eva Emery Dye. She had come to the region at the end of the century and soon became enamored with its romantic history from the stories told her by many old pioneers. She explored all the old landmarks and familiarized herself thoroughly with the source material. Her first in a series of novels was *McLoughlin and Old Oregon* (1900), to be followed two years later by *The Conquest*, and then *McDonald of Oregon* (1906).

To Mrs. Dye the pioneer epoch was more than a theme for her books. It represented a way of life and a spirit to such an extent that objectivity fell victim to overromanticizing. In reply to a letter requesting some background material about herself and her writings, she replied that her historic characters were founded on personal investigation and careful research. The surviving pioneers, she said, were her friends and neighbors and that nothing pleased them more than to recount the events of bygone days when they were building a civilization. "They are heroes as much as were the men of Homer, and the women were as fair as those of Tennyson. I have been amazed at the culture and refinement of many of the women whose lot it was to cradle their children in the land of red men. Soft voiced, white haird [*sic*] they are passing away, but the tales of their youth are like music in the solemn monotone of statistical history."

Mrs. Dye won instant acclaim in the Northwest, not only from the popular press, but also from the *Quarterly* of the Oregon Historical Society. In a review of the McLoughlin book it commented that it was "a series of pictures almost as vivid as real life" and that Mrs. Dye had an "inimitable power of representation." The reviewer commented in passing that there might be some errors of historical fact, but ended by saying that the book was one of the finest introductions to Oregon history for the layman.

She was dealt with a good deal more critically by Frances Fuller Victor, who deplored "the mingling of fiction with historical truth in a work which is likely to be mistaken for a serious one." Mrs. Victor devoted a page to pointing out distortions and inaccuracies of historical fact and also commented on Mrs. Dye's weakness as a literary artist. The figure of McLoughlin which emerges is blurred, she felt, because of the author's ineptitude in characterization.

This weakness is equally true of all her books which followed. Mrs. Dye's characters were glamorized far beyond the role they played in real life and were of such heroic proportions that they were completely unbelievable. The woodsmen, for example, were perfect specimens: "Each had his favorite accomplishment,—to shoot a bird on the wing or bring down a deer running, to slaughter an elk and in fifteen minutes have all its meat cooking and its skin laced on their feet for moccasins . . . fierce, fiery, and proud, every night they set out from the camping spot with enormous double-springed rat-traps on their backs, sure to snare a beaver or a bear for breakfast." In addition, she made the serious error of crowding into her books all the great and near-great who lived contemporaneously with her hero. The net result is that none of her characters could be well rounded for there is not enough space within the limits of the volume to do each justice and they emerge mere cardboard pieces. The *Quarterly* of the Oregon Historical Society, always friendly to her work, stated in one review that she undertook "a stupendous task" in trying to bring the campaigns of George Rogers Clark, the explorations of Lewis and Clark, and the career of William Clark as governor of Missouri and United States agent all between the covers of *The Conquest.*

The attempt to make her books Homeric epics of the Northwest brought reward in their warm reception in her adopted country. In a review of *The Conquest,* the Portland *Oregonian* wrote in a style to match her own:

> The characters in this book belong to the history of our country; heroes of the darkest days of the Revolution; heralds of the brightest days of Independence. Out of scraps and fragments, diamond dust of the past, their deeds have been revealed, and lo! the old-time centure [*sic*] is here with border armies hurrying by. Flintlocks gleam and sabers flash, and dangling fringes blend with uncut locks. . . .
>
> Clear and clearer as the years go by, under the dim forest shadows we catch glimpses of a primitive people, mighty in stature, courage and resources, battling like gods and demons for the future United States.

The Conquest was made into a play and produced in New York at the Belasco Theatre in 1905. It does not seem to have been too successful, for after it closed the producer wrote to Mrs. Dye that he was going to rewrite the play and take a good many more liberties with the book than he had before.

The popularity of her theme caused Mrs. Dye to be repetitious. When she sent her publishers the manuscript of *McDonald of Oregon,* the hero of which was Ranald McDonald, they wrote her that it was entirely too long and overloaded with material that had no connection either with McDonald or with her main theme, the part he played in opening up Japan. It contained, they said, such irrelevancies as the waves of immigration, the hardships of the pioneers on the trail, Indian fights, and so forth, which had been treated over and over again elsewhere. They suggested that at least a fourth of the manuscript could be cut. Mrs. Dye's books apparently sold well enough, however, for the publishers to say in the same letter that they were planning to issue the volume in the fall and were prepared to sign a contract immediately if she was amenable to their suggestion.

Though Eva Emery Dye cannot be said to have made a great contribution to a permanent literary tradition in the Northwest, her books served as a point of departure for the more artistic regional literature to come. As they were based on historical fact which was not too much distorted, they were not as trite as most of the romantic fiction written by her contemporaries, and they did help to make Easterners aware of the Northwest.

The first writer to use Idaho as a setting was Mary Hallock Foote. Her best known novel, *The Led Horse Claim,* is laid in Colorado; she wrote also of California, but the background of the major portion of her fiction is Idaho. It consists of two collections of short stories and her novels *The Chosen Valley* (1892), *Coeur D'Alene* (1894), *The Desert and the Sown* (1902), and *A Picked Company* (1912).

Like Bret Harte, Mrs. Foote might be considered a sojourner in the West where she had come with her husband, a civil engineer whose work had involved him in mining operations, but she possessed none of Harte's literary talent. Her books were superficial and romantic in the early nineteenth century tradition; her characters are puppets manipulated on strings, her situations contrived, and her descriptions of life in the mining regions of Idaho completely unrealistic. Her sheltered background and her husband's identification with the mining interests led her in *Coeur D'Alene* to put into her story a vicious and childish attack on the miners who had organized into a union. According to her they had precipitated the bloody mine riots of the nineties for no other reason than to raise hell and commit murder. After pages filled with incredible adventures, the book ends in sweetness and light, with the mine operators restored to their former position of preeminence under the law, the villains suitably punished, and the hero and heroine wed to live happily ever after.

Mrs. Foote's female-seminary education did not permit of any realism in either her characters' speech or manners, and thus her dauntless hero when angered uses "a strong expression." This was the type of writing that portrayed an artificial, technicolored West, collar-ad heroes, and beautiful, gentle, swooning heroines. Mrs. Foote's novels are of interest primarily as a reflection of the pioneering atmosphere in which they were written.

Another female writer was Ada W. Anderson of Washington. Her novels *The Heart of the Red Firs* (1908) and *The Strain of White* (1909), both published by Little, Brown and Company, contained, like so much of the writings of the region during that era, the local setting and nostalgic flavor characteristic of the time and place. The former book she dedicated "To those few remaining pioneers, who knew the Nisqually trail into the great solitudes, in times before the logging railroad devastated the Puget Sound hills, and the wilderness began to recede at the coming of the builder of townsites." Her books were distinguished for their honest attempts to delineate the true relationship between the red man and the white during the territorial period and to show how shabbily the native was treated. They fell far short of the standards of Helen Hunt Jackson's work, but Miss Anderson's books were similar in the objectivity with which the conditions of the aborigines were depicted.

A writer in a special category among Northwest literary figures was Charles Erskine Scott Wood, one of the most unusual and complex personalities this country has produced. In a long life—he was born in 1852 and died in 1944—his career included that of soldier, writer, lawyer, painter, humanitarian, and he achieved a national and international reputation in at least three fields. A man of considerable affluence, he was dubbed "The Philosophic Anarchist," and for the major part of his life he was in the forefront of any movement aimed at the amelioration of human misery.

Wood's early years were spent in a conservative atmosphere. He graduated from West Point, participated in the Indian campaigns in Oregon, Washington, and Idaho, received a law degree from Columbia University, retired from the army and practiced law in Portland for thirty years with phenomenal success. His clients were among the wealthiest men in the community, including the railroad monopolists. It may have been during the Indian campaigns that Wood began to acquire the humanitarian philosophy which influenced his activities for the rest of his life and put him on the side of any human being whom he felt was oppressed. Though he was often attacked in the newspapers, his extraordinary legal acumen apparently prevented his professional practice from being affected. As an instance of the high regard in which he was held as an attorney, a prominent Portland judge related that when the Northern Pacific Railroad wished to purchase a branch line between Walla Walla and Pendleton, Wood was asked to draw up the contract. He complied, writing it on one side of a sheet of paper in longhand and charged $50,000 for his services! His keen mind, extraordinary personal charm, and brilliant powers as a speaker may have influenced the Democratic party of Oregon to nominate him as their candidate for United States senator, and he ran on its ticket.

Though regarded as a radical, Wood was popular enough to be invited to contribute a column regularly to the *Pacific Monthly* magazine on anything he cared to write. The column, called "Impressions," ran for a number of years. He wrote as he spoke—trenchantly, bitingly, picturesquely, with complete lack of inhibition, flailing out in all directions. A typical column contained comments on the following assorted subjects: "The Embattled Missionary," "The Charter of the City of Portland," "The Russo-Japanese War," "The Prince of Peace and the Big Stick," "Beginnings of Life and Thought," "The Genesis of War," "International Arbitration," "Legislatures and Political Dishonesty," "The Beef Trust," "Police Tyranny," "The Churches and John D. Rockefeller," "Religious Liberty," "Direct Primary Nominations."

On one occasion Wood used Emma Goldman's visit to Portland to attempt to explode the popular impression that all anarchists carried bombs in their back pockets with which to destroy the pillars of the capitalistic system. After commending the city fathers for their tolerance in not following the example of Chicago, Butte, and other cities to prevent her from speaking, he rhetorically asked why Miss Goldman had such a reputation and replied in his characteristic style:

Why did the abolition Yankees have horns and hoofs? Why did the early Christians sacrifice infants and eat their flesh? Why, in the early Christian times, were all murders, all fires, all plagues, all riots laid at the door of the Christians? . . . Why was Dreyfus convicted? Why does the average reporter and average newspaper print a sensation rather than the truth? Why all the lies and superstitions of the world? . . . Dynamite! Bombs! Assassination! Rubbish! I have called it comedy. But the colossal American ignorance and gullibility is too tiresome to be comic.

Wood was also a prolific short-story writer, contributing under a pseudonym to magazines all over the country.

In a community that was still basically pioneer beneath the thin veneer of sophistication, a man of Wood's culture and charm who would have been outstanding in the most urbane society, was doubly so there. For that reason, and probably also because of his wealthy

clientele, his philosophical views seemed to have been regarded either
with amused tolerance or, as in the case of the *Oregonian*, as hypo-
critical. In an editorial headed "Petronius Arbiter," the paper wrote
that Wood's flaunting of anarchistic views was calculated to attract
the support of the masses at radical meetings, but he actually curried
the favor of the rich, who were his close associates and friends. It also
took a slap at those who looked to Wood in cultural matters: "Mr.
Wood is a great authority on art, as well as on anarchy. . . . His decision 'goes' on all affairs in which our 'upper classes' are interested,—
on duds, music, painting, poetry, . . . architecture, . . . hair dressing, perfumes, latest fads in furniture . . . face powders, chafing dish
specialties, and what not. People who know nothing themselves, who
merely have their inherited wealth and nothing else, look to the
Colonel."

Wood was an artist of not inconsiderable skill. His paintings were
exhibited at the Portland Art Museum and he numbered among his
intimate friends some of America's foremost artists and sculptors.
The digs by the *Oregonian*, therefore, did not prevent Portlanders
from consulting him on any artistic matters.

Not until fairly late in life did C. E. S. Wood turn to writing belles-
lettres. His first poetry, *A Masque of Love*, was published in 1904,
and *The Poet in the Desert*, a dialogue between Truth and a Poet
protesting social injustice and championing humanitarian ideals, when
he was sixty-three. The work for which he is most famous, *Heavenly
Discourse*, appeared when he was seventy-five and was written during
World War I. His other works are *A Book of Tales: Being Some
Myths of the North American Indians* (1891), *Maia* (1918) a sonnet
sequence, *Poems from the Ranges* (1929), and *Earthly Discourse*
(1937). In commenting on his work one reviewer wrote: "His style
is reminiscent both of Walt Whitman and of the Hebrew prophets,
but his ideas are his own. . . . [The poet has endeavored] to throw
aside the trappings of civilization, to get back to nature, to face naked
truth, to denounce capitalism, and incidentally to preach various
kinds of revolution."

Like Joaquin Miller, Ces Wood, as he was familiarly called, spent
the last years of his life in California, but unlike the "Poet of the
Sierras," he received effortlessly the fame and recognition that the
other tried so desperately to attain. Excerpts from his works can be
found in a number of anthologies of American poetry, dozens of articles were written about him in magazines, he numbered among his

friends the great in every walk of life, and he was constantly sought after to lend his name or give his support to various movements for human rights. When he died, one of the outstanding literary journals in the country eulogized:

One of the last of the Old Guard of American Letters; a man of the highest idealism; of a lifetime devoted to courageous battling for the rights of the underprivileged. . . . More and more it will be borne in upon the American people that in Col. Chas. Erskine Scott Wood they possessed a poet certainly superior in keenness of intellect to Walt Whitman, if not by any means so voluminous in rhetorical output; and a social satirist of the first order.

There were many faint, flickering flames in the Northwest that struggled to burst into a blaze. Edward Everett Hale once told an audience that he believed probably everyone present had at some time or other written a poem or had the urge to express himself in verse. When a hopeful Northwestern writer found it impossible to get his brain child into print through the ordinary channels, he found a solution which, if not simple, did solve the problem—he published the book himself, even if he had to set the type by hand. Valentine Brown of Oregon resorted to that extreme, printing almost one thousand pages of narrative and other verse. In his postlude to *Poems*, the first of five volumes printed between 1900 and 1917, Mr. Brown explains why he was impelled to do his own publishing: "A poet without reputation is not a poet any more than a light encompassed by a fog is a light. Each may glory in their own luster, but the world will not remark on their brightness. I have been shining in my own room for a number of years, still my nearest neighbors have not acknowledged that any unusual brilliance has emanated therefrom. . . ." His future, he went on, did not depend on public appreciation of his book—which was, indeed, fortunate. In the preface to his fourth volume, *Tales and Other Verse*, he informed the reader that he was composing as he set the type, "even as much of my verse was composed while in the process of being placed in book form. . . ." The results give every indication of that type of "composing."

Few writers were their own compositors, but a number printed privately a hundred or two hundred copies of the results of their creative urge. Olive S. England, J. H. Cradlebaugh, Dennis Along Waters, John Minto, Marion Cook, E. E. Eberhard were all in that group. A few, like Joseph Blethen, managing editor of the *Seattle Daily Times* and popular short-story writer, and Frank Carleton Teck, editor of the (Washington) *Whatcom Blade*, were more successful in terms of wider recognition and commercial reward from beyond the region. Winona Godfrey of Seattle had her short stories published in such magazines as *Harper's*, *Pearson's*, and *McClure's*.

Those who wrote exclusively for the local market never tired of rhapsodizing about the region, writing about the mountains as though they were majestic shrines to which homage should be paid for the privilege of enjoying their inspirational beauty. They sang with an almost mystical enthusiasm of the joy of living in the new region, the "land of their dreams." Oregon and Washington were the crown jewels of the continent, Gardens of Eden where free men could live in freedom and happiness. The poems of lyrical praise of the Northwest surpassed in volume and exuberance the literature of the chamber of commerce. History became myth and the past took on a magical, rapturous beauty in verse which no toastmaster at an annual pioneer reunion would be ashamed to recite:

> Where adown the mountain glaciers
> Grinding, crashing, blend their flashing
> With the sunlit snows eternal
> Pictured on the walls of dawn—
> Where the crags and coves are hiding
> Mighty rivers dashing, gliding,
> Comes a praise unto thy grandeur,
>   Oregon.
>
> .   .   .   .
>
> Pearl of all the golden Westland,
> Thou art peerless, like the fearless
> Pioneers who from thy mountains
> Gazed upon thy vales and sea;
> Pioneers, the noblest yeomen,
> Aiding friend, and daring foemen,
> Fighting, toiling, knowing ever
>   They were free.

Even academicians were guilty of distortions and exaggerations. John B. Horner, professor of literature at Oregon State College, holding high the torch of the covered-wagon immigrant, wrote a half-century after his own arrival in the region:

Despite ferocious attacks of the savages, these pilgrims—schooled in the hardships of pioneer life—hewed the forests into homes, schoolhouses, churches and cities; they cultivated the sod into fields, gardens and orchards; and they taught the treacherous Indian to worship the God of our fathers. Under their touch, the hunting ground became the scene of a harvest home, the tepee, a college, and the battlefield, a sanctuary.

Earlier, in a volume on Oregon literature, Professor Horner asserted proudly that his native state had produced more literature of a genuine kind during its brief history of only fifty years than all the thirteen original colonies had produced in a century and a half. And how could this literature be analyzed in order to ascertain its origins and quality? Horner presents a unique climatic and geographic interpretation of the reasons why there will always be a permanent distinction between the literature of eastern and western Oregon. After a disquisition on the "Webfoot" rain which will make the western Oregonian "an indoor plant, a reader of books, a student of indoor ethics," and the eastern Oregonian "an outdoor plant . . . a bold man, a brave man, a courageous man, a cultured man, nature's man," he goes on to say that the mildness of the climate will attract those who could not endure the rigors of eastern Oregon. Therefore the literature of western Oregon would not be characterized by the "rugged sayings" which would be evident in the writings east of the Cascades. In addition to the climate, the soil is also influential:

In Western Oregon there is much acid, little lime; much fruit, yet little to neutralize it; the teeth decay early, and there is but little bone material. In Eastern Oregon there is less fruit and more lime or bone-making material; hence the generations growing there will develop larger bones and frames. They will be bigger, consequently more rugged. The people of Western Oregon will be constructed on a frame-work of smaller bones; they will, therefore, possess a more delicate nature—fine physique true enough, but they will not be so strong and sturdy, hence more sensitive to warmth and cold and on this account, more sensitive to feeling and sentiment. There promises to be a whole-souled air in the literature of Eastern Oregon somewhat after the Dryden type, while finish and fine feeling of the Pope style will characterize the literature of Western Oregon.

Even after the turn of the century, a narrow provincialism dominated the literary landscape, militating against a successful fusion of the regional literature with the mainstream of the nation. Mrs. Eva Emery Dye once complained that Oregonians were interested in having native authors treat only with indigenous subjects and were reluctant to see them branch out. Writers were urged to concentrate on the exquisite scenery, the Indian life and legends, the pioneer beginnings, and other themes relating to the new society in the far Northwest. Out of these materials great literature would emerge, the local boosters insisted. And by and large the writers complied, but in a way that hindered the development of a genuine regional literature.

The pioneer attitude resulted in the tendency to indulge in glorification of the local hero or heroine, in the penchant for romanticizing. Objectivity of treatment was almost always lacking and the characters were lifeless, historical marionettes placed on the stage to speak their part, artificially contrived and made to fit the author's sense of history and loyalty to his region. Writers exalted the work of building and settling and idealized the founders of the pioneer society, creating noble personalities of those whose only major claim to nobility was their early arrival in the Oregon country. They displayed the same sense of destiny for their region as has always been demonstrated by writers of the frontier. They regarded the mouth of the Columbia River as the headwaters of the Missouri had been considered by other Western writers—the inevitable future center of the world's commerce and the point of convergence for the cultures of the East and West. The climate was superb, the scenery magnificent, the people earnest, conscientious, hard-working makers of history. The explorers, fur traders and trappers, missionaries and Indians combined to form a grand theme which, they believed, artistic integrity required them to relate over and over. Writers were unable to sever the umbilical cord which bound them to the past and so were limited by the provincial nature of their subject matter.

Yet, despite the large number of literati conscious of the historical past of their region, despite their intense local pride, and despite the fact that this feeling was shared by many persons in the new Northwest, literary critics and authors found the lack of popular support given native writers lamentable. On the one hand, any literary endeavor, no matter how insignificant, was enthusiastically welcomed, but on the other, the writer received no adequate financial returns. Apparently, it seemed to be necessary for a local writer first to achieve a degree of fame in the East before his neighbors accorded him the recognition which his work merited. Why, complained authors, should a Seattle or Portland or Spokane short-story writer or poet have to depend entirely on whatever financial rewards he could obtain from periodicals like *The Century* or *Scribners?* Why did not the population at home extend a helping hand to a deserving writer who was struggling for recognition? Must every poet emulate Joaquin

Miller and go to the East, Europe, and California to receive accolades before the Northwest recognized him and showed its appreciation? Samuel Simpson was beloved in Oregon and his "Beautiful Willamette" recited continually at annual pioneer gatherings, but he had never been paid anything for it. Of all the poems he wrote, the only one for which he had received remuneration was an obituary he had been asked to compose.

The sparsity of population was undoubtedly partly responsible for this condition. Even by 1910, the Northwest was still relatively unsettled, with miles of land separating homesteads in certain areas and large-scale industrialization still a vision on the horizon. Another reason might be termed the "colonial complex." The people were as yet unsure of their tastes, and publishing in the older centers, such as Boston and New York, gave a work the stamp of approval, testifying to the worth of an author. They were inordinately proud of their region and the things the West represented, but they were not yet self-confident enough to proclaim its literary independence. So the regional newspapers and periodicals paid for poems and stories received from the East, but offered no compensation to local literary talent unless the writer had already achieved a reputation outside the region.

Agitation among the literati mounted, especially as their numbers increased to respectable proportions after the turn of the century. They pointed to a Western Author's Week at the Lewis and Clark Fair held in Portland in 1905 to demonstrate that the creative force of literature as an indigenous product had at last been generated; to the literary magazines which were being founded in Seattle and other cities as proof that the literary manpower existed and all that was lacking was public appreciation. Curiously enough, the complaint was often heard that writers were leaving home, that the Northwest was being drained of its most productive and creative literary talent. Writers were not being adequately supported, but they were regarded as regional traitors, in a sense, for deserting their homeland in search of greener pastures.

The general feeling about the situation was summed up in a letter to the editor of a local magazine. The writer said that the *Spokesman-Review* had asked for "A literary genius to transfigure with the glowing colors of romance the stern realism of the early settlement of the Pacific Northwest," but, "I beg leave to suggest that the press of this state is doing miserly little to hasten this state's stunted literary art out of its nighties." Newspapers, she continued, maintained regular literary review departments, but instead of giving prominent space to local people, they are "letting the sorely needy and certainly worthy home talent squirm along, allowing only at rare intervals a bare mention to help it to public consideration, and that mention is given as one tosses a bone to a stray dog." Home talent needed support. "There was a great Concord in the East. Have no fear, we can make a greater Concord in this more inspiring realm—and it all depends vastly more upon the spirit of our journalism than upon the mood of the people, or upon the independent bursting forth of a possible Emersonian genius of philosophy or the call of a Cooper out of slumbering wilderness."

The indignant letter writer was correct in one respect: the development of a vital literary movement did not depend on the emergence of a genius or two, and it would only partly be helped by a friendlier journalistic attitude. A vigorous movement would emerge when writers freed themselves from the fetters of the past, when, in short, having overcome the pioneer complex, they would then be able to write on themes that had universal meaning and appeal, though the settings were local. But that was not to happen for some time yet.

Fourteen

Widening the Intellectual Horizons

In a pioneer society there is an almost tender reluctance to let go of the past, lest its aspects, romantic in retrospect to the participant, be eclipsed by the passage of time. This is responsible for the desire to preserve in print the events that occurred, whether significant or trivial, so that in later years the past could be reanimated for the pioneer's children and grandchildren. As in every new society, the Oregon country had writers, professional and otherwise, who undertook to perpetuate its heritage. The temptation to personalize history was great, and the writings of the pioneer recollectors of events were characterized by a coloring and romanticizing of facts. One of the few contemporary cynics about pioneer historical writing, and completely skeptical of its value, was Jesse Applegate. "I have assured all who have applied to me for information respecting the early history of Oregon that I did not think it worth writing," he once stated; "that I knew of no incident connected with it worth preserving—nor a single character that rose above mediocrity—no display of heroism, patriotism, or other of the sterner virtues—that exalt and preserve the names of men."

It was not unusual for a pioneer who had played a prominent part in the settlement and development of the region to be solicited personally by a writer for an advance subscription to his book. Its title was generally something like "A History of Oregon of 500 pages full of thrilling incidents, heroic acts, and hair-breadth escapes." It would contain the portraits and biographies of the "chief actors" and the price was to be about $5. The author also came to gather firsthand information; he would promise to devote a sizable amount of space in his work to the exploits of the person being interviewed and publish his portrait. For these favors, the honored and privileged subject was asked to contribute a few hundred dollars to aid publication. The more affluent settler often responded, but the one who could not afford to do so, or was reluctant to part with his money, received only brief mention in the volume or none at all.

Material for pioneer histories was drawn almost exclusively from personal reminiscences, a frequently unreliable source, as too many years had generally elapsed for faithful recollection. And, of course, accounts could not help but be colored by personal prejudices and special interests. Typical among the pioneer histories was a two-volume work, *Pioneer Days of Oregon History* (1905), written by a journalist, Samuel A. Clark. The volumes "do not follow chronological method, nor strictly the analystic," wrote the *Oregonian* in an editorial review. A thread of history did run through them, but "the narrative is interrupted at all points by a recital of reminiscences collected by the author in person," and the historic episodes were "embellished with legends and anecdotes about men, women and affairs, with excellent effect. It has romantic touches, but it is not romance. Doubtless there are errors of fact and incident, such as must occur in a work so largely written from the recollections of others. But we do not think them numerous or important." The great value of the work, the paper felt, lay in its "reminiscent character," as it contained accounts by and about almost every pioneer who had played some part in the early history of Oregon.

Few of the numerous histories written by old residents could be considered scholarly. William H. Gray's rambling *History of Oregon* (1870), contained the myth of Marcus Whitman's ride to the nation's capital and bristled with the missionary's personal biases. Horace Lyman, in his book which has the same title and was published thirty-three years later, was more objective but not free from pioneer limitations.

Perhaps the most illustrious representative of the early school of Northwestern historians was Edmond S. Meany. For almost a lifetime, he was associated with the University of Washington, first as professor and then head of its history department, with only a brief interruption when he served for two years in the state legislature. A pioneer himself, he had not only a firsthand knowledge of the history of the Northwest, but was intimately acquainted with almost every aspect of its geology, topography, plant and animal life. As a teacher he undoubtedly was an influence in perpetuating the tradition of the pioneer.

Completely and sentimentally devoted to the region, Meany's countless articles and books bore the unmistakable stamp of the frontier historian and romanticizer of the "heroic past." Indicative of much of his writings are the following excerpts from his *Vancouver's Discovery of Puget Sound:* "Nootka, wild, romantic Nootka, deserted and neglected by white men for more than a century, though once the most frequented harbor on the Pacific Coast . . . what a lure is this Nootka to one who has searched for truths among the rare and scattered records. . . . In the summer of 1905 the present writer made the journey on foot from Gray's Harbor to Neah Bay. It may be imagined what thoughts filled his mind as he visited these scenes of these tragedies of long ago."

A contemporary reviewer of the book commented with perhaps undue harshness: "In point of quality it is more like what one might expect from a student in essay or thesis than from a professing historian. As a student's essay or thesis it might be considered good as far as it goes, which is not very far." This was not, of course, the typical attitude.

Meany's next major work was a *History of the State of Washington* (1909) which is filled with many of the intimate details that could be known only to one who has either lived in the state or spent years in studying it. He also contributed countless articles to historical magazines, the newspapers, and periodicals of the region and still found time to edit the *Washington Historical Quarterly*, which he helped found in 1906. At his death, twenty-nine years later, the journal devoted sixteen pages to a listing of his publications and the balance of half of the issue to tributes. The bibliography is divided into sections on manuscripts, books and pamphlets, laws, magazine and newspaper articles, which in turn are subdivided into the topics of geography, history, coast history, state history, Seattle, University of Washington, pioneers, Indians, mountains, and natural history. Every conceivable topic within these subjects is covered, from "The Conifers of Puget Sound" to "The First Japanese Graduate of the University of Washington" to "The Name of Mount Robson a Puzzle"; Meany also tried his hand at verse, which was published in a book called *Mountain Camp Fires*. His services to the state and University of Washington were memorialized by naming a building for him on the campus.

It was difficult to write pioneer history without getting involved in all kinds of partisan disputes. Readers who would dig down into their memories and seek to disprove some statement made in a narrative had

to be considered. One of Oregon's leading historians, afraid to precip-
itate a controversy in which she would be identified with one
faction or another if she named the sources from whom she had obtained information for her book, omitted them from her acknowledg-
ments. A violent altercation once occurred in the downtown section
of Portland between two gentlemen because one denounced as "a lie"
the statement in a historical work that the first brick house in the city
had been built by William S. Ladd. And, on another occasion, great
exception was taken to a history because the river on which Portland
is situated was spelled "Wallamet" instead of "Willamette."

The controversy over the spelling of the river's name is of interest
as an indication of the intensity with which the pioneers regarded
local history. It went on for years, and before it was over it had involved historians, judges, and prominent citizens generally. The Honorable Matthew Deady entered the fray in support of "Wallamet"
with an article in the San Francisco *Bulletin* in 1864. Six years later the
discussion came up again when the legislature of Oregon was considering the spelling so that it might give legal status to the name. Judge E.
Strong, who had once served as a member of the Territorial Supreme
Court, wrote a lengthy article defending "Willamette." The matter
rested for a while until 1874, when the legislature again discussed the
question and Archbishop F. Blanchet published an article in the *Willamette Farmer* giving his view of the correct spelling. Whereupon
Deady again rushed into print: "When and how the spurious Gal-
licism and orthographic anomaly—Wi-la-met-te, Wil-la-METTE, or
Wil-LAM-ette first found its way to Oregon and was applied to the
Wallamet river and valley, no one appears to know."

That really began it in earnest. The *Pacific Christian Advocate* entered the battle on the side of the "Will's," provoking a reply by the
Oregonian; this led the Oregon legislature to pass a resolution calling
for the establishment of the correct spelling of the name of the river.
Judge Strong then replied to Judge Deady in the *Bulletin*, which in
turn editorialized in favor of the former. And then the *Willamette
Farmer* again entered the lists with Strong's reply to Deady, which
was followed by Deady's rebuttal in the *Oregonian!* The combat
raged with character assassination as a by-product until the legislature
finally settled the issue.

Deady, however, never gave up. As late as 1883, he was still doing
research on the name and communicating the results to the historian
Hubert Howe Bancroft. That year he wrote to Bancroft that he had

found, through a friend, an original copy of Franchère's narrative which was owned by someone in the Treasury Department at Washington, D.C. Franchère, he said, who spelled the name of the river "Wollamat," was the first person, so far as it was known, to have put it in writing. That in itself, he stated, should be conclusive that the name had an Indian origin and that "the sound of the first syllable is properly represented by the broad *A* as in 'father' or its equivalent the short *O*." He also pleaded with the historian who was to issue a work on Oregon that "I hope you will not allow your book to issue with this orthographical abomination and historic falsehood—Willamette. The history of a country is largely contained in its geographical names, and can best be preserved by giving them correctly."

The amount of time that was spent in research and in letter writing must have been prodigious for so unimportant a question, but no issue relating to the beloved Oregon country was too small to have its violent partisans.

The nature of the personalized and romanticized pioneer history was inevitable in a society where many contributed to it out of the reservoir of memory. Love of, and faith in, the new homeland imbued almost all the settlers, and they would have been reluctant to read any book that marred the glamorized picture. Many years were to elapse before history measured up to the standards of a social science, when it could be objective and not be regarded as detracting from the accomplishments of the past.

By the end of the century, historians like Frederic G. Young and Joseph Schafer were beginning to replace the older group, and with them, historical writings began to mature. Young served for almost thirty-three years as Professor of History, Economics, and Sociology, as well as dean at the University of Oregon. Soon after his arrival in the Northwest, he began to do research on its history. This led to the discovery of the journal and letters of Nathaniel J. Wyeth, which he edited for publication. Young was instrumental in the organization of the Oregon Historical Society and served as its secretary and editor of its *Quarterly* for almost thirty years, until his death.

Joseph Schafer published his *History of the Pacific Northwest* (1905) five years after he came to the University of Oregon to assume the chairmanship of its history department. Though fairly brief, it remains one of the standard works on the subject. The author, wrote the *Oregonian* in reviewing the book, "devotes his entire intellect to setting forth the processes by which the wilderness was subdued,

homes multiplied, cities built, commerce extended to all parts of the
world and a great civilization developed in this remote and once inaccessible portion of the continent."

Neither Young nor Schafer was a prolific writer, and in that respect
they were surpassed by the female historian of the Northwest, Mrs.
Frances Fuller Victor. Before she came to live in the Oregon country,
Mrs. Victor had been a poet and short-story writer and contributed
humorous editorials and society items to the San Francisco *Bulletin*
under a pen name. Like most immigrants she soon became devoted
to the new land and expressed her enthusiasm in letters, articles, and
a book, *All Over Oregon and Washington* (1872), which dealt with
its early history, scenery, climate, geologic history, and resources. A
biography of Joseph L. Meek, *River of the West*, published two years
before, was a sound, scholarly work which historians such as Chittenden found a valuable source.

In 1878 Mrs. Victor joined the staff of Hubert Howe Bancroft, who
was running a literary mill in California much on the style of Dumas
fils, employing a staff of writers to compile a history of the West. Her
contribution was the two volumes of the *History of Oregon* (1886,
1888), *History of Washington, Idaho and Montana* (1890), both of
which she alone wrote, almost all of the *History of Nevada, Colorado
and Wyoming* (1889), and a substantial portion of two of the six
volumes of the *History of California* (1884–1890). The entire series
of thirty-three books was edited and published by Bancroft under his
own name.

Mrs. Victor worked for Bancroft for eleven years, unhappy most
of the time because she felt she was grossly underpaid, and dissatisfied
with Bancroft's editing. She accused him of changing history to suit
his personal predilections, omitting figures whom he disliked or distorting their personalities and misconstruing the nature of their activities.

As a writer of the Northwest, Mrs. Victor should have been acclaimed by her fellow Oregonians, but during her lifetime she seems
to have been shunted to a back seat in their esteem. As the years passed
she grew increasingly bitter at what she considered the lack of recognition, which was in large part financial. To Professor Young, who
asked for her assistance in connection with the *Oregon Historical
Quarterly*, she replied coldly that unless he could see to it that she received monetary returns, she might do better by writing children's

stories. She felt that there was a conspiracy of silence regarding her contributions to Oregon history:

Take Mr. Lyman's article in the December Quarterly where he names *literary* people of note in Oregon. Does he mention me? When Mrs. Dye wrote a similar article for the Pacific Monthly she ended it by a paragraph of half a dozen lines, or less, in which she named me as a writer who had been industrious in research . . . giving me no place as a literateur, poet or historian. And she had just published a popular book, whose popularity was wholly derived from my *researches*. There are some people in Oregon who have a private opinion, no doubt, on this subject, which might be as flattering as I could wish: but they *keep it private*. . . . No one in this state, in any proper way has acknowledged my services, in many ways, to the State.

Some time after her death an article in a Northwest magazine commented that she had received so meager a return for her labors that she was compelled in her old age to peddle cosmetics from door to door to earn a living.

She was frequently despondent and one of her poems addressed "To Mrs. ———," published in a collection of her verse in 1900, sums up her philosophy:

> I have not found the meaning out
>   That lies in wrong, and pain and strife;
> I know not why we grope through grief,
>   Tear-blind, to touch the higher life.
>
> .   .   .   .
>
> Nay, own the truth, and say that we
>   Are but the bonded slaves of doom,
> Unconscious to the cradle came,
>   Unwilling must go to the tomb.
>
> I wait to find the meaning out
>   That lies beyond the bitter end;
> Comfort yourself with wearying heaven,
>   I find no comfort, O my friend.

Though Frances Fuller Victor was a pioneer historian, she was a careful, meticulous writer, using more of the techniques of modern scholarship than most of her contemporaries. She had little of the pioneering ax to grind and sought to have her work as accurate as possible. She was the first to expose the Whitman-saved-Oregon myth, and her efforts to be completely honest and not to romanticize facts may have been a factor contributing to her unpopularity. Not until after her death was she acclaimed in articles written about her.

With the exception of Joseph Schafer, neither Frances Fuller Victor nor Frederic G. Young nor Edmond S. Meany, and certainly none of the lesser historians, achieved much of a reputation beyond the borders of the Pacific Northwest. The first scholar to be elevated to national stature was J. Allen Smith, a professor at the University of Washington. He came there after his peremptory dismissal from his teaching post at Marietta College in Ohio for supporting William Jennings Bryan in the election of 1896. Smith had begun his academic career as a bold challenger of the existing social order. College professors then lived in what a contemporary sociologist described as "a tight little intellectual world . . . bounded by Presbyterianism, Republicanism, protectionism and capitalism." Smith's views opposing the principles of the high tariff, the gold standard, and the unregulated private ownership of monopolies were well known on the campus, and his vote for "radicalism" added the final touch. Two colleagues who also supported Bryan were discharged at the same time. He was recommended to the newly appointed president of the University of Washington, who, as it happened, was a Populist and a fellow alumnus. Smith was promptly hired to teach economics, sociology, and government. Though he was kept so busy that, as he wrote of himself, "He had to spend his last summer vacation at another state university library to get his work done," he managed to do a great deal of writing. His publications made him nationally known among students of American government, while at the university "the handsome man with the kindly, almost sad, face, who spoke deep convictions out of deep study, in quietly stirring tones," was extremely popular.

No ivory-tower intellectual, Smith was constantly concerned with, and participated in, the community controversies. His trenchant, carefully documented argument before a City Council which was prepared to grant a fifty-year franchise to the Seattle Electric Company was largely responsible for limiting the period of the franchise, an agreement to provide free transfers, and a reduction in fares on books of tickets. He was a firm advocate of municipal control, frequently warred with political bosses, and supported labor.

Smith worked on his manuscript *The Spirit of American Government* (1907) for ten years before it was published. Written in a vein similar to many of the critical books of that day, it attacked the alliance between business and government, the undemocratic character of the Supreme Court and the Senate (whose members were then elected by state legislatures), the system of checks and balances, and other features of American government. Smith attributed most of the evils of our political order to the Constitution, describing it as an instrumentality contrived by the wealthy and privileged for the maintenance of power, as contrasted with the Declaration of Independence, which was a democratic document.

Before the book came off the press, the *Seattle Times* obtained the proofs and, in a front-page story, quoted the sections attacking the Supreme Court. The views expressed infuriated prominent members of the Seattle bar. "The man writes like an anarchist," ran one denunciation; ". . . in a case in the Criminal courts . . . [Smith's attack on the Supreme Court] would make good evidence to substantiate a plea of insanity," was another. Demands were made for Smith's dismissal on the grounds that he was not fit to teach. It brought to a head a long period of agitation against the "nest of anarchists" at the university which included Smith and a number of other liberal professors in the Social Science Department. For years every president of the university and every governor of the state had been urged to get rid of Smith and his colleagues, but he was too popular and well liked among too many people of all political persuasions. Now they and a large segment of the student body rallied to his support, holding mass meetings, writing letters to the newspapers, to the governor, to the president of the university, and applying pressure generally in his behalf. Smith remained.

In 1911 a committee representing every county in the state was formed to try to persuade him to be the gubernatorial candidate on the Progressive ticket. That same year he was asked to run on the Democratic ticket. "So wide a following did Smith have in Washington, the Professor was told, that he would have to do nothing but assent to the nomination and his election was assured." He refused both offers because he felt that he could be more effective in his academic post.

The Spirit of American Government exerted a profound influence on men like the sociologist E. A. Ross, Wisconsin's Senator Robert La Follette, Sr., who distributed the book as part of his campaign literature; Theodore Roosevelt, who was strongly impressed with it, and William Allen White, who told a friend, "I think I have bought a half-dozen copies of that book and have referred a score of people to it."

Published during an era when a plethora of works by sociologists, economists, political scientists, and reporters analyzing and muckraking American institutions poured off the press, Smith's was outstanding as both a provocative and scholarly book. As a teacher, perhaps no other man at that period, with the exception of Charles A. Beard, played so vital a part in fostering an analytic approach toward the American government and its political institutions. J. Allen Smith elevated the standing not only of his own department, but of the university in the same manner as Vernon Louis Parrington, in another field, was to do some years later.

Smith created a rumpus in Washington with a book, but at the University of Oregon, two years later, a tempest in a teapot raged for weeks because an English professor stated in a lecture to some of his students after class hours that Jesus Christ was not divine and that the doctrine of atonement "was simply a relic of barbarism from a bloodthirsty age." The following Sunday the *Oregonian* had a front-page story that was headlined, "Howe's Belief Is Flayed in Pulpit." It seemed that a clergyman in Eugene took exception to Professor Herbert C. Howe's talk and violently attacked the college professor in a sermon entirely devoted to him. The newspaper story went on to say that the minister attended the lecture because he was familiar with Howe's attitude on the New Testament: "I felt it important to be there to hear what he was going to say, and the hope that my presence might in a way be a check to what he said." Other preachers joined in the denunciation and, according to the paper, the incident became an almost exclusive topic of discussion among the students, whose sympathies were overwhelmingly with the professor.

In Portland another clergyman joined the fray and gave a discourse on the subject "Are the Young People Safe at the State University?" Said he: "From press reports we learn that there is a conflict in Eugene. Several pastors of the city and a teacher in the State University are the principals. Students and church people have been on the firing line. It is a religious warfare."

Reeling, but not defeated, Professor Howe took time out to put his lecture on paper and submitted it to the *Oregonian*, which published it in full, without editorial comment. It occupied about five columns of six- or eight-point type and began: "I regret that I must open these remarks with a personal statement. But it has been made a very personal matter, various persons having, since we last met, called into question my moral right either to have any religious views, or to express any, if I have them."

This storm subsided, too, and the little town of Eugene settled down to consider weightier matters.

The world of learning in the Pacific Northwest was immeasurably enriched by Thomas Lamb Eliot, a Unitarian minister in Portland, whose influence extended far beyond that locality and far beyond the ministry. When he arrived in the city in 1867 to assume his duties as the congregation's first minister, Portland had a population of seven thousand. The streets had no lights and no sidewalks, the railroad had not yet reached it, and travelers arrived by overland coach from California or by one of the steamers which made the trip once or twice a month. Eliot did not confine himself to the pastorate of the new religious group. A man of wide interests, erudite and worldly, he gave lavishly of his time to the young city, providing strong moral and social leadership.

Laboring under the handicap of vision so defective—as the result of an injury in his youth—that he was unable to read for more than fifteen minutes without excruciating pain, he managed to participate actively in dozens of organizations. His influence resulted in either the creation or the strengthening of virtually all the educational, charitable, and humanitarian institutions of the city. Among other positions, he held those of County Superintendent of Education, Commissioner of Prisons for Oregon, president of both the Children's Home and the Oregon Humane Society, and trustee of the Portland Associated Charities. He also helped to organize the Art Association of Portland, which he served for a quarter of a century as, respectively, director, vice president, and president, and he was the vice president of the Library Association.

Eliot sponsored public lectures at his church on significant topics ranging from ethnology, jurisprudence, politics and government to the Australian ballot, civil-service reform, economics, the insane, education, and art. His greatest and most lasting contribution was in the field of education. Simeon Reed, the Oregonian who had amassed a fortune in the railroad business, was a parishioner of long standing in Mr. Eliot's congregation. The clergyman had proposed that he found a "Reed Institute of Lectures and Art and Music and Museum," modeled after the Lowell Institute in Boston or the Cooper Institute in New York, where men and women of average income could hear the outstanding authorities of the nation. Though frequently prompted, Reed died without doing anything about it. Mrs. Reed had evidently been impressed with the idea of the project and she left a provision in her will for the establishment of "an institution of learning having for its object the increase and diffusion of practical knowledge among the citizens of Portland . . . to be named and known as the Reed Institute." By the terms of the bequest, Eliot was named head of a board to administer the trust. When the college was later established on the basis of the Reed $2,000,000 endowment, he was chosen president of the board of trustees and served from 1904 to 1920.

With all these activities, Eliot managed to keep up with his scholarly interests, and he was awarded three honorary degrees—Doctor of Divinity from Harvard, Doctor of Laws from Washington University, and Doctor of Letters from Reed College. His career left an indelible imprint on the world of thought in the city and state and region which he had adopted early in his life.

The region for whose progress Eliot had devoted his energies possessed aspects that had intrigued men in the field of science. Its geologic wonders and mysteries, its strange plant and animal life, were objects of early investigation. The mariners who sailed along its thickly wooded shores occasionally took time to examine the curious rock formations, the alien vegetation, the brilliantly plumaged birds, and to make some notes about them in their logs. The later overland pathfinders described southeast Washington as a lava country and speculated as to the possible sources of the flow, some attributing it to Mount Adams and Mount Hood and other volcanic peaks in the Cascade range. The mighty, spectacular gorge of the Columbia had probably resulted, they believed, from a tremendous dislocation in the earth's structure which created a chasm between the mountains.

Later, natural scientists in every category, alone or accompanying expeditions, came to investigate those features of the Oregon country in which they were interested, and some perpetuated their names in the trees, flowers, and birds. The famous Northwest fir, named after another man, was discovered by the naturalist and botanist Dr. Archibald Menzies, who accompanied the Vancouver expedition. He also found the salal and large-leafed maple and his name is commemorated in a number of common wild flowers.

Lewis and Clark were not primarily scientists, but on their exploratory mission they performed the functions of ethnologists, geologists, zoologists, and botanists, obtaining a great deal of valuable information. Tribute was paid to their scientific work in giving the name "Lewisia" to the Montana state flower and "Clarkia" to a flower of eastern Oregon; also, one of the mountain birds, a crow, has been called the "Clark," and the beautiful western tanager, the "Louisiana."

In the early years of the nineteenth century, the Royal Horticultural Society sent a Scotch botanist, David Douglas, on two trips to the Oregon country; the stately fir bears his name. Another Scotsman, John Jeffry, was sent about twenty years later by a group of patrons to collect specimens of horticultural interest. The botanist, Dr. David Lyall, came with the International Boundary Survey. Dr. John Scouler, who was at Fort George, wrote about his scientific observations on trips made between 1824 and 1826 in his *Journal of a Voyage to Northwest America*.

The fur trader, Nathaniel Wyeth, was accompanied to Oregon in 1834 by Thomas Nuttall, a botanist and ornithologist, and John Kirk Townsend, an ornithologist. The Wilkes Exploring Expedition also brought along a number of scientists: James Dwight Dana, geologist, Dr. Charles Pickering and W. D. Brackenridge, both botanists.

The obstacles which a visiting scientist had to surmount in the primeval land were a testimony to the endurance engendered by the scientific spirit. In describing one of his trips, Douglas wrote: "We returned [from the mouth of the Umpqua] nearly by the same way we had come in 12 days hard labor, with great misery, hunger, rain and cold; but what gave me most pain was the nearly total loss of my collections crossing the river Sandiam." Despite these vicissitudes and countless others, he succeeded in getting a great deal of valuable material back to Europe, either by ship from the mouth of the Columbia, or by the fur brigades across Canada to the Hudson's Bay Company, and, from there, across the Atlantic to England.

The outstanding geologist during and after the pioneer period was Thomas Condon, Oregon's "Grand Old Man of Science," who came to the Northwest as a missionary in 1852. His youth had been spent around the Central Park section of New York when that area was virtually wilderness, scouring the neighborhood for fossils and rock specimens. It was, however, an urban center by contrast with the primitive land he and his bride found in Oregon.

Ministers' homes, like most others on the frontier, were unpretentious dwellings, and, having no library or study, Condon prepared his sermons during long walks through the neighboring hills. He always took a geologist's hammer along, and while one part of his mind was occupied with the talk he would deliver from the pulpit, the other was busy examining the fossil specimens along his path. With a gift for stimulating interest in his interests, he soon had the soldiers of the near-by fort, the teamsters, packers, and trappers collecting for him.

Condon supplied the Smithsonian Institution with many valuable specimens. His work came to the attention of Professor O. C. Marsh of Yale University, director of its geologic museum. Marsh was working on a manuscript dealing with the Tertiary and Cretaceous vertebrate animals, and he requested Condon to send him as complete a collection of the region's specimens as he could obtain. He enclosed $100 in his letter and offered to send more funds should they be needed.

Condon traced and recorded the geologic history of a large section of Oregon. Working alone in an area completely cut off from research facilities and specialized publications in the field, a good many of his discoveries and conclusions nevertheless remain valid today. In the sixties he unearthed some fossil remains of the horse which led him to conclude that in this country the Northwest was the birthplace of the animal. He published an article on the subject in the *Oregonian*, unaware that previous disclosures in the East discounted his theory. This circumstance later led the historian, Edmond S. Meany, to unfairly accuse Professor Marsh of not giving Condon credit in his book for the "discovery." Condon's investigations, however, provided an important link in the history of the horse in America.

Thomas Condon left the ministry in 1872 to become Professor of Geology and Natural History in Pacific University. Four years later, when the state university of Oregon opened, he was appointed to the same chair at that institution. He remained there for the rest of his life, teaching and carrying on his research.

Scientific works dealing with the region were promptly brought to the attention of the inhabitants by the newspapers. Typical is the announcement in an early paper of Washington Territory: "We have before us a copy of a work by Drs. Geo. Suckley and J. G. Cooper, Naturalists to the late North Pacific Railroad Expedition, entitled 'The Natural History of Washington Territory and Oregon.' It is a large volume, of 400 pages, with fifty-eight plates, and full catalogues and descriptions of plants and animals collected from 1853 to 1860 . . . a book of great interest to our citizens . . . it deserves special attention, and we trust it will meet that commendation which it merits."

Under the heading "MUSEUM! MUSEUM!" a paper in Eugene City announced in 1862 the formation of an organization which was to be devoted entirely to the advancement of science in the Northwest. It requested specimens of any sort: "Skins of all kinds of animals wanted, whether common or rare, whether feathery or hairy. If persons do not wish to spend their time in removing the skin, send us the bird or animal and we will attend to it ourselves. . . . As the skull is also a fair index to the structure, nature and habits of animals, a collection of the . . . whether they be of things which walk, crawl, fly or swim, are wanted. Entire skeletons would be preferred." Rocks, especially those containing fossils and plants, and ten bushels of bird eggs with which to study the "new science of Oology" were also wanted.

Among the settlers were a number of amateur scientists who soon began to investigate the land to which they had come. Alone or in groups they explored the countryside, carefully collecting and classifying, to the best of their ability, specimens of all kinds. A few accumulated extensive collections which were considered valuable enough to be placed in the herbariums of the universities. The collection of one layman, Thomas Howell, was acquired by Oregon State University.

Howell was a grocer who, for twenty years, spent every cent he could save and every moment he could spare in wandering over the country, gathering, classifying, and describing the natural flowers and plants. Unable to find a publisher for the book he subsequently wrote, and also unable to afford the services of a professional printer, he spent months learning to set type and then seven years in printing *A Flora of Northwest America*. It has been described as the only existing work "of all plants, shrubs and trees growing naturally in the states of Oregon, Washington and Idaho."

Not many, however, were imbued with Howell's passionate interest in nature study and his innate scientific spirit; or, if there were some, they lacked his stamina. Life on the frontier was rigorous and the average man had to be content with a less demanding avocation, a more passive type of diversion.

Fifteen

Front Bench, Center Aisle

The need for distraction from the daily monotonous grind, for relaxation of stiff muscles and a weary body, was especially great in the pioneer country, for, added to the toil was the often bare, cheerless house and the loneliness caused by widely scattered dwellings. When, therefore, some form of entertainment was offered, it was received gratefully and enthusiastically.

The first theatrical performance in the Oregon country brought out the people of the countryside for miles around, though it was given by a group with no pretensions even to amateur status as actors. The British man-of-war, H.M.S. *Modeste*, was anchored off Vancouver on the Columbia River while negotiations were being conducted between the United States and Great Britain over occupation of the area. Tired of wading through mud each day during their shore leave —it was the "rainy" season—and bored with the lack of activity, the officers and men formed a theatrical unit and spent their time rehearsing plays which they had decided to perform. The news quickly spread and soon everyone who possibly could was making preparations to attend, children and all.

For many it was no small trip. Some had to travel a great distance over difficult trails, some journeyed by water, and others had to use both routes. One group, having missed the regular small boat which plied the waters between Oregon City, Portland, and Vancouver, hunted up a large, old canoe, hired some Indians to assist in paddling, took their lunch baskets and set off. It was a whole day's journey on the wide Columbia, contending against a strong current, but the passengers passed the time exchanging jokes, singing Chinook songs, and discussing the future of Oregon. They arrived in time for the show, remained with the others for the dancing that lasted well into the

night, and for the picnic next day, to which the captain had invited
everyone.

The crew of the *Modeste* gave several plays, among which were
Three Weeks of Marriage, Mayor of Garratt, and *The Deuce Is in
Him,* all of which were received with hearty acclaim. One of these
plays was a popular comedy and the *Oregon Spectator* reported that
the house was held in continuous laughter from beginning to end.
Under the heading of "Theatrical Intelligence," the paper published
a dramatic criticism, the first to appear in the Oregon country, which
concluded:

Everyone did their [*sic*] part almost faultless, but we cannot omit specially to notice Roberts as inimitable in *Jerry Sneak*—it would take the
most descriptive mind to do him justice; suffice it to say, we even doubt
if the great *Liston* himself could *come it* as he did, in the comical twist of
the muscular fibre; and his *"I'll have a bit of the brown"* almost sent everyone into fits—it was tho't at one time that two gentlemen present would
require to be held, the risible faculties being so acted upon. Mr. Bynon's
Snuffle was also done to perfection—the jesters gestures and face were
first rate—even some of the children called out *"look at the man making
faces."* The orchestra was well got up, with violin, flute, and the *harmonious* bagpipes. . . . We conclude by saying that we wish these supporters of the drama every prosperity and success and bid them God-
speed! Gratified, I think, I may safely say, in my own name, with that
of the other settlers in Oregon, shall we be, when we see the "curtain
raised" in our infant city, and entertainment afforded us equal to that of
the *"Modest"* blue jackets.

It was some years, however, before the professional theater, good,
bad, or indifferent, came to the Northwest. In the interim the inhabitants had to content themselves with home talent. The first native
minstrel troupe—not blackface—gave a performance in 1850 in Portland, then a town of only about eight hundred inhabitants. No public
hall was available and so the dining room of one of the wealthier citizens, Simeon G. Reed, was hired. The performers paid $50 for its use
for two hours, with Mr. Reed furnishing the candles for lighting.
Despite the "full house" and the $1 admission charge, the actors found
it necessary to save expense by walking back to Oregon City, from
which they had come in style by canoe. They gave successive performances at Oregon City, Butteville, Champoeg, and Salem that
netted them very little profit but contributed a great deal to their own
and the communities' entertainment.

A few other groups blossomed out here and there, and then the Northwest was invaded by traveling magicians, circuses, blackface minstrel troupes, comedians, and individual performers of various kinds who put on one-man shows. An early and noted performer was Stephen Masset, who was a traveling trouper in the old tradition, a rolling stone who wandered the globe from Australia to the far Northwest. In his performance in Portland in 1856, he sang romantic ballads, some of which were original, gave vivid impersonations of seven different people attending a Yankee town meeting, and the inevitable readings. He was shrewd—and learned—enough to begin with a recital of Bryant's *Thanatopsis*, which has the famous line "where rolls the Oregon," and, of course, created a sensation.

Touring the region on horseback when he could find no other means of conveyance, with his precious melodeon following behind on a mule, Masset covered the area from Portland to Victoria. One of the amusing incidents of his career occurred in Salem. He was giving a performance in the courthouse, the only hall the town possessed, to the light of six tallow candles. While in the middle of a mournful ballad, "The Light of Other Days," a puff of wind extinguished them, and he was drowned out by hilarious laughter.

One of the first and most colorful of the professional entertainers, and for a while almost an institution, was the "professor." He was a man of many skills, singing, dancing, reciting monologues, playing the violin—sometimes on one string to make his talent the more unique—or bewildering and delighting with feats of legerdemain. He traveled leisurely up and down the coast, returning year after year. An intuitive psychologist, he had a deep understanding of people and knew how to please his audiences.

The "professor" was also an excellent publicity man who would have done well if he were hired to write copy for "supercolossal" Hollywood films. His descriptions of himself and his accomplishments did not suffer from excessive modesty:

Prof. Hermann, the World-renowned Prestidigitateur . . . has by special command, had the honor of appearing at the palaces of the following crowned heads of Europe: Queen Victoria of England, Emperor of Russia, Emperor of Prussia, Emperor of Austria. He has also given special entertainments for the gratification of three Presidents of the United States—Abraham Lincoln, Andrew Johnson and U. S. Grant, who all pronounced him to be the Greatest Living Magician Eclipsing in his marvelous feats of Legerdemain the great Hindoo Jugglers. The Professor has successfully performed at Egyptian Hall, London, for 1,000 nights; and at the Academy of Music, New York, for 200 nights and from 20 to 100 nights in Boston, Philadelphia, Baltimore, Washington, Chicago, Cincinnati, St. Louis, Mobile, New Orleans, and for 48 performances at McGuire's New Opera Theatre, San Francisco.

His audiences apparently never questioned why this "World-renowned figure should condescend to waste his energy traveling from backwoods hamlet to hamlet, or his great talents on a handful of common, unknown people. The inhabitants of the Northwest towns poured out to see him whenever he appeared and accorded him a generous welcome. But as the towns became cities and the population increased in size and sophistication, the simple, genial, and individualistic entertainment of the "professor" no longer had appeal, and he gradually disappeared from the scene, unmourned and forgotten. Some of the "professors" lingered, performing in saloons to aid in the sale of liquor. "Professor Ferdinand Zink from San Francisco, has been engaged at this establishment," ran an advertisement for the Bella Union Lager Beer & Billiard Saloon in Portland, "and will perform every evening on the Pianoforte. . . . The Bar will be supplied with the best assortment of Wines, Liquors, and Segars."

Close behind the "professor," and gently pushing him out of the way, came the blackfaced minstrels whose peculiar type of entertainment originated in San Francisco and was the forerunner of variety vaudeville. They were also particularly suited to the time and place in that they provided much with a minimum of manpower and trappings. All the men in the group—there were usually four—possessed a variety of talents. Characteristic of all minstrel shows was the opening number, an ensemble; each man played a different instrument, usually a banjo, bones, violin and tambourine combination, while they all sang. The middle part of the show, when every member of the troupe was given an opportunity to display his special talent—singing, dancing, jigging, stump-speaking, jokes—was a hodgepodge. The concluding part was generally a burlesque of some popular opera, such as *Giroflé-Girofla* or *The Bohemian Girl*, or a short farce.

That the minstrel show originated in the West is not surprising, for it was a natural expression of the boisterous and tempestuous aspects of the boom era that characterized the gold-rush days in California and the land-rush days of the Northwest. To the "Forty-niners" it represented the excitement of their own lives, and the more sedate Northwesterners welcomed it as a release from monotony and drudgery.

Two kinds of minstrel shows were given in the Oregon country—sometimes by the same performers in different halls—one for the robust male citizens and the other "toned-down" to make it acceptable to women and children.

In Washington Territory the minstrel shows were preceded by the dancing and singing in the saloons and squaw dance halls. This type of entertainment was especially popular in the mining towns and fishing villages of that area and later in the similar towns of Oregon and Idaho. An earthy kind of amusement was required by the hardy folk of the region and this supplied it. The places were aptly described as "furnishing both horizontal and vertical entertainment." As soon as white women saw that there was a demand for this type of diversion, they took it over. These "Frisco Lillies," as they were called, have been described as "women with dresses (?) reaching nearly to the point above their knees, with stained and sweaty tights, bare arms and necks uncovered over halfway to their waists, with blondined hair and some with powdered wigs, with faces rouged and powdered, lips dyed crimson with paint, eye-brows with winkers smutted up and blackened." Although severely censured by the more "respectable" members of the community, this form of entertainment continued because, it was said, prominent and influential citizens who owned or controlled the halls or the property on which the halls were located were reluctant to give up a profitable source of revenue.

One type of amusement to which a man did not hesitate to expose his family was the circus. A number of these toured the Northwest, especially during the early years. Caldwell's New York Circus exhibited in Oregon City in 1852. Among others were the Mammoth Circus, which boasted that it had been organized at an enormous expense and was coming directly from California, where it had been seen by more than 70,000 people; Kimball's Olympic Circus, which promised its patrons new performers, horses, wagons, and costumes regardless of expense; and Lee's National Circus and Roman Amphitheatre, which was "decidedly the most complete in the United States." The audience gaped at the daring equestriennes who could throw four consecutive forward somersaults on horseback over as many canvases while the horse went at full speed, the acrobats, the "La Perce Bearer." They laughed at the antics of the clown, one of whom was advertised as having a style which was "entirely new and void of everything approaching vulgarity."

This emphasis on "respectability" appeared over and over again in the notices and reviews of almost any type of entertainment offered. When a Mrs. Lesdernier, a monologist, came to Portland in 1857, the *Oregon Weekly Times* urged all to attend her "high-toned and refined intellectual entertainment." And in a brief comment on a theatrical group, another paper stated that the performance had been given to "full and respectable houses" and that the principal characters were supported by a few "respectable" actors.

In an "unguarded moment," as he claimed, one of Portland's most eminently "respectable" citizens wandered into a show that claimed to be an opera on the playbills but which was, alas, "a melodeon, moderated and subdued to this market." With horror he reported that the audience was composed entirely of men who "sat with their heads covered, and smoked and talked as if they were delivered from restraint. Upon the stage there were both sexes—doing high stepping in tights, called dancing, negro songs, and sweettoned [*sic*] melodies that sounded sadly out of place among the *bizarre* and coarse surroundings." Deady could endure this only briefly. "I soon turned away, thinking of Coleridge's splenetic lines upon the concert room:

> —I detest
> These scented rooms, where to a gaudy throng
> Heaves the proud harlot her distended breast,
> In intricacies of laborious song.

Though traveling was difficult, often hazardous and expensive—$50 from Seattle to San Francisco, for instance—the larger cities of Oregon Territory did not seem to suffer from lack of diversion, of one kind or another, which could be acceptable even to a Deady. During one month in 1857, Portlanders were offered three types of entertainment: a circus, a variety show, and the legitimate theater. One newspaper apparently felt that there were too many opportunities for diversion, for it wrote that theatricals, shows, and exhibitions had become a drug on the market and that too much was as bad as too little.

Various theatrical troupes found their way to the Oregon country by the late fifties. One of the most popular was the Chapman family, consisting of George Chapman and his wife, his sister Caroline, and brother William. The group, which had a national reputation, traveled up and down the coast, presenting plays, short skits, songs, and dances. They were among the first of the theatrical performers to visit California during the hectic gold-rush days of 1849, including in their itinerary every mining camp or mushrooming boom town they could possibly reach. The lack of an appropriate theater, or a theater of any kind, never stopped them. In one mining town they converted a huge tree trunk into a stage, to the delight and admiration of the miners.

The repertoire of the Chapmans included the popular Kotzebue melodrama *The Stranger*, the moralistic *Rosina Meadows*, or *The Roué of Boston*, and another favorite, *The Lady of Lyons*. Caroline, an actress of versatility and considerable talent, had appeared on occasion with Edwin Booth. She performed in vehicles that ranged from such classics as *The Rivals* and *She Stoops to Conquer* to the melodramatic *The French Spy*, and some of her roles included Ophelia, Lady Macbeth, and Desdemona.

Another group which was eagerly welcomed was the Stark Troupe. Of Mr. Stark, the Portland *Times* wrote that he was the finest actor to have visited Oregon, "and we can fully endorse the opinions of the entire California press, who have for many years conceded that he is one of the first Tragedians of the age." During visits, the group presented Schiller's *The Robbers*, the farce *Grimshaw & Co., The Warlock of the Glen*, and *Hamlet*.

Shakespeare seems to have been exceedingly popular, for his plays were given repeatedly. For the Stark performance, theatergoers came from as far as Oregon City. One young man from that locality wrote to his sweetheart that about fifty townspeople had traveled to Portland by boat and that the theater, which was capable of holding several hundred persons, had been filled to capacity. Mlle. Duret, a distinguished actress well known in Europe and the East, gave Shakespearean readings in drawing-room entertainments and kept her audiences in almost breathless silence for nearly three hours. She also appeared in several plays, one of which was *The Stranger*, about which performance the *Oregonian* commented: "Never have we seen more genius exhibited than in the personation of 'Mrs. Haller' by this great artiste. When stout and rugged hearts are softened and melted into tears, as was the case, who shall say it was not sublime. As we looked around the house and saw the eyes of all moistened with tears, we said to ourself, here is an audience of souls, what great lever could move them thus? Genius: there in the person of a weak-looking but mighty woman."

The hardy troupers who wandered up and down the country, from town to hamlet, on horseback, by canoe, boat or stagecoach, must have been men and women of unusual endurance or burning with an unquenchable fire of devotion to the stage. The country was rough and wild, "hotels" were frequently such in name only, and coping with unwelcome "visitors" in his bed was sometimes the least of an actor's housing problem. One of the early thespians recalls the various experiences "with good and bad business, ice, snow, colored cooks, high-toned piano players and too-proud-to-post-up-bills advance agents." During the death scene of Little Willie in one performance of *East Lynne*, while the audience sat in rapt silence, clutching moist handkerchiefs, the city marshal stomped up the aisle, climbed over the footlights and boomed: "What have you done with Kelly's cookstove?" The property man, it seemed, had borrowed a little sheet-iron camp stove to use in a scene of one of the plays and had forgotten to return it.

From time to time amateur theatrical companies were formed. Oregon City had an Edwin Booth Club in 1867 which erected the first stage in the town, and the Salem Dramatic Troupe that same year gave *The Warlock of the Glen* and *Five Shillings* in a benefit performance for the city's fire department. The following year, a group was organized in Portland and one in Vancouver, though at the latter place the female roles had to be taken by men!

On the whole, the theater was considered "decent," so that the redoubtable Matthew P. Deady could devote an entire article to "A Passing Touch at the Players" in his regular column in a San Francisco paper. One winter, he wrote that Portland was having an unusually productive dramatic season and that for the first time theatrical performances were being held regularly. He discussed in some detail "the stars and starlings, male and female, that have twinkled in this horizon during the season." The following year he must have left his readers bewildered by a complete change of tack. In an article inveighing against the participation of school children, especially girls, in amateur theatricals, he concluded: "But, moralizing apart, while man is man and woman is woman, the drama will exist and be patronized. With us, as among the Greeks and Romans, with the advance and ripening of what is called civilization—the multiplication of luxuries and the cultivation of the gross and sensual appetites—the tendency of the drama is downward, to substitute exhibitions of female nudity and the putrescent *Camilles* of the French for the manly English morals of Shakespeare." Apparently Deady, who was a scholar, had not read the Bard very carefully.

When, some years later, the intrepid Billy Sunday came to the Northwest and, at a meeting in Spokane, raved and ranted about the theater as a sink of iniquity and a den of vice, he received no popular support. For several days papers carried letters and editorials vigorously opposing his stand. One local actress, who wrote that she was the daughter of a minister and a student of the Bible, inveighed against his "coarse and offensive language," which, she said, would not be tolerated in a respectable theater, and called his statements maliciously untruthful. Even Harvey Scott rose to the defense of the stage. Although, he wrote, he himself rarely attended theatrical performances, most members of his family did go and always commented on the general intelligence of the theatergoers, with many of whom he was personally acquainted.

Regardless of moralists, people wanted entertainment, and so, almost as soon as a clearing in the wilderness took on the semblance of a town, a place of some sort was provided for the purpose. At first the mess hall of a mill or a large barn or warehouse or other similar structure was the only building large enough to hold an audience of any substantial size. In Seattle, from 1852 to 1859, the Cook House of Yessler's mill was the sole "theater" in the city. Later Yessler built a hall, but, like others in the region, it was a crude structure. The halls which served as theaters for many years, even long after the arrival of professional entertainers, were usually constructed of bare boards and lighted by candles and fish-oil lamps behind reflectors. Only the more elegant had a calico curtain stretched on a wire in front of the stage and some rudimentary props. The stage floor frequently was made just of loose boards that on occasion jumped up and slapped the actor at a particularly inappropriate moment.

One actor who made the circuit in the early days recalls an amusing experience which occurred in the little town of Silver Lake, Oregon. When the troupe arrived, it found that the only public hall had burned down some years back and had never been replaced. Determined to give a performance so that they could earn some necessary cash, the actors consulted the landlord of the hotel where they were staying and found that he had an empty barn which could be used as a makeshift theater. Rolling up their sleeves, the players swept up the hay, built a temporary stage with the horse stalls for dressing rooms, put up lanterns for footlights, made seats out of kegs, boxes, blocks of wood, and old boards. Everything was in fine order and the small handbills passed around town brought out a good-sized audience. Only one thing had been overlooked. The actors-turned-theater-builders had forgotten to sprinkle the floor so as to lay the sneeze weed

with which it was generously covered. That night the group put on
The Fatal Wedding, which was guaranteed to wring every last tear
from the most hard-hearted audience. No sooner had the curtain gone
up than the chorus began. "The actors, the audience and the horses
were sneezing. Every horse sneezed ten times a minute. The audience
was sneezing, crying and laughing . . . and the actors were playing
codas as the end of every speech."

Often theaters were only part of a structure, such as the one housed
in the three-story building which C. A. Reed built in Salem in 1870
and which was known throughout the state as Reed's Opera House.
The first floor was used as a storeroom and hotel, the second floor was
the theater proper, and the third was the "gallery." It was a barnlike
place with only two stoves to heat it, so that the audience had to remain in their wraps, and even at that, on especially cold nights the
actors frequently were accompanied by the music of chattering teeth.
The stage manager was an ancient of seventy who believed that anything is most enjoyed when it has to be waited for. As there was no
designated time for the performance to begin, he would keep the audience waiting until they were impatient and restless. On one occasion
the manager of the show asked, "Hawkins, when do we ring up the
curtain?" "Well," the worthy replied, "when you hear folks out there
stomp, then I reckon it's time to begin." So every show was preceded
with a rumbling tattoo on the floor and an ear-splitting whistle from
the gallery.

The completion of a theater was frequently the occasion for a celebration attended by people from miles around. When Plummer's Hall
in Seattle was completed in 1859—it was a two-story building with a
store below—a grand ball was held to observe the event, with guests
invited from Port Townsend, Port Madison, Olympia, and Steilacoom.
The steamer *Julia* brought two hundred persons from the cities on the
Sound. A grand free supper and ball was widely advertised, and the
evening was spent in dancing the polka, lancers, and Virginia reel to
the merry tunes of a fiddle.

The Willamette, or Stewart's Theatre, the first and most famous of
all the pioneer playhouses in Oregon, opened in 1858. "From a brief
inspection," wrote the *Oregonian*, "we think it will not soon be surpassed. The stage is large, the scenery all new, the boxes comfortable,
the pit commodious, the ventilation good, and the whole arrangements
designed to make the theatre comfortable and pleasant to the lovers of
the drama." Within its wooden walls angry words hurled at Copper-

heads, and jeering retorts directed at Union sympathizers were frequently heard in the tense days before Appomattox. During intermission, oratorical bombast was hurled forth freely, and political spellbinders like Senators Stark, Lane, and Nesmith stirred up passions that often made the play itself anticlimactic. The Willamette served not only to house visiting thespians, but as a town meeting hall in which to discuss and demand more satisfactory street lighting to replace the smoky, smelly kerosene lamps or agitate against the "invasion" of the Chinese.

A new type of theater, attached to a public market, was erected in 1875. The structure was three stories high, finished in brick and iron and with long, Corinthian columns. The two top floors were used for the theater while the ground floor housed a public market with twenty-eight arched stalls, each wide enough to accommodate a team and wagon. The ceiling of the market was twenty feet high and the asphalt floors and solid marble counters throughout gave it an imposing appearance. A decade later the combination of market and theater was considered inappropriate and the building was no longer used for dramatic productions.

On the other side of the tracks, and existing contemporaneously with the "respectable" theaters, were the "box houses," successors to the squaw dance halls. They housed variety vaudeville, which followed minstrelsy. In this type of diversion each performer was a specialist in a particular type of act, of which there were several on the bill. Box houses were so called because the balcony was partitioned off into curtained boxes from which the patrons could see the show without being seen themselves.

Entertainment was merely an adjunct to the sale of liquor. Some theaters hired women whose sole job was to visit the boxes and encourage the purchase of drinks on which they would later collect commissions. In others the female entertainers performed on the stage until midnight, then went into the boxes while another company took over, presenting melodrama. Performances were continuous, the curtain being lowered only when the fights, which were always going on, became too noisy and extensive. The women were not usually promiscuous, but scraps over them occurred frequently when two patrons who had imbibed too freely vied for the attention of the same damsel. One commentator of the social scene described one of these houses:

The place was located in a basement under a liquor saloon and cigar stand. . . . Into the mouldy and uncomfortable depths the pure atmosphere and sunlight never have an opportunity to enter. . . . A nervous opium eating individual was hammering away at a piano. In the hall-like space, before the stage, were a hundred or more men and boys. Not a woman was to be seen in the rows of seats—only men smoking and chewing tobacco and boys eating peanuts. Around the sides of the room and at the end opposite the stage were built out of thin pine boards, small apartments with an opening towards the platform and a barn-like door leading into the narrow passageway along the wall. In each room was an electric touch button which communicated with a bar fitted up behind the stage. The boxes were unlighted save as a stray beam might enter at the windows. In these places were women, one in some, more in others. The law was that not a drop of liquor be sold on the floor, but in the boxes . . . ?

During the nineties the managers of the box houses carried on a delaying action against the forces of righteousness and morality arrayed against them. There was objection to women encouraging the sale of liquor in the boxes, there was objection to liquor being sold at all, and there was opposition to the generally loose atmosphere. In a few towns the reform element succeeded in getting bills passed which outlawed some of the features of the box houses. Women were excluded from variety theaters in Tacoma in 1899, and six years later the state legislature passed an act prohibiting "the employment of females in places where intoxicating liquors are sold as beverage." The net result of this measure, because of its broad application, was to prevent even actresses from appearing in theaters, whether or not they helped sell liquor.

A powerful agency of reform and a strong "competitor" in some towns was the Salvation Army. In Walla Walla, which seems to have been more moralistic than a good many other places, it caused one theater to shut down by drawing away patronage to its own hall. In other places the Army was not quite so successful. The theater bands would lie in wait for the "soldiers of the Lord," and when they began to march past, a musical free-for-all would take place, with the Salvationists generally drowned out.

Competition was keen among the various houses, and bands were used in front of the theaters each evening to attract customers. If there were two theaters across the street from each other, the crowd really had a treat in the efforts of the two bands to outdo one another. If it seemed that despite their best efforts the opposition was winning the attention of the audience, a male performer was called out to create interest. The musicians were the best obtainable, and those people who were offended at the mere existence of the box houses did not consider it beneath them to park their carriages near by and listen to the music.

Prize fights were another feature of the box houses. Although they had been prohibited by law, the public demanded pugilistic entertainment and managers evaded the legal proscriptions by having plays written which would give boxers an opportunity to display their physical prowess. All the great names visited the Northwest in the nineties—John L. Sullivan, Jim Corbett, Bob Fitzsimmons, Jim Jeffries. "See Fitz: spar three rounds, make a horseshoe, punch the bag, shoe a horse, sing a funny song," ran an advertisement about Fitzsimmons's performance in *The Honest Blacksmith*. Corbett for several years received one of the largest salaries ever paid a single performer up to that time and was considered a good actor, but about Sullivan there is the legend of the time that he marched on the stage and bellowed, "I'll save you, Mudder." "Save her?" came a shout from the gallery. "You can't even pronounce her." The champion paused, removed his coat, and stepped to the footlights. "Who said that?" he demanded. No reply. He put his coat back on, returned to the wings and made a second entrance. "I'll save you, Mudder," he thundered and stopped, looking out into the audience. Silence. With a triumphant smile he clasped his hands over his head in the symbol of victory and proceeded with the performance amid vociferous applause.

Women who performed in the theaters were outcasts, morally suspect and regarded as a group apart, though their attire on the stage was more concealing than revealing—they would have been horrified at the modern girl's bathing costume. The skirts of the chorus girls modestly covered their knees, with two inches more for good measure, and underneath were the generously ruffled pantaloons fastened just above the knees. Opera-length hose were worn and the upper arms were hidden by little puffed sleeves. A sleeveless tunic or a skirt that reached above the knee could have brought a fine upon the management. Only the ballet dancers were somewhat more exposed, and when the stage manager of one of the Seattle theaters advertised for fifty girls to play in the ballet of his production, *Around the World in Eighty Days,* he received only a single reply, and she was forced to withdraw when her family threatened to disown her. "It is impossible to secure fifty young women in Seattle who would brave an audience in the slender costume of the ballet," was his regretful conclusion.

Vaudeville shows, "cleaned up" for the family trade, were given occasionally in the regular theaters by the same troupes who performed in the saloons and box houses. John Cort, who operated a chain of variety theaters in Butte, Spokane, Portland, San Francisco, and several smaller towns, tried to attract the respectable audience to his houses by advertising "a special grand matinee every Saturday at 2 P.M. for ladies and children." His efforts failed. It was not until John F. Cordray came to the west coast in 1888 that a theater devoted to vaudeville without the greater attraction of liquor was introduced in the Pacific Northwest. He opened in a tent in Portland with a stock company offering farce and melodrama, with specialty acts for curtain raisers, and was so successful that within a few years he was operating a circuit which included a number of cities. Cordray offered special attractions for children who were admitted on Saturday afternoons at half price, and, realizing whence sprang his success, his programs carried notices that no intoxicating liquors could be sold or permitted on the premises. Eating peanuts was prohibited in the theater and boys were cautioned against catcalling, whistling, and stamping their feet. Profane or boisterous language was not tolerated. Intoxicated or rowdy characters were not admitted. "We regard all our patrons as ladies and gentlemen and expect all to conduct themselves as such and anyone who cannot comply with the rules of the house must not be surprised if they are invited by a police officer of the house to vacate immediately."

John Considine, a box-house operator in Seattle, started the first legitimate, popular-priced vaudeville chain in the world. Using some acts from his box house, he was able to charge an admission price of only ten cents. He received financial backing from a Tammany politician, Timothy Sullivan, and the chain included theaters in Butte, Portland, San Francisco, Tacoma, Astoria, and Vancouver. The Considine-Sullivan combine owned twenty-one houses in the Pacific Northwest, twenty in California, and booked theaters all over the country, maintaining agencies in New York, Chicago, San Francisco, and Seattle. In the last-named city, Considine remodeled the Coliseum, which had originally been a skating rink. It was the largest theater west of Chicago—the "block-long theater," it was called—and so deep that patrons in the last rows could not hear the acts and were only barely able to see them.

As the box houses gradually gave way to the more respectable theaters, the nature of vaudeville changed. In the early days the performers
tried to keep the show going as long as possible, since the profit lay in
the sale of liquor. But when entertainment alone was the attraction, a
set program came into existence. A typical one in 1887 opened with
an overture by the orchestra, followed by the comedy *Married in the
Dark; or, Tricks on the Old Man*, and then the variety. This included
a "versatile song and dance lady," the "greatest lady banjo soloist in
the world," who was making her debut in the city; another "side-
splitting comedy," another overture, the "Three Solitaires" in a new
and novel specialty "abounding in new and sparkling music and refined comedy," the queen of the balladists, the empress of song "in
choice selections of vocal gems," the king of Irish comedians, the great
fire king in a new fire act, the queen of the African harp, a male singer
and dancer, "the beautiful and petite song bird," an accomplished
vocalist and dancer to whose magnificent costumes particular attention was called, a blackface farce, yet another overture, and, to conclude, another comedy, *The Roasted Lovers*.

An important feature of vaudeville was the topical nature of the
skits. They were frequently satires on the social, economic, and political events of the day, and the clever comedian or stage manager who
usually wrote them included something about the city in which the
performance was given. Even the dancers who swirled in skirts made
of dozens of yards of silk had pictures of national personalities, in addition to the customary colored lights, flashed on their moving
skirts.

With the appearance of variety vaudeville, the traveling troupes
faced almost insuperable competition in some towns. The John Jack
Theatrical Combination, headed by Captain Jack, to give one example, struggled along for a few years, offering in addition to plays a
comic Negro act, ballads, farces, and even holding a public dance after
the show. Captain Jack tried all kinds of plays, from *Life in New York*
to *Captain Jack; or, A Life on the Border*. In the latter melodrama he
tried to give his audience everything possible in the way of excitement
—it included four abductions, one attempted poisoning, two bowie-
knife combats, one chloroforming, twenty-four homicides, all to the
accompaniment of a continuous fire of pistols, so that passers-by
thought the Chinese were celebrating their New Year. Despite all the
effort and energy expended, the troupe was finally forced to disband.
In 1877 one newspaper cautioned theatrical groups against coming to

Walla Walla, because those that had been there failed to make expenses.

Troupes nevertheless continued to visit, and late in the nineties, stock companies began to operate. Cordray in Seattle managed the first one in that area, and others followed. Laurette Taylor got her start in a Seattle stock company, but few great actors emerged from Northwest stock. Public taste was the same in that region as elsewhere in the country, and ran in cycles. For a few years melodrama was the rage, then Shakespearean revivals, to be followed by grand opera, which, in turn, gave way to comic opera—including the ever popular Gilbert and Sullivan—and farce comedy. Dramas were generally saccharine, sensational, melodramatic. Unless they left theatergoers with their eyes dripping and their handkerchiefs soaked, they were failures. *Uncle Tom's Cabin* and *East Lynne* were among the favorites, as were such heartrending melodramas as *Bertha the Sewing-Machine Girl* and *A Mad Love*. Two of the many temperance plays have survived to this day but are performed as farces: *Ten Nights in a Barroom* and *The Drunkard*. Audience reaction was spontaneous and uninhibited. The black-mustached villain was loudly hissed and the handsome hero wildly cheered, while the women wept unashamedly at the trials and tribulations of the noble heroine and the men self-consciously blew their noses or surreptitiously wiped away a tear.

Stage manners and clothes were so stereotyped that one paper commented sarcastically:

When an actress makes a dab at her right eye with the middle finger of her right hand, followed by a show of throwing something into space, and then repeats the performance with respect to her left eye, it signifies that she is indulging in tears.

When an actress has something particular to confide to her papa or mama, it would be the height of ill-manners did she not crouch down on the floor by the side of her parent.

When an actor comes upon the stage, faultlessly dressed, with a flower in his button-hole, you may be sure he is a villain of the deepest dye.

When an actor has all manner of hard luck, and is seedy as to clothing and chronically empty as to stomach, he is to be congratulated, for he is shortly to wed the young lady of his choice and to arise by spasmodic bound to affluence.

Every attempt was made to have the staging completely realistic. About one play it was advertised that in addition to "its world-chronicled saw mill sensation . . . shoes are mended, wood sawed, a barn painted, bread kneaded, lamps filled and potatoes pared." In another a genuine fire engine, two horses, and three railroad effects were put on the stage. And in still another a pit was dug under the stage so that the hero could jump fifteen feet into a ten-thousand-gallon tank of real water.

Apart from the conventional theaters, the picturesque Chinese theater, of which there were three at different times in Portland, afforded the often homesick Orientals an opportunity to experience a little of the cultural atmosphere of their homeland. One remained in existence for almost a quarter of a century, until 1904, in the large upstairs room of a building. The auditorium was about a hundred feet square with a stage of about twenty-five feet in depth. In the center of the room were wooden benches, each of which had a shelf along the back for teapots or food (Chinese plays ran for at least five hours); and stalls, every one large enough to accommodate several people, were built around the room.

As in Shakespeare's day, the Chinese theater depended on the imagination of its audience; the stage, a raised platform about five feet high, was uncurtained, without wings or footlights. The few props used were tables or chairs, banners painted with clouds or a city wall, all of which were moved on and off as occasion required. For the rest, the "scene" was provided by words or actions, and mighty battles were fought out in pantomime.

The Chinese play depends for its effect on a highly specialized and traditional pantomime, and the action is symbolic. When an actor lifts his foot, it indicates that he is entering a room; if he carries a whip, it means that he is on horseback; and when he lays it down, he has dismounted. An actor is no longer part of a scene when he mounts a chair and hides his face. Rivers are crossed by imitating a rowing motion with an oar handed to the actor by the property man, who, though he wanders about the stage in street clothes, is invisible to the audience. After lying down on the floor for a moment or two, slain villains or generals simply get up and walk off the stage.

The orchestra performed almost constantly, as Chinese plays are operatic in form, with dialogue being sung rather than spoken, and the various instruments were used to underscore the action in the same manner as musical accompaniment is used in the films today. The brass percussion instruments and the drums and tom-toms accented a particularly dramatic scene, such as a battle or duel, while the flute or two-stringed violin was used for the lighter portions. On the rare occasions when the musicians rested, they sat at the back of the room, smoking and chatting.

Equally informal, and similar in a sense to a county fairground, was the general atmosphere. The plays had no intermissions and the audience wandered in and out while the performance went on; the din of the stage mingled with the sounds of chatter, crunching of watermelon seeds or sipping of tea, the cries of the venders of cakes, nuts or fruits and the clatter of dishes, while the air overhead was thick with the smoke of pipes.

Traveling Chinese troupes from San Francisco or even China visited, and for a period of weeks presented a cycle of plays in gorgeous costume taken from the rich and extensive reservoir of Chinese history. Townspeople frequently attended the Chinese theater and for twenty-five cents enjoyed its unique and exotic spectacles.

By the end of the century, theaters had become elaborate structures. The Seattle Theatre, which was completed in 1892, was built of blue stone, in Italian Renaissance style, with tiled floors, wainscoted lobby, and stained-glass windows. The orchestra and first-gallery seats were leather covered, with plush backs, and lighting arrangements were as modern as any in existence. The central switchboard had sixty switches which controlled the four hundred lights in the house, more than half of them for the stage alone. The orchestra lights had the new bronze hoods that confined the illumination to the music.

The orchestra leader could be signaled electrically to begin the performance. The two galleries, the orchestra leader, the manager, and the ticket office could be reached by means of speaking tubes. Three minutes before curtain time, a gong was sounded in the foyer and in the fashionable Rainier Club adjacent to the theater. The opening night of the Seattle Theatre brought out everyone in the city who could possibly get there, and the newspapers devoted columns to descriptions of its magnificence.

Other theaters were half-million-dollar architectural projects, with seating capacities of from two thousand to twenty-five hundred. Portland and Seattle had the finest houses in the region. When the Marquam Grand Opera House opened in Portland in 1910, it was not surpassed anywhere on the coast in the lavishness of its appointments.

Those were the rich years for the road shows in which leading actors and actresses of the country appeared. Ellen Terry, Sarah Bernhardt, Thomas Keene, and other luminaries traveled the Western circuit, whose main line included Los Angeles, San Francisco, Portland,

Tacoma, Seattle, and Spokane. Smaller companies visited the inland cities, such as Walla Walla and Lewiston. The plays in which they appeared were, as a rule, the same ones given in the East. Still popular, as indicated by their frequent repetition, were the old melodramatic favorites, *East Lynne, Uncle Tom's Cabin*, and *Ten Nights in a Barroom*, with Shakespeare following close behind.

With the development of the motion picture came the decline in stock and the traveling companies and, eventually, in vaudeville. At first the flickering films were used as an added attraction to variety or as a "chaser" to clear the house for the next show. But gradually, as they improved in quality and quantity, vaudeville became the secondary feature. The theater wave receded to the large cities of the East, with only an occasional company venturing forth into the no longer "Wild West." Residents now had to rely on canned entertainment or, as in the case of their pioneer forebears, resort to their own devices for amusement.

Sixteen

Adventures in Aesthetics

In a caravan of the heavily laden prairie schooners which dragged their way across a continent, perhaps one wagon might contain a melodeon, carefully wrapped and carefully placed among the numerous household items. Little room could be found in the jam-packed vehicles for many of the niceties of living, and only a very few women were able, in some miraculous way, to squeeze in this symbol of the civilization left behind. The smaller musical instruments were less of a problem, and those who owned guitars, violins, violas, or wind instruments generally carried them along. They were played occasionally to cheer the travelers on or to provide a little diversion when they stopped to rest in the evening, or at little celebrations of a holiday, a wedding, a betrothal.

From the accounts left by the pioneers, there seems to have been a good deal of singing on the way. The songs were those the emigrants brought with them, and no popular piece emerged like the famous "O Susannah" of another overland migration. Of the indigenous music later composed in the Oregon country, only fragmentary records could be found; if more had been written, it was either lost beyond recall or may yet be unearthed from a long-neglected attic. A few Oregon historians feel that the paucity of original compositions is due to negligence in collecting and preserving, but since every other relic of pioneer life was carefully treasured by the emigrants and their descendants, it seems more likely that there was little worth keeping.

The fact is that the American frontier was not a conducive milieu for the creation of a purely indigenous folk music; the nation's rapid growth militated against it, for the speed with which institutions on the frontier germinated and flowered soon turned a frontier into a stable and settled region, a jumping-off place for new sections. The southern Appalachian area is perhaps an exception to the rule, but in the main, frontier characteristics did not last long enough for any of the culture areas of the westward movement to produce a genuine "native" music.

The music which was sung and played on the frontier was not a frontier product but—as in the case of the English sacred songs of early New England, the Scotch and English ballads of the southern mountains, the folksongs of the French fur traders and voyageurs of the Northwest—a transplantation from the older areas. The immigrants had carried with them popular songs and ballads, and sometimes new words, reflecting the local conditions of the new environment, were substituted for the old. This adaptation of lyrics to indigenous circumstances is most apparent in the songs of the "Forty-niners" and the river boatmen.

Group singing was one of the most popular expressions of musical interest in the early days. Within a few years after settlement, choral instruction was being offered to children and adults. A Mr. Newell announced in the *Spectator* that he was organizing a juvenile singing school for boys and girls between the ages of six and fifteen and an adult group for "Ladies and Gentlemen who wish to learn to 'sing at sight.' " The following year Mr. Newell, now "Professor," was giving instruction on the pianoforte and melodeon in addition to voice. From all indications he found his field profitable, for he soon opened an "Academy of Music" in conjunction with a music store, and was selling instruments and sheet music in addition to giving lessons.

Similar activity was taking place in other cities. In Olympia, when a Mrs. Hamm let it be known that she was organizing a class in vocal music, the paper in that city ran an item giving the details and stated: "Mrs. Hamm, as a teacher of sacred music, has probably few superiors living, and the leisure hours of the ladies and gentlemen of Olympia cannot be more profitably subserved than by giving their attention to a course of lessons from her." A. L. Francis of Salem offered instruction on brass and stringed instruments, as well as musical arrangements for bands.

Lessons were given by "professors," some of whom had had good training, by married woman to earn a little pin money, and by maiden ladies as a genteel means of support. As a rule, the women had learned to sing or play the pianoforte after a fashion because it was considered an essential part of a female education. While they could read music

or strum out a tune, they were rarely equipped to teach. As their incomes naturally depended on whether or not their students learned
to play the instrument, they often resorted to all kinds of devices to
keep the youngsters glued to the bench and to make the unwilling
fingers master a piece.

The method of Auntie McMillan, as related by Homer Davenport,
was probably one of the most unique. With a pen, she wrote numbers
beneath the notes of the score, on the keys of the organ, and on the
nails of her pupils. This worked like a charm, and Homer was learning
to play the piano through his superb coordination of numbers from
score, to nails, to instrument. So well did he progress that a concert
was arranged to show off his skill as a result of Auntie's inimitable
teaching and thereby, perhaps, secure additional pupils for her. But
alas and alack! On the night of the performance, Homer got his hands
wet milking the cows, the numbers which had been put on that afternoon ran—and the rest is history. Auntie MacMillan left town the next
day.

That there was a demand for musical instruments is evidenced by
the many advertisements in the newspapers, though the cost of shipping them around the Cape must have made them almost prohibitive.
As early as the fifties, papers carried announcements of anticipated
arrivals of clipper ships from the East bringing instruments, and prospective purchasers were asked to place their orders promptly before
they were snatched up. A number of tuners toured the region and
their arrival in a city was always noted in the local paper.

The art of dancing, too, was not neglected. Professor Coggeshall,
"late of Boston, Mass.," started an academy in Salem in 1852. He gave
a course of twelve lessons in the "fashionable" dance and announced
that he was interested in forming classes in the other river towns.
Olympia had a school of the dance in 1854 where Professor Louis
Bach taught quadrilles, polkas, contradances, Scottish and Spanish
dances and waltzes "by theory and by practise." It flourished for a
number of years, and at one point its director announced that he had
thirty-five students, with more coming in each day. In addition to
instruction, students were offered the inducements of weekly "Soirée"
parties and occasional fancy-dress balls.

Professor Bach took his art seriously and tried to convince the settlers of the benefits of tripping the light fantastic. "Dancing! At the
very sound of the word, the blood leaps more cheerily through the
veins, the face brightens, the step lightens," he rhapsodized in a news-

paper advertisement. Those who performed physical labor would immediately be relieved of fatigue; the sedentary worker needed the muscular exercise, and as his movements harmonized with the inspiring music, his whole nature would be brought into more harmonious action; and the thinker could not find a better diversion from serious thoughts, stated the professor. Dancing also served to bring together people of all ages so that "each is benefitted by contact with the other: the old, by the elasticity and hilarity of youth; the young, by the decorum and prudence of age."

Concert artists visited the region as early as 1849. One of the first was a Mr. Morgan, who, according to the town paper, was a singer of distinction and was warmly appreciated by the audience. He was scheduled to give another concert the following week and the paper urged all music lovers who had not yet heard him to attend. "The immortal Bard," it stated, "to dissent from whom on such points is nothing short of literary heresy says that

> He that has no music in his soul
> Nor is not moved with concert of sweet sounds,
> Is fit for treasons, etc."

The following year the city was treated to a grand vocal and instrumental concert which featured, among other new selections, the "Hungarian Marriage Happiness Galloppe" (in imitation of a baby's cry), three popular favorite songs with instrumental music by a full band, and, to complete the evening, the *pièce de résistance*, the celebrated railroad steam galloppe in imitation of a railroad.

Mr. John McFarland, "the World Renowned Violinist and Paganini of the World!" accompanied by Mr. Joseph Pickering, "the Unrivalled Pianist! and Original Melodeonist!" toured the Northwest in 1858. A few years later came the "Old, Original Troupe of CAMPANALOGIANS, or SWISS BELL-RINGERS, in their Chaste and Elegant Entertainments, Playing 249 Bells, being seven and a half octaves on a perfect Chromatic Scale." They also offered harp, violin, and flute solos, vocal selections, and Irish, Scotch, Dutch, and Yankee characters in song, dance, and burlesque.

One of the most popular traveling groups of the seventies and eighties was the famed DeMoss family who had migrated to eastern Oregon in 1862. Father, mother, and five children sang and played forty-one different instruments in various arrangements of duets, trios, quartets, and quintets. It was said that the children learned to sing as they learned to talk. Originally the DeMosses had no professional aspirations. They enjoyed performing at home for friends who came regularly each Sunday from miles around. Finally, after long urging, they were persuaded to go on tour. The DeMosses visited the remotest mining villages and the most distant outposts of the frontier. So successful were they that their reputation spread throughout the country and they were booked in the East and in Europe. They always maintained their loyalty to their adopted state, ending every concert with "Sweet Oregon," which Mr. DeMoss had composed and for which he also wrote the lyrics. For many years it was virtually a state song:

> I'm thinking now of a beautiful land,
> > Oregon, Oregon.
> With rivers and valleys and mountains grand,
> > Oregon, sweet Oregon.
> From mountains' high peaks, all covered with snow,
> A swift, limpid streamlet doth flow
> By the home of my youth, which I ever adore,
> > Oh! Oregon, my home.
>
> I think of thy forests and prairies wide,
> > Oregon, Oregon.
> The mines, the fish, and the ocean tide,
> > Oregon, sweet Oregon.
> Where the mighty Columbia rolls down to the seas,
> And the pines gently echo the breeze,
> Like a beautiful dream to my memory come.
> > Oh! Oregon, my home.

DeMoss wrote several other laudatory songs about Oregon, and during the World's Columbian Exposition he published *The Columbian Souvenir*, which contained a song dedicated to each state in the Union.

The pioneers did not rely solely on visiting artists or groups to provide their musical fare. In 1859 Portland organized a Philharmonic Society which began with eighteen members and held weekly song fests. It continued off and on for a few years and was resuscitated seventeen years later with a greatly increased membership. That spring, the new organization gave its first concert with a chorus of about forty voices, offered several duets, quartets, solos, and two instrumental pieces by a band. The chorus presented the "Gloria" from Mozart's *Twelfth Mass* and the "Soldiers' Chorus" from Gounod's

Faust. With not a little snobbishness, Matthew P. Deady reported in his column that the *aria* "Toi que j'aime" from *Robert le Diable* was received "with storms of applause and showers of bouquets by many good people who would be troubled to give a reason for their approbation, except the very common one in such matters, that the music appeared to be very difficult of execution and altogether above their comprehension." The most impressive part of the evening, he said, was the audience of six hundred, which was the largest and "most superb" that had thus far gathered in the city outside of the churches. He closed his article with a few acid remarks about the elaborate criticism of the performance in the daily papers, which, he stated, was crammed with technical terms, artistic paraphrases, and personal allusions to such an extent that the reader might imagine he was looking at the musical report of the New York *Herald* instead of his local journal. The Philharmonic Society continued to meet and perform for a number of years.

Brass bands, so called because at first they had no reed sections, were the earliest form of instrumental musical organization, and almost every town could boast a large or small one. With the players dressed in colorful uniforms, weekly concerts were given on the courthouse square or some other central point in the city, and many bands went on tour. The East Portland Brass Band had sixteen pieces and gave free concerts each week on the Plaza. Newspapers kept readers informed of band activities. Items such as the following were typical: "The Tacoma Military Band left yesterday for North Yakima where they will furnish the music for the State Fair next week. Professor Adler has secured an engagement for the band at Seattle, Sunday, Oct. 1, at the Madison Street Pavilion, Lake Washington. He is also arranging for a series of 28 concerts to be given at the Tacoma Theatre every Sunday afternoon during the winter." Probably the most famous in the region, and always in great demand, was the Aurora Band.

The first orchestral group in Portland, the Amateur Musical Society, was formed in 1875 with five violinists, two double-bass players, a trombonist, a pianist, and a director. Its first concert that year was a social and financial success, with the "élite" of Portland crowding the hall to capacity. Additional members joined the organization, which lasted for two years. The next group was not formed until 1882, when the Orchestral Union was organized with thirty-four performers and gave its first concert the same year. It was well supported, but since the orchestra was merely a hobby with the players, it was difficult to get them to attend rehearsals. The group finally disbanded about ten years later, but a nucleus remained and, under the name of the Haydn Symphony, continued to give performances occasionally for the next fifteen years.

In the interim musical Portland—or, rather, the "Four Hundred"— was surprised one day by an invitation in the mails from a musician, Charles L. Brown, to attend a concert. He had assembled thirty-five local musicians and rehearsed them so well in the short space of seven weeks that, according to the *Oregonian*, the concert was an overwhelming success. The program consisted of the Overture to *A Midsummer Night's Dream*, Schubert's *B Minor Symphony*, two selections from *Tannhäuser*, and *Serenade* by Moszkowski. An appeal was made by community leaders that Brown continue the concert series, and he did for the next three years, until Edgar E. Coursen was appointed conductor. By that time there were forty performers. The organization was partially supported by a group known as "The Musical Club," composed of musicians and music lovers, but it was constantly in debt. It dissolved in 1904. Several attempts were made in later years to revive it. A few concerts were given but not enough financial support could be mustered to keep it going.

Although the Northwest was still largely a frontier in the seventies, a definite social-caste system had already developed, especially in the large cities. Society was divided on musical lines, too. The days of the little choral groups, when everyone who was not a monotone could participate, were over. The "people" attended band concerts in the parks and the squares and the third-rate light opera company performances, but grand opera and symphony concerts were reserved mainly for the social élite. When Mme. Ilma De Murska and an operatic group performed in Portland, the *Oregonian* gave them a "rave" review and commented: "With scarcely an exception, the audience was composed of the most cultivated, refined and fashionable ladies and gentleman of Portland."

This situation was true throughout the country, of course, but in the Northwest it hampered the development of the indigenous symphonic orchestras, especially in staid Portland. "Scala," who conducted a column on music in the *Rose City Magazine*, discussed the suggestion of a local critic that Portland should have a symphony orchestra along the lines of Boston, Chicago, and New York and stated: "We should remember that there are more millionaires in the city of

Pittsburgh than there are voters in Portland. Who then would do the financiering of such a project, which for the first half decade or so would mean a tremendous deficit to be made up out of private pockets or the guarantors of the enterprise?" "Scala" could see only one way out of the difficulty—popular concerts at popular prices.

That the "masses" whom "Scala" urged the Portland Symphony to embrace would support orchestral music was proven by the experience of Portland's neighbor and competitor to the north, Seattle. The city on the Sound began its orchestral career in 1903 with a concert organized and directed by Harry West, a talented violinist who until then had been taking his cues in an orchestra pit in one of the Seattle theaters. It proved so successful that others were given during the next four years by the amateur organization which had no regular payroll and was held together simply by the players' love of music.

A group of women organized the Seattle Symphony Society in 1907 and invited an outstanding conductor, Michael Kegrize, to direct the orchestra. He served for two years, during which time it was put on a professional level. Kegrize was succeeded by Henry Hadley, who, though still a young man, had already achieved a notable reputation as a composer. He instituted weekly "pop" concerts which helped to support the symphony. Hadley raised the orchestra to a new high standard of performance and engaged leading soloists, such as Fritz Kreisler and Josef Hofmann, to play with it. When Walter Damrosch and his New York Symphony came to Seattle in 1910, the main attraction of the two concerts was Hadley's direction of his cantata *In Musical Praise*.

There were no other symphony orchestras in the region, but almost every town had organizations devoted to musical activities. In Walla Walla the Symphony Club gave concerts and devoted its regular meetings to the presentation of papers and solo performances by its members, and the Whitman Conservatory had a Choral Union led by its director of voice. Seattle had an Evening Musical Club, a Mozart Society, and a Ladies' Musical Club, all of which gave concerts. Portland had a Philharmonic Society, a Philo Musical Society, whose programs included essays, lectures, and debates, a Swiss Male Chorus, and a choral branch of the Turnverein which sang German songs.

With all the interest in music, magazines decried the lack of support of home talent and deplored the general tendency to withhold it until after the artist had made a success in Europe or in the East. It was pointed out that excellent music teachers were compelled to leave

Seattle or Portland because they were unable to get enough pupils to earn a decent living. Here the difficulty was the same as in the field of belles-lettres—an indication that the region was still self-conscious and timid about its taste. The population was also too small to offer remuneration to musical artists on the same scale as in the older sections of the country. As a consequence, home talent was constantly being drained off, which, in turn, led to the complaint that there were not enough talented artists in the region.

Yet, by the turn of the century, the larger cities and even some of the smaller ones supported and carried on musical activities as actively as any in the country. "Seattle is very rapidly arriving at a point in the development of its musical affairs," wrote a local magazine in 1906, "where much that has heretofore been provincial and uncouth is being eliminated and superseded by an attitude that is at once suggestive of a wider point of view, a broader and more thorough culture, and a technical intelligence that are only the result of the city's growing attraction for good musicians and musical productions." The same might have been said of Portland, Tacoma, or other cities with equal validity.

Musical activity thrived as a result of popular participation by the public both as performers and as audience. Participation in the medium of art both active and passive, however, lagged behind. A painting is the product of highly individualized craftsmanship and natural endowment; even an intelligent appreciation of a work of art requires some measure of specialized knowledge. Nevertheless, the Oregon country was not barren of art and artists, even in the beginning years of settlement.

The earliest artists to put the Northwest on canvas were outsiders who were drawn to the region by reports of unparalleled vistas and scenic grandeur found nowhere else in the country. The first of whom a record could be found was Paul Kane, "a Canadian gentleman" and "an artist of great merit," as the *Oregon Spectator* reported, who arrived in 1847. His oils of the city and the falls were described by the paper as "faithful and beautiful, extremely attractive and strikingly correct." Easterners who had erroneous ideas of the physical nature of Oregon were informed that in Mr. Kane's work they would find "correct delineations" of the country.

Paul Kane was a finished artist who had spent several years studying with masters in Italy and other parts of Europe. He had come to the Northwest primarily to record Indian life and customs. The frontier, he saw, was rapidly being pushed back, and with the swift disintegration and even disappearance of the Indian, it would soon be impossible to represent him in his native habitat. Kane's work was purely a labor of love, for commercial success lay in the direction of more conventional subjects.

Through the assistance of the governor of Rupert's Island, Sir George Simpson, who had been impressed with Kane's paintings of Indians of the Eastern tribes and provided passage with a brigade of Hudson's Bay fur trappers, the artist arrived in the Northwest a year before the Oregon newspaper wrote about him. He traveled throughout the area, working steadily. The glimpses of Indian life which he transferred to canvas are especially significant because almost none of the few artists who penetrated the region were interested in the subject. His painting of a Clallam woman weaving a blanket—an occupation which has long since ceased to exist—is probably unique of its kind.

Shortly after Kane's departure, an American artist, William Mix Stanley, came up from California, where he had been with General Kearny's topographical corps. He was a guest for some time of John McLoughlin in Oregon City and painted sketches of the Columbia River area in the vicinity of what is now Portland. About a decade later, Albert Bierstadt, of the Hudson River school of painting, made the long trek and painted Mount Hood and other scenic views.

A few artists of various kinds drifted into the new country with the intention of settling. In 1859 a Mr. Charles Elveena, who was described as an "Artist and Teacher of Landscape Painting and Perspective Drawing," wandered over the state making sketches. The *Oregon Weekly Union* commented that it had seen his work and considered it "well excuted [sic] and truthful." It recommended him to anyone who wished to "acquire the art of taking pictures from Nature's great book" while Mr. Elveena was in the vicinity.

From time to time announcements appeared in the press that artists were forming classes for instruction. One young man exhibited his work at the post office so that prospective students could judge his ability, and he secured the cooperation of the postmaster to take the names of those who were interested in studying with him. He offered reasonable terms, with the fee payable at the conclusion of the lessons, and guaranteed thorough instruction. His forte was "oriental" paintings. Miss Pauline Shelton advised the public that she had taken lessons in landscape and portraiture from one of the finest artists in San Francisco and was now equipped to teach. She also offered to tint photographs in oil or water colors.

Undoubtedly a number of the early settlers tried their skill with paint and brush and some, apparently, were able to commercialize their work. A Portland store proprietor who had recently migrated from Buffalo, mentioned casually in a letter to a friend that he had painted a picture for the state fair for which he had received $110 in gold. The writer may have exaggerated the amount, but the fact that an amateur artist could sell his work at all indicates that interest in art did exist, though it was understandably slight.

Exhibitions were held at infrequent intervals. In 1873, when Olympia, the capital of Washington Territory, was still a frontier outpost, an exhibit of paintings attracted a "large and appreciative audience" during the week in which it was held, according to the local press. Nothing was mentioned about the artist, and the only clue to his name is the heading of the article, "Reed's Panorama." Nor was anything said about the media in which the paintings were done. The emphasis was entirely on content, which included views of the Columbia River, Astoria, the Cascades, The Dalles, Mounts Rainier and Baker, Portland, Oregon City, Salem, Roseburg, and the Lava Beds. The paintings were regarded solely from the viewpoint of their functional value in popularizing the region, and the critic commented that "so far as the artist has attempted to deliniate [sic] landscapes or the topography of of [sic] cities and towns, they are absolutely correct." He took exception, however, to the view of Oregon City, to which he felt full justice had not been given. Only a small portion of the town had been portrayed, and he recommended that another be made from the Linn City side so that it could be seen in all its natural beauty.

Seattle in 1885 had a combination art and bric-a-brac exhibition with musical accompaniment for an hour every afternoon. One hundred and twenty-five pictures in crayon and oil, etchings, tile work, chinaware "so skillfully done as to almost pervade the air with the fragrance of the fruits and flowers thereon portrayed" were on display. The exhibit was sponsored by, and was the work of, members of the Seattle Art Association.

The Portland Art Club presented the work of fourteen of its members the following year. The paintings were mostly scenes of the Oregon coast and mountains, and some of them were named "Light and Shadow," "Adversity," "Morning," "Springtime," "Christmas," "Home," "Action and Solitude." Among them was the work of Edward Espey, who is regarded as the first native Oregon artist. He had little time to develop whatever talent he possessed, for he died when he was only twenty-nine. Espey left as his best creation an oil called "Repose," which had been purchased by subscription and still hangs in the main branch of the Portland Library Association. Another exhibitor was C. Rockwell, whose paintings of the Oregon coast and mountains can still be found in the homes of old Oregonians.

Meetings of the Portland Art Club were held twice a week—once for a discussion of business matters and once for sketching from models. Each second Friday all members were required to present a finished work on some subject that had previously been assigned. These were then judged by the group and the three paintings receiving the highest number of votes became the property of the club.

During the nineties, the Sketch Club was established in Portland. It was a group of young amateurs who met to paint and criticize each other's work, but several in later years made some phase of the field of art their profession. One became curator of the art museum in the city; another attracted the attention of a famous artist and went abroad to study under his guidance; a third became the art supervisor in the public schools; a fourth taught art at Pacific University and in well known Eastern schools. One summer the club brought from New York Frank du Monde, who taught at the Students' Art League in that city. He gave the members instruction for several months, and when he returned East some followed him for additional tutelage or went to Europe to study.

One of the earliest Washington artists to achieve a reputation outside of the state was Ella Shepard Bush, who came to Seattle in 1888. She did landscapes, portraits, and miniatures but is perhaps better known for her activities to develop an appreciation of art in the city than for her paintings. She founded the Seattle Art School in 1894, attracting a group of enthusiastic members who worked in oils, water color, pencil, pen and ink. Many of them left Seattle to continue their studies in the art centers of the world and some made national reputations.

Two other female artists also achieved some fame in Washington— Mary G. Allen and Harriet Fletcher Beecher. Both painted the scenes and people of Puget Sound, leaving a valuable historical record of the area. One of the former's best known paintings is a portrait of Narcissa Whitman, a completely creative piece of work, as it is based entirely on fragmentary descriptions of the unfortunate missionary's appearance and personality. Miss Beecher's canvases of Indians on the beaches are an especially important contribution, as they record scenes which have since passed into history.

Seattle soon had enough art devotees to form an organization called the Society of Seattle Artists. It sponsored annual exhibitions of the work of its own members and also brought in collections on loan. The society did a good deal to develop an appreciation of art in the growing city on Puget Sound, and, because of its success, a more formal organization, the Seattle Fine Arts Association, was founded in 1908. Its members were "to give particular attention to municipal art, pictorial art, plastic art, art in architecture, interior decoration, ceramic art, applied design, landscape gardening and art in apparel." The first exhibit under its sponsorship was a collection of Japanese prints borrowed from Seattle residents.

A small museum, housed on the second floor of the old city library, was established in Portland under the aegis of the Portland Art Association, which had been organized in 1892. Six years later, the Portland Art Class was formed to take advantage of the many gifts that were coming in to the museum. The collection soon outgrew its facilities and the first public art museum in the Pacific Northwest was opened in 1905, offering art instruction to the public as one of its services.

In the decades following the end of the century, indigenous art was making noticeable strides, although many of the artists were not native Northwesterners. Colonel Charles Erskine Scott Wood exhibited some excellent canvases in oil and water colors. Childe Hassam visited Oregon at the invitation of Wood and two other art lovers and painted forty canvases of the high desert country of Harney County, an area of arid and semiarid land stretching to the far horizon of hazy, desert hills. Several were purchased by the museum. Other artists were working at this time, painting landscapes for the most part: Louis B. Akin, Rockwell W. Carey, C. C. McKim, and Merle DeVore Johnson. The Museum Art School was opened in 1909, sponsored by the Art Association of Portland and the Arts and Crafts Society. Washington had its State Art Association, which sent traveling exhibits to towns throughout the state and even up to Alaska. A museum, however, was not erected there for a number of years.

The foundations of a true art consciousness in Portland and Seattle were being laid, and civic-minded citizens of both cities were vying with each other to make theirs the art center of the Pacific coast.

There were enough wealthy families to make at least a start in that direction, and both cities had advanced far enough from the days of the frontier to regard art patronage as a real social distinction. Magazines interested in art development in the Northwest began to be published, and here, as in allied aesthetic fields, a genteel tradition was being fostered.

The extent to which a community can genuinely and without subservience evaluate any of the art media, and be receptive to new developments, indicates the degree of its maturity. In the field of architecture, however, other factors in addition to intellectual independence operate to stimulate or hinder experimentation with new designs. The necessity for adaptation to a unique climate, for example, may sometimes compel an immediate departure from known forms. The types of dwellings found by settlers; the conditions under which settlement is effected; the nature of the immigrant groups—all these, too, exert an influence in determining the character of architectural development.

During the pioneer period, and even after, the only indigenous and original architecture in the entire Far West region was to be found in the Southwest. It was an adaptation of the picturesque California missions—for whose attractive designs the Spanish explorers and Spanish missionaries were largely responsible—resulting in new, individualistic patterns suitable to the Pacific environment. The settlers who came to the Northwest found only the architecturally crude trading posts of the fur men and the hastily improvised stations of the New England missionaries.

Early trading posts, for which the Hudson Bay Company provided the general pattern, were constructed with a view to protection against the Indians. Their outstanding feature was the rectangular stockade which was composed of sharp-pointed logs driven close together into the ground and bastions (built with loopholes into which the muzzles of rifles would fit) projecting over each corner. It enclosed cabins ranging from tiny shacks of bark-covered logs, to sturdy, roomy dwellings, with the logs not only peeled but squared. At first, joints were rudely notched and the cracks caulked with mud, chips and moss; later they had mortise and tenon, dovetail, tongue and groove work. Missionaries, who established themselves in the inland area where the rigors of the cold winters had to be considered, sometimes filled in the frames of their houses with mud. A rare example of adobe construction was the Whitman station.

The log cabin era was a brief one. Craftsmen of various kinds soon arrived, as did sawmills and other paraphernalia needed for home construction, and the pioneers were ready to erect permanent dwellings. Without any precedent in their immediate environment, they resorted to the forms with which they were familiar, and their homes afford a ready clue to their place of origin. The traditional Colonial of the East and South provided the structural motif during the 1840's and 1850's. Many of these homes were attractive and well proportioned, with clean, uncluttered lines. A few had imported parts such as sash, trim, sidings and frame. Also prevalent was the unimaginative salt-box, some with two stories, some embellished with bay windows and porches, but all monotonously alike. In the towns where they followed each other, row upon row along the rutted, muddy streets, they created a dull, drab landscape. In the countryside they were flanked or backed by the inevitable milkhouses, stables, woodsheds and smokehouses.

When the Greek revival swept the East in the fifties, it also invaded the West. Heedless of the setting, public buildings—hotels, schools, post offices—resplendent with Greek columns, friezes and cornices, arose to tower incongruously over the miscellaneous structures crowding around them. The style was more successfully adapted to homes which were generally set on sufficient acreage to provide the necessary balance. One good illustration of classic architecture was the Territorial University of Washington, which had a two-story portico with four Ionic columns and classic entablature. It was erected in 1861 and "was an imposing structure sitting proudly upon one of Seattle's hills . . . ," wrote a native historian. "Artists and experts always praised the structure as a remarkably proportioned, clean cut example of the Grecian style."

As population increased during the next three decades and the railroads made the region more accessible, building activity and styles became frenzied. The ornate Victorian Gothic was extravagantly and tastelessly used. Towers were piled upon towers, chimneys of all dimensions cluttered roof tops and roofs were edged with scalloped shingles; bay windows had small diamond panes of colored glass; scrolls, brackets, patterned wood panels, jigsaw fretwork, dormers, cupolas, were generously scattered over all. Byzantine, Romanesque, Georgian, the various Gothics and Renaissance were not neglected. Sometimes a fantastic conglomeration of two or more of these styles was used for one building. After the disastrous fire of 1889, which ravaged almost all the wooden structures in the business sections of Washington's four largest cities, heterogeneous edifices of brick, stone and cast iron were erected.

At the end of the century, a Tacoma hotel was designed in imitation of a Norman château and its public library in French Renaissance. Portland's public library was Italian Renaissance, and a national bank, Roman; a Presbyterian church, English Gothic; and a high school, Maryland Colonial. The rococo splendor was somewhat modified by the Neo-Classic which reached the Northwest as part of a national trend that had been initiated by a group of conservative architects.

Northwesterners spared no effort to make their region a replica of the parent East. Elegance, lavishness, even bad taste, were slavishly copied. Any number of Western homes or public buildings could have been interchanged with Eastern, and none would have appeared out of place in their new environments. Even after a substantial number of trained architects supplanted the builder-designers towards the beginning of the twentieth century, little or no departure from standard and accepted forms was made for a number of years. Their contribution consisted of more careful planning, more faithful adherence to a particular style.

One historian comments that Oregon copied the architecture prevailing in the more established regions because its isolation "prevented those cultural contacts usually operating as a stimulus to creative culture. And, as in so many lines, the thought was merely that of the old transferred to a new environment. There was little that was indigenous and even little use of the new materials for old themes. The people were truly conservative and despised change from the established patterns. Pride in their culture they had, but scarcely the pride of achievement."

This may be entirely true of the Northwest, architecturally speaking, but so was it for the rest of the country. With the possible exception of Southern California an architecture indigenous to the American setting was slow in developing. This country is still a monument to Greek temples in our banks and museums, to Europe in our Gothic cathedrals, and, with rare exceptions, these institutions are still being erected in those styles. This clinging to the known and the tried is typical of the frontier mentality or, to use an oft-repeated phrase, the "colonial complex." All America, artistically speaking, was a frontier, a colony of the Old World until after the first World War, and remnants of that psychology still cling. The Pacific Northwest was merely a frontier within a frontier.

Epilogue

The land of the wide open spaces has in past years received a generous share of publicity from the movie industry; from magazines devoted solely to stories about it; even from books, though not as much as in the days of the dime novels published by the enterprising Erastus Beadle. He sold them by the millions, and every boy in America managed to smuggle them into the house to be read in secret. For some reason parents frowned on them, though they were as pure and moral as the stories of Horatio Alger—and completely unrealistic in their idyllic descriptions of life in the West.

To Easterners, the West today is still the land of the cowboy with his ten-gallon hat, colored handkerchief around his neck, trousers tucked into high-heeled shoes, spurs jingling as he walks, and his trusty six-shooter at his side. The West is Buffalo Bill and Wild Bill Hickok, cowboys in deadly combat with cattle rustlers, no-good hombres who run things their own illicit way until the fearless United States marshal arrives and establishes law and order with his two fists and his handy Colt. It is heroic exploits, sublime courage, breath-taking escapes, endless conflict between lawless desperadoes and the forces of righteousness, ending inevitably in the triumph of justice, dramatic battles with Indian hordes, romance between the handsome cowboy and the rancher's fair daughter. Zane Grey has made a fortune on novels of the West which he wrote at the average rate of about one a year. All are substantially the same, with slight variations in plot, heroes and heroines; and the American public has gone on devouring them insatiably.

The West is also the heroic, intrepid pioneer—and here we leave fiction and turn to the more scholarly works. Even in these, however, the view has been distorted by idealization. Out of the pages of Americana, the pioneer emerged as a fearless son of Nature, a trail blazer, a builder of homes in the wilderness, a dauntless Indian fighter. He grappled with the almost unconquerable forces of nature around him, and with his bare hands subdued them. He was a maker of history, a mover of events, imbued with a deep democratic fervor—in short, a man of destiny on whose broad shoulders rested the future of the nation and in whose veins flowed the sterling quality of individualism which impressed itself so deeply on the American consciousness. He is the picturesque man in buckskin, with an ax in one hand and a rifle over his shoulder. Daniel Boone is the classic prototype.

In an effort to right the balance, the debunkers of the pioneer myth have gone to the other extreme. The true picture lies somewhere midway between glorification and detraction. To divest the pioneer of the romantic halo drawn around him by professional commemorators is not to minimize his genuine accomplishments. And they were many.

It is true that the pioneer beat a new trail mainly because of the promise of cheap land and an opportunity to "better my condition," as many put it. But while he did not consider himself as being impelled by a historic mission, he did uproot himself from a stable existence and leave a familiar pattern for a strange one. And he did set his course toward a land which was largely unknown and inhabited by savages. It took courage and imagination to do that, and he undoubtedly had both. Life in the new land, too, was not easy. If he had not known luxury in his old home, he did, at least, enjoy the ordinary conveniences of nineteenth century civilization—a more or less organized system of communications, schools, churches, established cultural activities. In the Northwest all of these had to be forged anew.

If he had a model on which to base his new society, it *was* a new one, none the less, that he was creating. If the Indian menace was not as great as it had been portrayed, it did exist potentially and was enough to give the women—and the men, too—many uneasy hours. If he was not completely cut off from civilization, he was far enough away to have to do without a good many things that would have made life easier for him.

When all that is said, what remains is a picture of men and women who played no more heroic a role in our history than did other Americans when the country was young. In a sense all Americans, during the early part of the nation's history, were pioneers. They participated in the creation of a new society, they built homes in a new world, they established new patterns, set their own precedents, formulated their own rules.

The hardships which were experienced by the pioneer had their compensations. If the frontier necessitated the organization of a new society, it meant also that people were not restricted by precedent or inhibited by the heavy weight of tradition. Business establishments could be launched in as novel a manner as pleased the fancy. Newspapers could be started on a whim and a shoestring. Land could be bought so cheaply that, almost overnight, substantial profits could be realized on a small investment. Vocal opposition could be freely and effectively expressed against laws and regulations, for legislative assemblies had not as yet become austere bodies far removed from the people. Life was, on the whole, much simpler. Few failed to enjoy the comradeship and neighborliness that a common undertaking makes possible and for which the West became famous. In their isolation from the national mainstream, the pioneers had a bond in their collective purpose which is not present in the larger and more established communities.

Perhaps the pioneer lived in a different setting for a somewhat longer period than had his fellow countrymen in the East, but after a while his social environment came to assume the same qualities and characteristics as the one he had left behind. Relatively few of the pioneers in the Northwest had to reside in primitive log cabins, and those who did, for only brief periods. Sawmills soon began to operate, and houses as comfortable and even as elaborate as their former dwellings rose up in the cities and dotted the countryside. The work, the amusements, the social relationships were shortly as standardized.

Culturally, the Northwest soon became as advanced as any other section of the country, with few distinguishing characteristics. Perhaps learning and scholarship were not as polished as in Boston or Charleston, but neither were they as provincial and backward as many readers of fiction dealing with the West had come to imagine. Schools, churches, libraries, and even museums were quickly established, and there was nothing particularly "backwoods" about the development of journalism. If newspapers were badly and somewhat naïvely written and furnished the news late, they did keep their readers in touch with the outside world. The migratory entertainers were the same as those who performed in other parts of the country. Medical progress, in general, followed the same course in the Northwest as it had elsewhere; when the legitimate medical profession succeeded in cleaning house and expelling the pretenders and charlatans, the Northwest followed suit, albeit more slowly, for the "wide-open" atmosphere was more conducive to the success of quacks.

To say that the pioneer quickly went about setting up schools, churches, and libraries, organizing lyceums, and so forth, while he was still felling trees to clear the ground for homes, is not, however, to make him out to be an avid searcher for knowledge and truth. There is nothing especially unique or distinctive about Northwesterners providing intellectual stimulation and educational opportunities in a new land they had decided to make their home. They, too, were legatees of a long-standing tradition of free and representative institutions and were moved by the democratic impulse to widen their horizons. They had to provide their own "culture" if a two- or three-thousand-mile distance from the centers of activity was not to result in intellectual stagnation for themselves and their children. The pioneer in the Pacific Northwest did what his counterpart had done on every other frontier and what his forebears had done after arriving in the New World. He laid the foundations of an enduring society and, in so doing, followed the dictates of his own feelings, acted in pursuance of his own inclinations, and satisfied some innate desires which he carried with him from the old environment to the new.

To the frontier has also been attributed unique characteristics. For many years it was a segment of the American scene neglected by professional historians. And when Frederick Jackson Turner rescued it from the minor place to which it had been relegated, the natural reaction was for the pendulum to swing the other way to overemphasis. From the frontier, said Turner, and not the *Mayflower*, sprouted the seeds of democracy which blossomed throughout the land. As long as hardihood and fortitude were the badges of merit, there was no room for a class or caste system. Nowhere else did the simple virtues like ambition, resourcefulness, and honesty count as much, and since, on the whole, equality of wealth existed, no rigid social lines developed. The frontier was also responsible for the distinguishing characteristic of individualism, for, in the isolated backwoods, men and women perforce had to develop independence and self-reliance, not as virtues but as essentials for survival. Since they constantly had to meet new situations and were not hedged about by the restrictions of precedent in creating their society, they became social and political radicals. The frontier was also a gigantic melting pot, assimilating all national strains. It served as a safety valve for the labor discontent in the East and therefore lessened and perhaps cushioned the shock of depression and panics. And, concluded Turner's thesis, it contributed to the emergence of a crystallized and effective nationalism, an indestructible faith in the future of the country.

Turner's point of view has since been challenged and, with further study, the contribution of the frontier has been placed in more balanced perspective. It is regarded as a factor, but not the dominant one, in the shaping of the American tradition. Qualities like individualism and the democratic spirit are attributed to a number of influences, including that of the frontier. As much social distinction and cleavage existed in the West as in the sophisticated and developed East, though the fact that the society was new and growing made it easier to cross the line. The little tradesman of one day might be the merchant prince of the next.

Most social and economic reforms had Eastern origins. Western farmers, under the stress of economic depressions and railroad strangle holds, did join militant and often radical organizations which brought about considerable amelioration. And in the political sphere such innovations as the initiative, the referendum, and the recall found the most receptive hearing in the West. But these were parts of larger waves of progressivism that had swept across the country and were not confined to the frontier. Westerners were, on the whole, imitators, not originators, and conformists rather than nonconformists. What they wanted most of all was the kind of life they had envied back East but had been unable to attain there and had hoped to achieve in the new land. It is now seen that the greatest movements of population to the West occurred during the years of prosperity and not during depressions. It is probably valid to say that the cities, rather than the frontier, have served as safety valves, in that it was toward the urban centers that migration took place during periods of agricultural distress.

Whatever its significance, the frontier in American life no longer exists, for there are no more vast, continuous stretches of land to settle and cultivate. Yet, in a sense, the Pacific Northwest is still frontier country. A region where the chambers of commerce continue to boast of its glories and invite settlement is still open country. During the great depression of the thirties, half a million wanderers from Oklahoma and other Dust Bowl states wended their way into the Inland Empire, seeking to escape the scourge of economic distress. They followed the same northern star on which the eyes of thousands had been fixed during the great crossings of a century back. During the recent war, the cities of the Northwest became the thriving arsenals of democracy, and many who came remained to make their home in the land of mountains and "mist" that had attracted Americans before. In less than a decade, the population of the region has increased more than 40 per cent. Whether it is the covered wagon or the railroad that brings hopeful immigrants to the Northwest, it is the old Oregon Trail which they are crossing in spirit to the land of promise.

Notes

CHAPTER I

Page 1, Northwest Passage: Alan P. Stuckey, "The Influence of Juan de Fuca on Captain Vancouver," M.A. thesis, University of Florida (1948), pp. 2, 21.

Page 5, Sacajawea: C. S. Kingston, "Sacajawea As a Guide: The Evolution of a Legend," *Pacific Northwest Quarterly*, XXXV (1944), pp. 3–18.

Page 11, Joe Meek's story: Frances Fuller Victor, *River of the West* (Hartford, 1870), pp. 154–157.

Page 11, Fitzpatrick's adventure: Le Roy R. Hafen and W. J. Ghent, *Broken Hand* (Denver, 1931), pp. 94–96.

Pages 12–13, "Fur Traders' Ballad": a typewritten copy of this song is in a collection under the general title of Oregon Folklore at the Oregon State Library in Salem.

Page 14, the wooing of Virginia: "Colonel Joe Meek," *Pacific Monthly*, XIV, (1905), pp. 494–495.

Page 14, Chittenden's comment: quoted in Frances Fuller Victor, "The American Fur Trade in the Far West," *Quarterly of the Oregon Historical Society*, III (1902), pp. 265–266.

Page 14, "saving of Oregon," *ibid.*, p. 267.

CHAPTER II

Page 17, Captain Bishop's report: T. C. Elliott, "The Journal of the Ship Ruby," *Oregon Historical Quarterly*, XXVIII (1927), p. 267.

Page 17, Clark's observations: Reuben Gold Thwaites, ed., *Original Journals of the Lewis and Clark Expedition* (New York, 1905), III, p. 239.

Pages 18–19, Townsend on diseases among Indians: quoted in Leslie M. Scott, "Indian Diseases As Aids to Pacific Northwest Settlement," *Oregon Historical Quarterly*, XXIX (1928), p. 154.

Page 19, smallpox among Indians: John Minto, *Rhymes of Early Life in Oregon* (Salem c. 1912), pp. 41–43; Scott, *op. cit.*, p. 151.

Page 19, thesis of Northwestern historian: Scott, *op. cit.*, pp. 144–145.

Page 20, introduction of liquor: quoted in F. W. Howay, "The Introduction of Intoxicating Liquors Among the Indians of the Northwest Coast," *British Columbia Historical Quarterly*, VI (1942), p. 157.

Pages 20–21, "King Alcohol," *Oregon Argus* (Oregon City), Oct. 13, 1855.

Pages 21–22, Franchère: Gabriel Franchère, "Voyage to Northwest Coast, 1811–1814," *Early Western Travels, 1748–1846*, ed., Reuben Gold Thwaites (Cleveland, 1904), VI, p. 239.

Page 22, Chinook hymn: Rev. Myron Eels, *Hymns in the Chinook Jargon Language,* quoted in Charles D. Schreibeis, *Pioneer Education in the Pacific Northwest* (Portland, Ore., 1936), p. 74.

Pages 22–23, Nesmith anecdote: quoted in Rena V. Grant, "The Chinook Jargon, Past and Present," *California Folklore Quarterly,* III (1944), pp. 274–275.

Page 25, "Bridge of the Gods": George Gibbs, government geologist, who visited the Northwest in 1853, gives what is probably the first published account of the legend in his report on a Pacific railroad in *House of Representatives Documents* for 1853–1854. Many of the explorers, scientists, travelers, and literary figures who toured and later wrote about the region gave versions of Indian myths and legends, some of which were obtained directly from the natives. Among these were Gabriel Franchère, who in his *Narrative* records one of the myths of creation which was told him by the son of a Chinook chief. Alexander Ross in his *Adventures* tells an interesting tale of the origin of the Indians, or Skyloo, as they called themselves. They originally had white skins, but the island which they inhabited became detached and floated out into the ocean. As a result of living under the blazing sun for some time, their skin became darkened to its present color and so remained. Others were Samuel Parker (*Exploring Tour*), Captain Charles Wilkes (*Narrative*), Theodore Winthrop (*The Canoe and the Saddle*), James G. Swann (*The Northwest Coast*), Samuel A. Clarke (*Pioneer Days of Oregon History*). In a pamphlet, *Indian Myths of the Northwest,* William D. Lyman discusses in detail these and other works containing Indian legends.

Pages 27–28, Chief Joseph's plea: Young Joseph, "An Indian's Views of Indian Affairs," *North American Review,* Vol. 269 (April, 1879), pp. 422–423.

CHAPTER III

Page 30, letter by New York merchant: the writer was G. P. Disoway and his letter was published in the *Christian Advocate and Journal* (New York) March 1, 1833. At this time the paper was temporarily combined with another and was called *Christian Advocate and Zion City Herald,* but to avoid confusion most writers on the subject use the former name.

Page 31, Fisk's appeal: *Christian Advocate and Journal,* March 22, 1833.

Page 35, missionary's letter: Rev. H. Campbell to Ezekiel Pilcher, Sept. 12, 1840. Copied from *Sangamo Journal,* May 21, 1841. Typescript in the Oregon Historical Society Library. This library will hereafter be referred to as OHSL.

Page 37, Walker's letter (both quotations): Elkanah Walker to Dr. David Greene, Oct. 3, 1842, MS, OHSL.

Page 38, Waiilatpu massacre: *Oregon Spectator* (Oregon City), Jan. 20, 1848.

Pages 38–39, 40, Spalding's myth: Edward Gaylord Bourne, *Essays in Historical Criticism* (New York, 1901), pp. 8–9.

Page 39, circulation of Whitman myth: the literature on Whitman is vast. See Charles W. Smith, "A Contribution Toward a Bibliography of Marcus Whitman," *Washington Historical Quarterly,* III (1908), pp. 3–62.

Page 39, Mrs. Victor refutes myth: Frances Fuller Victor, "Did Whitman Save Oregon?" *The Californian,* II:9 (1880), p. 233; see also her letters to F. G. Young, Dec. 10, 1900, and Jan. 25, 1901, MS, OHSL.

Page 40, letter of Spalding's grandniece: Frances Whitman Montieth to Mrs. Mary A. Killam, March 4, 1915, MS, OHSL.

Page 40, myth revived in 1943: Donald Culross Peattie, "Marcus Whitman,

Martyr for Oregon," *Reader's Digest* (July, 1943), p. 25. See also "Marcus Whitman and His Famous Ride," *Life*, Sept. 27, 1943.

Page 41, Spalding attacks Catholics: *Walla Walla Statesman*, Feb. 9, 1866.

Page 41, Catholic's attack on Protestants: Father J. B. Z. Bolduc, Mission of the Columbia, Second Letter and Journal, MS, OHSL.

Page 43, John McLoughlin: see questionnaire circulated by McLoughlin and testimonial replies, MS, OHSL.

Page 43, Bancroft's opinion: Hubert Howe Bancroft to Matthew P. Deady, Nov. 29, 1884, MS, OHSL.

Page 43, Nesmith on missionaries: J. W. Nesmith, "Annual Address," *Transactions of the Oregon Pioneer Association, 1880* (Salem, 1881), p. 19.

CHAPTER IV

Pages 45–46, genesis of Kelley's crusade: quoted in Fred W. Powell, "Hall Jackson Kelley—Prophet of Oregon," *Quarterly of the Oregon Historical Society*, XVIII (1917), p. 12, and Fred W. Powell, ed., *Hall J. Kelley on Oregon* (Princeton, 1932), p. ix.

Page 46, Kelley denounced: quoted in Archer B. Hulbert, ed., *The Call of the Columbia*, IV (Denver, 1934), p. 89.

Page 47, Kelley's personality: Fred W. Powell to F. G. Young, Jan. 30, 1908, MS, OHSL.

Page 47, "tissue of errors": John Adams, *Memoirs*, V, as quoted in Charles H. Ambler, *The Life and Diary of John Floyd* (Richmond, 1918), p. 60.

Page 48, manifest destiny: *St. Louis Reporter*, March 18, 1845, as quoted in Melvin C. Jacobs, *Winning Oregon: A Study of an Expansionist Movement* (Caldwell, 1938), footnote p. 37.

Page 48, letter of Iowa minister: Dr. William Slater to his fiancée, Oct. 4, 1845, *Annals of Iowa*, Third Series, No. 5, IX, pp. 363–364.

Pages 49–50, Iowa emigrant company: local newspaper account of Bloomington group reprinted in "Documents," *Quarterly of the Oregon Historical Society*, III (1902), pp. 390–393.

Page 50, Palmer's instructions: Reuben Gold Thwaites, ed., *Palmer's Journal of Travels Over the Rocky Mountains*, XXX (Cleveland, 1906), pp. 259–260.

Page 52, on to Oregon, pro and con: *Daily Missouri Republican*, Nov. 21, 1843, and June 11, 1844. Quoted in *Publications of the Nebraska State Historical Society*, XX (1922), pp. 123–125 and 126–128.

Pages 52–53, cannibal story: Emeline L. Fuller, *Left by the Indians; or, Rapine, Massacre and Cannibalism on the Overland Trail in 1860* (Mount Vernon, Iowa, 1892), pp. 19–27.

Pages 53–54, accidents on the trail: "Diary of Mrs. Elizabeth Dixon Smith Geer," *Oregon Pioneer Association Transactions, 1880* (Salem, 1881), p. 164.

Page 54, poem: Joaquin Miller, "Pilgrims of the Plains," quoted in John Steele, *Across the Plains in 1850*, Joseph Schafer, ed. (Chicago, 1930), p. xxxviii.

Page 56, graves along the trail: before the migrations became heavy and the Indians were either friendly or afraid of the "pale faces," markers were placed on the graves of those who died on the trail. Later on, to deceive the Indians who might violate the grave, the earth was packed down hard and wagons were driven over the spot to hide it.

Page 56, cholera epidemic: quoted in Georgia Willis Read, "Diseases, Drugs and Doctors on the Oregon–California Trail in the Gold Rush Years," *Missouri Historical Review*, XXXVIII (1944), p. 261.

Page 57, song: Origen Thompson, *Crossing the Plains* (Greensburg, Ind., 1896), p. 81.

Pages 57–58, life on the trail: Jesse Applegate, "A Day with the Cow Column," *Quarterly of the Oregon Historical Society*, I (1900), pp. 372–374.

CHAPTER V

Pages 60–61, buckskin garment: Jesse Applegate, "Recollections of My Boyhood," in *The Oregon Trail and Some of Its Blazers*, Maude A. Rucker, ed. (New York, 1930), pp. 193–194.

Pages 64–65, letters: Roselle Putnam to Mrs. Susan Putnam, June 8, 1851, MS, OHSL.

Pages 66–67 Chappellier store: Isabel J. Szewcynski, "A Pioneer Store," typewritten MS, University of Washington Library.

Pages 67–68, letters to the East: *Oregon Spectator* (Oregon City), Feb. 5, 1846.

Page 68, mail delivery: *The Columbian* (Olympia), July 16, 1853.

Page 68, mailman's romance: *Centralia, the First Fifty Years, 1845–1900*, Herndon Smith, ed. (Centralia, Wash., 1942), p. 37.

Page 69, newspapers and magazines: Agnes Ruth Sengstacken, *Destination West!* (Portland, 1942), pp. 185–187.

Pages 69–70, pioneer describes conditions: S. H. Taylor to the *Watertown Chronicle* (Wisc.), Dec. 17, 1853, *Quarterly of the Oregon Historical Society*, XXII (1921), pp. 156–159.

Page 70, Seattle boom: David E. Blaine to his brother Saron, Nov. 20, 1854. "Letters and Papers of David E. and Catherine P. Blaine," typewritten MS, OHSL, pp. 117–119.

Page 70, Eugene, Oregon, described: George Belshaw to a friend, Aug. 20, 1858. Glen Castle, ed., "The Belshaw Journal, Oregon Trail, 1853," *Oregon Historical Quarterly*, XXXII (1931), pp. 238–239.

Page 70, farm prosperity: Wilson Blain to John Gray, July, 1851; John Withers to John Adair, Oct. 29, 1854, MS, OHSL.

Page 71, housing shortage: H. W. Williams to Mrs. Shumway, March 14, 1865, MS, OHSL.

Page 71, Winthrop's description: Laura Winthrop Johnson, ed., *Life and Poems of Theodore Winthrop* (New York, 1884), pp. 140–141, 154–155.

Pages 71–72, Applegate's leadership: Joseph Schafer, "Jesse Applegate," in Rucker, *op. cit.*, p. 59.

Page 73, Applegate's political philosophy: Joseph Schafer, "Jesse Applegate: Pioneer, Statesman and Philosopher," *Washington Historical Quarterly*, I (1907), pp. 228–233.

Page 73, Applegate on the marital relationship: Jesse Applegate to Mrs. B. A. Owens, June 22, 1872, MS, OHSL.

Page 74, Applegate's intimate feelings: Jesse Applegate to Mrs. B. A. Owens, Nov. 3, 1874, MS, OHSL.

Page 74, Applegate's inferiority complex: Jesse Applegate to Elwood Evans, Oct. 13, 1867, MS, OHSL.

Page 75, Mrs. Victor on Applegate: Frances Fuller Victor to Matthew P. Deady, Aug. 21, 1883, MS, OHSL.

Page 76, child marriages: *Oregonian*, Feb. 18, 1861.

Page 76, sale of squaws: Theodore Winthrop, *The Canoe and the Saddle* (Boston, 1863), p. 273.

Page 77, bachelor's meeting: quoted in Charles Prosch, "Puget Sound Society in Early Days," *Pacific Magazine*, IV (1891), p. 49.

Page 77, bachelor's complaint: *Puget Sound Herald* (Steilacoom), Dec. 3, 1858.

Page 79, Mercer's election urged: *Seattle Gazette*, May 28, 1864.

Pages 79-80, Mercer's experiences in the East: C. B. Bagley, "When Marriageable Girls Were Brought to Seattle," Seattle *Sunday Times*, Nov. 8, 1903.

Page 80, Mercer girls' departure: "Emigration to Washington Territory of Four Hundred Women on the Steamer 'Continental,'" *Harper's Weekly*, X (Jan. 6, 1866), p. 8.

Pages 80-81, poem: quoted in *Washington Standard* (Olympia), Oct. 28, 1865.

Page 81, cotillion party: *Oregon Spectator*, Oct. 17, 1850.

Pages 82-83, early dances: interview with George Duffy, Dec. 27, 1938, Oregon Folklore Studies, Oregon State Library, Salem.

CHAPTER VI

Page 86, almanac: *Fisher's Comic Almanac, 1847* (Philadelphia & New York, 1848) unpaged.

Page 88, letter: to Governor Addison C. Gibbs, signature of writer cut out, May 29, 1863, MS, OHSL.

Page 89, Mrs. Lincoln's ball: James W. Nesmith to his wife, Feb. 5, 1862, MS, OHSL.

Pages 89-90, trial stories: Robert G. Bailey, *River of No Return* (Lewiston, Ida., 1935), p. 116.

Pages 90-91, removal of capital: *Washington Standard*, Jan. 21, 1865.

Page 93, separation for Oregon: quoted in Dorothy Hull, "The Movement in Oregon for the Establishment of a Pacific Coast Republic," *Quarterly of the Oregon Historical Society*, XVII (1916), pp. 183-186.

Page 94, separation denounced: *Oregonian*, July 28, 1855.

Pages 94-95, separatists scored: *Washington Standard* (Olympia), Jan. 12, 1861.

Page 95, Deady chided: Jesse Applegate to Matthew P. Deady, April 13, 1862, MS, OHSL.

Page 96, writing for posterity: *ibid.*, March 23, 1862.

Page 96, Deady on slavery: Matthew P. Deady to Sampson, July 28, 1857, MS, OHSL.

Page 97, attack on Lincoln: *Oregon Weekly Union* (Corvallis), Sept. 16, 1861.

Page 99, miners' brawls: quoted in Eugene B. Chaffee, "Early History of the Boise Region, 1811-1864," M.A. thesis, University of California at Berkeley (1927), p. 66.

Page 99, Applegate's reactions: *Oregonian*, Oct. 19, 1861.

Pages 100-101, Canyon City election: W. W. Wells to Governor Addison C. Gibbs, June 10, 1864, MS, OHSL.

Page 101, suffrage campaign: Abigail Scott Duniway, *Path-Breaking: An Autobiographical History of the Equal Suffrage Movement in Pacific Coast States* (Portland, 1914), p. 45.

Page 101, report on suffrage: Phoebe Goodell Judson, *A Pioneer's Search for an Ideal Home* (Bellingham, Wash., 1925), p. 277.

Pages 102-103, future in Portland: Charles Stevens to his brother and sister, Feb. 26, 1854, MS, OHSL.

CHAPTER VII

Page 104, Wright's trip: William Wright to D. W. Craig, Sept. 9, 1854, MS, OHSL.

Page 106, Barlow's plan: S. H. Lewis, "A History of the Railroads in Washington," *Washington Historical Quarterly*, III (1912), pp. 186-187.

Pages 106–107, the Barlow road: Mary S. Barlow, "History of the Barlow Road," *Quarterly of the Oregon Historical Society*, III (1902), pp. 71–81.

Page 107, agent to Jay Cooke: quoted in George R. Leighton, "Seattle, Washington, the Edge of the Last Frontier," *Harper's Magazine* (February, 1939), p. 311.

Page 107, Chase to Cooke: quoted in *ibid*.

Pages 110–111, travel route: quoted in Lewis, *op. cit.*, p. 186.

Page 111, Oregon City and Linn City: *Oregon Spectator* (Oregon City), June 26, 1851.

Page 111, visiting journalist: Ray Stannard Baker, "The Great Northwest," *Century Magazine*, LXV (1903), p. 648.

Pages 111–112, census exaggeration: *Oregon State Journal* (Eugene), June 28, 1890.

Page 112, Frankfort defended: *Frankfort Chronicle*, May 10, 1892.

Page 112, northern Oregon climate: *Columbian* (Olympia), Nov. 6, 1852.

Pages 112–113, greatness of Tacoma: Jas. A. Sproule, "The Wonder of the World," Tacoma *New Herald Annual* (1909), p. 20; *West Shore*, XI:5 (1885), pp. 129–130.

Page 113, webfoot rain: John B. Horner, *Oregon Literature* (Corvallis, 1899), p. 22.

Pages 113–114, Seattle rain: *The Town Crier*, I:5 (1910), p. 7.

Page 114, high-school magazine: *The Cardinal* (Portland), January, 1897, p. 19.

Page 114, ditty on rain: *Daily Oregonian*, March 8, 1873.

Page 117, support of domestic manufactures: *West Shore*, XI:4 (1885), p. 94.

Page 118, Washington ports: *Washington Standard* (Olympia), Oct. 17, 1863.

CHAPTER VIII

Pages 119–120, miner's verse: *Oregon Statesman* (Oregon City), July 20, 1851.

Page 120, California correspondent: quoted in Eugene B. Chaffee, "Early History of the Boise Region, 1811–1864," M.A. thesis, University of California at Berkeley (1927), p. 67.

Page 120, Sunday in mining town: *ibid*.

Page 123, Boise editor: quoted in *Idaho Lore*, Vardis Fisher, ed. (Caldwell, 1939), pp. 101–102.

Page 125, slaughter of sheep: *Oregonian*, Dec. 12, 1904.

Page 126, crossing a puddle: *Weekly Oregonian*, Feb. 28, 1852.

Page 126, lady on horseback: *Washington Standard* (Olympia), May 24, 1862.

Pages 126–127, Betsy Jane and Hibernian: *ibid.*, Sept. 19 and 26; Dec. 5, 1863.

Page 127, scandal at The Dalles: *Weekly Mountaineer*, May 28, 1862.

Page 128, on kissing: *Democratic Era* (Portland), July 7, 1871.

Pages 128–129, temperance oath: *Oregon Spectator* (Oregon City), Sept. 16, 1853.

Pages 129–130, "Temperance Call": J. E. Clark, comp., *Selected Song Exercises for the Olympia Public Schools, Dist. 1* (Olympia, 1874) unpaged.

Page 130, female prohibitionists: Frances Fuller Victor, *The Women's War With Whisky* (Portland, 1874), p. 11.

Pages 130–131, "Inebriate's Soliloquy": *The Echo: A Temperance Journal*, II, (Oct. 22, 1869), unpaged.

Page 135, Spokane society: Julian Ralph, "Washington—the Evergreen State," *Harper's New Monthly*, LXXXV (1892), p. 597.

Pages 135–136, Western vice: Ella R. Higginson, "Fact and Fancy," *West Shore*, XVI:232 (1890), p. 212.

Page 136, "Box house": a description of this type of theater will be found in Chap. XV.

Page 136, cartoon: *West Shore* XV:171 (1889), p. 32.

Page 138, visiting journalist: Julian Ralph, *op. cit.*, p. 602.

Pages 138–139, *P.-I.* editorial: Seattle *Post-Intelligencer*, Dec. 3, 1910.

Page 139, vice in Seattle: "Our Great Restricted District Under Mayor Gill," Report of the Grand Jury, November, 1911, University of Washington Library.

Page 140, boast of native writer: Alfred Holman, "Oregonian Characteristics," *Overland Monthly*, XXV (1895), pp. 204–205.

Pages 140–141, Skidmore fountain: Charles Erskine Scott Wood, "The Skidmore Fountain," *Oregon Historical Quarterly*, XXXIV (1933), p. 101.

Page 142, primacy of the *Oregonian:* Alfred Holman, *op. cit.*, p. 205.

Page 143, natural selection: Thomas Condon, "The Process of Natural Selection in Oregon Pioneer Settlement," *Quarterly of the Oregon Historical Society*, I (1900), pp. 63–65.

Page 143, pioneer reunion: *Transactions of the 25th Annual Reunion of the Oregon Pioneer Association for 1897* (Portland, 1898), pp. 7–8.

Page 144, membership eligibility: *Transactions of the 18th Annual Reunion of the Oregon Pioneer Association for 1890* (Portland, 1892), pp. 21–22.

Page 144, pioneer spirit: Harvey W. Scott, "Pioneer Character of Oregon Progress," *Oregon Historical Quarterly*, XVIII (1917), pp. 259–261.

CHAPTER IX

Page 146, bar to Negroes: quoted in W. Sherman Savage, "The Negro in the History of the Pacific Northwest," *Journal of Negro History*, XIII (1928), p. 263.

Pages 146–147, William Bush: *The Republican* (Seattle), Jan. 4, 1896.

Page 148, Negro conditions: Daniel G. Hill, "The Negro in Oregon, a Survey," M.A. thesis, University of Oregon (1932), p. 29.

Page 150, anti-Japanese sermon: *Sunday Oregonian*, Oct. 27, 1907.

Page 150, Jews attacked: *Weekly Oregonian*, Sept. 11, 25; Oct. 9, 16, 1858.

Page 150, Dryer denounced: *Oregon Statesman* (Corvallis), Oct. 5, 1858; *Oregon Weekly Times* (Portland), Sept. 25, 1858.

Page 151, contributions of Jews: *Morning Oregonian*, Dec. 3, 1903.

Page 151, Scandinavian papers: quoted in Carlton C. Qualey, *Norwegian Settlement in the United States* (Northfield, Minn., 1938), pp. 189–190.

Page 153, Kiel's views: John E. Simon, "Wilhelm Keil, Founder of Aurora," M.A. thesis, University of Oregon (1935), p. 78.

Page 154, Puget Sound Colony: George Venable Smith, *Puget Sound Colony, A Model Co-Operative Commonwealth* (San Francisco, 1896), title page and pp. 23–28; G. M. Louridsen, *et alii, The Story of Port Angeles—An Historical Symposium* (Seattle, 1937), p. 59.

Page 155, Equality: Helen L. Young, "A Western Utopia," *The Dilettante*, II (May, 1900), p. 18.

Pages 155–156, the *P.-I.* on Equality: Seattle *Post-Intelligencer*, May 15, 1898.

Page 156, reasons for failure: *Industrial Freedom*, May 27, 1899.

Page 157, *Silverton Appeal:* quoted in *The Torch of Reason*, April 24, 1902.

Page 159, "The Nudes and the Prudes": *The Agitator*, July 1, 1911.

Pages 160–162, tall story: *Oregon Statesman*, June 9, 1857.

Page 162, bedbug story: *ibid.*, Aug. 4, 1855.

Pages 162-163, Fay Hubbard's dog: *Idaho: A Guide in Word and Picture,* Vardis Fisher, ed. (Caldwell, 1937), pp. 393-394.

Pages 164-165, Paul's Blue Ox: quoted in Ida Virginia Turney, *Paul Bunyan Comes West* (Boston, 1928), pp. 12-20.

Page 165, Stevens on Bunyan: "Paul Bunyan, Giant," *Fortune,* XXX (1944), p. 149.

CHAPTER X

Page 167, medical ethics: *Dental Register* (Cincinnati, Ohio), November, 1869, quoted in Olaf Larsell, "History of Medical Journals," *Oregon Historical Quarterly,* XLVII (1946), pp. 5-6.

Pages 168-169, Dr. Webber's advertisement: *Oregon Argus* (Oregon City), May 5, 1860.

Page 169, Dr. William Hall's advertisement: *ibid.,* Dec. 22, 1860.

Page 169, Perry Davis's advertisement: Astoria *Marine Gazette,* June 13, 1866.

Pages 169-170, mustang liniment: *Washington Standard* (Olympia), Nov. 3, 1866.

Page 170, "A Rich Puff": *Pioneer and Democrat* (Olympia), Oct. 30, 1857.

Pages 170-171, cancer remedies: *Oregon Weekly Times* (Portland), Oct. 8, 1853, Feb. 6, 1858.

Page 171, Czapkay's advertisement: *Pioneer and Democrat,* Oct. 15, 1858.

Pages 171-172, San Francisco specialist: *Washington Standard,* Nov. 3, 1866.

Page 172, verse: *ibid.,* Sept. 15, 1866.

Page 172, warning against quacks: *West Shore,* IV:38 (1878), p. 42.

Pages 172-173, Dr. Slocum: *ibid.,* XI:12 (1885), p. 61.

Pages 173-174, Dr. Kessler's advertisement: *Sunday Oregonian,* Dec. 6, 1903.

Page 174, Dr. Hudson's lectures: *Overland Press* (Olympia), Jan. 25, 1864.

Pages 174-175, verse: "Quacks and Doctors," *Proceedings of the Third Annual Meeting of the Medical Society of the State of Oregon, 1876* (Portland, 1876), pp. 26-27.

Page 175, laboratory equipment: quoted in Olaf Larsell, "An Outline of the History of Medicine in the Pacific Northwest," *Northwest Medicine,* XXXI (1932), pp. 483-484.

Pages 177-178, enterprising doctor: Dr. W. F. Allen to his brother, May 4, 1851, MS, OHSL.

Pages 180-181, Applegate's advice: Jesse Applegate to Mrs. B. A. Owens, Nov. 3, 1874, MS, OHSL.

Page 181, affection for Mrs. Owens: *ibid.*

Page 182, distant calls: Urling C. Coe, *Frontier Doctor* (New York, 1939), p. 12.

Page 182, race with the stork: Lois M. Small, "Remarkable Frontier Doctor," *Sunday Oregonian,* July 16, 1939.

Pages 182-183, medical standards: Samuel Eliot Morison, *Three Centuries of Harvard* (Cambridge, 1936), pp. 338-339; Olof Larsell, *The Doctor in Oregon* (Portland, Ore., 1947), p. 349.

Pages 183-184, medical faculty: Olaf Larsell, "The Development of Medical Education in the Pacific Northwest," *Quarterly of the Oregon Historical Society,* XXVII (1926), pp. 72-73.

Pages 184-185, Oregon University Medical Department: *Morning Oregonian,* July 16, 1896.

Pages 186-189, medical journals: The material in these pages is drawn in part from Larsell, "History of Medical Journals" (*op. cit.*), pp. 3-15.

CHAPTER XI

Page 191, Oregon Lyceum: undated document, MS, OHSL.

Pages 191–192, first number: *Oregon Spectator,* Feb. 5, 1846.

Page 192, "prospectus": *ibid.,* July 25, 1850.

Page 194, "copperhead journal": *Washington Press Association Annual Proceedings, 1887–1890* (Hoquiam, Wash., 1891), p. 38.

Page 195, *Daily Standard: Oregon Vidette* (Salem), June 23, 1883.

Page 196, verse: *Oregon Statesman* (Corvallis), Oct. 24, 1854.

Page 197, Elizabeth Markham: *Oregon Spectator,* June 15, 1848.

Pages 197–198, fashion expert: *Oregon Weekly Times* (Portland), Aug. 7, 1851.

Page 198, "bloomers": *ibid.,* Sept. 25, 1851.

Page 198, marriage ceremony: *Oregon Argus* (Portland), July 5, 1862.

Pages 198–199, on kissing: *Washington Standard,* Nov. 4, 1871.

Page 200, appeal for funds: *Pioneer and Democrat* (Olympia), Oct. 7, 1859.

Page 201, newspaper mortality: *Oregon Statesman* (Oregon City), Oct. 14, 1856.

Page 202, T'Vault's farewell: *Oregon Spectator,* April 2, 1846.

Page 203, Bush and Gaines: *Oregon Statesman* (Oregon City), Jan. 27, 1852.

Page 203, *Graphic* editor: quoted in "Oregon Oddities," No. 32, p. 1, Oregon State Library Folklore Collection.

Page 203, *People's Press: Oregon Argus,* June 30, 1860.

Pages 203–204, shooting affrays: *Democratic Era* (Portland), June 16, 1871.

Page 204, epithets: Jeanette E. Roberts, "Asahel Bush—Pioneer Editor, Politician and Banker," M.A. thesis, University of Oregon (1939), p. 45.

Page 204, Bush against Dryer: *Oregon Statesman,* April 4, 1851.

Page 205, country editors: *Sunday Oregonian,* Sept. 25, 1907.

Page 206, on the *Oregonian:* "A Hearst Publication," *The Guide and Town Topics,* III:2 (1903), p. 8.

Page 207, Scott's opinion: quoted in Otho Clark Leiter, "Scott and the Oregonian," *Journalism Quarterly,* V:4, p. 5.

Page 207, power of Scott and Oregon writer's comment: Alfred Powers, *History of Oregon Literature* (Portland, 1935), pp. 351, 358–359.

Page 209, number of newspapers: George S. Turnbull, *History of Oregon Newspapers* (Portland, 1939), pp. 526–527; Lancaster Pollard and Lloyd Spencer, *History of Washington,* I (New York, 1937), pp. 359–360.

Page 210, McCormick's magazine: *Oregon Spectator,* Dec. 16, 1851.

Page 211, jokes: *West Shore,* II:2 (1876), p. 25.

Page 211, story: *ibid.,* I:5 (1875), p. 6.

Pages 212–213, *New Northwest:* Abigail Scott Duniway, *op. cit.,* pp. 31–32.

Pages 214–215, prophecy for Pacific: *The New West,* I:1 (1910), p. 4.

Pages 216–217, literary future: *The State,* II:5 (1898), p. 115.

CHAPTER XII

Page 218, editorial chastisement: *Oregon Argus* (Portland), April 21, 1855.

Pages 219–220, Mrs. Thornton's school: *Oregon Spectator* (Oregon City), Oct. 12, 1848.

Page 221, quarterly examinations: *Pioneer and Democrat* (Olympia), Oct. 31, 1856.

Page 221, Bush on free education: *Oregon Statesman* (Salem), Sept. 29, 1857.

Pages 222–223, Walla Walla schools: *Washington Statesman* (Olympia), March 15, 1862.

Page 224, Oregon City public schools: *Oregon Argus,* July 7, 1855.

Page 225, Scott versus high schools: *Morning Oregonian,* Feb. 21, 1880.

Page 225, opposition to high schools: *ibid.*

Page 227, examination questions: Forest Grove *Independent,* April 5, 1873.

Pages 227–228, Teachers' Institute program: *Oregon Statesman,* April 19, 1889.

Page 228, Washington Institute: *Seventeenth Annual Session of the King County Teachers' Institute* (Seattle, 1895), unpaged.

Pages 228–229, demand for salary increases: *Oregon Teachers' Monthly,* VII:5 (1903), p. 93.

Page 229, Washington journal: quoted in *ibid.,* p. 94.

Page 229, opening of university: *Washington Standard* (Seattle), Sept. 27, 1862.

Page 229, Deady opposes state university: Matthew P. Deady to Logan, Jan. 2, 1851, MS, OHSL.

Page 230, university discipline: *Overland Press* (Olympia), Aug. 31, 1863.

Page 231, aim of college: *Catalogue of the University of Oregon, 1885.*

Page 231, evening amusements: *Oregon Spectator,* Nov. 29, 1849.

Page 234, lecture series: *Weekly Oregonian,* Dec. 8, 1860.

Page 234, Academy of Sciences: *Morning Oregonian,* Jan. 2, 1893.

Page 234, B. F. Underwood: *New Northwest,* Aug. 29, 1873.

Page 235, lecture on *Hamlet: Morning Oregonian,* Dec. 11, 1895.

Page 236, McCormick's advertisement: *Democratic Standard* (Portland), Oct. 18, 1855.

Page 238, library report: *Fifth Annual Report of the Library Commission* (Seattle, 1895), p. 3.

Page 239, library procedure: Cornelia Marvin Pierce, "Beginnings of Library Service in Oregon," typewritten MSS of talk delivered April 3, 1939. Oregon State Library.

Pages 239–240, library progress: "Second Biennial Report of the Library Commission to the Twenty-Fifth Legislative Assembly," *Oregon Messages and Documents,* I (Portland, 1908), p. 26.

CHAPTER XIII

Page 242, intellectual productions: Matthew P. Deady, "The Budding Literature of Oregon," *McCormick's Almanac,* Nov. 20, 1863; Deady's Scrapbook, p. 55, OHSL.

Page 243, Trail diary: quoted in Alfred Powers, *History of Oregon Literature* (Portland, 1935), pp. 102–103.

Page 244, critic on *Prairie Flower: ibid.,* p. 200.

Page 244, excerpt: Emerson Bennet, *The Prairie Flower* (Cincinnati, 1849), p. 249.

Pages 245–246, Mrs. Bailey's marriage: Herbert B. Nelson, "First True Confession Story Pictures Oregon 'Moral,'" *Oregon Historical Quarterly,* XLV (1944), pp. 169–170.

Page 246, review: *Weekly Oregonian,* Sept. 9, 1854.

Page 247, review: *Oregon Weekly Times* (Portland), Sept. 2, 1854.

Page 248, reviews: See, for example, *Pioneer and Democrat* (Olympia), May 6, 1859; *Oregon Weekly Times,* April 30, 1859.

Page 248, excerpt: Abigail Scott Duniway: *Captain Gray's Company; or, Crossing the Plains and Living in Oregon* (Portland, 1859), p. 241.

Page 249, Mrs. Duniway on Belle W. Cooke: *New Northwest,* June 30, 1871.

Page 249, Bret Harte on Cooke: *Overland Monthly,* VII (1871), p. 584.

Pages 249–250, *Notes by the Way: Washington Standard* (Olympia), May 2, 1863.

Page 250, "Another Oregon Poet": *Democratic Era* (Portland), July 28, 1871.

Pages 250–251, author of history: John B. Horner, *Oregon Literature* (Corvallis, 1899), p. 25.

Page 251, grammar criticized: *Weekly Democratic Press* (Salem), April 24, 1869.

Page 251, genius of Miller: *Eugene City Guard*, April 24, 1869; see also *Democratic Era*, Jan. 18, 1872.

Pages 251–252, Miller abroad: for much of the material on Joaquin Miller, I am indebted to Martin Severin Peterson's *Joaquin Miller, Literary Frontiersman* (Stanford University, 1937).

Page 252, Mrs. Miller's letter: *New Northwest*, Nov. 10, 1871.

Page 254, autobiography: Martin Severin Peterson, "The Border Days of Joaquin Miller, 1854–70," *The Frontier*, XI (1931), p. 363.

Page 256, evaluation of Miller: Peterson, *Joaquin Miller*, p. 178.

Page 256, Simpson: Fred A. Dunham, "Sam Simpson As I Knew Him," *Pacific Monthly*, II:4, pp. 168–169.

Page 257, "Beautiful Willamette": quoted in Manche Irene Langley, "Sam L. Simpson, Author of the Gold-Gated West," *The Lariat*, II (1923), p. 424.

Page 258, portrayal of the Indian: Frederic Balch, *Bridge of the Gods*, 7th ed. (Chicago, 1902), p. 114.

Page 260, on Herbert Bashford: Frank Carleton Teck, "Songs from Puget Sea," *The Dilettante*, II:2 (1900), p. 27.

Pages 260–261, poem: *The State*, V:1 (1900), p. 29.

Page 262, on Ella R. Higginson: quoted in John B. Horner, "Mrs. Ella Higginson," *Oregon Native Son*, I:5, p. 239.

Page 262, contemporary critic: *ibid.*

Page 263, Mrs. Dye on pioneers: Eva Emery Dye to Mrs. Clarke, Aug. 12, 1910, MS, OHSL.

Page 263, Mrs. Victor's criticism: Frances Fuller Victor, "McLoughlin and Old Oregon: A Chronicle," *American Historical Review*, VI, (1900), p. 148.

Page 264, review: *Sunday Oregonian*, Nov. 2, 1902.

Pages 264–265, publisher's comment: A. C. McClurg & Co. to Mrs. Eva Emery Dye, March 15, 1906, MS, OHSL.

Page 265, Mrs. Foote: for much of the material on this writer I am indebted to Richard Martin Keller's "Regionalism in Novels of the Northwest," M.A. thesis, State College of Washington (1938).

Page 267, on Emma Goldman: Charles Erskine Scott Wood, "Impressions," *Pacific Monthly*, XX (1908), p. 227.

Page 268, "Petronius Arbiter": *Morning Oregonian*, Nov. 27, 1906.

Page 268, review of Wood: "Poetic Tribute to the Western Desert," New York *Times*, June 20, 1915.

Page 269, eulogy: editorial by W. R. B., *Saturday Review of Literature*, Jan. 29, 1944, p. 12.

Page 269, poet's statement: Valentine Brown, *Poems* (Portland, 1900), p. 335; *Tales and Other Verse* (Portland, 1904), Preface.

Page 270, poem: Brown, *Poems*, pp. 238–240.

Pages 270–271, pilgrims: G. W. Kennedy, *The Pioneer Campfire* (Portland, 1913), Foreword by John B. Horner, p. 7.

Page 271, literature and geography: Horner, *op. cit.*, p. 25.

Pages 273–274, failure of press: "Bloom and Bramble," *The Dilettante*, IV:6 (1901), p. 9.

CHAPTER XIV

Page 275, Applegate on pioneer history: Jesse Applegate to Elwood Evans, Oct. 13, 1867, MS, OHSL.

Page 275, pioneer history: *ibid.*

Page 276, review of Clark: *Morning Oregonian*, June 17, 1905.

Page 277, quotation: Edmond S. Meany, *Vancouver's Discovery of Puget Sound* (New York, 1907), p. 46, footnote p. 66.

Page 277, criticism of Meany: Porter Garnet, "History, Fiction and the Point of View," *Pacific Monthly*, XVIII (1907), p. 262.

Page 278, altercations: Frances Fuller Victor to Matthew P. Deady, May 3, 1872, MS, OHSL.

Pages 278–279, spelling of "Willamette": Phillip Overmeyer, "The Oregon Justinian: A Life of Matthew Paul Deady," M.S. thesis, University of Oregon (1935), pp. 288–291.

Pages 279–280, review of Schafer: *Sunday Oregonian*, June 18, 1905.

Page 280, criticism of Bancroft: "The Woman Historian," *Sunday Call*, July 7, 1895; *Frances F. Victor's Scrapbook*, p. 146, OHSL; *cf.*, Hubert Howe Bancroft, *Historian of the West* (Berkeley & L.A., 1946), pp. 273–275.

Page 281, lack of recognition: Frances Fuller Victor to F. G. Young, Feb. 18, 1902; see also letter of Jan. 23, 1900; MS, OHSL.

Page 281, verse: Frances Fuller Victor, *Poems* (author's edition, 1900), pp. 83–84.

Page 282, sociologist's views: quoted in Eric F. Goldman, "J. Allen Smith; the Reformer and His Dilemma," *Pacific Northwest Quarterly*, XXXV (1944), p. 196.

Page 283, Smith attacked: quoted in *ibid.*, p. 205.

Pages 284–285, professor in religious controversy: *Morning Oregonian*, Oct. 25, 1909; *Sunday Oregonian*, Oct. 31, 1909.

Page 287, Douglas's trip: quoted in B. A. Thaxter, "Scientists in Early Oregon," *Oregon Historical Quarterly*, XXXIV (1933), p. 336.

Page 288, newspaper announcement: *Pioneer and Democrat* (Olympia), Nov. 23, 1860.

Page 289, museum: *State Republican*, Feb. 8, 1862.

CHAPTER XV

Page 291, dramatic criticism: *Oregon Spectator* (Oregon City), Feb. 19, 1846.

Pages 292–293, Professor Hermann: *Weekly Intelligencer* (Tacoma), Jan. 1, 1876.

Page 293, Professor Zink: Portland *Daily Advertiser*, March 12, 1860.

Page 294, "Frisco Lillies": quoted in Bernard Berelson and Howard F. Grant, "The Pioneer Theater in Washington," *Pacific Northwest Quarterly*, XXVIII (1937), p. 116.

Page 295, Deady's comment: "The 'Melodeon' at Portland," Sept. 8, 1862. *Matthew P. Deady's Scrapbook*, p. 11, OHSL.

Page 296, Stark troupe: *Daily Portland Times*, Jan. 5, 1861.

Page 296, Mlle. Duret: *Weekly Oregonian*, Feb. 26, 1859.

Page 297, thespian's experiences: Edwards Hoag Meade, *Doubling Back, Autobiography of an Actor* (Chicago, 1916), p. 119.

Page 297, Deady on drama: "A Passing Touch at the Players," April 2, 1864; "Some Thoughts on Theatricals—A Blast Against the 'Acting' of Children," Feb. 25, 1865; Deady, *op. cit.*, pp. 75 and 127.

Pages 297–298, Billy Sunday and the theater: Rev. Henry Brown, comp., *War On the Theatre* (Spokane, 1909), pp. 6 and 20.

Page 299, sneezing actors: Meade, *op. cit.*, pp. 139–141.

Page 301, box houses: quoted in Berelson and Grant, *op. cit.*, p. 20.

Page 302, John L. Sullivan: quoted in Eugene Clinton Elliott, *A History of Variety-Vaudeville in Seattle,* University of Washington Publications in Drama, No. 1 (Seattle, 1944), p. 16.

Page 302, Cordray's theater: *ibid.*, pp. 29–30.

Page 304, typical program: *Tacoma News,* Sept. 28, 1887.

Page 305, stage manners: *Every Sunday* (Tacoma), Dec. 26, 1891.

Pages 305–306, stage props: *Seattle Telegraph,* July 2, 1892, March 26, 1893.

CHAPTER XVI

Pages 309–310, frontier music: Robert M. McHargue, "Studies in the Popular Music of the American Frontiers," M.A. thesis, University of California at L.A. (1940).

Page 310, Mrs. Hamm: *Pioneer and Democrat* (Olympia), Aug. 19, 1854.

Pages 311–312, Professor Bach: *ibid.*, Dec. 24, 1858.

Page 313, Oregon song: "Sweet Oregon," *Oregon Teachers' Monthly,* VIII:10 (1904), pp. 34–35.

Page 314, Deady's comment: "The Portland Philharmonic and the Oregon Opera," June 21, 1866, *Matthew P. Deady's Scrapbook,* p. 165, OHSL.

Page 314, band activities: *Pacific Musical Times,* II:3 (1899), p. 4.

Pages 315–316, orchestra proposed: "Scala," "A Portland Symphony Orchestra?" *Rose City Magazine,* I:10 (1909), pp. 8–9.

Page 317, Seattle music: "Music," *The Week-End,* I:10 (1906), p. 6.

Page 317, Paul Kane: *Oregon Spectator* (Oregon City), Feb. 18, 1847.

Page 319, "Reed's Panaroma": *Washington Standard* (Olympia), Aug. 30, 1873.

Page 323, Territorial university: quoted in Charles H. Alden, "The Historic Precedent in Coast Architecture," *Architect and Engineer,* XXIX (1912), p. 83.

Page 324, no indigenous architecture: John T. Ganoe, "The Pacific Far West One Generation After the Frontier," *Pacific Historical Review,* IX (1940) p. 216.

Bibliography

Adams, W. L., *History of Medicine and Surgery in Oregon and Washington.* Portland, 1888.

——, *A Melodrame Entitled "Treason, Stratagems and Spoils," in Five Acts, By Breakspear.* Portland, 1852.

——, *Oregon As It Is* . . . Portland, 1873.

Alden, Charles H., "The Historic Precedent in Coast Architecture," *Architect and Engineer,* Vol. XXIX, No. 3, pp. 80–83 (1912).

Almack, John C., "History of Oregon Normal Schools," *Quarterly of the Oregon Historical Society,* Vol. XXI, No. 2, pp. 95–169 (1920).

Ambler, Charles H., *Life and Diary of John Floyd, Governor of Virginia* . . . *the Father of the Oregon Country.* Richmond, 1918.

Anderson, Eric D., "A Comparative Study of the Contributions of Public and Private Schools to Oregon Life, 1865–1895." M.A. thesis, University of Oregon, 1941.

Applegate, Jesse, "A Day with the Cow Column," *Quarterly of the Oregon Historical Society,* Vol. I, No. 4, pp. 371–383 (1900).

——, "Views of Oregon History, 1878." Manuscript, Bancroft Library.

"Art Survey of Portland." American Association of University Women, Portland branch, May, 1940. Typewritten volume in Library Association of Portland.

Atkinson, Rev. G. H., "Early History of the Public School System of Oregon . . ." *Biennial Report of the Superintendent of Public Instruction of Oregon.* Salem, 1876.

Atkinson, Nancy Bates, comp., *Biography of Rev. G. H. Atkinson, D.D.* . . . Portland, 1893.

"Authorship of 'The Prairie Flower,'" *Washington Historical Quarterly,* Vol. XIX, No. 2, pp. 155–156 (1928).

Bagley, Clarence B., "The Mercer Immigration: Two Cargoes of Maidens for the Sound Country," *Quarterly of the Oregon Historical Society,* Vol. V, No. 1, pp. 1–25 (1904).

Bailey, Margaret Jewett, *The Grains; or Passages in the Life of Ruth Rover.* Portland, 1854.

Bailey, Robert G., *Hell's Canyon* . . . *together with historical sketches of Idaho* . . . *mythology, poetry and stories.* Lewiston, 1943.

——, *River of No Return: A Century of Central Idaho and Eastern Washington History and Development.* Lewiston, 1935.

Bain, Read, "Educational Plans and Efforts by Methodists in Oregon to 1860,"

Quarterly of the Oregon Historical Society, Vol. XXI, No. 2, pp. 63–94 (1920).

Baker, Ray Stannard, "The Great Northwest," *Century Magazine*, Vol. LXV, No. 5, pp. 647–667 (1903).

Balch, Frederic Homer, *The Bridge of the Gods*. Chicago, 1910.

——, *Genevieve: A Tale of Oregon*. Portland, 1932.

——, *Memaloose*. Portland, 1934.

Bancroft, A., "Diary of Journey to Oregon in 1862." Manuscript, Bancroft Library, Berkeley, Calif.

Bancroft, Hubert Howe, *History of the Northwest Coast*, 2 vols. San Francisco, 1884.

——, *History of Oregon*, 2 vols. San Francisco, 1886.

——, *History of Washington, Idaho and Montana*. San Francisco, 1890.

——, *The Native Races*. San Francisco, 1882.

Banks, Louis A., *An Oregon Boyhood*. Boston, 1898.

Barrett, Myrna A., "History of Oregon Public Libraries." M.A. thesis, University of Oregon, June, 1940.

Barry, J. Neilson, "Astorians Who Became Permanent Settlers," *Washington Historical Quarterly*, Vol. XXIV, No. 3, pp. 221–231 (1933).

Bartlett, Laura B., *Chinook-English Songs*. Portland, 1914.

Barzee, C. Louis, *Oregon in the Making—'60's to Gay '90's*. Salem, Oregon, 1936.

Bashford, Herbert, *Nature Stories of the Northwest*. San Francisco, 1898.

——, *Songs from Puget Sea*. San Francisco, 1898.

——, *Wolves of the Sea and Other Poems*. San Francisco, 1901.

Bauer, Emilie F., "Musical Conditions in Portland, Oregon," *Oregonian*, Aug. 20, 1905.

Beal, Merrill D., *A History of Southeastern Idaho*. Caldwell, Idaho, 1942.

Bell, James Christy, *Opening a Highway to the Pacific, 1838–1846*. New York, 1921.

Bennett, Emerson, *The Prairie Flower; or, Adventures in the Far West*. New York and London, 1881.

Benson, H. K., "History of Chemical Education in Washington," *Washington Historical Quarterly*, Vol. XX, No. 3, pp. 174–177 (1929).

Berelson, Bernard and Howard F. Grant, "The Pioneer Theatre in Washington," *Pacific Northwest Quarterly*, Vol. XXVIII, No. 2, pp. 115–136 (1937).

Bergman, Hans, *History of Scandinavians in Tacoma and Pierce Counties* . . . Tacoma, 1936.

Bibb, Thomas W., *History of Early Common School Education in Washington*. Seattle, 1929.

Birney, Hoffman, *Vigilantes; A Chronicle of the Plummer Gang . . . in the Early 'Sixties*. Philadelphia, 1929.

Bischoff, William N., *The Jesuits in Old Oregon, 1840–1940*. Caldwell, Idaho, 1945.

Blaine, David E. and Catherine P., "Letters and Papers." Typewritten manuscript, Oregon Historical Society Library.

Blair, Mirpah, "Some Early Libraries of Oregon," *Washington Historical Quarterly*, Vol. XVII, No. 4, pp. 259–270 (1926).

Blegen, Theodore, *Norwegian Migration to America* . . . Northfield, Minn., 1940.

Boas, Franz, *Chinook Texts*. Government Printing Office, Washington, D.C., 1894.

Bolton, Frederick E., "High Schools in Territorial Washington," *Washington Historical Quarterly*, Vol. XXIV, No. 3, pp. 211–220, 271–281 (1933).

——, and Thomas W. Bibb, *History of Education in Washington.* U.S. Office of Education Bulletin, IX, Washington, D.C., 1934.

Booth, Margaret, ed., "The Dinwiddie Journal—Overland from Indiana to Oregon," *The Frontier*, Vol. VIII, No. 2, pp. 115–130 (1928).

Booth, R. A., "History of Umpqua Academy," *Quarterly of the Oregon Historical Society*, Vol. XIX, No. 1, pp. 1–26 (1918).

Bourne, Edward G., *Essays in Historical Criticism.* New York, 1901.

Bowden, Mrs. Angie, *Early Schools of Washington Territory.* Seattle, 1935.

Bradley, Marie M., "Political Beginnings in Oregon," *Quarterly of the Oregon Historical Society*, Vol. IX, No. 1, pp. 42–72 (1908).

Brosnan, Cornelius J., *Jason Lee, Prophet of the New Oregon.* New York, 1932.

Brouillet, Rev. J. B. A., *Protestantism in Oregon.* New York, 1853.

Brown, Arthur J., "The Promotion of Emigration to Washington Territory 1854–1909," *Pacific Northwest Quarterly*, Vol. XXXVI, No. 1, pp. 3–17 (1945).

Brown, Rev. Henry, comp., *War on the Theatre.* Spokane, 1909.

Bruneau, Lyda H., *Stories of Idaho from Pioneer Days to the Present Time.* Lewiston, 1940.

Burnett, Peter H., *Recollections and Opinions of an Old Pioneer.* New York, 1880.

Bushnell, David I., *Drawings by George Gibb in . . . the Northwest, 1849–51.* Smithsonian Misc. Collections, Vol. 97, No. 8. Washington, D.C., 1938.

Butterworth, Hezekia, *Log School House on the Columbia—A Tale of the Pioneers.* New York, 1890.

Canse, John Martin, "The Oregon Mission—Its Transition," *Washington Historical Quarterly*, Vol. 25, No. 3, pp. 203–209 (1934).

Capell, Letitia Lee, "A Biography of Abigail Scott Duniway." M.A. thesis, University of Oregon, 1934.

Carey, Charles H., *A General History of Oregon Prior to 1861*, 2 vols. Portland, 1935.

——, ed., *The Oregon Constitution and Proceedings and Debates of the Constitutional Convention of 1857.* Salem, 1926.

Carkeek, E. G., "Historical Sketch of the Seattle Public Library." Typewritten manuscript, University of Washington Library, Seattle.

Cass, Frank Hadley, *Looking Northwest.* Portland, 1938.

Castle, Gwen, ed., "Belshaw Journal, Oregon Trail, 1853," *Oregon Historical Quarterly*, Vol. XXXII, No. 3, pp. 217–239 (1931).

Caughey, John W., *History of the Pacific Coast.* Los Angeles, 1933.

——, *Hubert Howe Bancroft, Historian of the West.* Berkeley and Los Angeles, 1946.

Chafee, E. B., "Early History of the Boise Region, 1811–1864." M.A. thesis, University of California at Berkeley, 1927.

Chapman, Charles N., "Extensive Library of Harvey W. Scott as Gauge of His Broad Scholarship and Literary Activity," *Quarterly of the Oregon Historical Society*, Vol. XIV, No. 2, pp. 134–139 (1913).

Cheney, Charles B., "Political Movements in the Northwest," *Review of Reviews*, Vol. XXI, pp. 337–341 (March, 1905).

Chittick, V. L. O., *Ring-tailed Roarers: Tall Tales of the American Frontier, 1830–60.* Caldwell, 1941.

Churchill, Claire W., comp., "Speech Expressions from Letters of Matthew P. Deady to Asahel Bush, 1855–1859," Oregon Folklore Studies, Oregon State Library, Salem.

Clark, Dan E., "The Movement to the Far West During the Decade of the

'Sixties." *Washington Historical Quarterly*, Vol. XVII, No. 2, pp. 105–113 (1926).

Clark, Dan E., *The West in American History*. New York, 1937.

Clark, Robert C., *A History of the Willamette Valley, Oregon*. Chicago, 1927.

Clarke, Samuel A., *Pioneer Days of Oregon History*. Portland, 1905.

Clay, Claud A., "The First Woman Born in the West," *Ladies Home Journal*, Vol. XXX, No. 8, pp. 14, 38–40 (1897).

Cleveland, Alfred A., "The Educational History of Astoria," *Quarterly of the Oregon Historical Society*, Vol. IV, No. 1, pp. 21–32 (1903).

——, "Social and Economic History of Astoria," *Quarterly of the Oregon Historical Society*, Vol. IV, No. 2, pp. 130–149 (1903).

Coe, Urling C., *Frontier Doctor*. New York, 1939.

Coldwell, O. B., "Electricity in Oregon." Manuscript, Oregon Historical Society Library.

Cole, George E., *Early Oregon—Jottings of Personal Recollections of a Pioneer of 1850*. Spokane, 1905.

"Colonel Joe Meek," *Pacific Monthly*, Vol. XIV, No. 5, pp. 494–495 (1905).

Condon, Thomas, "The Process of Selection in Oregon Pioneer Settlement," *Quarterly of the Oregon Historical Society*, Vol. I, No. 1, pp. 60–65 (1900).

Connelley, William E., "National Aspects of the Old Oregon Trail," *Kansas State Historical Society Collections*, Vol. 13, pp. 415–423 (1913–1914).

Cook, James, and James King, *A Voyage to the Pacific Ocean*. London, 1784.

Cooke, Belle W., *Tears and Victory and Other Poems*. Salem, 1871.

Costello, J. A., *The Siwash, Their Life, Legends and Tales*. Seattle, 1895.

Cox, Ross, *The Columbia River*, 2 vols. London, 1832.

Crawford, Medorem, "Journal, 1842," *Sources of the History of Oregon*, Vol. 1, No. 12, Dept. of History and Economics, University of Oregon. Eugene, 1897.

Cummins, Mrs. S. J. W., *Autobiography and Reminiscences*. La Grand, Oregon, 1914.

Dale, Harrison C., "The Organization of the Oregon Emigrating Companies," *Quarterly of the Oregon Historical Society*, Vol. XVI, No. 3, pp. 205–227 (1915).

Davenport, Homer, *The Country Boy: the Story of His Own Early Life*. New York, 1910.

Davenport, T. W., "Slavery Question in Oregon," *Quarterly of the Oregon Historical Society*, Vol. IX, Nos. 3, 4, pp. 189–253, 309–373 (1908).

Dawson, Charles, *Pioneer Tales of the Oregon Trail and of Jefferson County*. Topeka, 1912.

Deady, Matthew P., "Scrapbook." Oregon Historical Society Library Collections.

Denny, Arthur A., *Pioneer Days on Puget Sound*, ed. Alice Harriman. Seattle, 1908.

Denny, Emily Inez, *Blazing the Way; or, True Stories, Songs and Sketches of Puget Sound* . . . Seattle, 1909.

DeVoto, Bernard, *Across the Wide Missouri*. Boston, 1947.

Dewey, Henry B., comp., *History of Education in Washington*. Olympia, 1909.

DeWolf, Captain David, "Diary of the Overland Trail, 1849, and Letters, 1849–50," *Illinois Historical Society Transactions*, No. 32 (1925).

Dickson, Albert J., *Covered Wagon Days: A Journey Across the Plains in the 'Sixties and Pioneer Days in the Northwest*. Cleveland, 1929.

Dillon, Lee A., "The Portland Public School System from 1873 to 1913." Typewritten manuscript, Oregon Historical Society Library.

Dobie, Edith, "Looking at Oregon Territory Through Advertisements," *Wash-*

ington Historical Quarterly, Vol. XVIII, No. 2, pp. 103–109 (1927).

Donaldson, Thomas C., *Idaho of Yesterday*. Caldwell, 1941.

Douthit, Mary Osborn, ed., *Souvenir of Western Women*. Portland, 1905.

Drake, Elizabeth, ed., "Public Education in Boise in Territorial Days," *Idaho State Historical Society, 18th Biennial Report*. Boise, 1942.

Drury, Clifford M., *Elkanah and Mary Walker*. Caldwell, 1940.

———, *Henry Harmon Spalding*. Caldwell, 1926.

———, *Marcus Whitman, M.D., Pioneer and Martyr*. Caldwell, 1937.

Duniway, Abigail Scott, *Captain Gray's Company; or, Crossing the Plains and Living in Oregon*. Portland, 1859.

———, *David and Anna Matson*. Portland, 1881.

———, *Path Breaking: An Autobiographical History of the Equal Suffrage Movement in Pacific Coast States*. Portland, 1914.

Dunlap, Leslie W., "Oregon Free Press," *Pacific Northwest Quarterly*, Vol. XXXIII, No. 2, pp. 171–185 (1942).

Dunn, John, *History of the Oregon Territory*. London, 1844.

Dye, Eva Emery, *The Conquest*. Chicago, 1902.

———, *McDonald of Oregon*. Chicago, 1906.

———, *McLoughlin and Old Oregon*. Chicago, 1900.

———, "Oregon Writers," *Pacific Monthly*, Vol. IV, No. 6, pp. 253–257 (1900).

"Early History of Washington," *The Republican* (Seattle), Vol. II, No. 34 (Jan. 4, 1896).

Eaton, Allen H., *The Oregon System: The Story of Direct Legislation in Oregon*. Chicago, 1912.

Eaton, W. Clement, "Nathaniel Wyeth's Oregon Expeditions," *Pacific Historical Review*, Vol. IV, No. 2, pp. 101–113 (1935).

Edwards, Jonathan, *Marcus Whitman*. Spokane, 1892.

Eels, Myron, *Reply to Professor Bourne's "The Whitman Legend."* Walla Walla, Wash., 1902.

Elliott, Eugene C., *History of Variety-Vaudeville in Seattle to 1914*. University of Washington Publications in Drama, No. 1, Seattle, 1944.

Elliott, T. C., "David Thompson and Beginnings in Idaho," *Quarterly of the Oregon Historical Society*, Vol. XXI, No. 2, pp. 49–61 (1920).

———, "David Thompson's Journeys in the Spokane Country," *Washington Historical Quarterly*, Vol. VIII, No. 3, pp. 183–187 (1917).

———, "The Earliest Travellers on the Oregon Trail," *Quarterly of the Oregon Historical Society*, Vol. XIII, No. 1, pp. 71–84 (1912).

———, "Jonathan Carver's Source for the Name Oregon," *Quarterly of the Oregon Historical Society*, Vol. XXIII, No. 1, pp. 53–69 (1922).

———, comp., *The Coming of the White Woman, 1836, As Told in the Letters and Journals of Narcissa Prentice Whitman*. Portland, 1937.

Ellison, Joseph, "Designs for a Pacific Republic, 1843–62." *Oregon Historical Quarterly*, Vol. XXXI, No. 4, pp. 319–342 (1930).

———, "The Sentiment for a Pacific Republic, 1843–1862," *American Historical Association Preceedings*. Los Angeles, 1929.

Ernst, Alice H., "Eugene's Theatres and Shows in Horse and Buggy Days," *Oregon Historical Quarterly*, Vol. XLIV, No. 2, pp. 127–139; No. 3, pp. 232–248 (1943).

Estes, George, *The Stage Coach*. Portland, 1925.

Feary, Amelia A., "Origin and Development of Family Social Work in Portland, Oregon." M.A. thesis, University of Oregon, 1936.

Fee, Chester Anders, *Chief Joseph: a Biography of a Great Indian*. New York, 1936.

Finck, Henry T., *My Adventures in the Golden Age of Music*. New York, 1926.

Fisher, Vardis, ed., *Idaho: A Guide in Word and Pictures*. Caldwell, 1937.

——, *Idaho Lore*. Caldwell, 1939.

Fiske, John, "Oration at the 20th Annual Reunion of the Oregon Pioneer Association, 1892," *Transactions of the Oregon Pioneer Association*, Vol. 20, p. 31. Portland, 1893.

——, *Unpublished Orations*. The Bibliophile Society, Boston, 1909.

"Folklore Studies: Interviews with Pioneers." W.P.A., Federal Writers' Project. Manuscript Collection, Oregon State Library, Salem.

Foote, Mary Hallock, *The Chosen Valley*. Boston and New York, 1892.

——, *The Desert and the Sown*. Boston and New York, 1902.

——, *In Exile and Other Stories*. Boston and New York, 1894.

——, *A Touch of the Sun and Other Stories*. Boston and New York, 1903.

——, *A Picked Company*. Boston and New York, 1912.

Franchère, Gabriel, *Narrative of a Voyage to the Northwest Coast of America*. New York, 1854.

French, Hiram T., *History of Idaho*, 3 vols. Chicago and New York, 1914.

Fry, F., *Fry's Traveler's Guide and Descriptive Journal of the Great Northwestern Territories of the United States of America*. Cincinnati, 1865.

Fuller, George W., *A History of the Pacific Northwest*. New York, 1931.

——, *The Inland Empire of the Pacific Northwest*, 3 vols. Spokane and Denver, 1928.

Gabriel, Ralph H., *The Lure of the Frontier*. London, 1929.

Ganoe, John T., "The Pacific Far West One Generation After the Frontier," *Pacific Historical Review*, Vol. IX, No. 2, pp. 205–217 (1940).

Garnett, Porter, "Facility and Felicity in Western Letters," *Pacific Monthly*, Vol. XVII, No. 3, pp. 333–337 (1907).

——, "History, Fiction and the Point of View," *Pacific Monthly*, Vol. XVIII, No. 2, pp. 259–264 (1908).

Garth, Jr., Thomas R., "Early Architecture in the Pacific Northwest," *Pacific Northwest Quarterly*, Vol. XXXVIII, No. 3, pp. 215–232 (1947).

Gass, Patrick, *Lewis and Clarke's Journey to the Rocky Mountains . . . 1904, 1905, 1906 . . .* Dayton, 1847.

Gates, Charles, ed., *Messages of the Governors of the Territory of Washington to the Legislative Assembly, 1854–1889*. Seattle, 1940.

Gatke, Robert M., *Chronicles of Willamette: the Pioneer University of the West*. Portland, 1943.

Gay, Theressa, *Life and Letters of Mrs. Jason Lee*. Portland, 1936.

Ghent, W. J., *The Road to Oregon*. New York, 1929.

Goldman, Eric F., "J. Allen Smith: The Reformer and His Dilemma," *Pacific Northwest Quarterly*, Vol. XXXV, No. 3, pp. 195–214 (1944).

Goodrich, Frederick W., "Oregon Orchestral Music, 1868–1932," *Oregon Historical Quarterly*, Vol. XXXIII, No. 2, pp. 136–142 (1932).

Gowen, Herbert H., "Problem of Oriental Immigration in Washington," *Annals of the American Academy*, Vol. XXXIV, pp. 329–337 (September, 1909).

Grant, Ethel Austen, "Old Buildings in Seattle, Tacoma, Spokane: Descriptions of Early Theatre Buildings." Typewritten manuscript, University of Washington Library, Seattle.

——, "Theatrical Performances in Yesler's Hall . . ." Typewritten manuscript, University of Washington Library.

Grant, Howard F., comp., *Story of Seattle's Early Theatres*. Seattle, 1934.

Grant, Rena V., "The Chinook Jargon, Past and Present," *California Folklore Quarterly*, Vol. III, No. 4, pp. 259–276 (1944).

Gray, William Henry, *History of Oregon, 1792–1849.* Portland, 1870.

Haehlen, Gottlieb, *Historical Sketch of the Pine Street Coffee House; Also Early History of the City of Portland.* Portland, 1914.

Hafen, LeRoy R., *The Overland Mail, 1849–1868.* Cleveland, 1926.

Hailey, John, *History of Idaho.* Boise, 1910.

Haines, Francis, "The Nez Percé Delegation to St. Louis in 1831," *Pacific Historical Review,* Vol. VI, No. 1, pp. 71–78 (1937).

Hamilton, S. Watson, *A Pioneer of Fifty-three.* Albany, Oregon, 1905.

Hargreaves, Sheba, ed., "The Letters of Roselle Putnam," *Oregon Historical Society Quarterly,* Vol. XXIX, No. 3, pp. 242–264 (1928).

Harkness, Ione B., "Basque Settlement in Oregon," *Oregon Historical Society Quarterly,* Vol. XXXIV, No. 3, pp. 273–275 (1933).

——, "Certain Social Settlements of Oregon." M.A. thesis, University of California, 1925.

Hebard, Grace R., *Sacajawea.* Glendale, Oregon, 1933.

Hedges, James B., *Henry Villard and the Railways of the Northwest.* New Haven, 1930.

Hendrick, Burton J., "The 'Recall' in Seattle," *McClure's Magazine,* Vol. XXXVII, No. 6, pp. 647–663 (1911).

Henry, Gladys J., "Paul Bunyan Twenty-five Years After," *Journal of American Folklore,* Vol. LV, No. 217, pp. 155–168 (1942).

Herndon, Mrs. Sarah P., *Days on the Road: Crossing the Plains in 1865.* New York, 1902.

Hewitt, R. H., *Notes by the Way: Memoranda of a Journey Across the Plains From Dundee, Illinois to Olympia, W.T.* Olympia, 1863.

Higginson, Ella R., "Fact and Fancy," *West Shore,* Vol. XVI, No. 232, p. 212 (1890).

——, *A Forest Orchid.* New York, 1897.

——, *From the Land of the Snow Pearls.* New York, 1897.

——, *Mariella of Out-West.* New York, 1902.

——, *The Snow Pearls.* New York, 1897.

——, *The Voice of April Land.* New York, 1903.

——, *When the Birds Go North Again.* New York, 1898.

Hill, Jr., Daniel G., "The Negro in Oregon, a Survey," M.A. thesis, University of Oregon, 1932.

Himes, George H., "An Account of Crossing the Plains in 1853," *Transactions of the Oregon Pioneer Association, 1907.* Portland, 1908.

Hines, Harvey K., "Overland in Winter," *Ladies' Repository,* Vol. XXIX, pp. 297–300 (April, 1869).

——, *Missionary History of the Pacific Northwest.* Portland, c. 1899.

Hodge, Frederick W., ed., *The Handbook of American Indians North of Mexico.* Smithsonian Institute, Bureau of American Ethnology, Bulletin 30, Pts. 1–2, Washington, 1907–1910.

Holman, Alfred, "Oregonian Characteristics," *Overland Monthly,* Vol. XXV, No. 146, pp. 202–206 (1895).

——, "Review of Harvey W. Scott's Half-Century Career as Editor and Estimate of His Work," *Quarterly of the Oregon Historical Society,* Vol. XIV, No. 2, pp. 87–133 (1913).

Holman, Frederick F., "A Brief History of the Oregon Provisional Government and What Caused Its Formation," *Quarterly of the Oregon Historical Society,* Vol. XIII, No. 2, pp. 82–139 (1912).

Holt, Joseph, *The Relation of Music to the Civilization of the Northwest.* Portland, 1890.

Holt, William S., "The Chinese of the Pacific Coast," *Pacific Monthly*, Vol. III, No. 5, pp. 201–206 (1900).
Horner, John B., *Oregon: Her History, Her Great Men, Her Literature*. Corvallis, Oregon, 1919.
——, *Oregon History and Early Literature* (rev. ed.). Portland, 1931.
——, *Oregon Literature*. Corvallis, 1899.
Howard, Charles. A., "A History of High School Legislation in Oregon to 1910." M.A. thesis, University of Oregon, 1923.
Howard, Helen A. and George D. McGrath, *War Chief Joseph*. Caldwell, 1941.
Howay, F. W., "Early Literature of the Northwest Coast," *Proceedings and Transactions Royal Society of Canada*, Series 3, Sec. 2, Vol. XVIII (1924).
——, "The Introduction of Intoxicating Liquors Amongst the Indians of the Northwest Coast," *British Columbia Historical Quarterly*, Vol. VI, No. 3, pp. 157–169 (1942).
——, "Origins of the Chinook Jargon on the North West Coast," *Oregon Historical Quarterly*, Vol. XLIV, No. 1, pp. 27–55 (1943).
——, *Voyages of the "Columbia" to the Northwest Coast* . . . Boston, 1941.
Howe, Frederick C., "Oregon—the Most Complete Democracy in the World," *Hampton's Magazine*, Vol. XXVI, pp. 459–472 (April, 1911).
Howell, Thomas, *Flora of Northwest America*. Portland, 1903.
Hulbert, Archer B., ed., *The Call of the Columbia*. Denver, 1934.
——, "Western Trails: Work of the Stewart Commission," *The Frontier*, Vol. IX, No. 1, pp. 52–54 (1928).
——, *Where Rolls the Oregon: Prophet and Pessimist Look Northwest, 1825–1830*. Denver, c. 1933.
Hulbert, Archer B. and Dorothy P., eds., *Marcus Whitman, Crusader*, 3 vols. Denver, 1936–1941.
——, *The Oregon Crusade: Across Land and Sea to Oregon*. Denver, 1935.
Hull, Dorothy, "The Movement in Oregon for the Establishment of a Pacific Coast Republic," *Quarterly of the Oregon Historical Society*, Vol. XVII, No. 3, pp. 177–200 (1916).
Hunter, George, *Reminiscences of an Old Timer*. San Francisco, 1887.
Ingalls, Gertrude Balch, "Frederic Homer Balch, Author of 'The Bridge of the Gods,' " *Pacific Monthly*, Vol. V, No. 2, pp. 85–86 (1900).
Irving, Washington, *The Adventures of Captain Bonneville*. London, 1837.
——, *Astoria*. Philadelphia, 1836.
Jacobs, Melville, "Historical Perspectives in Indian Languages of Oregon and Washington," *Pacific Northwest Quarterly*, Vol. XXVIII, No. 1, pp. 55–74 (1937).
Jacobs, Melvin C., *Winning Oregon: A Study of an Expansionist Movement*. Caldwell, 1938.
Jennings, Frederick, "The Most Notable Architecture and Landscape Architecture of Spokane, Washington," *Architect and Engineer*, Vol. LXV, No. 3, pp. 49–94 (1921).
——, "The Most Notable Buildings of a City—What Are They?" *Architect and Engineer*, Vol. LVI, No. 3, pp. 40–76 (1919).
Joergenson, G. B., *Early Migrations in the Northwest*. Manuscript, University of Washington Library, c. 1925.
Johnson, C. T., "The Evolution of a Lament," *Washington Historical Quarterly*, Vol. II, No. 3, pp. 195–208 (1908).
Johnson, Mrs. Laura Winthrop, ed., *The Life and Poems of Theodore Winthrop*. New York, 1884.

Johnson, Overton and William H. Winter, *Route Across the Rocky Mountains, With a Description of Oregon and California* . . . Lafayette, Ind., 1846.

Johnson, Robert C., *John McLoughlin: Patriarch of the Northwest*. Portland, 1935.

Jones, Nard, *Scarlet Petticoat*. New York, 1941.

Judson, Katharine Berry, *Early Days in Old Oregon*. Chicago, 1916.

———, *Myths and Legends of the Pacific Northwest* . . . Chicago, 1910.

Judson, Phoebe Goodall, *A Pioneer's Search for an Ideal Home*. Bellingham, Wash., 1925.

Kane, Paul, *Wanderings of an Artist Among the Indians of North America* . . . London, 1859.

"Katharine," *Letters from an Oregon Ranch*. Chicago, 1905.

Kehoe, James P., "History of the Catholic Missionary Activity Among the Indians of the Oregon Country, 1839-1936." M.A. thesis, University of Oregon, 1936.

Keller, Richard M., "Regionalism in Novels of the Northwest." M.A. thesis, State College of Washington, 1938.

Kelley, Hall Jackson, *History of the Colonization of the Oregon Territory*. Springfield, Mass., 1849.

Kelly, Clara J., comp., "Publications of the University of Washington Faculty, Nov. 4, 1861-March 31, 1938." Manuscript, University of Washington Library.

Kelly, Sister M. Margaret Jean, *The Career of Joseph Lane, Frontier Politician*. Washington, D.C., 1942.

Kidd, Kenneth, "The Wanderings of Kane," *The Beaver*, Outfit 277, December, 1946, pp. 3-9.

Kingston, C. S., "Sacajawea As a Guide: The Evaluation of a Legend," *Pacific Northwest Quarterly*, Vol. XXXV, No. 1, pp. 3-18 (1944).

Knapp, Ralph R., "Divorce in Washington," *Washington Historical Quarterly*, Vol. V, No. 2, pp. 121-128 (1914).

Ladd, James W., "A Survey of the Legitimate Theatre in Seattle Since 1856." M.A. thesis, State College of Washington, 1935.

Landes, Henry, "History of the Geology of the State of Washington," *Washington Historical Quarterly*, Vol. XIX, No. 4, pp. 243-249 (1928).

Lange, Edwin F., "Oregon City Private Schools, 1843-59," *Oregon Historical Quarterly*, Vol. XXXVII, No. 4, pp. 308-328 (1936).

———, "The Oregon City Public School," *Oregon Historical Quarterly*, Vol. XXXVIII, No. 1, pp. 92-108 (1937).

Langford, N. P., *Vigilante Days and Ways* . . . New York and St. Paul, 1893.

Langley, Manche Irene, "Sam L. Simpson—Author of the Gold-Gated West," *The Lariat*, Vol. II, No. 5, pp. 423-425 (1923).

Larsell, Olaf, *The Doctor in Oregon*. Portland, 1947.

Lash, Frederick M., "An Historical and Functional Study of Public Education in Seattle." Ph.D. thesis, University of Washington, 1934.

Laut, Agnes C., *The Conquest of the Great Northwest*, 2 vols. New York, 1908.

———, *The Overland Trail: the Epic Path of the Pioneers to Oregon*. New York, 1939.

———, *Pioneers of the Pacific Coast*. Toronto, 1920.

———, *Vikings of the Pacific*. New York and London, 1905.

Ledyard, John, *A Journal of Captain Cook's Last Voyage to the Pacific Ocean* . . . Hartford, 1783.

Leighton, George R., "Seattle, the Edge of the Last Frontier," *Harper's Magazine*, Vol. 178, pp. 306-328, 422-440 (February, March, 1939).

Leiter, Otho Clarke, "Scott and the Oregonian," *The Journalism Quarterly*, Vol. V, No. 4, pp. 1–10 (1929).

Lincoln, Fred, "Vaudeville in the Northwest," *Washington Magazine*, Vol. II, No. 1, pp. 29–30 (1906).

Littell, L., "Mimes and Minstrels," Oregon Folklore, W.P.A. Project. Oregon State Library, Salem.

Lockley, Fred, *Oregon's Yesterdays*. New York, 1928.

Long, Mrs. S. A., "Mrs. Jesse Applegate," *Quarterly of the Oregon Historical Society*, Vol. IX, No. 2, pp. 179–183 (1908).

Lord, Mrs. Elizabeth L., *Reminiscences of Eastern Oregon*. Portland, 1903.

Lord, William R., *A First Book on the Birds of Oregon and Washington*. Portland, 1902.

Lyman, H. S., "An Oregon Literature," *Quarterly of the Oregon Historical Society*, Vol. II, No. 4, pp. 401–409 (1901).

Lyman, William D., *The Columbia River: Its History, Its Myths, Its Scenery, Its Commerce*. New York, 1909.

——, *Indian Myths of the Northwest*. Worcester, Mass., 1915.

McArthur, Lewis, *Oregon Geographic Names*. Portland, 1928.

McConnell, W. J., and H. Driggs, *Frontier Law: A Story of Vigilante Days*. New York, 1924.

McCornack, Ellen Condon, *Thomas Condon: Pioneer Geologist of Oregon*. Eugene, 1928.

McCoy, Bernice, "Early Territorial Day Schools, 1863–1880," *Lewiston Morning Tribune*, Spaulding Centennial Edition, May 3, 1936.

McCrea, Mary H., *Growth of School Libraries in the State of Washington*. Olympia, 1938.

McHargue, Robert M., "Studies in the Popular Music of the American Frontiers." M.A. thesis, University of California at Los Angeles, 1940.

McMurtrie, Douglas C., *Pioneer Printing in Washington*. Chicago, 1931.

——, *Washington Newspapers, 1852–1890 Inclusive; a Supplement to Prof. Meany's List*. Seattle, 1935.

MacQueen, Joseph, "Pioneer Music of the Oregon Country," Manuscript, No. 3, Federal Emergency Relief Administration MMS Project. Portland, 1935.

Manning, James W., "Literacy on the Oregon Trail—Books Across the Plains," *Oregon Historical Quarterly*, Vol. XLI, No. 2, pp. 189–194 (1940).

Marcy, Captain, Randolph B. (U.S. Army), *The Prairie Traveler, a Handbook for Overland Expeditions*. Washington, 1863.

Marshall, William I., *Acquisition of Oregon and the Long Suppressed Evidence About Marcus Whitman*, 2 vols. Seattle, 1911.

——, *The Hudson's Bay Company's Archives Furnish No Support to the Whitman Saved Oregon Story*. Chicago, 1905.

Mason, J. Tate, M.D., "Seattle's First Physician—Dr. David Swinson Maynard," *Western Journal of Surgery, Obstetrics and Gynecology*, Vol. XLI, Nos. 1, 2, 3 (January, February, March, 1933).

Matthew, Harry V., "A History of the Certification of Teachers in Oregon, 1849–1932." Ph.D. thesis, University of Oregon, 1932.

Meade, Edwards H., *Doubling Back: Autobiography of an Actor . . .* Chicago, 1916.

Meany, Edmond S., "Has Puget Sound a Literature?" *Washington Magazine*, Vol. 1, No. 1, pp. 8–11 (1889).

——, "History of Science in Washington," *Washington Historical Quarterly*, Vol. XIX, No. 3, pp. 163–164 (1928).

——, *History of the State of Washington*. New York, 1910.

——, *Newspapers of Washington Territory.* University of Washington Press, Seattle, 1923.

——, "Professor Thomas Condon, the Remarkable History of Oregon's Famous Geologist," *Pacific Monthly*, Vol. XVI, No. 5, pp. 566–569 (1906).

——, "The Towns of the Pacific Northwest Were Not Founded on the Fur Trade," *American Historical Association Annual Report*, 1909.

——, *Vancouver's Discovery of Puget Sound.* New York, 1907.

Meares, John, *Voyages Made in the Years 1788 and 1789 from China to the North West Coast of America.* London, 1790.

Meeker, Ezra, *The Busy Life of Eighty-five Years.* Seattle, 1916.

——, *The Oxteam; or, The Old Oregon Trail, 1852–1906.* Omaha, 1906.

Mercer, Asa Shinn, *The Pioneer.* Chicago, 1913.

Miles, Charles and O. B. Sperlin, *Building a State: Washington, 1889–1939.* Tacoma, 1940.

Miller, Joaquin, *Complete Poetical Works.* San Francisco, 1902.

——, *My Life Among the Indians.* Chicago, 1892.

Mills, Randall V., "Frontier Humor in Oregon and Its Characteristics," *Oregon Historical Quarterly*, Vol. XLIII, No. 4, pp. 339–356 (1942).

——, "A History of Transportation in the Pacific Northwest," *Oregon Historical Quarterly*, Vol. XLVII, No. 3, pp. 281–312 (1946).

Mitchell, Mrs. Rebecca, *Historical Sketches: Pioneer Characters and Conditions of Eastern Idaho.* Idaho Falls, 1905.

Montgomery, Richard G., *The White-Headed Eagle: John McLoughlin, Builder of an Empire.* New York, 1934.

Morris, William A., "Historian of the Northwest, a Woman Who Loved Oregon," *Quarterly of the Oregon Historical Society*, Vol. III, No. 4, pp. 429–434 (1902).

——, "The Origin and Authorship of the Bancroft Pacific States Publications: A History of a History," *Quarterly of the Oregon Historical Society*, Vol. IV, No. 4, pp. 287–364 (1903).

Morse, Eldridge, "Puget Sound Literature in 1910," *Washington Magazine*, Vol. I, No. 4, pp. 5–7 (1889).

Mudge, Zachariah A., *Sketches of Mission Life Among the Indians of Oregon.* New York, 1854.

Munford, Kenneth, *John Ledyard, An American Marco Polo.* Portland, 1939.

Nolder, Mae M., "The Academy Era in the State of Washington." M.A. thesis, State College of Washington, 1934.

Nichols, M. Leona, *Joab Powell, Homespun Missionary.* Portland, 1935.

Nixon, Oliver W., *How Marcus Whitman Saved Oregon.* Chicago, 1895.

O'Hara, Edwin V., "De Smet in the Oregon Country," *Quarterly of the Oregon Historical Society*, Vol. X, No. 3, pp. 239–262 (1909).

——, *Catholic History of Oregon.* Portland, 1916.

Oregon Pioneer Association Transactions. 1873–1928. Portland, published yearly.

Oregon Writers' Program: *Oregon: End of the Trail.* Portland, 1940.

——, *Oregon Trail: the Missouri River to the Pacific Ocean.* New York, 1939.

Overmeyer, Philip H., "The Oregon Justinian; A Life of Matthew Paul Deady." M.S. thesis, University of Oregon, 1935.

——, "Villard and the University of Oregon," *Oregon Historical Quarterly*, Vol. XXXV, No. 4, pp. 340–347 (1934).

Owens-Adair, Bethenia, *Dr. Owens-Adair; Some of Her Life Experiences.* Portland, n.d.

Pacific Northwest Library Association Proceedings. 1909–1949. Seattle, published yearly.

Pacific Northwest Number, *Harper's Weekly*, Vol. LIII, No. 2728 (April 3, 1909).

Palmer, Joel, *Journal of Travels over the Rocky Mountains, to the Mouth of the Columbia River . . . 1845, 1846 . . .* Cincinnati, 1847.

Parker, Rev. Samuel, *Journal of an Exploring Tour Beyond the Rocky Mountains, 1835–1837 . . .* Ithaca, N.Y., 1838.

Parrish, Philip H., *Before the Covered Wagon.* Portland, 1931.

"Paul Bunyan," *Fortune*, Vol. XXX, No. 1, pp. 148–150 (1944).

Pearce, Stella E., "Suffrage in the Pacific Northwest, Old Oregon and Washington," *Washington Historical Quarterly*, Vol. III, No. 2, pp. 106–114 (1908–1912).

Peattie, D. C., "Marcus Whitman, Martyr for Oregon," *Readers Digest*, July, 1943.

Penrose, Stephen B. L., *Whitman, An Unfinished Story.* Walla Walla, c. 1935.

Peterson, Martin S., "The Border Days of Joaquin Miller, 1854–1870," *The Frontier*, Vol. XI, No. 4, pp. 362–375 (1931).

———, *Joaquin Miller: Literary Frontiersman.* Palo Alto, Calif., and London, 1937.

Phillips, Paul C. and W. S. Lewis, eds., "The Oregon Missions as Shown in the Walker Letters, 1839–1851," *The Frontier*, Vol. XI, No. 1, pp. 74–89 (1930).

Phillips, William, *Crossing the Plains in '46.* Oregon City, 1900.

Pierce, Cornelia M., "Beginnings of State Library Service in Oregon." Typewritten manuscript, 1939, Oregon State Library, Salem.

Pike, C. J., "Petitions of Oregon Settlers, 1838–48," *Oregon Historical Quarterly*, Vol. XXXIV, No. 3, pp. 216–235 (1933).

Pittock, Henry L., "Story of the Daily Oregonian Told by Its Founders," *Morning Oregonian*, 50th anniversary number, Feb. 4, 1911.

Pollard, Lancaster, "A Check List of Washington Authors," *Pacific Northwest Quarterly*, Vol. XXXI, No. 1, pp. 3–96 (1940).

———, "A Check List of Washington Authors: Additions and Corrections," *Pacific Northwest Quarterly*, Vol. XXXV, No. 3, pp. 233–266 (1944).

———, "Washington Literature: A Historical Sketch," *Pacific Northwest Quarterly*, Vol. XXIX, No. 3, pp. 227–254 (1938).

———, and Lloyd Spencer, ed., *History of Washington*, 2 vols. New York, 1937.

Porter, Kenneth W., "Jane Barnes, First White Woman in Oregon," *Oregon Historical Quarterly*, Vol. XXXI, No. 2, pp. 125–135 (1930).

Portland Art Association: *Nineteenth Annual Report, June 1, 1911.*

Powell, Fred W., *Hall J. Kelley on Oregon.* Princeton, 1932.

———, *Hall Jackson Kelley, Prophet of Oregon.* Portland, 1917.

Powell, Lawrence Clark, *Philosopher Pickett: The Life and Writings of Charles Edward Pickett.* Los Angeles, 1942.

Powers, Alfred, *History of Oregon Literature.* Portland, 1935.

———, and Mary-Jane Finke, "Survey of First Half-Century of Oregon Hotels," *Oregon Historical Quarterly*, Vol. XLIII, No. 3, pp. 232–281 (1942).

Powers, Kate Ball, Flora Ball Hopkins and Lucy Ball, comps., *Autobiography of John Ball.* Grand Rapids, 1935.

"Prominent Writers and Literary Folk of Oregon Today," *Sunday Oregonian*, May 21, 1905.

Prosch, Charles, "Puget Sound Society in Early Days," *Pacific Magazine*, Vol. 4, No. 2, pp. 49–51 (1891).

———, "Washington's Pioneers," *Washington Magazine*, Vol. I, No. 3, pp. 20–22 (1889).

Prosch, Thomas W., *David S. Maynard and Catherine T. Maynard.* Seattle, 1906.

———, "Dr. David S. Maynard, Pioneer Physician of Seattle," *Northwest Medicine*, Vol. II, No. 4, pp. 3–6 (1904).

Qualey, Carlton C., *Norwegian Settlement in the United States*. Northfield, Minn., 1938.

Rader, L. E., "A Washington Literarium," *Washington Magazine*, Vol. II, No. 1, pp. 11–12 (1890).

Ray, Verne F., "Native Villages and Groupings of the Columbia Basin," *Pacific Northwest Quarterly*, Vol. XXVII, No. 2, pp. 99–152 (1936).

Raymer, Robert G., "Educational Development in the Territory and State of Washington, 1853–1908," *Washington Historical Quarterly*, Vol. XVIII, No. 3, pp. 163–180 (1927).

Read, Georgia W., "Diseases, Drugs and Doctors on the Oregon-California Trail in the Gold-rush Years," *Missouri Historical Review*, Vol. XXXVIII, No. 3, pp. 260–276 (1944).

Reid, William, *The Progress of Oregon and Portland From 1868 to 1878*. Portland, 1879.

Rice, Ben H., "Spokane's War With Vice," *Pacific Monthly*, Vol. XI, No. 6, pp. 407–410 (1904).

Rigg, George B., "Notes on the History of Botany in the State of Washington," *Washington Historical Quarterly*, Vol. XX, No. 3, pp. 163–173 (1929).

Roberts, Jeanette E., "Asahel Bush; Pioneer Editor, Politician and Banker." M.A. thesis, University of Oregon, 1939.

Robertson, James R., "The Social Evolution of Oregon," *Quarterly of the Oregon Historical Society*, Vol. III, No. 1, pp. 1–37 (1902).

Rollins, Philip Ashton, ed., *Robert Stuart: Narratives of His Overland Trip Eastward from Astoria in 1812–1813; The Discovery of the Oregon Trail*. New York, 1935.

Rorher, Mary K., *History of Seattle Stock Companies from Their Beginnings to 1934*, University of Washington Publications in Drama, No. 2. Seattle, 1945.

Ross, Alexander, *Adventures of the First Settlers on the Oregon or Columbia Rivers*. London, 1894.

Rucker, Maude A., *The Oregon Trail and Some of Its Blazers*. New York, 1930.

Santee, J. F., "Thomas Milton Gatch, Educator," *Oregon Historical Quarterly*, Vol. XXXII, No. 2, pp. 114–122 (1931).

Savage, W., "The Negro in the History of the Pacific Northwest," *Journal of Negro History*, Vol. XIII, No. 3, pp. 255–264 (1928).

Schaefer, Ruth E., "The Influence of Methodism in Early Oregon History." M.A. thesis, University of Oregon, 1929.

Schafer, Joseph, *Acquisition of Oregon Territory*, University of Oregon Bulletin No. 3, Vol. 6. Eugene, 1908.

———, "Career of Frederic George Young," *Oregon Historical Quarterly*, Vol. XXX, No. 1, pp. 1–8 (1929).

———, "Jesse Applegate: Pioneer, Statesman and Philosopher," *Washington Historical Quarterly*, Vol. I, No. 4, pp. 217–233 (1907).

———, "Trailing a Trail Artist of 1849," *Wisconsin Magazine of History*, Vol. XII, No. 1, pp. 97–108 (1928).

———, ed., John Steele, *Across the Plains in 1850*. Chicago, 1930.

Schmid, Calvin F., *Social Trends in Seattle*. Seattle, 1944.

Schreibeis, Charles D., *Pioneer Education in the Pacific Northwest*. Portland, 1936.

Schulz, John, "Oregon Population of Foreign Born by Country." Typewritten manuscript, 1945, Oregon Historical Society Library.

Scott, Harvey W., "Jason Lee's Place in History," *Washington Historical Quarterly*, Vol. i, No. i, pp. 21–33 (1906–1907).

——, "The Pioneer Character of Oregon Progress," *Quarterly of the Oregon Historical Society*, Vol. XVIII, No. 4, pp. 245–270 (1917).

Scott, Leslie M., "Indians' Diseases As Aids to Pacific Northwest Settlement," *Oregon Historical Quarterly*, Vol. XXIX, No. 2, pp. 142–161 (1928).

——, "Modern Fallacies of Champoeg," *Oregon Historical Quarterly*, Vol. XXXII, No. 3, pp. 213–216 (1931).

——, "Oregon History Writers and Their Materials," *Quarterly of the Oregon Historical Society*, Vol. XXV, No. 3, pp. 284–293 (1924).

——, "Review of Mr. Scott's Writings on Favorite and Most Important Topics," *Quarterly of the Oregon Historical Society*, Vol. XIV, No. 2, pp. 140–204 (1913).

——, comp., Harvey Scott: *History of the Oregon Country*, 6 vols. Cambridge, 1924.

——, comp., Harvey Scott: *Religion, Theology and Morals*, 2 vols. Cambridge, 1917.

Seattle: *First Annual Report of the City Superintendent of Seattle, Washington Territory*, 1884–1885. Seattle, 1885.

Seattle Grand Jury Report, "Our Great Restricted District Under Mayor Gill," November, 1911. University of Washington Library.

Seattle Library Commission, *Fifth Annual Report*. Seattle, 1895.

Seattle Museum of Arts and Sciences of the Washington Art Association Bulletin. Seattle, 1910.

Seattle Public Library, *Annual Report*, 1891–1893; 1895–1899.

Sengstacken, Agnes R., *Destination, West!* Portland, 1942.

Sheldon, Henry D., *History of the University of Oregon*. Portland, 1940.

Shephard, Esther, *Paul Bunyan*. Seattle, 1924.

Sheppard, Edward and Emily Johnson, "Forty Years of Symphony in Seattle, 1903–1943," *Pacific Northwest Quarterly*, Vol. XXXV, No. i, pp. 19–28 (1944).

Shortess, Robert, "First Emigrants to Oregon," *Oregon Pioneer Association Transactions, 1897*. Portland, 1898.

Simon, John E., "Wilhelm Keil, Founder of Aurora." M.A. thesis, University of Oregon, 1935.

Simpson, Samuel L., *The Gold-Gated West*. Philadelphia, 1910.

Skiff, Fred W., *Landmarks and Literature*. Portland, 1937.

——, *Adventures in Americana*. Portland, 1935.

Small, Hugh, *Oregon—For the Use of Immigrants*. 1875.

——, *Oregon—For General Information*. 1879.

——, *Oregon For General Information*. 1880. Three pamphlets bound together under "Oregon Description," New York Public Library.

Smith, Charles W., "Early Library Development in Washington," *Washington Historical Quarterly*, Vol. XVII, No. 4, pp. 246–258 (1926).

——, *Pacific Northwest Americana: A Checklist of Books and Pamphlets Relating to the Pacific Northwest*. New York, 1921.

Smith, George Venable, *Puget Sound Colony: A Model Co-operative Commonwealth*. San Francisco, 1896.

Smith, Herndon, comp., *Centralia, the First Fifty Years, 1845–1900*. Centralia, 1942.

Smith, Mrs. Susan W., *The Legend of Multnomah Falls*. Portland, 1905.

Snowden, Clinton A., *History of Washington*. New York, 1909.

Spier, Leslie, "Tribal Distribution in Southwestern Oregon," *Oregon Historical Quarterly*, Vol. XXVIII, No. 4, pp. 358-365 (1927).

Steele, Oliver G., *Western Guide Book and Emigrants' Directory* . . . Buffalo, 1849.

Stern, Bernhard J., *The Lummi Indians of Northwest Washington*. New York, 1934.

Stevens, James, *Paul Bunyan*. New York, 1925.

Stine, Thomas Ostenson, *Scandinavians on the Pacific, Puget Sound*. Seattle, 1900.

Stuckey, Alan P., "The Influence of Juan de Fuca on Captain Vancouver." M.A. thesis, University of Florida, 1948.

Swan, James G., *The Northwest Coast*. New York, 1857.

Szewcynski, Isabel J., "A Pioneer Store, Lewis County, Washington." Type-written manuscript, University of Washington Library.

Tacoma Public Library, *Annual Report, 1908-09*. Tacoma, 1909.

Talkington, Henry L., "Removal of the Capital from Lewiston to Boise." *Idaho Journal of Education*, Vol. XIII, No. 7, pp. 258-259 (1932).

Taylor, S. H., "Documentary Letters of S. H. Taylor to the Watertown (Wisc.) Chronicle, 1853," *Quarterly of the Oregon Historical Society*, Vol. XXII, No. 2, pp. 117-160 (1921).

Teeter, C. N., "Four Years of My Life; or, My Adventures in the Far West . . . 1862-65." *State Historical Society of Idaho, 13th Biennial Report, 1931-32*. Boise, 1932.

Thomson, Origen, *Crossing the Plains*. Greensburg, Ind., 1896.

Thwaites, Reuben Gold, ed., *Early Western Travels, 1748-1846*, "Narrative of a Journey Across the Rocky Mountains" by John K. Townsend, Vol. XXI. Cleveland, 1905.

——, *Original Journals of the Lewis and Clark Expedition*, 8 vols. New York, 1905.

——, "The Story of Lewis and Clark's Journals," *Quarterly of the Oregon Historical Society*, Vol. VI, No. 1, pp. 26-53 (1905).

Tobie, H. E., "Joseph L. Meek, A Conspicuous Personality," *Oregon Historical Quarterly*, Vol. XXXIX, Nos. 2-4, pp. 123-146; 286-306; 410-424 (1938); Vol. XL, No. 1, pp. 19-39 (1939).

Todd, Ronald, "Bibliography of the Writings of Edmond Stephen Meany," *Washington Historical Quarterly*, Vol. XXVI, No. 3, pp. 176-191 (1935).

Tomlinson, Laurence E., "Factors Influencing the Immigration of the Foreign Born to the United States and Oregon." Typewritten manuscript, Oregon Historical Society Library.

Troth, Dennis C., *History and Development of Common School Legislation in Washington*, University of Washington Publications in the Social Sciences, Vol. III, No. 2 (1927).

Turnbull, George I., *History of Oregon Newspapers*. Portland, 1939.

Turney, Ida V., *Paul Bunyan Comes West*. Boston, 1928.

Turner, William M., "Pioneer Justice in Oregon," *Overland Monthly*, Vol. XII, No. 3, pp. 224-230 (1874).

Vancouver, George, *A Voyage of Discovery to the North Pacific Ocean*. London, 1798.

Van Dusen, W. W., *Blazing the Way; or, Pioneer Experiences in Idaho, Washington and Oregon*. Cincinnati, 1905.

Van Male, John, *Resources of Pacific Northwest Libraries*. Seattle, 1943.

Victor, Frances Fuller, *Atlantis Arisen; or, Talks of a Tourist About Oregon and Washington*. Philadelphia, 1891.
——, "Did Whitman Save Oregon?" *The Californian: a Western Monthly Magazine*, Vol. II, pp. 229–233 (July–December, 1880).
——, "The Literature of Oregon," *West Shore*, Vol. I, No. 6, pp. 2–3 (1876).
——, *The River of the West*. Hartford, 1870.
——, "Scrapbook," Oregon Historical Society Library.
——, *The Women's War with Whisky; or, Crusading in Portland*. Portland, 1874.
Vincent, F. G., "Herbert Bashford, the Poet of the West," *Washington Magazine*, Vol. III, No. 1, p. 202 (1890).
Wagner, Harr, *Joaquin Miller and His Other Self*. San Francisco, 1929.
Walgamott, Charles S., *Six Decades Back*. Caldwell, 1936.
Ward, Dillis B., *Across the Plains in 1853*. Seattle, 1911.
Washington (State) W.P.A., "Told by the Pioneers—Tales of Pioneer Life." Olympia(?) 1937–1938.
Washington Writers' Program: *Washington: A Guide to the Evergreen State*. Portland, 1941.
Watkins, Albert, ed., "Oregon Trail," *Publications of the Nebraska State Historical Society*, Vol. XX. Lincoln, 1922.
Webber, William L., *The Thunderbird "Yootooch" Legends: Folk Tales of the Indian Tribes of the Pacific Northwest Coast*. Seattle, 1936.
Webster, Jean, "The Myth of Pioneer Hardships on the Oregon Trail," *Reed College Bulletin*, Vol. 24, No. 2. Portland, 1946.
Weed, George L., "When Dr. Whitman Added Three Stars to Our Flag," *Ladies' Home Journal*, Vol. 14, No. 12, pp. 9–10 (1897).
Wheeler, Olin D., *The Trail of Lewis and Clark, 1804–1904*, 2 vols. New York, 1904.
Wilbur, Earl M., *Thomas Lamb Eliot, 1841–1936*. Privately printed, Portland, 1937.
Williams, Joseph, *Narrative of a Tour from the State of Indiana to the Oregon Territory . . . 1841–42*. New York, 1921.
Winther, Oscar Osburn, "The Place of Transportation in the Early History of the Pacific Northwest," *Pacific Historical Review*, Vol. XI, No. 4, pp. 383–396 (1942).
——, *Via Western Express and Stagecoach*. Stanford University, 1945.
Winthrop, Theodore, *The Canoe and the Saddle*. New York, 1862.
Wissler, Clark, *The American Indian*, 2nd ed., New York, 1931.
Wood, Charles Erskine Scott, *A Book of Tales; Being Some Myths of the North American Indians*. New York, 1929.
Woodward, Walter C., *The Rise and Early History of Political Parties in Oregon, 1843–1868*. Portland, 1913.
Wrenn, Sara, "Strange Fruit of the Juniper," Sagebrush and Bunchgrass. Oregon Folklore Studies, Oregon State Library, Salem.
York, Harold A., "History of the Placer Mining Era in the State of Idaho." M.A. thesis, University of Oregon, 1939.
Young, Frederick G., ed., *The Correspondence and Journals of Captain Nathaniel J. Wyeth, 1831–1836*. Eugene, Oregon, 1899.
——, "The Oregon Trail," *Quarterly of the Oregon Historical Society*, Vol. I, No. 4, pp. 339–370 (1900).
Young, Helen L., "A Western Utopia," *Dilettante*, Vol. II, No. 4, pp. 17–21 (1900).

Index